Marcel Szabó | Laura Gyeney | Petra Lea Láncos [Eds.]

Hungarian Yearbook

of International Law and European Law

2025

Nomos

iustum æquum salutare

Main professional partner:
The National Media and Infocommunications Authority (NMHH).

Nemzeti Média- és Hírközlési Hatóság

The Deutsche Nationalbibliothek lists this publication in the Deutsche Nationalbibliografie; detailed bibliographic data are available on the Internet at http://dnb.d-nb.de

1st Edition 2025

Published by
Nomos Verlagsgesellschaft mbH & Co. KG
Waldseestraße 3–5 | 76530 Baden-Baden
www.nomos.de

Production of the printed version:
Nomos Verlagsgesellschaft mbH & Co. KG
Waldseestraße 3–5 | 76530 Baden-Baden

ISBN 978-3-7560-2011-9 (Print)
ISBN 978-3-7489-5548-1 (ePDF)

ISSN 2666-2701 (Print)
ISSN 2666-271X (Online)

DOI https://doi.org/10.5771/9783748955481

Online Version
Nomos eLibrary

Table of Contents

Part II - Developments in international law

Part III - Developments in European law

János Bruhács – Remembering the Scholar

*Mátyás Kiss – Bence Kis Kelemen – Ágoston Mohay**

Abstract

We, the new generation of the University of Pécs, Faculty of Law's International Law research hub would like to express our utmost respect towards the late János Bruhács, professor emeritus of international law with this short article, the purpose of which is to remember Professor Bruhács, the scholar. In this article, we present the prestigious life path of Professor Bruhács, alongside some of our fondest memories of him (Section 1). Furthermore, we dive into some of Professor Bruhács's favourite subjects within international law, namely the responsibility of states for internationally wrongful acts, with an emphasis on the pollution of international rivers, and the sources and overall nature of international law (Section 2). Finally, we conclude (Section 3).

Keywords: János Bruhács, in memoriam, University of Pécs, international watercourses, responsibility of states

* Mátyás Kiss: assistant research fellow, University of Pécs, kiss.matyas@ajk.pte.hu.
Bence Kis Kelemen: senior lecturer, University of Pécs, kis.kelemen.bence@ajk.pte.hu.
Ágoston Mohay: associate professor of law, University of Pécs, mohay.agoston@ajk.pte.hu.

1. Professor Bruhács the Scholar, the Doktorvater and the Practicing Professional

János Bruhács was born on 23 September 1939, in Pécs, where he later completed his secondary and higher education. In 1964, he was awarded his doctorate with the distinction *Sub auspiciis Rei Publicae Popularis.* He began his teaching career in 1963, initially at Janus Pannonius University of Pécs, and later at its successor institution, the University of Pécs. He started as an assistant lecturer, and later he was appointed as a senior lecturer in 1969, associate professor in 1979, and professor in 1994. A *professor emeritus* since 2009, he remained actively involved in academic and teaching activities at the University of Pécs. In 1977, he earned the title of Candidate of Sciences (CSc), and habilitated in 1994. Professor Bruhács was the head of the Department of International and European Law and its predecessors at the University of Pécs, Faculty of Law, between 1988 and 2004. Simultaneously, he served as vice-dean of the Faculty of Law in 1989, and between 1990 and 1993, he served as the dean of the Faculty. Besides Pécs, he also taught at the Faculty of Law of the Károli Gáspár University of the Reformed Church between 2001 and 2009 and continued to participate in the work of the latter institution as *professor emeritus* as well.[1]

Professor Bruhács was deeply committed to mentoring future generations. He placed emphasis on mentoring and supporting young scholars specializing in international law. He served as the head of the sub-program "International Legal Issues of Territory and Space" within the Doctoral School of Law at the University of Pécs and he was a member of the Doctoral School of Law at Károli Gáspár University as well. On numerous occasions, he acted as an opponent and as a member of the evaluation committee at public doctoral defences. Under his supervision, 8 researchers were awarded a Ph.D. degree, among them prestigious Hungarian international and European law scholars and – thus far – one high ranking public

1 *See* at https://almanach.pte.hu/oktato/573?from=http%3A//almanach.pte.hu/oktatok%3Fdirection%3Dasc%26f1%3Dff%26o1%3Din_any%26page%3D1%26sortBy%3Dnev%26v1%255B0%255D%3DPTE%252FJPTE%2520%25C3%2581JK.

official.[2] Throughout his nearly sixty-year-long teaching career, he authored a widely used textbook, published in multiple editions, which introduced generations of law students to the fundamentals of international law.

Professor Bruhács was among the most highly regarded international legal scholars in Hungary. His research interests prominently included the law of international watercourses, international environmental law, space law, and the law of international responsibility. One of his most significant works is a monograph titled "The Law of Non-Navigational Uses of International Watercourses."[3]

Due to his expertise on the law of international watercourses and international environmental protection, Professor Bruhács represented Hungary in the activities of the Danube Commission (1979). As a member of the Hungarian delegation, he participated in the Hungarian-Czechoslovak negotiations concerning the Gabčikovo-Nagymaros Waterworks project. Subsequently, he was a member of the Hungarian legal team in the *Gabčikovo-Nagymaros Project Case* before the ICJ (1993–1997) and took part in the negotiations aimed at implementing the ICJ's judgment. Professor Bruhács represented Hungary in the negotiations leading up to the adoption of the Danube River Protection Convention (1991–2001) and participated in the Pan-European Environmental Conference (2003). He served as head of the Hungarian delegation in a working group of the UN Economic Commission for Europe on environmental liability (2000–2003). Professor Bruhács was actively involved in the work of several prestigious organizations, in different capacities. He was a member of the Permanent Court of Arbitration in The Hague. Additionally, he participated in the work of the International Institute of Space Law, the Hungarian Branch of the International Law Association, and the International Water Law Association. He was a member of the Pécs Academic Committee, serving as the chairman of one of its specialized committees between 1993 and 1999. Furthermore, he was a member of the Hungarian Atlantic Council, the Governing Council of the UN Association of Hungary, the Hungarian UNESCO Committee, the Hungarian Foreign Affairs Society, and the Hungarian Astronautical Society.[4]

---

2 *See* at https://doktori.hu/index.php?menuid=192&lang=HU&sz_ID=2710&show=1.

3 *See* at https://pte.hu/hu/hirek/gyaszhir-elhunyt-dr-bruhacs-janos; https://portal.kre.hu/index.php/2581-elhunyt-bruhacs-janos-egyetemunk-professor-emeritusa.html.

4 Melinda Szappanyos & Zsuzsanna Csapó, 'Bruhács János Életpályája', *in* Zsuzsanna Csapó (ed.), *Ünnepi Tanulmánykötet Bruhács János Professor Emeritus 70. születésnapjára,* Pécsi Tudományegyetem Állam- és Jogtudományi Kar, Pécs, 2009, pp. 14–15.

Throughout his decades-long teaching career, Professor Bruhács introduced thousands of students to the complexities and beauty of international law. His lectures were always outstanding– precise, thought-provoking, and highly informative. His students consistently showed exceptional attentiveness and deep respect for both him and his teaching. In recognition of his contributions, the University of Pécs, Faculty of Law awarded him the *Pro Facultate Iuridico-Politica Universitatis Quinquecclesiensis* gold medal of merit. As a guest lecturer, he also participated in the academic activities of the Panthéon-Assas University in Paris. In addition to his lectures on international law, he conducted specialized seminars on topics such as the law of international watercourses, international environmental law, the jurisprudence of international courts, and the international law of the Cold War. His contribution extended to postgraduate education as well, including teaching in the Environmental Law Specialist program at the Institute for Postgraduate Legal Studies at ELTE Law School, Budapest, and the COPERNICUS program established by the European Rectors' Conference.[5]

Professor Bruhács's distinguished career and professional achievements were recognized by the government of Hungary with the Officer's Cross of the Order of Merit of Hungary (2011) and the Commander's Cross of the Order of Merit of Hungary (2023).[6]

Professor Bruhács was an extraordinary man, whose academic and professional career serves as an example for anyone who wishes to start their own journey in this field. One of our fondest memories of him is when he demonstrated that he could stay up to date with what was happening in the world, despite the fact that he *literally* never used a computer. It was almost comical how well informed he was despite the limitations inherent in the analogue technologies he used and was so fond of. Professor Bruhács wrote all his manuscripts by hand, with pen and paper, and his memory was also excellent. Somehow, he could instruct us to find him an article that was published roughly 40 years ago that he read at that time in a particular journal. He not only knew the name of the journal and the decade, but often the exact issue in which we later actually found the article he was looking for.

5 Id. pp. 15–16.

6 *See* at https://almanach.pte.hu/oktato/573?from=http%3A//almanach.pte.hu/oktatok%3Fdirection%3Dasc%26f1%3Dff%26o1%3Din_any%26page%3D1%26sortBy%3Dnev%26v1%255B0%255D%3DPTE%252FJPTE%2520%25C3%2581JK.

2. *Selected Fields from the Research Interests of Professor Bruhács*

2.1. International Responsibility

International responsibility is a compelling and at the same time an ever-current topic of international law. It is therefore not a coincidence that Professor Bruhács was also especially interested in this field, and published extensively on it, in particular, on the responsibility in connection with environmental damages.[7] Professor Bruhács pointed out that international responsibility was for long not considered as one of the key problems of international law – besides enforcement of obligations.[8]

Due to his long career, Professor Bruhács was one of the first Hungarian scholars who commented on the International Law Commission's codification efforts on the responsibility of states for internationally wrongful acts, already in the 1980's, when only the first half of the preliminary draft was available to the public.[9] In this early work, Professor Bruhács observed that international legal practice even in the early 1980's already relied on the provisionally adopted chapters of the draft articles, referring to the *Tehran Hostage* case.[10] This process finally culminated in the adoption of the *Draft Articles on the Responsibility of States for Internationally Wrongful Acts* (hereinafter: ARSIWA).[11] The ARSIWA is not a treaty, however it can be

7 *See e.g.* János Bruhács, 'Az államok nemzetközi felelősségéről szóló végleges tervezet', *Acta Universitatis Szegediensis: Acta Juridicita et Politica,* Tomus LXI, 2002, pp. 117–132; János Bruhács, 'International Legal Problems of Environmental Protection', *Questions of International Law,* Vol. 4, 1988, pp. 31–45; János Bruhács, 'A környezeti károk miatti nemzetközi felelősség', *in Az államok nemzetközi jogi felelőssége – tíz év után. In memoriam Nagy Károly (1932–2001),* Pólay Elemér Alapítvány, Szeged, 2013, pp. 57–66; János Bruhács, *Nemzetközi jogi felelősség a nemzetközi folyóvizek szennyezéséért,* Budapest, 1983.

8 Bruhács 2002, footnote 35.

9 *See* Report of the International Law Commission on the work of its twenty-fifth session, 7 May – 13 July 1973, A/9010/Rev.1; Report of the International Law Commission on the work of its twenty-sixth session, 6 May – 26 July 1974, A/9610/Rev.1; Report of the International Law Commission on the work of its twenty-seventh session, 5 May – 25 July 1975, A/10010/Rev.1; Report of the International Law Commission on the work of its twenty-eight session, 3 May – 23 July 1976, A/31/10; Report of the International Law Commission on the work of its twenty-ninth session, 9 May – 29 July 1977, A/32/10; Report of the International Law Commission on the work of its Thirtieth session, 8 May – 28 July 1978, A/33/10.

10 *United States Diplomatic and Consular Staff in Tehran (United States of America v Iran),* Judgment of 24 May 1980, ICJ Reports 1980, p. 3; *See* Bruhács 1983.

11 56/83. Responsibility of States for internationally wrongful acts, adopted on 12 December 2001, A/RES/56/83. (hereinafter: ARSIWA)

characterized as a compilation of customary international legal norms,[12] binding upon the members of the international community as such. Professor Bruhács considered ARSIWA to not be that different from a multilateral treaty,[13] since the UN General Assembly has taken note of it and commended it to the attention of states.[14] We respectfully contend on this point, that it is not possible to put an equation between a treaty and customary international law. This is true even in a field where rules are generally accepted as binding norms for the international community. The constant need to establish the existence of a customary norm, and the possibility of persistent objection[15] makes it much harder to operate based on customary international law, than on the basis of an international treaty.

Professor Bruhács regularly emphasized that the state is not responsible for the conduct of private persons and individuals, save for those situations where it failed to comply with its obligations of prevention.[16] Of course, this statement is true in essence, especially when it comes to transboundary environmental pollution, however it needs to be noted, that the ARSIWA clearly establishes those situations, in which the state is responsible for the conduct of private individuals as well. To name a few examples, the conduct of persons or entities exercising elements of governmental authority (Article 5), or those who are directed or controlled by the state itself (Article 8). We realize that these are rarely the cases when it comes to environmental harm, however, other use cases might still be relevant *e.g.* conduct in the absence of, or default of the official authorities (Article 9).[17]

Another important aspect of Professor Bruhács's work is the underlining of the role and purpose of culpability in the law of international responsibility. Professor Bruhács noted that culpability is not a condition of responsibility, rather it is typically regulated by primary law, meaning that culpability should be examined at the level of primary obligations of states and not in connection with secondary – responsibility related – obliga-

12 Mirka Möldner, 'Responsibility of International Organizations – Introducing the ILC's Dario', *Max Planck Yearbook of United Nations Law*, Vol. 16, 2012, p. 286.

13 Bruhács 2002, p. 121.

14 ARSIWA, para. 3.

15 *Fisheries Case (United Kingdom v Norway)*, Judgment of 18 December 1951, ICJ Reports 1951, p. 116.

16 Bruhács 2002, p. 121; Bruhács 1983, p. 199.

17 It could be noted that even Professor Bruhács accepted that, in a socialist state (such as Hungary was for the majority of his career) a State-owned enterprise's conduct might be attributable to the state. However, Professor Bruhács paid excessive attention to the provisional-ARSIWA Article 5. *See* Bruhács 1988, p. 44.

tions.[18] Professor Bruhács also opined, that culpability is nevertheless part of some secondary obligations.[19]

From the regular mention of the transformation of international crimes and international delicts (Article 19) in the ARSIWA (provisionally adopted)[20] to serious breaches of obligations under peremptory norms of general international law (Chapter III),[21] it is evident that he truly lamented this change from the provisional text to the final version.[22] For example, in one of his pre-ARSIWA works he stated that Article 19 of the provisional ARSIWA was of great importance, since it designates as international crime among others, the serious breach of an international obligation of essential importance for the safeguarding and preservation of the human environment, such as the pollution of the atmosphere and of the seas. Professor Bruhács deduced from this, following an *a maiore ad minus* logic, that other cases of environmental pollution should be seen as 'simple' violations of international legal obligations.[23]

In one of his last publications, Professor Bruhács also touched upon the issue of the responsibility of international organizations and attempted to draw a picture of the relations between the ARSIWA and its 'younger brother', the *Draft Articles on the Responsibility of International Organizations* (hereinafter: ARIO) as adopted by the UN General Assembly.[24] The starting point of Professor Bruhács on this issue is the fact that the ARIO is an adaptation and analogy of the ARSIWA, therefore, it requires further analysis whether the ARIO – despite the lack of a binding treaty – also reflects customary international law as did its predecessor.[25] Professor Bruhács's answer to this question is negatory: he does not characterize the

18 Bruhács 2013, p. 63. *Cf.* ARSIWA, Article 2, which stipulates that there are only two conditions for establishing state responsibility: breach of an international obligation and attribution.

19 Bruhács 2013, p. 64.

20 Report of the International Law Commission on the work of its forty-eight session, 6 May – 26 July 1996, A/51/10 and Corr. 1, pp. 125–151.

21 ARSIWA, Articles 40–41.

22 János Bruhács, *Nemzetközi jog I. Általános rész,* Dialóg Campus, Budapest-Pécs, 2011, pp. 213–214.

23 Bruhács 1983, p. 48. It should be noted that Professor Bruhács also considers the prohibition of ecocide as a potentially jus cogens norm. *See* Bruhács 2013, footnote 41.

24 Report of the International Law Commission. Sixty-third session, 26 April – 3 June and 4 July – 12 August, 2011, A/66/10; János Bruhács, 'Az államok és a nemzetközi szervezetek felelősségének kapcsolatáról', *in* Ágoston Mohay *et al.* (eds.), *A nemzetközi szervezetek felelőssége – elmélet és gyakorlat határán,* Publikon, Pécs, 2023, p. 26.

25 Id. p. 27.

ARIO as part of customary international law,[26] however, he does argue that its adoption indicates the stabilization of the legal regime of international responsibility at its core (responsibility for internationally wrongful acts, requirement of attribution, conditions precluding wrongfulness, reparations and countermeasures).[27] We would like to note, that beyond these norms, we consider the International Law Commission's codification as a law development effort.[28] Professor Bruhács also emphasizes that at least some of the problems of ARSIWA were inherited by ARIO due to the close connection between the two systems,[29] although at the same time the crucial differences between the ARIO and ARSIWA need to be emphasized as well.[30]

All in all, we would like to end this segment with a recurring statement in Professor Bruhács's responsibility-related works: if the establishment of international responsibility is not possible, the cooperation of states (and international organizations) in this field, especially when it comes to environmental dagames, is pivotal.[31]

2.2. The Nature and Sources of International Law

As part of his extensive *oeuvre,* Professor Bruhács has, time and time again, reflected upon the nature, overall characteristics and sources of international law. His relevant works exude a certain duality: as a scholar of international law, Professor Bruhács was naturally mindful of the significance of the emergence of new international rules; however, as a follower of the sociological approach to international law, he was never one to stray from the reality of international relations and their effect on the implementation (and thus the overall effectiveness) of the norms of international law.

Among other things, this is true of his views on the peremptory norms of international law, also known as *ius cogens.* It should be noted at the outset that Professor Bruhács considers peremptory norms to be a separate category of the sources of international law. He positions said norms hierarchically above other sources of international law, including customary interna-

26 Id. p. 28.
27 Id. p. 30.
28 András Hárs, 'Felelősség/vállalás – Az ARIO 9. cikkének alkalmazhatósága az ENSZ békeműveleteire', *in* Mohay *et al.* (eds.) 2023, p. 78. *Cf.* Ágoston Mohay *et al.*, 'Bevezető: A nemzetközi szervezetek felelősségének alapproblémái', *in* Mohay *et al.* (eds.) 2023, p. 22.
29 Bruhács 2023, pp. 30–31.
30 Mohay *et al.*, 2023, p. 21.
31 Bruhács 1988, p. 45.

tional law, and notes that *ius cogens* plays a formative role in shaping international law into a legal order, as opposed to a mere assemblage of juxtaposed norms.[32] His point of view on what *ius cogens* is *not* is also quite clear: bearing in mind that the 1969 Vienna Convention on the Law of Treaties (hereinafter: VCLT) posits peremptory norms as capable of amendment (even if only via peremptory norms),[33] a clear distinction can (and should) be made between peremptory norms on the one hand, and the concept of natural law on the other; the latter being, by its very nature, unchangeable.[34] He does however note that, by adopting an axiological approach, one can come to the conclusion that *ius cogens* represents the values of the current (*i.e.*, post-1945) regime of international law, although this statement does not enjoy complete consensus neither in theory, nor in state practice.[35] This statement is further accentuated by the fact that the application of peremptory norms is an area of international law where actual examples of application are rather scarce – increased importance must however be given to instances where the ICJ and the UN Security Council have indeed engaged with the concept of *ius cogens* in earnest.[36] Thus his analysis leads Professor Bruhács to a conclusion similar to that of Brownlie's, who compared *ius cogens* to a car that does not leave the garage too often.[37]

In the later years of his career, Professor Bruhács often commented on the overall tendencies of the development of international law in the era of the Cold War and afterwards. As he himself remarked, the fact that his career in teaching and research essentially overlapped with this period gave his observations on the topic a personal touch.[38] As a starting point, he often noted the anachronism observable in the fact that the creation of the UN (1945),

32 János Bruhács *et al.*, *Nemzetközi jog I*, Ludovika Egyetemi Kiadó, Budapest, 2023, pp. 32, 106 and 171.

33 Vienna Convention on the Law of Treaties, 1969, Article 53.

34 Bruhács *et al.* 2023, p. 172.

35 János Bruhács, 'A nemzetközi jog doktrínáiról', *in* Tibor Nochta & Gábor Monori (eds.), *IUS EST ARS: Ünnepi tanulmányok Visegrády Antal professzor 65. születésnapja tiszteletére*, Pécsi Tudományegyetem Állam- és Jogtudományi Kar, Pécs, 2015, p. 106.

36 *Cf.* the detalied analysis of the application of peremptory norms in Bruhács *et al.* 2023, pp. 174–177.

37 Ian Brownlie, 'Comment', *in* Antonio Cassese & Joseph H. H. Weiler (eds.), *Change and Stability in International Law-Making*, De Gruyter, Berlin, 1988. Professor Bruhács references this metaphor himself, although refers, instead of a mere vehicle, to a Rolls Royce. This unintentional enhancement of Brownlie's metaphor suits Professor Bruhács's elegant and eloquent style rather well. *See* János Bruhács, 'A nemzetközi jog átalakulása', *Jogtörténeti Szemle*, Vol. 17, Issue 3, 2015, p. 27.

38 János Bruhács, 'A nemzetközi jog tegnap és ma', *Állam- és Jogtudomány*, Vol. 54, Issue 3–4, 2013, pp. 9–10.

the Charter of which envisioned a peaceful, united world based on cooperation, coincided with the start of the Cold War (1945–1989).[39] The period of the Cold War was characterised by antagonistic opposition between the two opposing centres of power (often portrayed as a battle between "good" and "evil", or between democracy and totalitarianism), but this – perhaps somewhat surprisingly – did not prevent the 1960s from being regarded as the most successful period of the codification of customary international law.[40] Professor Bruhács noted how the newfound 'dynamic' nature of international law-making spearheaded by the UN reinforced the relevance of multilateralism in international law, but underlined that none of these multilateral ventures – not even ones as fundamental as the VCLT or UNCLOS – achieved truly universal status.[41] Commenting on the end of the Cold War, he often pointed out a paradox: namely that the end of this historical period did not, in fact, improve the conditions for the further development of international law: on the contrary, the adoption of 'grand' multilateral agreements seemed to have slowed down, and many treaties did not enter into force.[42]

One cannot help but wonder how Professor Bruhács would have evaluated the current turbulent state of international relations. As regards the prohibition of the use of force, at least, this can be inferred from his earlier works. Commenting on the state of international relations throughout and following the Cold War, Professor Bruhács noted the Janus-faced attitude of states towards this core tenet of the post-1945 international order: states do not dispute or denounce the prohibition of the use of force *per se,* but instead focus on *legitimizing* their external action via international law, albeit interpreting the exceptions to the prohibition of the use of force rather extensively or, one could also say, creatively[43] – a practice of interpretation Professor Bruhács preferred to describe as 'rabulistic'.[44] This aforementioned practice even characterises Russia's behaviour in the context of its 'special military operations' (or more appropriately: aggression) against Ukraine initiated in February 2022: a so-called Article 51 letter was indeed addressed

39 Bruhács *et al.* 2023, p. 71.
40 Bruhács, 'A nemzetközi jog átalakulása', 2015, p. 30.
41 Bruhács 2013, p. 14.
42 Id.
43 János Bruhács, 'Jus contra bellum – glosszák az erőszak nemzetközi jogi tilalmához', *in* László Blutman & Mária Homoki-Nagy (eds.), *Ünnepi kötet Dr. Bodnár László egyetemi tanár 70. születésnapjára,* Szegedi Tudományegyetem Állam- és Jogtudományi Kar, Szeged, 2014, pp. 72–73.
44 Bruhács, 'A nemzetközi jog doktrínáiról', 2015, p. 112.

by Russia to the UN Security Council[45] – on its own, of course, the sending of the letter does not prejudge the legality or lack thereof of Russia's action, but clearly illustrates the aforementioned trend. (The fact that the letter consisted entirely of a speech by Vladimir Putin is also irrelevant in this regard.)

3. Concluding Thoughts

It is an honourable, but quite difficult task to write an article in remembrance of a former colleague. In the foregoing, we have concentrated on his achievements and scientific findings. The authors have – to varying degrees and for varying periods, but – known János Bruhács first as students, later as Ph.D. students, and finally as colleagues, and have thus collected many cherished memories about his character as well. To round off our commemoration, let us recall two anecdotes that showcase his sense of humour.

During his career, he took part as an expert in the drafting of two multilateral treaties, both relating to the international environmental law: the 1993 Council of Europe Convention on Civil Liability for Damage resulting from Activities Dangerous to the Environment[46] and the Draft Protocol on Civil Liability and Compensation for Damage caused by the Transboundary Effects of Industrial Accidents on Transboundary Waters (elaborated in the framework of the UN Economic Commission for Europe and finalised in 2003).[47] In his very last conference presentation[48] in 2023, János referred to this fact with the following witty remark: "In my career I have participated in the drafting of two multilateral international treaties. The significance of my work is demonstrated well by the fact that neither of these treaties entered into force."

János was also a well-travelled man of culture and good taste, a quality that occasionally clashed with the inadequacy of reality. He once described

45 Letter dated 24 February 2022 from the Permanent Representative of the Russian Federation to the United Nations addressed to the Secretary-General (S/2022/154).

46 Convention on Civil Liability for Damage resulting from Activities Dangerous to the Environment (ETS No. 150).

47 UNECE MP.WAT/2003/1. The protocol would have supplemented the 1992 Helsinki Convention on the Transboundary Effects of Industrial Accidents, UN Treaty Series, Vol. 2105, p. 457.

48 At the conference entitled "The Responsibility of International Organisations: Theory and Practice" organised at the University of Pécs Faculty of Law on 28 April 2023. And edited volume based on the conference presentations, including a contribution by Bruhács was later published.

a holiday in a smaller Hungarian city where he and his wife wished to enjoy a cocktail in the sun. When the waiter appeared to take their order, János asked if they could have two daiquiris. "I'm sorry sir – the waiter replied – but I don't speak English." This rather aptly reflects the conflict between certain principles of international law and the often harsh world of international relations, which János Bruhács often described in his works.

Editorial Comments: The German and the Hungarian Constitutional Court's Climate Decisions

Similarities and Differences

*Petra Lea Láncos**

1. Introduction

About 25 years ago, my grandfather – a keen industrialist and mining engineer handed me a book. He said that this book is extremely important and I should keep a copy of it on my shelf. The book was titled *'The Limits to Growth'*[1] and was published in 1972. Half a century later, two groundbreaking European constitutional court decisions were brought which have the potential to effect change not only in the realm of climate change mitigation and adaptation, but also in the legislators' approach to the environment and the interests of future generations.

In what follows, I make a rough comparison of the German *Klimabeschluss*[2] and the Hungarian *Klímahatározat*,[3] without delving deeply into the individual decisions.[4] I will first describe the importance of the German

* Petra Lea Láncos: professor of law, Pázmány Péter Catholic University, Budapest; editor, Hungarian Yearbook of International Law and European law, lancos.petra.lea@jak.ppke.hu.

1 Donatella H. Meadows *et al.*, *The Limits to Growth,* Club of Rome, Potomac Associates, 1972.

2 BVerfG, Beschluss des Ersten Senats vom 24. März 2021 – 1 BvR 2656/18, Rn. 1–270, at https://www.bverfg.de/e/rs20210324_1bvr265618 (hereinafter: *Klimabeschluss*).

3 Decision No. 5/2025. (VI. 30.) AB.

4 For a more comprehensive study on the *Urgenda* decision and the *Klimabeschluss* and their impact on the Hungarian petition, *see* Petra Lea Láncos, 'The Possible Impact of Urgenda

Constitutional Court's jurisprudence for the development of Hungarian constitutional thinking. Then, I will briefly compare the petitions submitted in the German and the Hungarian case, and finally, I shall compare the two decisions on the basis of a limited set of aspects gleaned from scholarly literature discussing the *Klimabeschluss.* It is worth noting that the German petitioners' petitions were only available in summary through the text of the *Klimabeschluss,* while the Hungarian petition is publicly available on the Hungarian Constitutional Court's website.[5]

2. *Why Compare the German and the Hungarian Constitutional Courts' Decisions on the Climate Acts?*

Just 6 months after the *Klimabeschluss* was rendered in Karlsruhe, petition No. II/3536/2021 was submitted to the Hungarian Constitutional Court by 50 members of the Hungarian National Assembly. Similarly to the petitioners before the *Bundesverfassungsgericht,* the Hungarian petition challenged the national Climate Change Act for its insufficient and non-specific emission reduction targets. Indeed, the Hungarian petition expressly referred to the *Klimabeschluss* of the German Constitutional Court, and the constitutional legal bases invoked, arguments made by the petitioners also showed similarities.

In general, it is safe to say that Hungarian constitutional jurisprudence is inspired by the *Bundesverfassungsgericht's* rulings. The reasons for this are manifold: *(i)* the development of Hungarian law within the Austro-Hungarian Monarchy; *(ii)* the German language as an official language and then an important minority language within Hungary, and later, a popular foreign language among Hungarian speakers, making law and jurisprudence in the German language accessible to Hungarian lawyers; *(iii)* and finally, the focus of the first members of the Hungarian Constitutional Court on the practice of the *Bundesverfassungsgericht* afforded German constitutional law and jurisprudence a special place in the sources of inspiration for the development of Hungarian constitutional thinking.[6] When perusing Hungarian

---

and the Klimabeschluss on Climate Litigation on the Example of the Petition Pending Before the Hungarian Constitutional Court', *Wroclaw Review of Law, Administration & Economics,* Vol 13, Issue 1, 2023, pp. 1–23.

5 *See* at https://alkotmanybirosag.hu/ugyadatlap/?id=6E82DC86EA198AF3C1258764003 3C9F2.

6 László Sólyom, 'Az alkotmány őrei', *in* Mindentudás Egyeteme 6., Kossuth Kiadó, Budapest, 2006, p. 331.

Constitutional Court decisions, one can frequently find references to, and citations from, *Bundesverfassungsgericht* decisions. (Perhaps the new Hungarian constitution's title: Fundamental Law is also an allusion to the Basic Law of Germany.)

One can only speculate, but it is perhaps this strong connection with German constitutional law and jurisprudence (and the success of the German petition) why the Hungarian petitioners also sought inspiration from the *Klimabeschluss,* including both the German petitioners' arguments and the findings of the *Bundesverfassungsgericht.* While these tendencies in themselves would suffice as a reason for comparison, a brief look at the main pillars of the two constitutional courts' reasoning reveals similar structures, that may serve as a model for other courts in developing their environmental jurisprudence for the benefit of future generations.

3. *Petitions and Legal Bases*

There are important differences underlying the two decisions, which have to do with standing and the constitutional legal bases available for environmental related claims. While the petitioners before the *Bundesverfassungsgericht* proceeded in the framework of an *actio popularis,* with standing afforded to even petitioners residing outside of Germany, the Hungarian petitioners were 50 Members of Parliament, proceeding under their constitutional right to seek constitutional review of norms – without having to substantiate any impairment of rights or interests [Article 24(2)(e) of the Fundamental Law and Section 32(2) of the Act on the Constitutional Court]. Owing to the lack of *actio popularis* under contemporary Hungarian constitutional law, it was most expedient for the Hungarian MPs to make use of their privilege to initiate the procedure before the Hungarian Constitutional Court.

The petitioners proceeding before the *Bundesverfassungsgericht* sought the annulment of the German Climate Protection Act for an unconstitutional restriction of the right to life and limb, human dignity, the right to property and the non-fulfillment of the state's obligation to protect the environment. Meanwhile, the Hungarian petitioners sought the "examination of whether the Climate Act conflicts with international treaties", namely the Paris Agreement, as well as the review of the unconstitutional restriction of the right to human dignity, physical and mental health, the right to a healthy environment and Article P(1) foreseeing a general duty to protect natural resources, and to ensure legal certainty.

In fact, the Hungarian MPs expressly referred to the *Klimabeschluss,* noting the largely similar German and Hungarian constitutional provisions and related constitutional court practice. The Hungarian petitioners further referred to the findings of the *Bundesverfassungsgericht's* ruling on the state's obligation to protect the climate, the need to balance the increasingly important climate protection against other constitutional interests and principles, as well as the impossibility of avoiding liability for climate protection by pointing to scientific uncertainties or other states' violations.

Constitutional provisions referred to in	
the German petition *Grundgesetz*	**the Hungarian petition** *Fundamental Law*
Article 1(1) – human dignity	-
Article 2 – the right to life and physical integrity	Article XX – right to physical and mental health
-	Article XXI – right to a healthy environment
Article 14 – right to property	-
-	Article B) – clarity of norms, legal certainty (rule of law)
-	Article Q) – compliance with international law
Article 20a – state's obligation to protect the environment	Article P) – state's and everyone else's obligation to protect the environment

4. Similarities and Differences

In what follows I will concentrate on the main aspects of the two constitutional court's decisions, as highlighted in the (predominantly German scholarly) literature on the *Klimabeschluss.* In particular, the literature on the *Bundesverfassungsgericht's* decision highlighted the novelty of extending constitutional review to address future fundamental rights violations, the relevance of science as a legislative requirement and a yardstick of review, and the obligation of the state towards future generations. When comparing the two constitutional decisions along these aspects, they do show slight nuances in phrasing, however, the similarities between them are clear.

4.1. Framing Future Risks as Restrictions on Fundamental Rights

The *Bundesverfassungsgericht* frames the omission to set clear targets and measures in the German Climate Act as a fundamental rights violation through the figure of the so-called *Eingrifssähnliche Vorwirkung* (advance interference-like effect), stating that present fundamental rights are affected by legislative omission since this omission puts processes in motion which will cause irreversible harm to these fundamental rights.[7] Owing to the fact that when the restriction on the fundamental rights will be actually realized all remedies taken will be futile, claims regarding (future) fundamental rights restrictions in such situations are admissible.[8]

The Hungarian Constitutional Court does not explicitly state that the lack of clear and effective targets amounts to a (future) restriction of the fundamental rights invoked, however, it does arrive at the conclusion that the legislator's failure violates Hungary's constitutional obligation to safeguard fundamental rights.[9] In this regard, while side-stepping the issue of temporality, the Hungarian Constitutional Court does accept that restrictions, while not current, can lead to a finding of unconstitutionality.

4.2. Balancing the Rights of Present and Future Generations

Both the *Bundesverfassungsgericht* and the Hungarian Constitutional Court refer to the obligation to take into consideration and balance the rights and interest of present and future generations when considering legislative options for the protection of the climate. However, as the *Bundesverfassungerich*t points out, future generations' interests do not take precedence over those of others but must be balanced against other constitutional interests and principles. That is, freedom of action should be distributed propor-

7 Anna-Julia Saiger, 'The Constitution Speaks in the Future Tense: On the Constitutional Complaints Against the Federal Climate Change Act', *Verfassungsblog*, 29 April 2021; Petra Minnerop, 'The 'Advance Interference-Like Effect' of Climate Targets: Fundamental Rights, Intergenerational Equity and the German Federal Constitutional Court', *Journal of Environmental Law*, Vol. 34, Issue 1, 2022, pp. 135–162.

8 *Klimabeschluss*, marginal note 130.

9 Decision No. 5/2025. (VI. 30.) AB, Reasoning [130].

tionately between the generations.[10] This approach still ensures ample room for political choice in framing national environmental policy.

As for the Hungarian Constitutional Court, it draws attention to the fact that present generations have three obligations in respect of the environment: to preserve choice, quality and access for future generations. This means actual choices in plural; a quality of environment where the natural environment is passed on to future generations in at least the same condition as it was given by past generations, and an actual restriction on access for present generations to natural resources, since their access is dependent on taking the equitable interests of future generations into account.[11]

While the approach of the two courts is similar, the Hungarian Constitutional Court's requirement that the quality of the national environment must be the same as what we had inherited from the previous generation (prohibition of retrogression or non-derogation principle) is an extremely stringent requirement: it leaves no leeway for contemporary politicians regarding actions which possibly lead to a degradation of the environment.

4.3. The Constitutional Relevance of Science

An important aspect of the two decisions is the role of science in legislating against climate change and – incidentally – in reviewing the constitutionality of the respective legislative act. The German Constitutional Court's reasoning is that while

> "there is scientific uncertainty regarding causal relationships of environmental relevance, [the *Grundgesetz*] places constraints on the legislator's decisions – especially those with irreversible consequences for the environment – and imposes a special duty of care on the legislator, including a responsibility for future generations."[12]

In addition, the *Klimabeschluss* itself cites several scientific findings on climate change when reviewing the climate act.

The Hungarian Constitutional Court emphasizes that the legislator has a duty based on Article P of the Fundamental Law to evaluate the expected impact of its legislation based on the prevailing scientific consensus, the pre-

10 *Klimabeschluss,* marginal note 183.
11 Decision No. 5/2025. (VI. 30.) AB, Reasoning [49].
12 *Klimabeschluss,* marginal note 229.

cautionary principle and the principle of prevention.[13] This necessarily means a requirement of legislation based on scientifically grounded facts, but also a role for science in the constitutional review of legislation.

4.4. Duty of Care and Public Trust

The *Bundesverfassungsgericht* emphasizes that Article 20a of the *Grundgesetz* imposes a special duty of care on the legislator, who must take into account possible serious and irreversible damage caused by its legislation and in particular, its effect on future generations.[14]

This idea finds an expression in the public trust doctrine introduced into Hungarian constitutional jurisprudence with the 'forest act decision' [*Decision No. 14/2020. (VII. 6.) AB*]. According to this approach, the Hungarian state holds in trust the natural environment for future generations as beneficiaries, while present generations use this environment to the extent that these assets are not endangered. The Hungarian Constitutional Court explains that

> "[t]he public trust doctrine is a means of enforcing the principle of intergenerational equity: the public trust doctrine implies the responsible stewardship of the values belonging to the common heritage of the nation by the present generation, in accordance with the requirement of fiduciary trust, and intergenerational equity defines the framework for the use and exploitation of these values, taking into account equally and to the same degree the protection of natural, environmental and cultural values for their own sake, as well as the interests of the present and future generations".[15]

According to the constitutional courts, these obligations and guarantees amount to 'intertemporal guarantees of freedom' *(Bundesverfassungsgericht)* or 'intergenerational equity' (Hungarian Constitutional Court). In addition, both courts refer to international law sources, and arrive at the finding that the national climate acts are unconstitutional due to inadequate targets and lack of specificity regarding measures.

---

13 Decision No. 5/2025. (VI. 30.) AB, Reasoning [52].

14 *Klimabeschluss,* marginal note 229.

15 Decision No. 5/2025. (VI. 30.) AB, Reasoning [94].

	Bundesverfassungsgericht	**Hungarian Constitutional Court**
Core Finding	Post-2030 reduction targets lack specificity; violates future freedoms	2030 target (40 %) inadequate; lack of mitigation, adaptation, resilience measures; violates constitutional obligations
Intergenerational Justice	'intertemporal freedom'	intergenerational equity
International Law's Role	Paris Agreement, EU law	Paris Agreement, EU law, ECtHR (*KlimaSeniorinnen* judgment)

What is clear from this brief comparison is the palpable tendency of 'judicial learning' where courts, but also petitioners are strongly inspired by successful climate cases. Both the *Klimabeschluss* and the Hungarian decision highlight the increasing willingness of courts to interpret constitutional obligations and scientific evidence as requiring concrete action on climate change. In addition, an increasing focus is placed on future generations and their interests. These developments suggest a trend where the judiciary acts as a crucial actor in climate policy, when national legislators fall short of achieving climate goals. The German *Klimabeschluss* has shown that climate obligations are rooted in constitutional rights and must be implemented with specificity and urgency. The Hungarian petition and decision, for their part demonstrate openness to transnational legal learning, and an awareness that courts can correct legislative inertia, when legislative measures are vague, ineffective, and non-compliant with the constitution.

Part I
– AI and intellectual property rights: new developments, new challenges

If Legislation is a Hammer, Could AI Be a Nail?

The Possibility and Viability of AI Legislation in International and EU Copyright Law

*Dávid Ujhelyi**

Abstract

This paper addresses the growing tensions between technological advancements in artificial intelligence (AI) and the traditional frameworks of copyright law. The paper highlights that throughout history, copyright law has adapted to various technological pressures. The paper asserts that generative AI poses unique challenges that necessitate a re-evaluation of existing legal standards. The paper assesses the current landscape of legislative efforts regarding these challenges and discusses potential legislative solutions, advocating for a balanced approach that preserves the foundational objectives of copyright while accommodating the innovations brought by AI. The paper ultimately seeks to determine the necessity and viability of legislative action at both EU and international levels to address the implications of AI on copyright protection and creativity.

Keywords: generative AI, copyright, legislation, originality, compensation, sui generis right

* Dávid Ujhelyi: head of department, Department of Competition Law and Intellectual Property, Ministry of Justice of Hungary, Budapest; senior lecturer, Pázmány Péter Catholic University, Budapest, dr.ujhelyi.david@gmail.com. The views expressed in this paper do not necessarily reflect the views of the above institutions.

"Throughout its history, federal copyright law has flexed under the pressures of technological advancement. Developments in artificial intelligence will soon place even more tension on the scope and application of its traditional requirements."[1]

(Timothy L. Butler, 1982)

1. Introduction

In 1982, Timothy L. Butler wrote a visionary article in the Journal of Communications and Entertainment Law,[2] in which he correctly stated that new technologies tend to impact copyright law in ways that put pressure on existing legislation. (We may add that this tendency can be observed not only in US federal copyright law but also globally, affecting international, EU, and national legislation.) Butler also stated that artificial intelligence (hereinafter: AI) would soon place an even greater strain on traditional legal requirements. While 'soon' is a relative term, it is beyond doubt that copyright law – both in practice and in legislation – is currently facing a global challenge, mainly due to the legal questions raised by a technology that has only recently become widely available; this technology is generative AI. This development, once again, confirms Butler's insights.

This said, the challenges posed by new technological advancements are neither unique nor new to copyright law.[3] We may recall times when video cassettes (home copying),[4] the rise of the internet,[5] peer-to-peer file sharing,[6] or the increasing availability of streaming services[7] led some –

1 Timothy L. Butler, 'Can a Computer be an Author – Copyright Aspects of Artificial Intelligence', *Journal of Communications and Entertainment Law,* Vol. 4, Issue 4, 1981–1982, p. 747.

2 Id.

3 Péter Gyertyánfy, 'A mesterséges intelligencia hatályos szerzői jogi törvényünk szerint', *Iparjogvédelmi és Szerzői Jogi Szemle,* Vol. 19, Issue 5, 2024, p. 34 (hereinafter: Gyertyánfy 2024a).

4 *See* Franca Klaver, 'The Legal Problems of Video-Cassettes and Audio-Visual Discs', *Bulletin of the Copyright Society of the U.S.A.,* Vol. 23, Issue 3, 1976, pp. 152–185.

5 *See* Lewis A. Kaplan, 'Copyright and the Internet', *Temple Environmental Law & Technology Journal,* Vol. 22, Issue 1, 2003, pp. 1–14.

6 *See* Péter Mezei, *'A fájlcsere dilemma – a perek lassúak, az internet gyors',* HVG-ORAC, Budapest, 2012.

7 *See* Martin Senftleben *et al.,* 'Ensuring the Visibility and Accessibility of European Creative Content on the World Market: The Need for Copyright Data Improvement in the Light of New Technologies and the Opportunity Arising from Article 17 of the CDSM Directive',

or even many – IP scholars to question the adequacy of existing legislative solutions, sometimes even the very foundations of this field of law. Legal and practical problems were raised, studied, researched, and revisited many times before ultimately being addressed through scholarly papers, judicial decisions, or legislative actions. Over the decades, copyright law has continuously adapted to these challenges, shaping and reshaping our legal regimes.

In this sense, AI does not pose a new or unique challenge for copyright law, nor should it be considered as such (although the impact of this novel technology may require new solutions). Since the first public release of ChatGPT,[8] generative AI-based solutions have begun to permeate many aspects of our lives. For example, more than 350 years after his passing, a new Rembrandt painting was generated in the style of the original artist.[9] As a result of this technology, we can now listen to a (generated) hit song featuring Drake and The Weeknd,[10] as well as a (generated) song about Harry Potter, the North Korean wizard.[11] Additionally, AI-generated background music services are available, offering royalty-free tunes to enhance the atmosphere in elevators or hotel lobbies.[12]

Without a doubt, these new technological solutions and services are having a significant impact on copyright law. In my view, generative AI – at its current stage of development – does not constitute true intelligence,[13] because without the building blocks provided by training data and the creative prompts of human users, it is incapable of producing original works in the

---

Journal of Intellectual Property, Information Technology and Electronic Commerce Law, Vol. 13, Issue 1, 2022, pp. 67–86.

8 ChatGPT was first publicly available on 30 November 2022. Andrew Perlman, 'The Implications of ChatGPT for Legal Services and Society', *Michigan Technology Law Review*, Vol. 30, Issue 1, 2023, p. 2.

9 Kavya Rallabhandi, 'The Copyright Authorship Conundrum for Works Generated by Artificial Intelligence: A Proposal for Standardized International Guidelines in the WIPO Copyright Treaty', *George Washington International Law* Review, Vol. 54, Issue 2, 2023, p. 312.

10 Fallon Jones, 'Tune in or Tune out: AI Developments Urges Federal Proposal for Voice Protection in Right of Publicity', *University of Denver Sports and Entertainment Law Journal*, No. 28, 2024, p. 40.

11 Harry Potter – North Korea Wizard (Official Music Video) is available at: https://youtu.be/_Vv21pKqxUs?si=XX3GKZwT0OUxPc6B.

12 *See e.g.* artlist.io or beatoven.ai.

13 Yudong Chen, 'The Legality of Artificial Intelligence's Unauthorized Use of Copyrighted Materials under China and U.S. Law', *IDEA: The Law Review of the Franklin Pierce Center for Intellectual Property*, Vol. 63, Issue 2, 2023, p. 250.

copyright sense.[14] Based on this, predictions about the end of human creativity and copyright legislation seem unfounded; the final days of copyright law are not upon us just yet. Nevertheless, the impact generative AI is having on copyright law may leave a mark comparable to that of digitization and the widespread availability of the internet.

This impact is not merely an academic concept or something that lies in the near or distant future – it is already happening.[15] There is tangible competition between works created by human authors and outputs generated by AI,[16] with authors and other rightsholders already losing ground. From a purely commercial perspective, some works appear to be replaceable in the consumer market by AI-generated content.[17] In terms of copyright law, this signals a noticeable shift in the balance[18] established by legislators. There is nothing more crucial to copyright law than this delicate, ever-shifting, and constantly evolving balance[19] – one that copyright legislators must hold closest to heart.

It must be noted that copyright law is in a much better position than it was two or three years ago, as some of the most important questions that emerged alongside generative AI services have now been answered – or at least a reliable consensus is beginning to form. For example, we now have a fairly clear stance on outputs solely generated by AI services, the relevant economic rights, the role of CDSM Directive's[20] text-and-data mining (hereinafter: TDM) exception, and the potential infringing nature of AI training. Therefore, the second section of this paper aims to summarize the most significant uncertainties surrounding generative AI and their current solutions.

---

14 Some aptly refer to this process as the simple regurgitation of the training set: Stephen McJohn, 'Against Progress: Fundamental IP Values in Changing Technological Times', *New England Law Review*, Vol. 58, Issue 2, 2024, p. 203.

15 Anikó Grad-Gyenge, 'A mesterséges intelligencia által generált tartalmak értelmezésének lehetőségei a szerzői jog útján', *Magyar Jog*, Vol. 60, Issue 6, 2023, p. 337.

16 Faye F. Wang, 'Copyright Protection for AI-Generated Works: Solutions to Further Challenges from Generative AI', *Amicus Curiae*, Vol. 5, Issue 1, 2023, p. 93.

17 In principle, the replacement of works and other protected materials, from a competition perspective is not necessarily a problem. The displacement of the human author through unfair competitive advantage should be considered a relevant legal problem.

18 Christophe Geiger & Elena Izyumenko, 'Copyright on the Human Rights' Trial: Redefining the Boundaries of Exclusivity Through Freedom of Expression', *International Review of Intellectual Property and Competition Law*, Vol. 45, 2014, pp. 326–339.

19 Dávid Ujhelyi, 'The Long Road to Parody Exception in Hungarian Copyright Law – An Explorer's Log', *Iparjogvédelmi és Szerzői Jogi Szemle*, Vol. 17, Issue 2, 2022, p. 45.

20 Directive (EU) 2019/790 of the European Parliament and of the Council of 17 April 2019 on copyright and related rights in the Digital Single Market and amending Directives 96/9/EC and 2001/29/EC.

This is important because challenges in copyright law arising from technological advancements should only be addressed by legislators once the issues at hand and copyright law's position have reached a sufficient level of clarity[21] to allow for well-founded responses and sustainable, consistent modifications.[22]

The third section of this paper aims to provide a comparative summary of current legislative efforts responding to generative AI's impact on copyright law and rightsholders, as well as the various alternative legislative solutions proposed by academics to address copyright issues in recent years. Furthermore, this paper seeks to assess the necessity and viability of international and EU-level legislation based on the legislative alternatives identified in my research, while the final section presents the conclusion.

2. The Current Landscape of Questions (and Their Possible Answers)

When the first generative AI services became publicly available in 2022, prompt-based image generation and large language models (LLMs) seemed, to most of us, like concepts straight out of a science fiction movie. While the topic had not been entirely overlooked by researchers,[23] it remained largely within the domain of academics with an interest in technology and the futuristic challenges of copyright law. Moreover, it is beyond question that international, EU, and national copyright legislations did not contain a single rule specifically addressing generative AI-related issues.[24] Nevertheless, the principle of technological neutrality[25] in copyright law enables us to provide answers to most – if not all – legal questions that have emerged since the advent of generative AI services. This section aims to summarize the most

21 András Jókúti, 'Mesterséges feltalálók és intelligens találmányok: az MI és a szabadalmi jog fejlődési irányai', *Iparjogvédelmi és Szerzői Jogi Szemle,* Vol. 19, Issue 5, 2024, p. 23.

22 Shr-Shian Chen, 'The Dawn of AI Generated Contents: Revisiting Compulsory Mediation and IP Disputes Resolution', *Contemporary Asia Arbitration Journal,* Vol. 16, Issue 2, 2023, p. 309.

23 *See e.g.* Butler 1982; Dan Rosen, 'A Common Law for the Ages of Intellectual Property,' *University of Miami Law Review,* Vol. 38, Issue 5, 1984, pp. 769–828; or Dániel Necz, 'A mesterséges intelligencia hatása a szerzői jogra', *Iparjogvédelmi és Szerzői Jogi Szemle,* Vol. 13, Issue 6, 2018, pp. 52–76.

24 Natalia Opolska & Anna Solomon, 'Intellectual Property Rights to Objects Created by Artificial Intelligence', *Law Review of Kyiv University of Law,* 2021/3, p. 207.

25 *See* Carys J. Craig, 'Technological Neutrality: Recalibrating Copyright in the Information Age,' *Theoretical Inquiries in Law,* Vol. 17, Issue 2, 2016, pp. 601–632.

pressing copyright-related questions concerning generative AI and to elucidate the legal interpretations that have emerged in recent years. The objective of this summary is to distinguish between issues that do not require legislative intervention and those that may necessitate regulatory action, either now or in the future.

2.1. Does Generative AI Enjoy Copyright Protection?

The first – and perhaps the easiest – question to address is whether generative AI service itself can be eligible for copyright protection. Fundamentally, AI services consist partly of software and partly of databases,[26] both of which are (or can be) unquestionably protected under copyright law. The author(s) of the software and the rightsholder(s) of the database are granted exclusive rights, allowing them to control the use of the service. At the international level, Article 10 of the TRIPS Agreement[27] provides protection for computer programs and compilations of data. At the EU level, the Software Directive[28] and the Database Directive[29] establish the specific legal framework governing their protection.

2.2. Is Generative AI the Author of Its Output?

A fundamental principle, a deeply rooted axiom in copyright law is that authorship can only be attributed to natural persons. While the Berne Convention[30] does not explicitly define *'author'*[31] or expressly state that the author must be a human being,[32] this omission does not imply that its drafters, our copyright forefathers envisioned granting authorship to generative AI.

26 Grad-Gyenge 2023, p. 340.

27 Agreement on Trade-Related Aspects of Intellectual Property Rights, 1998, at https://wipolex.wipo.int/en/text/305907.

28 Directive 2009/24/EC of the European Parliament and of the Council of 23 April 2009 on the legal protection of computer programs.

29 Directive 96/9/EC of the European Parliament and of the Council of 11 March 1996 on the legal protection of databases.

30 Berne Convention for the Protection of Literary and Artistic Works (Berne Convention), at https://wipolex.wipo.int/en/text/283698.

31 Victoria Ellen Amos, 'Man v Machine: How AI is Testing the Legal Notion of Copyright', *Southampton Student Law Review*, 2024/14, p. 145.

32 *Cf.* Agnes Augustian, 'Authorship of AI-Generated Works: An Analytical Study', *Indian Journal of Law and Legal Research*, Vol. 4, Issue 6, 2022–2023, p. 6.

Rather, the Bern Convention states that "the author shall enjoy the exclusive right of making a collection of his works mentioned in the preceding paragraphs." The phrase "his works" strongly suggests that, at the international level, the legal framework at least assumes,[33] but definitely requires[34] that the author is a natural person.

That being said, the positivist approach takes us only this far on the international level. A broader perspective requires considering the fundamental aims and purposes of copyright law. One of the main purposes of copyright law – at least, in civil law regimes[35] – is to provide incentives for authors, by granting them exclusive rights over their works, thereby fostering the expression of creativity. AI services lack both real, substantive, and genuine creativity and the ability to be incentivized for original expressions. The originality requirement is not merely a formal threshold in copyright regimes; originality embodies the recognition that a human being's personality[36] is imprinted on their work in a unique and irreplaceable manner.[37] The foundations of copyright law rest on this very principle – that the personal imprint of the author, the mark of personality, the original element of the work is invaluable, and warrants protection and support from the legislator.

The EU copyright *acquis* and the CJEU's decisions mirror this approach of originality. Article 1(3) of the Software Directive states that "[a] computer program shall be protected if it is original in the sense that it is the author's own intellectual creation". Recital (16) of the Database Directive states that "[…] no criterion other than originality in the sense of the author's intellectual creation should be applied to determine the eligibility of the database for copyright protection." Article 3(1) of the Database Directive adds that "databases which, by reason of the selection or arrangement of their contents, constitute the author's own intellectual creation shall be protected as

33 Victor Habib Lantyer, 'Granting Legal Personality to Artificial Intelligences in Brazil's Legal Context: A Possible Solution to the Copyright Limbo', *University of Miami International and Comparative Law Review,* Vol. 31, Issue 2, 2024, p. 315.

34 Haochen Sun, 'Redesigning Copyright Protection in the Era of Artificial Intelligence', *Iowa Law Review,* Vol. 107, Issue 3, 2022, p. 1226.

35 Zhe Dai & Banggui Jin, 'The Copyright Protection of AI-Generated Works under Chinese Law', *Juridical Tribune,* Vol. 13, Issue 2, 2023, p. 253.

36 Péter Gyertyánfy, 'A hollywoodi takácsok és a szerzői jog', *Iparjogvédelmi és Szerzői Jogi Szemle,* Vol. 19, Issue 5, 2024, p. 225 (hereinafter: Gyertyánfy 2024b).

37 Anett Pogácsás, 'A plágium új jelentésrétege? A "társszerzőség" útjai és megítélése a mesterséges intelligencia vonatkozásában', *Iparjogvédelmi és Szerzői Jogi Szemle,* Vol. 19, Issue 5, 2024, p. 139.

such by copyright." Finally, Article 6 of the Copyright Term Directive[38] states that "[p]hotographs which are original in the sense that they are the author's own intellectual creation shall be protected [...]." All of the above-mentioned directives acknowledge the very same, self-evident, anthropocentric approach on originality.[39]

The CJEU's decisions, to no surprise, follow this interpretation of originality. *Infopaq*, filling the blank spots the directives left in respect of originality, states that "[i]t is only through the choice, sequence and combination of those words that the author may express his creativity in an original manner and achieve a result which is an intellectual creation."[40] Based on this, the CJEU adds in *Painer* that "copyright is liable to apply only in relation to a subject-matter, such as a photograph, which is original in the sense that it is its author's own intellectual creation".[41] In *Football Dataco* the CJEU refers back again to *Infopaq*, stating that "criterion of originality is satisfied when, through the selection or arrangement of the data which it contains, its author expresses his creative ability in an original manner by making free and creative choices [...]."[42] Finally, in *Cofemel*, the CJEU already and rightly refers to the question of originality as a matter that should be clear from the previous decisions: "[...] it follows from the Court's settled case-law that, if a subject matter is to be capable of being regarded as original, it is both necessary and sufficient that the subject matter reflects the personality of its author, as an expression of his free and creative choices."[43]

As seen above, the EU copyright framework provides a *harmonized approach* to the requirement of originality, which partially stems from and is consequently accepted by its Member States.[44] This unified position leaves little room for further interpretation: as a fundamental principle of copy-

---

38 Directive 2006/116/EC of the European Parliament and of the Council of 12 December 2006 on the term of protection of copyright and certain related rights.

39 Catherine O'Callaghan, 'Can Output Produced Autonomously by AI Systems Enjoy Copyright Protection, and Should It? An Analysis of the Current Legal Position and the Search for the Way Forward', *Cornell International Law Journal*, Vol. 55, Issue 4, 2022, p. 325 and 327.

40 Judgment of 16 July 2009, *Case C-5/08, Infopaq*, ECLI:EU:C:2009:465, para. 45.

41 Judgment of 1 December 2011, *Case C-145/10, Painer*, ECLI:EU:C:2011:798, para. 87.

42 Judgment of 1 March 2012, *Case C-604/10, Football Dataco and Others*, ECLI:EU:C:2012:115, para. 38.

43 Judgment of 12 September 2019, *Case C-683/17, Cofemel*, ECLI:EU:C:2019:721, para. 30. *See also* Lilla Fanni Szakács, 'Átformálja-e a formatervezésiminta-oltalom világát a mesterséges intelligencia', *Iparjogvédelmi és Szerzői Jogi Szemle*, Vol. 19, Issue 5, 2024, p. 57.

44 Matt Blaszczyk, 'Impossibility of Emergent Works' Protection in U.S. and EU Copyright Law', *North Carolina Journal of Law & Technology*, Vol. 25, Issue 1, 2023, p. 32.

right law, authorship in the classical sense can only be granted to natural persons. Generative AI services, which currently fail to meet the criteria established in both international and EU copyright law, do not qualify as natural persons. It must be noted that even if generative AI services could be considered as persons (currently they cannot), they are still lacking in the aspect of creativity, being unable to make genuine creative decisions.[45] Consequently, AI cannot be recognized as the author of its generated outputs.[46]

2.3. Does AI-Assisted Output Enjoy Copyright Protection?

We have already clarified that generative AI service itself cannot be granted authorship. However, if the AI service does not meet the requirements to be considered an author, could any other party be eligible for this legal status? This preliminary question is of utmost importance, because without an author recognized by copyright law, there is no copyrightable work or copyright protection to speak of.

One potential candidate that comes to mind is the *developer* of the AI service, who makes substantial investments to ensure its operability. However, as previously discussed, authorship requires not only that the rightsholder be a natural person but also that the originality requirement be fulfilled. The developer of the AI service provides users with the means to utilize generative functions, but this has no direct – or even indirect – effect on the generating process, consequently, in this context it is not possible for the operator to expresses his creative ability in an original manner by making free and creative choices, to impact on the generating process in an original way. The AI service itself could only be interpreted – at this stage – as a tool, utilized by the user of the service,[47] and no more.[48] Therefore, seeking authorship for the developer would be somewhat analogous to claiming that this paper, written with the assistance of the text-editing software Microsoft Word, is at

45 Idan Zur, 'New Ownership Hierarchy for AI Creations', *IDEA: The Law Review of the Franklin Pierce Center for Intellectual Property,* Vol. 64, Issue 3, 2024, p. 655.

46 Blaszczyk 2023, p. 39.

47 Thomas F. Greene, 'Artificial Intelligence and Copyright: Why the United States Should Grant Full Copyright Protection to Works Produced Using Artificial Intelligence', *IDEA: The Law Review of the Franklin Pierce Center for Intellectual Property,* Vol. 64, Issue 3, 2024, p. 833.

48 Augustian 2022–2023, p. 8. *Cf.* Tzipi Zipper, 'Mind over Matter: Addressing Challenges of Computer-Generated Works under Copyright Law', *Wake Forest Journal of Business and Intellectual Property Law,* Vol. 22, Issue 2, 2022, p. 198.

least partially authored by Microsoft Corporation and subject to its exclusive rights. In my view, the developer of the AI service does not contribute to the generative process in an original manner and, as such, cannot be granted authorship under current international and EU copyright frameworks.

The other interested party is, of course, the *user*. From the perspective of copyright law, the user is in a much stronger position to claim copyright protection. *(i)* First, as a natural person,[49] the user possesses the ability to express their personality and the intellectual capacity to reflect it in the work through free and creative choices.[50] *(ii)* Second, on the input side of the service, the user has the opportunity to influence the generative process in a manner that may result in an original output. The primary means of exerting this influence is prompting. However, providing a prompt – essentially an instruction for the generative AI software to perform a task[51] – does not necessarily ensure that the output will be original and, therefore, eligible for copyright protection. In this regard, copyright law's longstanding thresholds are holding firm against every new technology that emerged so far. If a natural person can be identified and has exercised sufficient creative control over the generative process, such that the output reflects their personality, thereby fulfilling the originality requirement, copyright protection is available. Thus, the user has the potential to create works through generative AI and may, in certain cases, be recognized as the author of the work.[52]

While this sounds plain and simple, the spectrum of AI-generated outputs is remarkably broad, ranging from works created entirely by AI to those shaped by highly detailed and carefully crafted prompts. While the thumb rule of originality in copyright law is pretty straightforward, determining originality requires the assessment of each work and its creation process on a case-by-case basis.[53] In most cases, assessing the originality of traditional works is easy or even self-evident, in the case of AI generated outputs, outlining the amount and significance of the human contribution can be a complex task requiring both legal expertise in copyright law and technical knowledge of AI systems. Conducting a case-by-case analysis for every AI-generated work – or even a large number of them – could prove highly im-

---

49 Gergely Csősz, 'Áttekintés a generatív mesterséges intelligenciák szerzői jogi kérdéseiről', *Iparjogvédelmi és Szerzői Jogi Szemle,* Vol. 18, Issue 2, 2023, p. 64.

50 Wang 2023, p. 89.

51 Péter Somkutas, 'Kérdések és válaszok – A mesterséges intellgienciáról jogászoknak', *Iparjogvédelmi és Szerzői Jogi Szemle,* Vol. 19, Issue 5, 2024, p. 11.

52 Grad-Gyenge 2023, p. 343.

53 Péter Mezei, 'Szöveg- és adatbányászat és generatív mesterséges intelligencia', *Iparjogvédelmi és Szerzői Jogi Szemle,* Vol. 19, Issue 5, 2024, p. 103.

practical, placing an unreasonable burden on both users and the judiciary system.[54]

It is also important to note that the distinction between original works and unoriginal outputs has already led to divergent practices worldwide. For example, the US seems to follow a strict approach,[55] requiring a high level of, and direct human influence by the natural person on the generating process to be able to speak of originality. The U.S. Copyright Office's guidance states that "[i]f a work's traditional elements of authorship were produced by a machine, the work lacks human authorship and the Office will not register it." However, it also acknowledges that "[i]n other cases, [...] a work containing AI-generated material will also contain sufficient human authorship to support a copyright claim," further clarifying that "[i]n these cases, copyright will only protect the human-authored aspects of the work, which are 'independent of' and do 'not affect' the copyright status of the AI-generated material itself."[56] This approach has already been reflected in practice, as demonstrated in cases such as *A Recent Entrance to Paradise*[57] and *Théâtre d'Opéra Spatial*.[58] The *Zarya of the Dawn* registration process[59] is also a good example. None of the above mentioned cases resulted in copyright protection. In contrast, the People's Republic of China has adopted a more flexible approach,[60] interpreting the originality threshold more leniently and granting copyright protection to outputs that exhibit some identifiable level of human creative contribution. *Tencent*[61] and *Liu*[62] serve as

54 Gyertyánfy 2024b, p. 224.

55 Miriam Vogel *et al.*, 'Is Your Use of AI Violating the Law? An Overview of the Current Legal Landscape', *New York University Journal of Legislation and Public Policy,* Vol. 26, Issue 4, 2024, p. 1081.

56 U.S. Copyright Office, 'Copyright Registration Guidance: Works Containing Material Generated by Artificial Intelligence', *Federal Register,* Vol. 88, Issue 51, 2023, p. 16192–16193, at https://www.govinfo.gov/content/pkg/FR-2023-03-16/pdf/2023–05321.pdf.

57 *Thaler v Perlmutter,* Case 1:22-cv-01564-BAH (D.D.C., 18 August 2023). *See also* Ádám Miklós Sulyok, 'Utómunkák a generált tartalmakon', *Iparjogvédelmi és Szerzői Jogi Szemle,* Vol. 19, Issue 5, 2024, p. 132, and Blaszczyk 2023, p. 50.

58 *Jason Allen v Perlmutter,* Case 1:24-cv-02665-SKC-KAS (26 September 2024). *See also* Csősz 2023, p. 65.

59 Zarya of the Dawn (Registration # VAu001480196) (2023), at https://www.copyright.gov/docs/zarya-of-the-dawn.pdf. *See also* Sulyok 2024, p. 134.

60 Dai & Jin, 2023, p. 253.

61 *Tencent Company v Yingxun Company,* Case No. Y0305MC No. 14010 (December 21, 2019). *See also* Dai & Jin 2023, p. 248, Rallabhandi 2023, p. 335, and Greene 2024, p. 836.

62 *Li v Liu,* 2023 Jing 0491 Min Chu No. 11279 (27 November 2023). *See also* Gergely Csősz, 'A prompt szerepe az alkotásban', *Iparjogvédelmi és Szerzői Jogi Szemle,* Vol. 19, Issue 5, 2024, p. 117.

notable examples, both concluding that, in the specific circumstances of each case, AI-assisted generation met the requirements for copyright protection.

In my view, it is very clear that under international and EU copyright law, generative AI services' outputs could only qualify for protection when the user's contribution mirrors the author's personality. In this sense, the current copyright paradigm is capable of providing an Abstract, yet dogmatically consistent answer to the question of copyright protection. While the CJEU's stance on AI-assisted works remains to be seen, it seems reasonable – both from a practical and a competitiveness perspective – that the US' unusually high standard should not be followed, and the originality threshold should be kept on a low level (as is traditional in copyright law).[63] That being said, the existing, traditional originality requirement should be preserved, as there is no compelling argument or identifiable interest that would justify abandoning this fundamental criterion.

2.4. What Happens to Outputs Without an Author?

If the generation process is realized without any human contribution, or if the human contribution is inadequate to satisfy the requirement of originality, the output is considered to be a part of the public domain.[64] In such cases, neither the AI itself, nor the developer or the user could be recognized as the author. Since outputs without an author do not qualify as 'works' under the current copyright regimes, the only legally viable classification for such outputs is their placement in the public domain.[65]

For the sake of completeness, it should be noted that, following the United Kingdom's legal approach,[66] some jurisdictions (*e.g.*, New Zealand, India, Hong Kong, Ireland and South Africa) have a protection for computer-

---

63 Allison Dang, 'How International Precedence Can Inform Future U.S. Copyright Law Applications to Generative AI', *Notre Dame Journal on Emerging Technologies*, Vol. 5, Issue 2, 2024, p. 213.

64 Andrew Ahrenstein, 'AI Generated Art and the Gap in Copyright Law', *American University Intellectual Property Brief*, Vol. 15, Issue 2, 2024, p. 26, and Gyertyánfy 2024a, p. 45.

65 Isaac Sachdev Pereira, 'Exploring How Domestic Law Might Evolve to Deal with Copyright concerning Creative Works That Are Generated by an Artificial Intelligence Computer Program', *City Law Review*, 2020/2, p. 75, and Zur 2024, p. 656.

66 Section 9(3) of the UK's Copyright, Designs and Patents Act of 1988. *See also* O'Callaghan 2022, p. 331, and Liubov Maidanyk, 'Artificial Intelligence and Sui Generis Right: A Perspective for Copyright in Ukraine?', *Access to Justice in Eastern Europe*, 2021/3, p. 150.

generated works (CGWs), which allows for a special form of protection, even in absence of originality, but this legal instrument holds limited significance in the context of international and EU copyright law.[67]

2.5. Does AI Training Without a License Constitute Copyright Infringement?

Without delving into unnecessary technological details, we can confidently say that the neural networks of generative AI services are trained with the use of a significant amount of training data. These datasets may include works that are under copyright protection, particularly if they are acquired through internet scraping algorithms.[68] The training process itself requires the dataset to be reproduced on local storage, as the system needs to repeatedly access the data to establish and reinforce the correct – or at least expected – logical connections. As a result, the training of AI services inherently affects at least one of the author's economic rights – namely, the exclusive right of reproduction.[69]

It is evident that the use of a work requires a license from the author (or other rightsholder). As a general rule, this license may be acquired for a fee, except in cases where established exceptions apply (*e.g.*, the work is in the public domain) or limitations are in place (*e.g.*, codified cases of free use). Therefore, the first part of the answer must establish that the exploitation of a work for AI training purposes constitutes use, specifically in the form of reproduction. If such use occurs without a license and does not fall within the scope of currently regulated exceptions or limitations, it constitutes an infringement of the rightsholder's exclusive rights.[70]

Our next step is to determine whether any available exceptions for free use could apply to the reproduction that occurs during AI training. Interna-

67 Wang 2023, p. 93, and Marta Duque Lizarralde & Christofer Meinecke, 'Authorless AI-Assisted Productions: Recent Developments Impacting Their Protection in the European Union', *Journal of Intellectual Property, Information Technology and Electronic Commerce Law,* Vol. 14, Issue 1, 2023, p. 91.

68 Dennis Crouch, 'Using Intellectual Property to Regulate Artificial Intelligence', *Missouri Law Review,* Vol. 89, Issue 3, 2024, p. 821.

69 Csősz 2023, p. 76, and Mihály Ficsor, 'A WIPO válaszára várva – Mesterséges intelligencia és a nemzetközi szerzői jog', *Iparjogvédelmi és Szerzői Jogi Szemle,* Vol. 19, Issue 5, 2024, p. 203.

70 Gary Myers, 'Artificial Intelligence and Transformative Use after Warhol', *Washington and Lee Law Review Online,* Vol. 81, Issue 1, 2023, p. 26.

tional and EU copyright law sources provide several possible cases of free use, though few of them are relevant in this context. The Infosoc Directive's[71] exception for temporary acts of reproduction, as regulated in Article 5(1), appears to be a possible option. However, this exception applies only if the use has no independent economic significance – a condition that AI training does not meet. Furthermore, even if this exception were interpreted to encompass the training of generative AI systems, it would almost certainly fail to satisfy the conditions set forth in Article 5(5) of the Infosoc Directive,[72] known as the three-step test.[73] According to this provision, every exception should only be considered lawful, if it is "only [to] be applied in certain special cases which do not conflict with a normal exploitation of the work or other subject-matter and do not unreasonably prejudice the legitimate interests of the rightsholder." It would be highly challenging to substantiate a claim that training AI systems on a large volume of protected works without rightsholders' consent constitutes a "special case," does not interfere with normal exploitation, and does not unreasonably harm the legitimate interests of the rightsholder.[74]

Another potential candidate is the TDM exception under the CDSM Directive. Technically, Article 3 and 4 of the CDSM Directive regulate two distinct exceptions, both addressing a specific form of use but with different scopes. Article 3 of the CDSM Directive provides for a broader limitation on the author's exclusive rights, as it allows for the storage of mined data and does not allow rightsholders to opt out of this form of free use.[75] However, this broader exception is available only when the mining is conducted for scientific research purposes by research organizations or cultural heritage

---

71 Directive 2001/29/EC of the European Parliament and of the Council of 22 May 2001 on the harmonisation of certain aspects of copyright and related rights in the information society.

72 The test is regulated on the international level, see Article 9(2) of the Bern Convention, Article 13 of the TRIPS Agreement, Article 10(1) of the WIPO Copyright Treaty and Article 16(2) of the WIPO Performances and Phonograms Treaty. Article 6(3) of the Software Directive and the Database Directive also regulate this legal instrument, along with 10(3) of Directive 2006/115/EC of the European Parliament and of the Council of 12 December 2006 on rental right and lending right and on certain rights related to copyright in the field of intellectual property.

73 *See more* Richard Arnold & Eleonora Rosati, 'Are national courts the addressees of the InfoSoc three-step test?', *Journal of Intellectual Property Law & Practice,* Vol. 10, Issue 10, 2015, pp. 741–749.

74 Mezei 2024, p. 104, and Ficsor 2024, p. 204.

75 Serena Chu Lightstone, 'Train or Restrain? Using International Perspectives to Inform the American Fair Use Analysis of Copyright in Generative Artificial Intelligence Training', *Northwestern Journal of International Law & Business,* Vol. 44, Issue 3, 2024, p. 477.

institutions. By contrast, Article 4 of the CDSM Directive establishes a narrower limitation (as it is does not allow for storing data, and the rightsholders may opt out from the exception), but its scope is broader in terms of applicability, as it permits free use for any purpose and is available to a wider range of entities, not just research organizations and cultural heritage institutions.[76]

This, latter form of the TDM exception does cover uses for AI training purposes. Although neither the DSM Proposal of 2016,[77] nor the CDSM Directive of 2019 explicitly mention artificial intelligence or generative AI training – and it is certain that the legislative process did not originally contemplate such uses under this exception –,[78] the AI Act[79] has effectively repurposed Article 4 of the CDSM Directive for this context. Recital (105) of the AI Act states as follows:

> "[…] The development and training of such models require access to vast amounts of text, images, videos and other data. Text and data mining techniques may be used extensively in this context for the retrieval and analysis of such content, which may be protected by copyright and related rights. Any use of copyright protected content requires the authorisation of the rightsholder concerned unless relevant copyright exceptions and limitations apply. Directive (EU) 2019/790 introduced exceptions and limitations allowing reproductions and extractions of works or other subject matter, for the purpose of text and data mining, under certain conditions. Under these rules, rightsholders may choose to reserve their rights over their works or other subject matter to prevent text and data mining, unless this is done for the purposes of scientific research. Where the rights to opt out has been expressly reserved in an appropriate manner, providers of general-purpose AI models need to obtain an authorisation from rightsholders if they want to carry out text and data mining over such works."

---

76 Mohd Syaufiq Abdul Latif *et al.*, 'Proposal for Copyright Compensation for Artificial Intelligence (AI) Data Training for Malaysia', *IIUM Law Journal*, Vol. 32, Issue 2, 2024, p. 180.

77 Proposal for a Directive of the European Parliament and of the Council on copyright in the Digital Single Market, COM/2016/0593 final – 2016/0280 (COD).

78 Ficsor 2024, p. 209.

79 Regulation (EU) 2024/1689 of the European Parliament and of the Council of 13 June 2024 laying down harmonised rules on artificial intelligence and amending Regulations (EC) No 300/2008, (EU) No 167/2013, (EU) No 168/2013, (EU) 2018/858, (EU) 2018/1139 and (EU) 2019/2144 and Directives 2014/90/EU, (EU) 2016/797 and (EU) 2020/1828.

Although the applicability of the TDM exception was not explicitly addressed in the legislative text – an omission that would have enhanced legal certainty – the AI Act, already referred to as the "mother of all AI laws,"[80] has effectively broadened the scope of this limitation through the recital quoted above. It is important to note that my earlier reservations regarding the mass use of protected works and their compliance with the three-step test remain highly relevant to the TDM exception as well. Nevertheless, the question of whether the TDM exception applies to generative AI training appears to have been settled by the EU legislator.

If the TDM exception is applicable, the opt out mechanism in Article 4(3) of the CDSM Directive must also be considered. In this context, Recital (106) of the AI Act states that "[...] providers of general-purpose AI models should put in place a policy to comply with Union law on copyright and related rights, in particular to identify and comply with the reservation of rights expressed by rightsholders pursuant to Article 4(3) of Directive (EU) 2019/790." This recital, along with the transparency requirements set out in Recital (107) of the AI Act, constitutes the primary legislative support that the EU has provided to rightsholders thus far. However, despite the transposition deadline for the CDSM Directive having long lapsed, the concrete methodology for implementing the opt-out mechanism in practice remains unclear. There are, of course, some practical solutions for the machine readable opt outs, but many questions remain yet to be answered.

A key question concerns the temporal effect of the opt-out mechanism and whether it applies only *ex nunc*. This is most likely the case, as *ex tunc* opt-outs would be difficult for AI service providers to manage. Consequently, the opt-out mechanism does not extend to uses that occurred before the transposition deadline of the CDSM Directive.[81] Another point of uncertainty is whether the opt-out must apply to all works of a rightsholder or whether selective opt outs for specific works are permissible. Since there is no explicit regulation requiring the opt out to cover all works, it follows that rightsholders should be able to opt out only for selected works if they so choose. Similarly, the legal framework does not prohibit collective management organizations (hereinafter: CMOs) from declaring opt-outs on behalf of their rightsholders, suggesting that such a mechanism could be im-

80 Dorian Chang, 'AI Regulation for the AI Revolution', *Singapore Comparative Law Review,* 2023, p. 135.

81 Gábor Faludi, 'A generatív mesterséges intelligencia (MI) és a szerzői jog, kitekintéssel egyes nemzetközi és uniós közös jogkezelő ernyőszervezetek álláspontjára', *Iparjogvédelmi és Szerzői Jogi Szemle,* Vol. 19, Issue 5, 2024, p. 94.

plemented within the existing legal structure.[82] The only barrier here is Article 12(2) of the CDSM Directive, which states that collective licensing with an extended effect could only be applied by Member States

> "[...] within well-defined areas of use, where obtaining authorizations from rightholders on an individual basis is typically onerous and impractical to a degree that makes the required licensing transaction unlikely, due to the nature of the use or of the types of works or other subject matter concerned, and shall ensure that such licensing mechanism safeguards the legitimate interests of rightholders."

In my view, it is beyond doubt that the use for generative AI training fits this criterion. The technical implementation of the machine-readable requirement also remains unresolved. In principle, any method that allows a machine to process the opt-out should be legally valid. Current practices include robots.txt files, server protocols, and Hypertext Transfer Protocol (HTTP) response status codes,[83] but a standardized approach or further guidance from the European Commission would be highly beneficial in ensuring legal certainty and uniform application. Beyond these technical and procedural considerations, a fundamental issue arises concerning the ability of rightsholders to substantiate infringement claims and whether infringement can be effectively proven. While, in theory, the transparency obligations set forth in the AI Act should provide a degree of oversight, in my view, there are valid grounds for skepticism regarding their practical enforceability. The broader question of whether this new, expanded form of the TDM exception aligns with the three-step test remains a potential subject for legal debate. Although the EU legislator has clearly endorsed its validity, in my view, as discussed above, concerns persist about its conformity.[84] As the ECJ has not yet provided a definitive interpretation of these issues under EU law, their resolution remains an open question for future judicial review.

To summarize, the second part of my analysis should establish that under the current EU legal framework, the TDM exception applies to generative AI training.[85] Consequently, if the rightsholder has not exercised the opt-out mechanism in a manner that meets the "machine readable" requirement before the training occurs, and if the service provider complies with the

82 Gyertyánfy 2024a, p. 41, and Faludi 2024, p. 93.
83 Mezei 2024, p. 108.
84 Gyertyánfy 2024a, p. 42.
85 Dang 2024, p. 209.

transparency obligations set out in the AI Act,[86] no infringement may be found.

Again, for the sake of completeness, it is important to note that US copyright law has not yet established a definitive judicial position on whether the fair use doctrine extends to generative AI training. While some of the academic literature reviewed in this research advocates for recognizing AI training as falling within the scope of fair use,[87] I maintain that the large-scale use of protected works, combined with the tendency of AI-generated outputs to substitute certain types of works in the market, strongly suggests that AI training should not be considered fair use.[88]

2.6. Could the Output Be Considered a Reproduction of the Work?

Ideally, a generative AI service, once trained, does not store any part of the original work, nor should it reproduce the work in whole or in part. However, if the AI system does generate an output that reproduces the work or any original element of it, such use would constitute unlawful reproduction in the absence of rightsholder authorization or a relevant limitation or exception.[89]

In such cases, certain copyright exceptions may be applicable. Among them, the quotation, criticism, review, parody,[90] and pastiche exceptions hold particular significance, especially following the adoption of the CDSM Directive, which mandates the implementation of these exceptions across EU Member States. Quotation, criticism, and review are well established in national legal frameworks and will therefore not be examined in detail in this paper. Since *Deckmyn,* the conditions for invoking the parody exception – requiring both an evocation of an existing work and humor or mockery to

86 Article 50 of the AI Act.

87 David Silverman, 'Burying the Black Box: AI Image Generation Platforms as Artists' Tools in the Age of Google v. Oracle', *Federal Communications Law Journal,* Vol. 76, Issue 1, 2023, p. 118, Myers 2023, p. 2, Ahrenstein 2024, p. 33, Lightstone 2024, pp. 482–500, and Chen 2023, p. 261.

88 Nicoletta Gasparis, 'Drake or Droid?: A.I.-Generated Music and the Legal Challenges in Safeguarding Artist Rights', *Hofstra Law Review,* Vol. 52, Issue 4, 2024, p. 985.

89 Ficsor 2024, p. 205.

90 *See more* Ujhelyi 2022 and Dávid Ujhelyi, *A paródiakivétel szükségessége és lehetséges keretrendszere a hazai szerzői jogban,* Ludovika Egyetemi Kiadó, Budapest, 2021. *See also* Lindsey Joost, 'The Place for Illusions: Deepfake Technology and the Challenges of Regulating Unreality', *University of Florida Journal of Law and Public Policy,* Vol. 33, Issue 2, 2023, p. 321, and 325.

be expressed[91] – have been clearly defined. By contrast, the scope of the pastiche exception remains uncertain, as the CJEU has yet to provide a definitive interpretation of its precise conditions in the pending *Pelham* case.[92] A key concern regarding the pastiche exception is the risk of an overly broad interpretation by the CJEU. The requirement that a pastiche express 'respect' for the original work, a condition often associated with this exception,[93] is inherently ambiguous and open to varying interpretations. If interpreted too broadly, this could lead to a disproportionately expansive limitation on the exclusive rights of rightsholders, potentially undermining the fundamental balance of copyright protection.[94] There are already voices stating AI generation could basically be considered as pastiche of the training dataset.[95]

Another aspect of this analysis, though minor in practical terms but significant from a doctrinal perspective, concerns the topic of style, specifically the imitation of an author's artistic style. This issue is particularly intriguing, as an author's style is generally not protected under copyright law, with national legal frameworks often imposing limitations in this regard.[96] However, certain original elements of an author's style may still qualify for copyright protection, and if such distinctive elements are reproduced in AI-generated outputs, the right of reproduction could become relevant.[97] A prominent example of this phenomenon is the widespread use of ChatGPT to generate images that emulate the distinctive artistic style of Hayao Miyazaki (Studio Ghibli).[98]

91 Judgment of 3 September 2014, *Case C-201/13, Deckmyn and Vrijheidsfonds,* ECLI:EU:C:2014:2132, para. 36.

92 *Case C-590/23, Pelham,* pending.

93 Yatin Arora, 'Music Sampling and Copyright: Are the Courts Hung up on Restricting Creativity?', *Trinity College Law Review,* Vol. 25, 2022, p. 185.

94 Péter Mezei, 'Új általános szerzői jogi kivétel a láthatáron? Pastiche az Európai Bíróság előtt', *Iparjogvédelmi és Szerzői Jogi Szemle,* Vol. 19, Issue 3, 2024, pp. 69–99.

95 Derek E. Bambauer & Mihai Surdeanu, 'Authorbots', *Journal of Free Speech Law,* Vol. 3, Issue 2, 2023, p. 380.

96 Gasparis 2024, p. 987.

97 Grad-Gyenge 2023, p. 345.

98 Studio Ghibli Memes: 42 Memes Ghiblified by ChatGPT, Thunder Gundeon, 30 March 2025, at https://thunderdungeon.com/2025/03/28/studio-ghibli-memes-ghiblify-memes/.

Illustration 1. The 'Disaster Girl' meme (left) and the 'Ghibli-fied' version (right) (Source: nytimes.com; thunderdungeon.com)

The so-called 'Ghibli-fication' of images has gained immense popularity on the internet, despite Miyazaki himself having previously condemned AI-generated animation as "disgusting" and "an insult to life itself."[99] While the question of whether imitating Miyazaki's style constitutes copyright infringement based on economic rights – particularly reproduction – remains open to debate, an equally compelling issue arises concerning the potential infringement of moral rights, particularly the right of integrity. If an AI-generated work mimics an artist's style in a manner that distorts, misrepresents, or otherwise compromises the artistic vision of the original creator, it could arguably infringe upon the author's moral rights.[100]

3. The Necessity and Viability of Legislation

The previous section summarized the current state, the *status quo* of copyright law, the main legal questions, and their potential answers regarding generative AI services. This section aims to present the legislative alternatives that have emerged concerning AI systems, with the ambition to assess their necessity and viability. While this paper primarily focuses on proposals suggesting amendments to the international or EU legal framework,[101]

---

99 Greg Evans, 'Hayao Miyazaki's 'disgusted' thoughts on AI resurface following Studio Ghibli trend', Independent, 28 March 2025, at https://www.independent.co.uk/arts-entertainment/films/news/hayao-miyazaki-studio-ghibli-ai-trend-b2723358.html.

100 Anikó Grad-Gyenge, 'A (mesterséges) intelligencia és a stílus a szerzői jogban', *Iparjogvédelmi és Szerzői Jogi Szemle,* Vol. 19, Issue 5, 2024, p. 168.

101 Naturally, not all alternatives could be summarized here. For further proposed solutions, *see* Mauritz Kop, 'Public Property from the Machine', in Péter Mezei *et al.* (eds.), *Harmonizing Intellectual Property Law for a Trans-Atlantic Knowledge Economy,* Brill–

recommendations for national legislation or soft law instruments will also be provided when relevant or deemed particularly useful.

3.1. Changing the Threshold of Originality

The originality requirement has been discussed in detail in this paper. Some scholars are not satisfied with the current interpretation of this threshold, and calling for changes in this regard. Moldawer for example advocates for a 'spectral model of originality', based on the premise of the Turing test, thereby granting direct authorship to the AI service.[102] LEE essentially proposes further lowering the level of creativity required to meet the originality requirement, referring to this as the 'bare minimum approach'.[103] Rallabhandi suggests a similar idea, recommending the adaptation of Chinese court rulings on originality as a WCT Guidance, thereby establishing the flexible approach to originality as a best practice. Zipper's proposal aims to abandon the originality threshold altogether replacing it with an 'intelligence requirement,' wherein outputs that demonstrate 'only a modicum of intelligence' would qualify for copyright protection,[104] ultimately resulting in joint authorship between humans and AIs. At the same time, Gyertyánfy proposes raising the originality threshold to safeguard human creativity.[105] In my view, any significant modification to the current threshold appears practically unfeasible, as it would necessitate revisions not only at the national level but also at the EU and international levels of the copyright legislative system, besides the decades of established judicial practice. Simply put, such a change "would contradict not only the current prevalent opinion in the academic community, but also the contemporary conception of copy-

Nijhoff, Leiden–Boston, 2024, pp. 264–288 (Res Publicae ex Machina), or CISAC, 'Study on the economic impact of Generative AI in the Music and Audiovisual industries', November 2024, at https://www.cisac.org/services/reports-and-research/cisacpmp-strategy-ai-study, and Artisjus, 'Mesterséges intelligencia a zeneiparban – díjazzuk?', *Dalszerző,* 19 November 2024, at https://dalszerzo.hu/2024/11/19/mesterseges-intelligencia-a-zeneiparban-dijazzuk/.

102 Mira Moldawer, 'The Shadow of the Law versus a Law with No Shadow: Pride and Prejudice in Exchange for Generative AI Authorship', *Seattle Journal of Technology, Environmental & Innovation Law,* Vol. 14, Issue 2, 2024, p. 45.

103 Edward Lee, 'Prompting Progress: Authorship in the Age of AI', *Florida Law Review,* Vol. 76, Issue 5, 2024, pp. 1505, and 1578–1579.

104 Zipper 2022, pp. 231–232.

105 Gyertyánfy 2024b, pp. 224–225.

right in the EU."[106] That said, minor changes – whether increasing or decreasing the originality requirement – are not inconceivable. The CJEU or even national courts would be suitable forums for such adjustments. As discussed above, I believe that maintaining the expectation of originality at the lowest feasible level is the most appropriate approach to address the challenges posed by generative AI systems.

It should be noted that in connection with the realignment of the originality threshold, there are also voices supporting the reestablishment of the registration requirement for protected works, but since the prohibition of formality is deeply embedded in international copyright law, this alternative has low viability.[107]

3.2. Adapting the Work-for-Hire Doctrine

Some scholars have proposed applying the work-for-hire doctrine to AI-generated outputs.[108] Under this approach, following amendments to national regulations,[109] AI-generated works would be considered the property of the AI service.[110] However, since these works are produced on behalf of the developer (the 'employer'),[111] the associated economic rights would be automatically transferred. While EU law does not harmonize work-for-hire rules, many Member States recognize this legal instrument in some form.[112] The primary issue with this alternative is that transferring rights to the employer would first require granting authorship to generative AI services – an option that, as previously discussed, is not feasible.[113] As early as 1982, Butler had already deemed this alternative unviable.[114] Simply put, this proposal is nothing more than a reformulation of the argument advocating for AI services to be granted authorship.

106 Lizarralde & Meinecke 2023, p. 92.

107 Gyertyánfy 2024b, p. 225.

108 Laetitia Coguic, 'Forward Thinking or Right on Time?: A Proposal to Recognize Authorship and Inventorship to Artificial Intelligence', *Indonesian Journal of International & Comparative Law*, Vol. 8, Issue 3, 2021, p. 236.

109 Moldawer 2024, p. 7.

110 Sun 2022, p. 1233.

111 Augustian 2022–2023, p. 8.

112 *See* Article 30 of Act LXXVI of 1999 on Copyright Law (Hungarian Copyright Act).

113 Augustian 2022–2023, p. 9.

114 Butler 1981–1982, p. 740.

3.3. Generative AI Services as Legal Persons, Joint Authorship

Some scholars suggest that granting legal, 'electronic'[115] personhood to generative AI systems could be an innovative approach to addressing the legal challenges they present. This, they argue, "would provide legal security, creating a clearer and more predictable legal environment for determining rights and duties associated with Al creations."[116] According to this perspective, an AI system could fulfill the requirements of legal personhood[117] and, consequently, be eligible for some form of intellectual property protection over outputs generated solely by itself. If the generation of the output had a meaningful human contribution, AI systems and human authors could be granted joint authorship on the work.[118] However, this proposal is not only controversial,[119] but also seemingly unnecessary.[120] If some form of intellectual property protection – other than copyright – were deemed beneficial, it could instead be granted to existing legal persons, such as the entities behind the development of AI services. Establishing legal personhood for AI systems would constitute a significant departure from the current legal framework, and implementing such a fundamental shift solely to extend copyright protection – another major deviation from the *status quo* – appears premature and unsubstantiated. Regarding joint authorship, demarcating the line between the contribution of AI and the natural person would be also impossible, while the distribution of the exercise of exclusive rights also seems unclear.

3.4. Common Rights Management and Compensation for Use in AI Training

As discussed above, the use of protected works could be carried out under the TDM exception, but the legal use of works with opt-outs still requires a

115 Coguic 2021, p. 237.

116 Victor Habib Lantyer, 'Granting Legal Personality to Artificial Intelligences in Brazil's Legal Context: A Possible Solution to the Copyright Limbo', *University of Miami International and Comparative Law Review,* Vol. 31, Issue 2, 2024, p. 326.

117 Wong Pui Yuen, 'Rights for AIS: A Possible Solution to Accountability for Autonomous Artificial Intelligence Systems', *Hong Kong Journal of Legal Studies,* Vol. 17, 2023, p. 119.

118 Zur 2024, p. 655, Zipper 2022, p. 232, and Immidisetty Navya Raga Sravani & Kurella Venkat, 'AI-Produced Works and the Subject of Copyright – Its Legal Position', *Indian Journal of Law and Legal Research,* Vol. 5, Issue 2, 2023, p. 8.

119 O'Callaghan 2022, p. 341.

120 Wang 2023, p. 91.

license from the rightsholder. Regardless, the use of works and other protected material for AI training occurs on a mass scale and the resulting outputs directly compete with authored works.[121] This situation is further exacerbated by the fact that the AI Act's transparency requirements are not fully met in practice, and the TDM exception's machine-readable opt-outs are not uniform, and there is also a real risk that AI developers may not comply with them in any way whatsoever, while infringements are exceedingly difficult to prove in court. It should be noted that Spain already drafted legislation[122] in December 2024 that reflects this very proposal. Under this framework, certified CMOs would be authorized to issue non-exclusive licenses for the reproduction of copyrighted works needed for AI training.[123]

Consequently, scholars propose that economic rights – at least for the most vulnerable and exposed types of works and authors – should be centralized within CMOs to ensure that opt-outs are clear for AI developers and IPR enforcement is guaranteed.[124] For works remaining under the TDM exception, scholars suggest the establishment of a new compensation regime[125] to counterbalance the mass and uncontrollable use caused by AI training. This compensation system could be modeled on the private reproduction levy system[126] outlined in the Infosoc Directive.[127]

In my view, both proposals are well-founded. CMOs have traditionally and effectively been involved in cases where individual licensing is deemed ineffectual, while collective authorization ensures a stronger bargaining position for licensing fees, providing a competitive advantage for rightsholders and a more effective mechanism for enforcement. Since AI training is unsustainable when developers treat protected works as a renewable resource, and 90 % of authors feel that they should be compensated for the use of their works in AI training,[128] the establishment of a new compensation regime

121 Gary Myers, 'The Future Is Now: Copyright Protection for Works Created by Artificial Intelligence', *Texas Law Review Online,* Vol. 102, 2023, p. 26.

122 The draft text is available at https://www.cultura.gob.es/en/servicios-al-ciudadano/informacion-publica/audiencia-informacion-publica/cerrados/2024/concesion-licencias-colectivas.html.

123 Dávid Ujhelyi, 'Spain's Proposal for Extended Collective Licensing in AI Development', *Central European Lawyers Initiative,* 24 January 2025, at https://ceuli.com/spains-proposal-for-extended-collective-licensing-in-ai-development/.

124 Ficsor 2024, pp. 211–212., Wang 2023, p. 98.

125 Latif *et al.* 2024, pp. 171–172.

126 Id. p. 173.

127 Faludi 2024, p. 90. *See* Article 4(2)(b) of the Infosoc Directive.

128 Frank Pasquale & Haochen Sun, 'Consent and Compensation: Resolving Generative AI's Copyright Crisis', *Virginia Law Review Online,* Vol. 110, 2024, pp. 220 and 230.

appears justified. Furthermore, the EU copyright framework is not unfamiliar with compensation systems for free uses, as Member States already have implemented operable methods for imposing, collecting and distributing license fees. The introduction of a new compensation scheme for AI training would not impose a dogmatic strain on the existing copyright framework, but could, in fact, enhance the competitiveness of works on the market.

It should be noted that during its Presidency of the Council of the EU in 2024, Hungary issued a questionnaire[129] to Member States addressing various AI-related issues. The summary of this questionnaire (hereinafter: Summary) indicated that some Member States believed "it would be better to consider introducing extended or mandatory collective licensing mechanisms," while a significant number of Member States expressed the view that "a remuneration scheme should be guaranteed for generative AI activities."[130] Based on these findings, the proposals outlined here align with the existing copyright regime and could garner support from Member States.

3.5. Introduction of a New Sui Generis Right for AI Generated Outputs

As discussed above, granting AI services legal personhood or authorship does not appear viable in light of the existing legal framework, and introducing changes in this regard would also be unfounded. At the same time, copyright law does provide some form of protection even for non-original subject matter. One example is the previously mentioned protection for computer-generated works established in the UK.[131] This legal instrument will not be analyzed in detail in this paper, as there is no clear consensus on

129 Council of the European Union, '*Policy questionnaire on the relationship between generative Artificial Intelligence and copyright and related rights*', 11575/24, 27 June 2024, at https://data.consilium.europa.eu/doc/document/ST-11575-2024-INIT/en/pdf.

130 Council of the European Union, '*Policy questionnaire on the relationship between generative Artificial Intelligence and copyright and related rights – Revised Presidency summary of the Member States contributions*', 16710/1/24 REV 1, 20 December 2024, pp. 13 and 23, at https://data.consilium.europa.eu/doc/document/ST-16710-2024-REV-1/en/pdf.

131 *See* Antonije D. Zivkovic, 'Computer Programs Legal Protection Framework with Special Reference to Artificial Intelligence ChatGPT', *Strani Pravni Zivot,* 2024/3, pp. 317–388, and Sakshi Mittal, 'Digital Copyright and Trademark Issues in the Era of Artificial Intelligence', *International Journal of Law Management & Humanities,* Vol. 6, Issue 2, 2023, p. 3251.

its applicability to AI services. Another example is the *sui generis* protection of databases established by the Database Directive in the EU.[132]

Since *sui generis* protection is a recognized and accepted form of related rights in copyright law, and since this kind of protection is suitable for subject matters that do not fulfill the requirement of originality, scholars have identified the possibility of establishing a new *sui generis* right for AI-generated outputs.[133] These rights usually emphasize economic interests over artistic considerations,[134] which aligns well with the non-original nature of purely AI-generated outputs. The protection of databases was introduced to safeguard the investment of time, effort, financial resources, labor, and other skills necessary to create a database.[135] A similar situation arises in the context of AI-generated outputs, as AI developers are not eligible to be considered authors under the current copyright regime, yet they invest labor, resources, and capital – much like the rightsholders of a database. This could serve as a foundation for a related-rights form of protection.

That said, many details remain to be determined should the EU legislator decide to establish a new *sui generis* right. In this regard, Sun proposes that only AI developers should be deemed owners of such a right, with reproduction and distribution rights granted to the developer, while moral rights would be deemed unnecessary. The proposed term of protection is ten years, and the *sui generis* right should apply only to the verbatim copying of AI-generated works. Additionally, a verification obligation should be introduced, requiring AI system developers or users to disclose when their works have been generated by such systems.[136] At present, however, a comprehensive legal framework for this right has yet to be clearly formulated.[137]

Critics of this proposed related right argue that the economic impact of *sui generis* rights for databases remains unproven and that such rights have, in fact, led to significant legal uncertainty.[138] Furthermore, based on the

---

132 Sun 2022, p. 1236.

133 Ficsor 2024, p. 205, Yuen 2023, pp. 119 and 131, Augustian 2022–2023, p. 10, Zivkovic 2024, p. 336.

134 Michalina Kowala, 'Collective Work as an Inspiration for Legal Qualification of Computer-Generated Works – Comparative Analysis of the Institution from Polish and French Copyright Law Perspective', *Review of European and Comparative Law,* Vol. 45, Issue 2, 2021, p. 53.

135 Zur 2024, p. 668.

136 Sun 2022, p. 1237–1247.

137 Anna Shtefan, 'Creations of Artificial Intelligence: In Search of the Legal Protection Regime', *Journal of Intellectual Property, Information Technology and Electronic Commerce Law,* Vol. 14, Issue 1, 2023, pp. 104–107.

138 O'Callaghan 2022, p. 349.

Summary, the majority of EU Member States currently do not support the introduction of a new *sui generis* right,[139] and some scholars have deemed the proposal at least controversial.[140]

Nevertheless, a *sui generis* right for AI-generated outputs is not merely a theoretical construct. Ukraine proposed such a system in 2021,[141] and its Law No. 2811-IX on Copyright and Related Rights came into force on 1 December 2022.[142] Article 33 of this law regulates the alienable *sui generis* right for non-original objects generated by a computer program. This provision applies to non-original outputs, excludes moral rights, and grants protection for 25 years from the moment of generation.[143]

In my view, the development and effects of this new form of protection should be carefully monitored, as its adoption could serve as an incentive for innovation and may contribute to legal certainty. Nonetheless, it remains uncertain whether the EU legislator and Member States are prepared to take such a significant step at this time. Regardless, the European Commission should explore available options and closely follow the positions of Member States on this matter.

3.6. Amending Current Free Uses

As previously noted, the EU legislator has already repurposed the TDM exception, and the applicability of the existing fair use test is currently under consideration in the US.[144] While guidance from the European Commission on the TDM exception's opt-out mechanism and its connection to the AI Act's transparency obligations[145] would be welcome, I believe that no further amendments are necessary concerning AI. The CJEU's position on the conditions of the pastiche exception should also be closely monitored.

139 Summary 2024, p. 18.

140 Lizarralde & Meinecke 2023, p. 93, Shtefan 2023, p. 105.

141 Maidanyk 2021, pp. 150–151.

142 Law No. 2811-IX on Copyright and Related Rights, Ukraine, available in English at https://www.wipo.int/wipolex/en/legislation/details/21708.

143 Anca Parmena Olimid *et al.*, 'Legal Analysis of EU Artificial Intelligence Act: Insights from Personal Data Governance and Health Policy', *Access to Justice in Eastern Europe,* 2024/4, pp. 133–134.

144 Vaughn Gendron, 'A New Frontier: The Music Industry's Struggle against Generative AI', *University of Miami Business Law Review,* Vol. 33, Issue 1, 2024, p. 177.

145 *See* Kitti Mezei, 'A mesterséges intelligencia jogi szabályozásának aktuális kérdései az Európai Unióban', *In Medias Res,* 2023/1, p. 60.

It must be noted that some Asian countries, such as Japan[146] and Singapore adopted TDM exceptions that are far broader than their EU counterpart,[147] but these alternatives seem to limit the exclusive rights in a manner that may not comply with the three-step test.

3.7. Level of Legislation

Selecting the appropriate level of legislation is, without a doubt, of utmost importance. While the WIPO is actively engaged in ongoing discussions within the Standing Committee on Copyright and Related Rights,[148] no legislative process is currently underway. Based on previous legislative dossiers, it is highly unlikely that an international legislative framework[149] could be successfully established in the foreseeable future. This leaves the EU and national levels to be the primary avenues for legislative action.[150]

As previously cited in the Summary, Member States are generally supportive of international discussions, emphasizing that the EU's unified stance should be reflected in such debates. However, they consider legislation feasible only if pursued through a harmonized EU-level approach.[151] That said, there is currently no legislative proposal before the Council, making EU-level legislation unlikely in the near future.

While I support the principle that any legislation concerning AI should ideally be implemented at the EU level, there are already examples of national legislative initiatives within the EU. The Spanish model of extended collective licensing has been previously mentioned. In Italy, a proposed amendment to the Italian Copyright Act seeks to clarify that AI-generated works can be protected only if a demonstrable, creative, and substantial human intervention is present. Another proposed amendment would reinforce the principle that, except for scientific research purposes, copyright holders can

146 David Linke, 'AI Training Data: Between Holy Grail and Forbidden Fruit', *in* Mezei *et al.* (eds.) 2024, pp. 300–301.

147 Lightstone 2024, p. 479.

148 Kathleen Wills, 'AI around the World: Intellectual Property Law Considerations and beyond', *Journal of the Patent and Trademark Office Society,* Vol. 102, Issue 2, 2022, pp. 199–200.

149 *See more* Anett Pogácsás, 'One Hundred Years of International Copyright', *Hungarian Yearbook on International Law and European Law,* Vol. 10, 2022, pp. 246–259.

150 Ficsor 2024, p. 218, and Rallabhandi 2023, pp. 312–328.

151 Summary 2024, pp. 5 and 9.

opt out of having their content used for text-and-data mining for commercial purposes.[152]

In France, a legislative proposal introduced in 2023 aimed, among other objectives, to establish a collective management of rights generated by AI and to regulate the remuneration collected by collecting societies in this context.[153] Following the failure of this bill, another French proposal was introduced, seeking to prescribe the identification of AI-generated images published on social networks to combat disinformation and manipulation.[154]

In principle, as long as the EU legislator does not adopt relevant legislation and the issue remains unharmonized, national legislators retain some discretion to propose and adapt copyright rules concerning generative AI. In my view, it is foreseeable that, before an EU-level legislative proposal materializes, some Member States will experiment with different regulatory approaches.

4. Conclusion

What do stakeholders expect from good legislation? Good legislation, for example, should be flexible yet predictable, readily available and responsive while also well-founded and transparent, balanced and fair, comprehensible to all yet clear and precise, reciprocal, accountable, incentivizing, and responsible. It should be neither premature nor delayed and positioned at the appropriate regulatory level. Numerous expectations of this nature have been cited by scholars in discussions on generative AI legislation.[155] But what does this truly entail? Citing the fundamental criteria of sound legislation is akin to stating that cakes should generally be made of flour, butter,

152 Gianluca Campus, 'Artificial Intelligence and copyright: the Italian AI Law Proposal', *Kluwer Copyright Blog*, 28 May 2024.

153 Alain Duflot, 'Artificial Intelligence in the French Law of 2024', *Legal Issues in the Digital Age*, Vol. 5, Issue 1, 2024, pp. 52–53. Kevin Bercimuelle-Chamot, 'French Copyright framework for artificial intelligence: a half-hearted attempt', *The IPKat*, 16 October 2023, at https://ipkitten.blogspot.com/2023/10/french-copyright-framework-for.html.

154 Kevin Bercimuelle-Chamot, 'New French draft law on AI: Generated or not generated, that is the question', *The IPKat*, 13 December 2024, at https://ipkitten.blogspot.com/2024/12/new-french-draft-law-on-ai-generated-or.html.

155 Moldawer 2024, p. 6, Chang 2023, p. 135, Yuen 2023, p. 117. Mohammad Belayet Hossain *et al.*, 'From Legality to Responsibility: Charting the Course for AI Regulation in Malaysia', *IIUM Law Journal*, Vol. 32, Issue 1, 2024, p. 406.

and eggs, or that medical professionals are expected to exercise care when treating patients. While these principles are meaningful, they merely establish the foundational aspects of legislative efforts and offer little guidance on how generative AI should be regulated – if at all.

In my view, the alternatives and examples identified during my research indicate only a few viable directions. First, shifting the current legal paradigm is no closer to reality today than it was when the internet became widely accessible. This suggests that the foundational principles of copyright law remain intact and resilient in the tide of generative AI.[156] The traditionally low originality requirement and the principle of human authorship do not necessitate any substantive revision.[157] Similarly, the recognition of joint authorship with AI or granting legal personhood to AI systems appears to be a dead end at this stage.

That said, the widespread and unlawful use of protected works should not be tolerated, necessitating legislative intervention. In this regard, uses covered by the TDM exception should be subject to compensation, and licensing for opt-out uses should be centralized under collective rights management. However, I see no compelling reason for expanding other free-use exceptions, and the CJEU should proceed with caution when establishing harmonized conditions for the pastiche exception.

The introduction of a new *sui generis* right for generative AI outputs is an intriguing concept. However, EU legislators must thoroughly assess its potential and actual implications for creative industries and innovation before submitting any legislative proposals in this domain. It must also be emphasized that, ideally, any regulatory framework should be adopted at the EU level. Nevertheless, until such measures are enacted, national legislators retain the authority to regulate generative AI under domestic law (as far as the EU copyright *acquis* allows this).

There is no doubt that generative AI, as a novel technology, has placed significant strain on the copyright regime – more so than usual. However, this does not warrant an entirely different regulatory approach; rather, it calls for a more decisive response.[158] As is always the case in copyright law,

156 Anushka Dwivedi, 'Convergence of Artificial Intelligence with IP Laws', *Jus Corpus Law Journal,* Vol. 3, Issue 2, 2022, p. 789.

157 Dylan Jignesh Patel, 'Authored by Artificial Intelligence: An Analysis of AI Use in Copyright', *American Journal of Trial Advocacy,* Vol. 47, Issue 2, 2024, p. 423.

158 Marcia Narine Weldon *et al.*, 'Establishing a Future-Proof Framework for AI Regulation: Balancing Ethics, Transparency, and Innovation', *Transactions: The Tennessee Journal of Business Law,* Vol. 25, Issue 2, 2024, p. 345.

the proposed adjustments seek to recalibrate the balance that has shifted with the widespread adoption of generative AI. The protection and incentivization of human creativity, as well as the recognition of the inherent personal imprint in original works have always been, and should remain, the central objectives of copyright legislation.

AI as a Tool for IP Protection or IP Law Molded by the AI Boom?

*Anna Szilvia Perlusz – Szabolcs Stock**

Abstract

As artificial intelligence becomes more widespread, its role in intellectual property management – especially in trademark research and patentability – is expanding rapidly. Due to advanced image recognition softwares, technology offers new opportunities in trademarking, as artificial intelligence makes trademark research faster and more efficient. Still, its added value, future, and regulation remain unclear. In patent law, answering the age-old question of the patentability of machine inventions is more important than ever. AI systems question and challenge the long-standing doctrines of the PHOSITA requirement, non-obviousness, the inventive step and maybe even patent law itself.

Keywords: artificial intelligence, trademark, patent, TRIPS, AI Act, PHOSITA, European Patent Office.

* Anna Szilvia Perlusz: chief advisor, Ministry of Justice of Hungary, Budapest, szilvia.anna.perlusz@im.gov.hu.
Szabolcs Stock: junior associate in intellectual property, Dr. Krajnyák & Partner Law Office, sz.stocki@gmail.com. The ideas expressed in this study reflect the authors' own opinions, which do not necessarily correspond to the views of their institutions.

„The most effective way to manage change is to create it."

Peter Drucker[1]

1. Introduction

Imagine a world where Andy Warhol made his first *pop-art* creation using artificial intelligence (hereinafter: AI), and Leonardo da Vinci asked ChatGPT the key elements of an everlasting painting.

We do not have to go really far to collect more tangible examples in connection with AI and science. In Stanley Kubrick's *2001: a Space Odyssey,* AI played a major role as an immensely useful but also dangerous tool. As we could observe throughout the storyline, AI's malfunctions raised philosophical questions about the trust we place in AI, its potential for autonomy, and the ethical implications of creating machines with intelligence that might surpass human understanding.[2] In Dune, AI is banned after sentient machines dominated humanity, prompting their destruction and a subsequent societal shift. As a result, humanity arrived at the view that AI – just like in *Space Odyssey* – is dangerous and unethical, and the humans of the *Dune* prohibited the use of "thinking machines", or any form of AI. The famous line from the book clarifies the statement: *"Thou shalt not make a machine in the likeness of a human mind."*[3]

Apart from the artistic imagination surrounding the dangers inherent in AI described above, ideally, with AI handling routine tasks, humans can focus on more complex and creative roles. We know from experience, that AI can automate repetitive tasks like data processing, boosting efficiency, productivity, and accuracy.[4] It is highly relevant that AI has started making a mark in creative and industrial fields such as music composition, art, writing, or even technical solutions. While AI can generate impressive works in these fields, it raises questions regarding the role of human creativity and the ownership of AI-created contents for the near future. Many have claimed that AI is the next groundbreaking technology that will propel humanity

1 Peter Drucker, *Managing in the Next Society: Lessons from the Renown Thinker and Writer on Corporate Management,* St. Martin's Press, New York, 2003.

2 Arthur C. Clarke, *2001: a Space Odyssey,* New American Library, New York, 1968.

3 Frank Herbert, *Dune,* Chilton Books, Philadelphia, 1965.

4 Andy Johnson-Laird, 'Neural Networks: The Next Intellectual Property Nightmare?', *The Computer Lawyer,* Vol. 7, Issue 3, 1990, pp. 7–16.

into the next phase of evolution, transforming our lives in a way similar to how the internet reshaped the 20th and 21st centuries.

When any revolutionary innovation or concept emerges, its legal implications and applications often face the most scrutiny. In case of AI and intellectual property rights we expect the same, meaning that AI becomes a major focus for intellectual property systems worldwide, raising a host of new questions, discussions, and challenges.[5] This paper focuses on the field of industrial property rights, mainly analyzing AI's increasing effect on trademark law and patent law through the use of AI in practice, and the challenges raised by AI. Our aim is to stimulate debate on the impacts that this groundbreaking revolution brings on the table.

2. Living Revolution: AI's Effect on Trademarks

2.1. AI's General Effects on Trademarks

As trademark registrations continue to rise worldwide, brand owners are facing greater challenges in securing a distinctive and meaningful trademark that doesn't conflict with existing marks. Additionally, once a unique trademark is acquired, they must remain vigilant for potential infringements on their established portfolios. This highlights the crucial need for thorough trademark research before registration and ongoing monitoring afterward.[6]

In 2019 WIPO unveiled an enhanced AI-driven technology that appears to leverage advanced machine learning to analyze various features in an image, helping to identify similar registered trademarks.[7] Experts and users of the AI-powered search tool, accessible for free to all practitioners via WIPO's *Global Brand Database,* experienced more precise and tailored search outcomes, leading to reduced labor costs. Beyond WIPO's tool described above, AI-assisted search is advancing through various other methods and tools.[8] For instance, a 2019 article in the World Trademark Review introduced *TradeMarker,* an AI-assisted system, aimed at offering improve-

---

5 Aswin Pradeep, 'Artificial intelligence and intellectual property: potential and challenges', *Indian Journal of Law & Legal Research,* Vol. 3, Issue 1, 2021–2022, p. 2.

6 Ronda Majure, 'AI and Image Recognition: The Next Generation Brand Protection?', *The Journal of Robotics, Artificial Intelligence & Law,* Vol. 2, Issue 4, 2019, p. 6.

7 Agrata Jain *et al.*, 'Trademark law and AI's impact on it', *Indian Journal of Law and Legal Research,* Vol. 2, Issue 2, 2021, p. 52.

8 Ulrich Paschen *et al.*, 'Artificial intelligence: Building blocks and an innovation typology', *Business Horizons,* Vol. 63, Issue 2, 2020, pp. 147–155.

ments over other AI-based search platforms. The *TradeMarker* service enhances AI-driven image searches by organizing search results into four categories: subject similarity, pixel similarity, text similarity, and manually specified similarity criteria.[9]

Using free and easily accessible databases or search engines for trademark searching and clearance may appear to be a cost-effective solution for a brand owner, but it can ultimately be detrimental, leaving the brand exposed. Resources often fail to cover all relevant marks or search areas, lack expert guidance or analysis, and cannot provide the level of customization necessary to ensure a comprehensive and thorough search.[10] AI however can examine a wider range of images and interpretations to compare a specific trademark against, expanding the search and providing more opportunities to understand an image's meaning. This approach ensures that the results are as precise as possible, reducing the chance of overlooking any relevant marks.[11]

As of the date of completion of the present article, the image search tool of the European Union Intellectual Property Office's (hereinafter: EUIPO) seems rather unhelpful in case of some image similarity searches. When inserting a portrait of one of the co-authors to run a similarity search, the EUIPO search tool resulted in several hits, ranging from the infamous 'Uncle Sam' figurative mark,[12] through an 'Arvid Nordquist' coffee bag label[13] to the 'iSales mobile' figurative trademark,[14] all of which have only one thing in common: they have some kind of a figure or face on them. Based on this empirical evidence, we can ascertain that this particular search tool still has a long way to go. In this development AI will be indispensable (as we are of the view that the portrait input in the search tool does not look like the above referenced results).

2.2. The Role of AI in Transforming Trademark Registration Processes

By leveraging AI capabilities, businesses and legal entities can address the challenges of traditional trademark registration methods, creating a more

9 Id.
10 Id.
11 Id.
12 *See* at https://euipo.europa.eu/eSearch/#details/trademarks/014714901.
13 *See* at https://euipo.europa.eu/eSearch/#details/trademarks/018856885.
14 *See* at https://euipo.europa.eu/eSearch/#details/trademarks/012560991.

efficient, reliable, and responsive system.[15] Traditionally, this process has depended largely on human involvement, leading to inefficiencies, delays, and the risk of error. However, the emergence of AI has brought a new wave of innovation, presenting unique opportunities to transform trademark registration systems.[16]

(i) The essence of AI as a toolkit. The immense amount of data and information available online can make it difficult to perform thorough trademark searches and clearances manually. AI-powered tools can greatly improve the efficiency and accuracy of this process, when algorithms sift through large databases, detect potential conflicts, and offer valuable insights. These tools save time, while minimizing human errors, and assist businesses in making informed decisions when selecting and safeguarding their trademarks.

(ii) The accuracy of AI. AI's capacity to process data with remarkable precision reduces risks linked to human error. Traditional methods, on the other hand, depend largely on manual input and interpretation, which raises the chance for mistakes. Trademark searches are essential for a successful registration, ensuring a proposed mark doesn't clash with existing ones and complies with legal standards. AI has greatly enhanced the speed and accuracy of these searches, making it an indispensable tool for businesses.

(iii) AI-powered techniques. There are numerous AI-powered techniques, that can be used during the registration process, such as *natural language processing, machine learning,* and *computer vision;* all used to automate and enhance different stages of the trademark registration process. From initial trademark searches and clearance to application drafting, examination, and prosecution, AI-driven systems promise to streamline workflows, reduce conflict risks, and improve the accuracy of trademark assessments.[17]

(iv) Steps for the AI-based registration. There are five steps when it comes to AI-based registration in general. Firstly, the AI-driven search and clearance tools use *natural language processing* and *machine learning* algorithms to perform thorough searches of trademark databases and other pertinent sources, in which these algorithms analyze textual data related to trademarks to detect similarities, semantic connections, and potential conflicts.

15 Ananth Raja Muthukalyani, 'Analyzing the Adoption and Influence of AI in Retail Supply Chain Operations', *International Journal of Artificial Intelligence Research and Development,* Vol. 1, Issue 1, 2023, pp. 43–51.

16 Id.

17 Sundaram Balasubramanian, 'AI-powered trademark registration systems: streamlining processes and improving accuracy', *International Journal of Intellectual Property Rights,* Vol. 14, Issue 1, 2024, pp. 3–6.

Then for the second step AI-driven systems can help draft trademark applications by offering smart suggestions based on historical data and legal requirements. The third step is AI tools examining applications and reviewing reports to evaluate their adherence to legal requirements. Fourthly, AI-driven monitoring systems constantly monitor trademark registrations and potential infringements across multiple channels, such as online platforms and marketplaces. Lastly, predictive analytics models use AI algorithms to predict trademark registration trends, foresee legal challenges, and offer strategic insights.[18]

2.3. Recent Cases of AI-related Trademark Infringements.

While the use of AI in trademarks is a growing tendency, the legal background, or framework of this development has not yet been established. Tamás Lábady (former vice president of the Hungarian Constitutional Court) once noted that "*the law always follows life*" – clearly a crucial point when it comes to legislation, but the swiftness of creating the applicable legal framework is is also a key factor.

In a recent case of the High Court of Justice Business and Property Courts of England and Wales', named *Getty Images (US) Inc. v. Stability AI Ltd.*,[19] proceedings were brought for copyright infringement, database right infringement, trademark infringement and passing off against an open-source generative artificial intelligence ('AI') company, which generates synthetic image outputs in response to commands entered by users. The claimants' complaint was that the defendant has scraped millions of images from the Getty Images websites, all without the claimants' consent, and used those images unlawfully as input to train and develop Stable Diffusion. Further, the claimants asserted that the output of Stable Diffusion is itself infringing, not least because it is said to reproduce a substantial part of the claimant's copyrighted works and, or bears the claimant's trademarks. In the case at hand, a judgment is expected this summer; however, even at this stage, the shortcomings that may arise from inadequate training of artificial intelligence are already apparent.

In an other case, the well-known and worldwide famous Barbie brand of Mattel came under scrutinity as a possible victim of AI generated contents.

18 Id.

19 *See* at https://www.judiciary.uk/wp-content/uploads/2025/01/Getty-Images-and-others-v-Stability-AI-14.01.25.pdf.

Mattel, Inc. holds the intellectual property rights to Barbie, which encompass trademarks, copyrights, and design patents as well. These protections extend to the Barbie name, the distinctive bright pink handwritten logo, Barbie's image, her clothing, accessories, fashion style, packaging, and even her narrative. Any images or videos that use or recreate appearance in derivative works in connection with arts under intellectual property protection may violate Mattel's rights. Some probably come across the viral 'AI Barbie' trend, where users generate Barbie-inspired avatars, images, and videos using artificial intelligence. These creations often showcase the classic Barbie aesthetic – lots of pink, bold makeup, glamorous fashion, and the signature look. To join in, users upload their own photos, and use AI apps or tools, such as LinkedIn headshot or TikTok effects.[20] They give prompts to the AI detailing what their Barbie version should include: outfits, careers, packaging style, and more. The result is a customized, Barbie-styled avatar often paired with witty or aspirational captions, using Barbie's trademark. As generative AI evolves and influencer culture continues to shape digital trends, the AI Barbie craze serves as a vivid example of how pop culture, law, and technology are increasingly overlapping, and at times clashing. We can say that plastic is not always as fantastic as it seems – depending on the legal context.[21]

3. Machine Inventions in Patents

3.1. Patents and AI

Whether or not AI can be the inventor of a patent, has already been and will surely be one of the most exciting questions to answer in patent law in the foreseeable future. With AI models becoming smarter by the day, it is vital that the governing legislation or at least the practice of the relevant offices follow. A crucial factor regarding whether an invention can be patent-protected is its ability to meet the patentability criteria such as novelty, involving an inventive step, and the potential for industrial application. Regarding the question of the inventive step (*i.e.,* non-obviousness), if an AI system struggles to determine novelty, the likelihood of creating innovations on existing

20 *See* at https://www.bbc.com/news/articles/c5yg690e9eno.

21 *See* at https://timesofindia.indiatimes.com/etimes/trending/barbie-box-trend-goes-viral-how-to-turn-your-photos-into-ai-doll-avatars-using-chatgpt/articleshow/120183105.cms.

models or concepts that are not obvious to a person having ordinary skill in the art (hereinafter: PHOSITA), becomes even more challenging.[22]

Patent law is an adaptable system, capable of accommodating immense technological advances. Burk compares today's AI revolution to the huge leaps of biotechnology some 30–40 years ago.[23] The technologies that once seemed sci-fi-like, are now considered state of the art. AI was once considered the same, but that has now changed. Owing to these advancements, the long-standing patent law system may be due for a review with the spreading of ever smarter AI technologies, which, contrary to the above cited biotechnological advances, need less and less human contribution. We also note that patent law has been found to be applicable to the advances of software, biotechnology and genetic research.[24] Due to the dynamic nature of the law, when trying to solve new issues arising from technological advances, apart from existing laws *(lex lata),* one must also consider future legislation *(lex ferenda).*[25]

3.2. Views on the Patentability of AI

The patent systems' main incentive is to trigger innovation; an inventor may be encouraged by the prospect of a financial gain during their inventive activities. Of course, the argument can be made that human nature is curious by 'design' and therefore needs no further motivation to invent. On the other hand, an AI model does not need an incentive to invent, as it has no 'curious nature' – unless of course, it has been programmed that way. AI has been used extensively in order to simplify the execution of basic functions and primarily to reduce human effort.[26]

This raises the question, would AI systems capable of invention be developed in a world where their output could not be patented? Would a patent protecting the inventing machine be enough of an incentive to create such a machine or would the machines' outputs also need to be eligible for patent

22 *See* at https://robohub.org/should-an-artificial-intelligence-be-allowed-to-get-a-patent/.

23 Dan L. Burk, 'AI Patents and the Self-Assembling Machine', *Minnesota Law Review,* Vol. 105, Spring, 2021, p. 302.

24 Liza Vertinsky, 'Reorienting Patent Policy Towards Responsible AI Design', *University of Maryland Legal Studies Research Paper,* No. 2024-09. p. 14.

25 William Chindrawa *et al.,* 'Revolution in Intellectual Property Rights: Artificial Intelligence as the Inventor of a Patent', *Anthology: Inside Intellectual Property Rights,* Vol. 1, Issue 1, 2023, p. 19.

26 Id.

protection?[27] If innovators have no means to secure the output of their AI systems, what incentive do they have? By contrast, if every invention made by an AI system is granted patent protection, this gives the inventor an undisputable and huge incentive to pursue the creation of a machine capable of such output.[28]

There are several arguments for and against the responses patent law may need to give to the current AI revolution. Vertinsky summarizes these options as follows: firstly, even though patent law has been known to react well to new technologies, the AI-issue may need a unique response. Secondly, we should leave patents strictly to human inventors. Thirdly, responding to the changes occurring in the innovation ecosystem and incentivizing the private sector innovation would come with some changes to the current patent law system. Lastly, AI neutrality, *i.e.*, attributing AI inventorship the same role as that of human inventors.[29]

We live in an age where the danger of AI and inventive machines rendering human inventorship and research redundant may be imminent. While automation that generates innovation benefits society as a whole, it may also contribute to unemployment, deepen financial disparities and decrease social mobility. This aspect makes the present industrial revolution different to the previous ones. And while patent law alone will not be the decisive factor in all the above issues, it will undoubtedly play a significant role.[30]

3.2.1. Inventorship and Inventive Step

The inventive process of an AI system differs greatly from that of a human ('traditional') inventor. As mentioned before, a smoothly running AI can reduce the lengthy and costly trial-and-error method of an inventive process to a data-crunching, automated task,[31] it simplifies our lives, as does every tool humans have been using since the wheel.[32]

When discussing AI inventorship, we can pose the question 'Are we really talking about Artificial Intelligence systems'? Burk is of the opinion that the

27 Gaétan de Rassenfosse *et al.*, 'AI Generated inventions: Implications for the Satent System', *Southern California Law Review*, Vol. 96, Issue 6, 2024, p. 1458.
28 Id. p. 1459.
29 Vertinsky 2025, pp. 13–14.
30 Abbott 2018, p. 51.
31 de Rassenfosse *et al.* 2024, p. 1458.
32 Burk 2021, p. 310.

use of the term AI is a misnomer, as the systems we commonly refer to as AI are no more than machine learning routines, that possess no cognitive abilities and prospect. He argues that 'computer science has given up on building machines that can think in favor of machines that can learn'.[33] AI systems capable of generating outputs that seem unforeseen for humans may be taken as a sign of the cognitive abilities of the AI system, however such emergent outputs have long been around in several technical fields, *e.g.*, chemistry and biotechnology.[34]

An invention involves several crucial factors that determine whether a patent can be granted; however, certain criteria must be met for someone to be recognized as an *inventor.* While computers, which cannot feel emotions, are not motivated by such incentives, humans will continue to be driven to develop these technologies, recognizing the benefits of patent protection.[35] Patents are primarily intended to protect the inventor and acknowledge their personal contribution and connection to the invention, preventing others from exploiting it without restriction. Opponents of granting patent protection to AI-made inventions argue that computers lack such attachment, making them unable to have strong opinions on how their inventions should be used, thus undermining the fundamental purpose of patent protection.[36]

From a formalist perspective, one can argue that a machine cannot be considered as the inventor, since it has no mind in which the idea can be conceived. This is the core of the American patent legislation's approach to inventorship. In the landmark case, *Townsend v Smith,* the Court of Customs and Patent Appeals stipulated that "conception of the invention consists in the complete performance of the mental part of the inventive act."[37] Conception therefore has to be a definite and permanent idea of the inventor, and it should be applied in practice in the invention.[38]

---

33 Id. p. 303, and Marion Fourcade & Kieran Healy, 'Seeing Like a Market', *Socio-Economic Review,* Vol. 15, Issue 1, 2017, p. 24. The present article's scope does not cover the distinction and etymological differentiation between the use of the terms 'AI' or 'machine learning systems' and only uses 'AI'.

34 Burk 2021, p. 304.

35 Ryan Abbot, 'I think, therefore I invent. Creative Computers and the Future of Patent Law', *Boston College Law Review,* Vol. 57, Issue 4, 2016, p. 1095.

36 Id.

37 Burk 2021, pp. 306–307, and *Townsend v Smith,* 36. F.2d. 292 (C.C.P.A. 1929).

38 Yuan Hao, 'The Rise of 'Centaur' Inventors: How Patent Law Should Adapt to the Challenge to Inventorship Doctrine by Human-AI Inventing Synergies', *Journal of The Patent and Trademark Office Society,* Vol. 71, 2024, p. 64.

Patent law has been known to allow the patenting of 'accidental' inventions, when conception is simultaneous with reduction to practice. In such cases the inventor's role is to recognize the desirable qualities of the discovery (or invention). We can imagine a similar approach when an AI comes up with a solution that is recognized by the human element of the equation. It is inconceivable that a human present during the accidental discovery of a desirable molecule is not recognized as the inventor. This approach, according to Professor Burk, may be applied to outcomes from AI (as he says, machine learning) systems, which only become inventions after they have been perceived as useful by a human operator.[39] In case of AI-related inventing, the procedure seems to have more than one stakeholder most of the time.[40] However, how deep do we need to dive in recognizing the player? Do we only recognize the operators or should we go back all the way to the programmers and trainers of the AI system?

The above perspective poses the question: since AI inventors are different in so many ways from humans, should they be treated differently? If we start treating AI inventions differently from 'traditional' inventions, we can be sure that inventors and other stakeholders will quickly find ways to characterize their inventions as non-AI in order to circumvent the different treatment to obtain a potentially stronger protection. Such a differentiated treatment may also require a *sui generis* IP right, which would shake the patent system at its core. And even if we argue that separating different types of inventions is cost-free, such a distinction would quickly bring us back to the above issue where inventors circumvent the AI-related rules and claim inventorship on their own.

Hao argues that in order to resolve the issue with inventorship of AI, policymakers have three choices: first, leave inventorless inventions (*e.g.*, those, where the AI is the inventor and therefore patentability is challenged) in the public domain; second, fundamentally change the patent system to accommodate AI inventors; or third, update the long-standing doctrine of inventorship to allow the patentability of these inventions.[41] However, this last option would make such institutional changes to an internationally harmonized field, that it should only be considered if the goal of patent law as an innovation motivator can be safeguarded. A different approach could be to treat AI-related inventions similarly to software-related inventions. An in-

39 Burk 2021, pp. 307–308.
40 Vertinsky 2025, p. 16.
41 Hao 2024, p. 69.

vention with no technical features, *e.g.*, a neural network or its learning method itself is only used as an alternative to a data processing method previously disclosed in prior arts, it should not be regarded as fulfilling the requirement of the inventive step. However, if it includes a special technical feature rather than a substitution of previously known methods, the inventiveness criteria should be considered to have been met.[42]

Lastly, some argue that if one country opts to establish a new patent system, it could also raise issues connected to the international treaties governing patent law, such as the Trade-Related Aspects of Intellectual Property Rights (hereinafter: TRIPS).[43] TRIPS established minimum requirements for patent protection, by stating that "patents shall be available for any inventions, whether products or processes, in all fields of technology, provided that they are new, involve an inventive step and are capable of industrial application".[44]

3.2.2. Non-obviousness and the PHOSITA[45] Requirement

Is everything obvious for an AI system? What is obvious for the PHOSITA? Can we allow AI inventorship to potentially raise the bar for non-obviousness so high, that even a PHOSITA, by whose standards patentability has been judged for decades now, will consider everything to be non-obvious? Or on the contrary, will a PHOSITA using AI render everything to be obvious?[46]

---

42 Okakita Yuhei, *Patent examination practices regarding AI-related inventions: Comparison in the EPO, USPTO and JPO,* Munich Intellectual Property Law Center (MIPLC) Master Thesis, 2018/19, pp. 35–36.

43 de Rassenfosse *et al.* 2024, pp. 1467–1469.

44 Agreement on Trade-Related Aspects of Intellectual Property Rights, Article 27.1.

45 As per the TRIPS Agreement, "Members shall require that an applicant for a patent shall disclose the invention in a manner sufficiently clear and complete for the invention to be carried out by a person skilled in the art." (Article 29 TRIPS). The same requirement is set forth in the legislation of the US, the specification of an invention shall be made in such a way that enables "*any person skilled in the art to which it pertains, or with which it is most nearly connected, to make and use the same*" [35 U.S. Code § 112(a) In General]. Lastly, the Hungarian Act XXXIII of 1995 on the Protection of Inventions by Patents similarly states that "An invention shall be considered to involve an inventive activity if, in regard to the state of the art, it is not obvious to a person skilled in the art." [Hungarian Patent Act, Section 4(1)]. Based on the above, a person having ordinary skill in the art (the 'PHOSITA') can be regarded as a universal measure for assessing the novelty or non-obviousness of an invention.

46 de Rassenfosse *et al.* 2024, p. 1466.

If the use of AI can make everything obvious, assuring technical success without risk, cost or time-considerations, would we still need to issue exclusive patent rights? Burk argues that the above issue would deem patents obsolete and we could "enjoy the utopia of research certainty that AI ushered in."[47] However, he argues that obviously AI does no such thing[48] and that machine learning systems only find what human contributors intend and design for them to find within pre-specified statistical parameters.[49] Furthermore, the patent law term 'obvious(ness)' is not synonymous to 'obvious to try' a particular inventive combination of elements. In several fields unexpected (and therefore inventive or novel) results can often come from obvious combinations and can be eligible for patent protection nonetheless.[50]

Abbott asserts that if the PHOSITA requirement fails to evolve and follow the technological advancements of the AI revolution, it will result in setting the threshold for patentability too low. Keeping the skilled person in line with the actual practices and real world applications of AI is vital, and it must be done before inventive machines become commonplace[51] – if that did not already happen. Once such machines become the standard in research – which we may argue has already happened – the need may also arise for patent offices to require disclosure of the use of AI inventors.[52] The current standard can be problematic when the need to ascertain what another person found obvious, which results in 'inconsistent an unpredictable non-obviousness determinations' for policymakers, lawmakers and persons applying the applicable legislation as well.[53] This can put an even greater burden on legal professionals, especially judges with no technical expertise, who can find themselves in the position of ruling on complex technical issues. Of course this issue can be resolved by appointing judges who have relevant technical backgrounds, as do the Boards of Appeal of the EPO,[54] but until this becomes the standard legislative and judicial practice, judges will need to rule based on a subjective perception of obviousness.

It also has to be borne in mind that through the use of AI and inventive machines, 'average workers' may also become capable of creating patentable

---

47 Burk 2021, p. 309.

48 ...yet... – the authors.

49 Burk 2021, pp. 309–310.

50 Id. p. 310.

51 Ryan Abbott, 'Everything is Obvious', *U.C.L.A. Law Review*, Vol. 66, Issue 2, 2019, p. 5.

52 Id. p. 6.

53 Id. pp. 6–7, and 42.

54 *See* at https://www.epo.org/en/case-law-appeals/organisation/technical-boards-of-appeal.

innovations, which can pose further questions about the use of the long-standing PHOSITA requirement.[55]

An emerging argument regarding patentability of AI inventions is the turn in examination practices towards secondary, economical features of an invention and reproducibility. The latter would focus on answering whether the inventive machine could reproduce the subject matter of the patent application with ease. However, if we argued that determining what another person finds obvious is hard, how hard can it be to Abstractly imagine what a machine could reproduce? AI systems highly depend on available data, but what about data that is not publicly available? Abbott argues that as machines develop and become more advanced, they will be able to achieve more complex results using less data. A computer generating semi-random output, if given unlimited resources, would eventually be able to produce an invention that may be deemed patentable. At any given time, there are several inventions that humanity is capable of discovering or making[56] (meaning that the technical knowledge and means are available and advanced enough). In other words, if a 'normally-skilled' AI could have created a proposed invention, does that render the invention invalid? If yes, this could raise the bar for the PHOSITA requirement,[57] as above discussed. Maybe not the only, but possibly the most important question to answer remains, how long are we willing to wait for mathematically and scientifically possible inventions to happen (or be discovered)?[58]

The US Supreme Court tried to supplement the *non-obviousness* a long time ago with 'real-world' evidence of the reception of an invention in the marketplace. It can be argued that such an approach may need to be revisited for accommodating AI inventions and their relation to the PHOSITA and *non-obviousness* criteria. The features that would need to be examined instead of or in addition to the well-known criteria are those of commercial success, unexpected results, long-felt but unsolved needs, and the failure of others, as well as those of licensing, professional approval, initial skepticism, near-simultaneous inventing and copying. The widespread use of inventive

---

55 Abbott 2018, p. 6.

56 de Rassenfosse *et al.* 2024, p. 1463.

57 Id. p. 1464.

58 Abbott 2018, p. 7, and 41–43. This approach may be interpreted as a twist on the classic *'infinite monkey theorem'.* The 'infinite monkey theorem' states that if you give a monkey a typewriter and let it hit the keys at random an infinite amount of times, it will eventually write down the entire works of Shakespeare. (*See* at https://www.theguardian.com/science/2023/mar/20/can-you-solve-it-the-infinite-monkey-theorem). But how long should we wait for something patentable to be found among the huge amount of random output?

machines could spark the use of these economic factors in assessing patentability.[59]

Finally, further to the question of whether machines are capable of performing an inventive step, we need to keep in mind the question: would an invention be recognized as such, if the PHOSITA weren't present? Do we consider AI inventors or inventor machines to be so 'smart' that they are capable of recognizing their own work as patentable or is the PHOSITA still essential?[60] In Indonesia, this question has been answered as follows:

> "If AIs are unable to file an Application on its own, it would be impossible for an AI to have its invention patented but if an AI is able to autonomously file an Application on its own, as our Law is silent on non-human Applicant, very clearly the AI filing the Application can be deemed as an Applicant."[61]

We believe that in the coming years policymakers, competent courts and institutions will play an essential role in developing a somewhat uniform set of requirements that harmonizes patentability criteria with the unprecedented technological advancements.

4. Conclusion

Rene Descartes[62] was a groundbreaking mathematician, scientific thinker, and original metaphysician. In *The Discourse on the Method,* he described nonhuman animals as machines without minds or consciousness, thus lacking sentience. He argued that it must be morally impossible that there should exist in any machine a diversity of organs sufficient to enable it to act in all the occurrences of life, in the way in which our reason enables us to act.[63] In the seventeenth century, Descartes found it unimaginable that machines could function like humans. By contrast, Alan Turing[64] was one of the early thinkers to explore the possibility of learning machines. Turing's

59 Id. pp. 44–46.
60 Id. pp. 47–48.
61 Chindrawa *et al.* 2023, pp. 19–20.
62 Gary C. Hartfield, *Routledge Philosophy GuideBook to Descartes and the Meditations,* Routledge, London, 2014, p. 22.
63 Id.
64 David B. Fogel, *Evolutionary Computation: Toward a new Philosophy of Machine Intelligence,* Wiley-IEEE Press, London, 2005, p. 4.

most notable achievements were the series of articles and public lectures on the topic of machine intelligence. In his seminal article *Computing Machinery and Intelligence*[65] he introduced the well-known imitation game[66] and pondered the question, if machines are able to think or not. Although Turing had the foresight to envision computers designed to simulate intelligence, he still viewed them as learning machines.

Handling AI and industrial property rights is not an easy task. When it comes to legislation, we can observe that the two fields are mostly discussed separately, leaving the users and stakeholders without any safety belts. The AI Act[67] does not directly address IPRs. The EU is still exploring the possibilities of AI and since there are several unresolved legal and ethical debates on AI and IPRs, there is still no settled legal framework, there is no universally accepted definition of AI in legal contexts. Current legal and regulatory frameworks in various jurisdictions are making innovative attempts by incorporating technical aspects along with goals or objectives. The European Parliament declared that the notion of 'AI systems' should be clearly defined, harmonized with international organisations for legal certainty and flexibility, distinguishing AI from simple software and excluding systems defined only by human-set rules.[68] Reinforcing the previous statements, in the AI Act, the concept of AI system is defined as

> "a machine-based system that is designed to operate with varying levels of autonomy and that may exhibit adaptiveness after deployment, and that, for explicit or implicit objectives, infers, from the input it receives, how to generate outputs such as predictions, content, recommendations, or decisions that can influence physical or virtual environments."[69]

It is clear that having a practical and clear definition of AI is crucial for regulation and governance, as laws and policies rely on a definition for effective implementation and oversight.[70]

---

65 Alan Turing, 'I.-Computing Machinery and Intelligence', *Mind,* Vol. 59, Issue 236, 1950, pp. 433–460.

66 Also known as the '*Turing test*'.

67 Regulation (EU) 2024/1689 of the European Parliament and of the Council of 13 June 2024 laying down harmonised rules on artificial intelligence and amending Regulations (EC) No 300/2008, (EU) No 167/2013, (EU) No 168/2013, (EU) 2018/858, (EU) 2018/1139 and (EU) 2019/2144 and Directives 2014/90/EU, (EU) 2016/797 and (EU) 2020/1828 (hereinafter: AI Act).

68 AI Act, Recital (12).

69 AI Act, Article 3(1).

70 *See* at https://theconversation.com/why-we-need-a-legal-definition-of-artificial-intelligence-46796.

The current position of AIs under IP is however still problematic, wherein, recognition of work generated by Al is a step towards the future, but its implementation is the real problem.[71] While there is a clear distinction between the inventor and the invention, the rise of AI systems requires that lawmakers address whether AI-enabled systems should be included in this category. As the use of these technologies grows and the solutions they generate become more widespread, the issue of protection becomes a crucial concern.

71 Tripathi Swapnil & Ghatak Chandni, 'Artificial Intelligence and Intellectual Property Law', *Christ University Law Journal*, Vol. 7, Issue 1, 2018, p. 96.

The Concept of Originality in EU Copyright Law and the Effect of AI on the 'Margin of Manoeuvre'

*Anett Pogácsás – Zsófia Imre**

Abstract

This paper explores the evolving concept of originality within EU copyright law, focusing on its implications in the context of mass production and artificial intelligence (AI). While originality, defined as the author's own intellectual creation, has long served as a foundational yet low-threshold requirement for copyright protection, recent technological developments and legal harmonization efforts have challenged its adequacy and coherence. Drawing from legislative history, CJEU case law, and doctrinal literature, the authors investigate two core questions: (i) how the existing low originality threshold affects copyright in an AI-driven creative landscape, and (ii) whether this threshold should or could be adjusted or refined. The study highlights how the proliferation of creative content – both human- and AI-generated – narrows the 'margin of manoeuvre', i.e., the room for creative freedom, complicates originality assessments, and raises systemic questions about authorship, expression, and protection. Proposals such as AI-based originality assessments and a double-threshold system are examined for their potential to address these challenges. Ultimately, the paper argues for a re-evaluation of originality's role and criteria, with a stronger focus on the existing criteria regarding the author's 'personal touch', to maintain the integrity and adaptability of European copyright law in the digital age.

Keywords: EU copyright law, creative freedom, AI, narrow margin of manouvre, personal touch

1. Overview and Research Questions

Originality, as a minimum requirement for copyright protection, is the cornerstone of copyright law. Recently, the definition of originality has come under the spotlight in relation to its suitability to handle the reception of

* Anett Pogácsás: associate professor of law, Pázmány Péter Catholic University, Budapest; member of the Hungarian Copyright Expert Board, Budapest, pogacsas.anett@jak.ppke.hu.
Zsófia Imre: legal advisor, Private International Law Department, Ministry of Justice of Hungary, Budapest, zsofi.imre23@gmail.com.

non-human contributions, and its meaningfulness in the process of content produced by artificial intelligence (hereinafter: AI). This paper does not intend to contribute to this stream of research, but rather focuses on the impact of the extremely low threshold that has been set over the last few decades of the copyright law in the context of the shift to 'mass production'. Following a review of the international law and EU law foundations through a survey of the literature and a case law analysis, it examines two interrelated research questions that put the issue in a different perspective.

This paper aims to explore the impact and the effects of the very low entry threshold for copyright in the context of AI *(RQ1)*. Moreover, bearing in mind its side effects, the paper examines whether the low threshold needs to be raised, or whether other methods for examining and establishing the entry threshold might be a possible option *(RQ2)*.

Therefore, the first part of the paper gives a brief overview of how originality has become a central requirement for copyright protection in the EU. The concept signifies that a work must be the author's own intellectual creation, reflecting their personal choices, creativity, and perspective. EU copyright law is largely harmonized through directives and regulations, beginning with the Berne and Rome Conventions, followed by the EU's own legislative efforts such as the InfoSoc-, Term-, Software-, and Database Directives. These instruments set a unified standard of originality across the Member States, repealing additional national requirements such as artistic quality or significant labor.

The case law of the CJEU has further clarified this standard. In *Infopaq* and *Painer,* the CJEU emphasized that even small creative choices, applied for example in photography, can meet the originality threshold. In *Football Dataco,* the CJEU distinguished creativity from mere labor or skill, moving away from the UK's former 'sweat of the brow' approach. Later rulings like *Cofemel* and *Brompton Bicycle* reinforced that originality lies in the author's creative freedom, even when it comes to functional or industrial designs. Thus, EU copyright law embraces a low threshold of originality, fostering broad protection for creative expression across various forms and sectors.

In the second part, the paper examines the evolving nature and challenges of copyright law in light of the historically low entry threshold and automatic protection under the Berne Convention, which removed formalities such as registration. Initially rooted in the author's personal connection to their work, this approach emphasized originality as a binary threshold, not a qualitative one. However, the digital era has dramatically increased the volume and complexity of creative output, blurring lines between professional and amateur creators, and challenging traditional notions of originality.

As copyright attempts to encompass all creative expression, differentiation based on the type, purpose, and use of works becomes increasingly relevant. New questions arise about how to assess originality, especially in functional or AI-generated works, where the 'margin of manoeuvre', *i.e.*, the room for creative choices is narrower. Legal systems are struggling to adapt, particularly as mass production and digital tools flood the public domain with similar content, making it harder to identify truly original works.

Emerging proposals, like using AI to assess 'originality scores' or applying a double threshold, reflect attempts to redefine thresholds more clearly.

This paper explores both the current impact of originality in the context of AI and the theoretical and practical viability of modifying the threshold and its examination. In doing so, it seeks to contribute to a more coherent and forward-looking understanding of originality in European copyright law.

2. Originality in EU Copyright Law

Copyright is a legal framework which grants creators exclusive rights over their intellectual work;[1] it belongs to the author, the sole creator of a unique artwork.[2] Copyright protection aims to protect and value creativity, which is considered to be a uniquely human trait. For an artistic work to qualify for copyright protections, it must satisfy a set of standards, one of which is the requirement of originality. The threshold of originality is a concept to determine whether an artistic work is entitled to copyright protection. Creators can express themselves through their creations, using their imagination, creativity, intentionality, and their personal point of view. Artists infuse their work with emotional depth, allowing their works to reflect not only their individual personalities, but also their human consciousness.[3]

1 Nooshin Ardalan Manesh, 'The Nexus Between Creativity and Copyright Infringement: A Practical Guide in Nutshells', *Fashion Law Journal,* at https://fashionlawjournal.com/the-nexus-between-creativity-and-copyright-infringement-a-practical-guide-in-nutshells/.

2 Martha Woodmansee, 'On the Author Effect: Recovering Collectivity', *Case Western Reserve University School of Law Scholarly Commons,* Vol. 10, 1997, p. 279.

3 Deep Dream Generator Blog, *'AI-Generated Art and the Question of Originality',* at https://deepdreamgenerator.com/blog/ai-art-originality.

2.1. Concept of Originality in EU Primary Law

Copyright law is harmonized in the EU to a large extent. A total of 23 directives and 2 regulations harmonize the essential rights of authors, performers and producers. By establishing these harmonized standards, EU Copyright Law aims to reduce national discrepancies,[4] and guarantee the protection needed to foster creativity in the copyright field.[5]

The long road to harmonization will not be exhaustingly covered in all its significant stages, therefore only the most pertinent legislation regarding the threshold of originality will be outlined in this essay.

The first milestone in copyright law is the Berne Convention,[6] to which all EU Member States are parties. While the Berne Convention had created the foundations of copyright protection, the Rome Convention[7] emphasized the protection of performers, producers of phonograms and broadcasting organizations. Being parties to the above-mentioned conventions, Member States of the EU have already achieved a certain level of approximation, but there were still significant differences regarding copyright protection in national laws.

EU level harmonization began with the recognition of the need to create a unified legal approach to copyright protection, since the emergence of new technical innovations brought with them new challenges to copyright, which required a Community-level solution.

The first step towards further harmonization was undertaken by the Commission by releasing the '*Green Paper on copyright and the challenges of technology*'[8] in 1988. In this document the Commission instituted the harmonization of various areas of copyright law all at once, aiming to protect and elevate the recognition of intellectual and artistic creativity, which serves as a fundamental source of Europe's cultural identity.[9]

---

4 The EU Copyright Legislation, at https://digital-strategy.ec.europa.eu/en/policies/copyright-legislation.

5 EU Copyright, at https://eur-lex.europa.eu/legal-content/EN/TXT/?uri=legissum:eu_copyright.

6 Berne Convention for the Protection of Literary and Artistic Works of September 9, 1886 (as amended on September 28, 1979) (hereinafter: BC).

7 Rome Convention for the Protection of Performers, Producers of Phonograms and Broadcasting Organisations, Rome, Italy, 26 October 1961.

8 Green Paper on Copyright and the Challenge of Technology – Copyright Issues Requiring Immediate Action, at https://op.europa.eu/en/publication-detail/-/publication/f075fcc5-0c3d-11e4-a7d0-01aa75ed71a1

9 WIPO National Seminar on Copyright and Related Rights Organized by the World Intellectual Property Organization (WIPO) in Cooperation with the State Intellectual Property Office of the Republic of Croatia Opatija, 17–19 June 1998, p. 2.

Ten years later, in 1998 the Commission submitted a Proposal for a European Parliament and Council Directive on the harmonization of certain aspects of copyright and related rights[10] in the Information Society[11] which was later adopted as the InfoSoc[12] Directive. This enshrined the basis of copyright protection, but originality as a requirement was not yet defined in its provisions.

Originality was first defined in detail in the Term Directive,[13] the Database Directive[14] and the Software Directive.[15] Each of these directives contain similar provisions, stating that in order for a work to be considered original, it has to be the author's own intellectual creation, with no other criteria foreseen for its eligibility for protection.

The aforementioned directives laid the groundwork for defining originality, and in April 2010 the Wittem Group – formed by leading copyright academics – released the European Copyright Code.[16] Their main concern was, that EU-level copyright legislation lacked transparency and consistency. They intended to create a reference tool that could be used as a guideline for the future harmonization of copyright. Article 1.1(1) defined '*work*' as "any expression within the field of literature, art or science insofar as it constitutes its author's own intellectual creation" setting the general originality standard.[17]

The CDSM Directive,[18] one of the most recent EU directives aiming to adapt copyright law to the digital environment, has a special provision re-

10 Eleonora Rosati, '*Originality in Eu Copyright, Full Harmonization Through Case Law*', Edward Elgar, Cheltenham, 2013, p. 18.

11 Proposal for a European Parliament and Council Directive on the harmonization of certain aspects of copyright and related rights in the information society, COM(97) 628 final.

12 Directive 2001/29/EC of the European Parliament and of the Council of 22 May 2001 on the harmonisation of certain aspects of copyright and related rights in the information society.

13 Directive 2006/116/EC of the European Parliament and of the Council of 12 December 2006 on the term of protection of copyright and certain related rights.

14 Directive 96/9/EC of the European Parliament and of the Council of 11 March 1996 on the legal protection of databases.

15 Directive 2009/24/EC of the European Parliament and of the Council of 23 April 2009 on the legal protection of computer programs.

16 Eleonora Rosati, 'The Wittem Group and the Project of a European Copyright Code', *Journal of Intellectual Property Law and Practice,* Vol. 5, Issue 12, 2010, pp. 862–868.

17 P. Bernt Hugenholtz, '*The Wittem Group's European Copyright Code*', Chapter 17, at https://www.ivir.nl/publicaties/download/ILS_29_chapter17.pdf.

18 Directive (EU) 2019/790 of the European Parliament and of the Council of 17 April 2019 on copyright and related rights in the Digital Single Market and amending Directives 96/9/EC and 2001/29/EC.

garding the legal status of the reproductions of artworks belonging in the public domain, clarifying that in case the protection of a work of visual art has expired, the reproduction of the work is not eligible for copyright protection, unless it is original in the sense that it is the author's own intellectual creation.[19]

It is clear from the above that EU legislation establishes a relatively low threshold of originality, allowing for a broad range of creative works to be embraced. Before harmonization several Member States had national copyright laws that included additional requirements for protection beyond the minimum standards set by the EU, usually involving criteria like labor, quality or other subjective measures. For example, the German *Urheberrechtsgesetz*[20] required a certain level of creative artistry, whereas the French *Code de la propriété intellectuelle*[21] demanded a quality condition to be fulfilled, resulting in a higher threshold for originality.

2.2. The Secondary Sources on Originality

Besides legislation, harmonization has also been achieved through case law of the CJEU. The first outstanding decision which shaped the understanding of originality was *Infopaq*[22] in 2009. The CJEU laid down the definition of work in the context of copyright containing two conditions, particularly that *(i)* artworks must be original meaning that they are the author's own intellectual creation, and *(ii)* only those creations may be defined as a 'work' that are the expression of the author's own intellectual creation.[23]

Building upon *Infopaq*, the CJEU continued to refine the concept of originality in *Painer*,[24] where the preliminary matter to be decided by the CJEU was related to a question of free use and reproduction of a photograph by

19 Alexandra Giannopoulou, 'The new copyright directive: Article 14 or when the public domain enters the new copyright directive', *Kluwer Copyright Blog*, 27 June 2019.

20 Urheberrechtsgesetz (UrhG), Gesetz über Urheberrecht und verwandte Schutzrechte (Copyright Act) of 9 September as last amended by Article 28 of the Act of 23 October 2024.

21 Code de la propriété intellectuelle (CPI, Intellectual Property Code) consolidated version as of 22 May 2020.

22 Judgment of 16 July 2009, *Case C-5/08, Infopaq*, ECLI:EU:C:2009:465.

23 David Linke, 'Copyright work and its definition with regard to originality and AI – Conference report on the fourth binational seminar of TU Dresden and Charles University in Prague, 27 June 2019', *GRUR International*, Vol. 69, Issue 1, 2020, p. 41.

24 Judgment of 1 December 2011, *Case C-145/10, Painer*, ECLI:EU:C:2011:798.

the press, particularly, whether a realistic portrait photograph with a rather minor creative freedom can obtain copyright protection under Article 6 of the Term Directive. The ruling reflected the reasoning of *Infopaq,* as it made clear that the author of a photograph can also 'stamp the work with his personal touch' by using his creative freedom and own perspective – for example by choosing perspective, adjusting the lights or framing – therefore the creation can be protected by copyright.[25]

A similar approach to originality was followed in *Football Dataco,* when the CJEU held in the context of databases, that "the criterion of originality is satisfied when – through the selection or arrangement of the data which it contains – its author expresses his creative ability in an original manner by making free and creative choices and thus stamps his personal touch", however copyright protection is not granted solely on the basis that setting up a database required labor and skill. According to the decision's reasoning, solely the amount of labor and skill it took to create the artwork cannot justify copyright protection without an expression of originality which – in this case – is in the selection or arrangement of data.[26] Advocate General Mengozzi clarified in his Opinion that in terms of copyright protection a 'creative' aspect is required, and it is not sufficient that the creation required 'significant labor and skill'.[27] He also pointed out the huge difference between the common law tradition and the civil law tradition regarding the level of originality required for copyright protection. While the UK used to apply[28] the 'skill and labor' standard, also known as the 'sweat of the brow' doctrine – meaning, that they grant copyright protection based on the amount of labor, skill, diligence and effort it took for the author to create a work – countries of the civil law tradition require works to have a creative element in order to be eligible for copyright protection.[29]

---

25 Andreas Rahmatian, 'Originality in UK Copyright Law: The Old "Skill and Labour" Doctrine Under Pressure', *International Review of Intellectual Property and Competition Law,* Vol. 44, Issue 1, 2013, pp. 4–34.

26 Judgment of 1 March 2012, *Case C-604/10, Football Dataco Ltd,* ECLI:EU:C:2012:115.

27 Eleonora Rosati, 'Why originality in copyright is not and should not be a meaningless requirement', *Journal of Intellectual Property Law and practice,* Vol. 13, Issue 8, 2018, pp. 597–598.

28 Eleonora Rosati, *'Copyright and the Court of Justice of the European Union (Second Edition)',* Oxford University Press, Oxford, 2023, pp. 311–350. "After leaving the EU in 2020, United Kingdom had the chance to return to the previous interpretation of originality, but so far the court decisions regarding originality are in line with the CJEU case law."

29 Opinion of Advocate General Mengozzi delivered in 15 December 2011, *Case C-604/10, Football Dataco Ltd,* ECLI:EU:C:2011:848.

Jumping ahead in time to more recent rulings, both in *Cofemel*[30] and *Brompton Bicycle*[31] the CJEU delivered quite unique decisions involving originality. In 2013. G-Star, a clothing brand accused *Cofemel* of infringing their copyright regarding multiple clothing items, claiming, that their 'ARC' jeans and 'ROWDY' t-shirt and sweatshirt designs are original intellectual creations, they are to be considered 'works' and are therefore entitled to copyright protection. *Cofemel,* on the other hand, argued that clothing items could not be classified as 'works'. After the Portuguese Supreme Court made a referral to the CJEU for a preliminary ruling, the CJEU declared, that once a design is the original intellectual creation of the author, and therefore the subject matter fulfils the originality requirement, it is protected by copyright.[32] Aesthetic effects and the artistic value of the work cannot be a requirement for copyright protection, and any national provision is inadmissible, such as the 'aesthetic effect' requirement in Portuguese copyright law.[33]

The basis of the dispute in *Brompton Bicycle,* was a copyright infringement against a particular design of a bicycle made by *Brompton Bicycle,* which allowed the two-wheeled vehicle to fold into three different positions. The special feature was protected by a patent, which eventually expired, giving the opportunity for others to use it. Get2Get, a Korean Company marketed a bicycle called 'Chedech', quite similar to the iconic folding bike, allegedly infringing copyright protection. In response to the claim, Get2Get argued, that the appearance of their bike is dictated by the technical solution sought, to ensure that the bike can fold, and that the technique could only be protected under patent law.[34] In response, Brompton Bicycle highlighted, that the three positions could have been obtained in several ways, making the particular method of folding the creator's own creative choice, which is therefore eligible for copyright protection. The main question was, whether copyright protection under the InfoSoc Directive applies when the appear-

30 Judgment of 12 September 2019, *Case C-683/17, Cofemel,* ECLI:EU:C:2019:721.

31 Judgment of 11 June 2020, *Case C-833/18, Brompton Bicycle Ltd,* ECLI:EU:C:2020:461.

32 Simon Clark & Sara Witton, *'Cofemel v G-Star Raw (C-683/17) and its effect on UK copyright law before and after Brexit',* 2020, at https://www.bristows.com/viewpoint/articles/cofemel-v-g-star-raw-c-683-17-and-its-effect-on-uk-copyright-law-before-and-after-brexit/.

33 EU Copyright in Designs – CJEU Rule in Cofemel that 'Originality' is the Only Requirement for Protection, 2019, at https://cms-lawnow.com/en/ealerts/2019/10/eu-copyright-in-designs-cjeu-rule-in-cofemel-that-originality-is-the-only-requirement-for-protection.

34 *Case C-833/18, Brompton Bicycle Ltd,* para. 14.

ance of a product is necessary to achieve a technical result.[35] In its ruling the CJEU relied on *Cofemel,* and confirmed, that for a work to be considered original, it is both necessary and sufficient that the subject matter reflects the personality of the author, as an expression of their free and creative choices. In line with this reasoning, the CJEU ruled, that a creation could be eligible for copyright protection, if it satisfies the originality requirement, even if the realization is dictated by a technical consideration, as far as it does not prevent the author from reflecting his personality and express their free and creative choices when creating the subject matter.[36]

3. Side Effects of the Copyright 'Entry Point'

The low entry threshold cannot be considered by itself, but only within its context. One of the defining principles of this context – established in the Berne Convention[37] – is that copyright protection is formality-free, *i.e.* it arises automatically. This means that protection is generated by the creation of the work itself, without any registration, evaluation, approval or notification.[38] Despite the fundamental differences between the civil law and common law approaches, the principle of protection without formalities has become a fundamental concept in international copyright law. In the infamous *Wheaton v Peters,* Craig Joyce bitterly observes that by joining the Berne Convention, the United States' previously effective tool, the "statutory formalities beast", has suddenly become a "toothless tiger".[39] Furthermore, the prohibition of formality reinforced the approach of copyright as a fundamental, natural right of man, deriving from the personality of the creator. By

35 Eleonora Rosati, '*CJEU rules that functional shapes are eligible for copyright protection, in so far as they are original works*', 2020, at https://www.twobirds.com/en/insights/2020/global/cjeu-rules-that-functional-shapes-are-eligible-for-copyright-protection-in-so-far.

36 *Case C-833/18, Brompton Bicycle Ltd,* para. 38.

37 BC Article 5(2) "The enjoyment and the exercise of these rights shall not be subject to any formality; such enjoyment and such exercise shall be independent of the existence of protection in the country of origin of the work."

38 "[…] formality-free (or "automatic") protection ("automatic", since, in the absence of formalities, the creation – and where it is a condition, the fixation – of a work directly, "automatically" brings copyright protection into being." Mihály Ficsor, '*Guide to the Copyright and Related Rights Treaties Administered by WIPO*', 2003, at https://www.wipo.int/edocs/pubdocs/en/copyright/891/wipo_pub_891.pdf.

39 Craig Joyce, '"Curious Chapter in the History of Judicature": Wheaton v. Peters and the Rest of the Story (of Copyright in the New Republic)', *Huston Law Review,* Vol. 42, Issue 2, 2005, p. 389.

contrast, it is easier to fit the limitation of the entry point into the system of property right approach , *i.e.*, to impose some formality on the creation of copyright.[40] However, where copyright derives from the personality of the author, its limitation can be perceived within a different – narrower – framework. Thus, the principle of protection without formalities has – in addition to its original purpose – been coupled with the principles and objectives that define the basic characteristics and function of copyright and represent a choice of values. This principle arose from the need to ensure the absence of censorship and the orderly succession of rights, and which were of course justified by the specific nature of the legal relationship, such as the interdependence of moral and economic rights or the typically weaker position of the author in the contracting process.[41] Although originally it was mainly intended to close loopholes aimed at circumventing the principle of equal treatment of the Berne Convention,[42] more and more arguments have been brought forward to substantiate it: the position of unfinished but already original works and fragments of works had been added to this list.[43] Moreover, given that, as van Gompel points out, the historical justification for the principle of protection without formalities has now virtually disappeared,[44] having lost their original purpose and function, it is these new objectives and arguments that now serve as its rationale.

Another important factor that must be mentioned in order to accurately portray the context is the fact that, in the meantime, the 'mass production' of artworks has been accelerating, and there has been an increasing number of frequently complex and high quality works of art, even of new types, requiring incredible creativity (*e.g.*, animated films, software). This has created a particular environment in the light of the fact that, as we have explained, it is relatively easy for anyone to create a work that meets the requirement of originality.

As Bobrovszky explains, "the requirement of the individual-original work [...] is not a quality-evaluation scale, but a binary threshold of intellectual

40 "[...] the Court had made clear that copyright in the United States, at least respecting published works, was a creature of federal statute only." Id. p. 384.

41 Caterina Sganga, '*Propertizing European Copyright History, Challenges and Opportunities*', Edward Elgar, Cheltenham–Northampton, 2018, p. 28.

42 *See in detail* Anett Pogácsás, 'One Hundred Years of International Copyright', *Hungarian Yearbook of International Law and European Law*, Vol. 10, Issue 1, 2022, pp. 246–259.

43 Sam Ricketson & Jane C. Ginsburg, '*International Copyright and Neighbouring Rights: The Berne Convention and Beyond, 1*', Oxford University Press, Oxford, 2006, p. 321.

44 Stef van Gompel, '*Formalities in Copyright Law: An Analysis of Their History, Rationales and Possible Future*', Wolters Kluwer, Amsterdam, 2011, p. 292.

property."[45] Although it seems a contradiction in terms that there is a *mass* of *individual, original* works, since we typically imagine authorship and creativity as 'special' – in reality they are very 'common'.

3.1. Everything (and Anything) is Equally Original?

Several differentiation points have emerged within copyright law, and if we look closely at these 'breakpoints', we can see that they have essentially affected the concept and content of originality. Many of the points of differentiation that have emerged have become more pronounced over the last decade, new fracture points are taking shape, and others need to be smoothed over. The issue of eliminating differences in Europe was explicitly addressed in the context of national divergences that hamper the Digital Single Market: "[...] the rapid removal of key differences between the online and offline worlds to break down barriers to cross-border online activity."[46] However, this is another dimension of differentiation – in the context of our topic, we should focus on a number of systemic differentiations, their rationale and lack thereof.

The differentiation in copyright started with the protection of different types of works. Today, a clear separation of regulation along categories of genres would not be easy simply because of the mixed content and diversity of works, and their convergent use further complicates the matter. As we have seen, the digital/analogue dividing line alone is not a useful demarcation, although it will be an important aspect of differentiation. While different types of works and performances may require different approaches in the digital world, the distinction may increasingly be made on the basis of their other characteristics, which are already reflected to some extent in the regulation. In 1989, Boytha argued:

> "Let us pass to the structural changes within the law on authors' rights which are revolutionary all over the world. [W]e have to change the traditional interpretation of the role of authors' rights, according to which it is a somewhat exclusive branch of law, concerning only a few persons, and

45 Jenő Bobrovszky, 'A szellemi tulajdon néhány dilemmájáról a körte és a sajt között', *in* Miklós Király & Péter Gyertyánfy (eds.), '*Liber Amicorum. Studia Gy. Boytha Dedicata. Ünnepi dolgozatok Boytha György tiszteletére*', ELTE ÁJK, Budapest, 2004, p. 42.

46 Communication from the Commission to the European Parliament, the Council, the European Economic and Social Committee and the Committee of the Regions. A Digital Single Market Strategy for Europe, Brussels, 6.5.2015. COM(2015) 192 final, point 1.

which related only to the field of a narrowly defined culture. This interpretation follows from the traditional concept of culture. Culture should no more be confined to creations of literature and art, the activities of writers, artists, painters and sculptors, or composers. Today technology and technical creative activities represent an integral part of modern culture. The development of the quality of life is no more determined merely by the performances of the Opera house, by books sold in bookshops, by works of architecture or visual arts, *etc.* Culture covers also production of goods satisfying human demands, technical conditions of everyday life, the development of our scientific concept of the world, ecology and robotics, electronics in general, *etc.*"[47]

In the three decades since the above statement, this structural change has become even more pronounced. The smallest common denominator of the various protected works and performances is less and less the 'aesthetic' and increasingly the 'expression of creativity'. Whether it is correct that copyright law seeks to protect all forms of creative expression without distinction regarding the origin of protection,[48] and whether the uncertainty of users can be eliminated while maintaining the principle of the non-registration of the vast amount of 'creative content' are questions inseparable from the fight against censorship. However, even if the threshold of protection cannot be changed, precisely in order to guarantee the freedom of expression or participation in cultural life, the importance of the characteristics of the works/performances arises in regard to the substance of protection.

The importance of the original art copy is decreasing (even in the field of fine arts, and some works are even mass-produced using 3D printers, but in other cases the work is still expressed in a single or limited number of copies, for example of a painting or a ceramic piece, the digital copies of which have a different artistic value). The form of expression of the work (digital/analogue, number of copies, significance), the recording of the performance and the way it is recorded have a considerable impact on regulation and its application.[49] This is because in the digital medium, the focus is less and less

47 György Boytha, 'Topical Questions Concerning the Development of the Protection of Computer Programs', *in Proceedings of the Hungarian Group of IAPIP, No. 16,* 1989, p. 56.

48 According to Naughton, protection that goes beyond the protection of printed books necessarily produces a dysfunctional result. John Naughton, *From Gutenberg to Zuckerberg. Disruptive innovation in the age of the internet,* Quercus, New York–London, 2012, p. 7.

49 This soon became clear in the context of music. *See e.g.* Mihály Ficsor, 'Szerzői jog: változtatás és megőrzés – avagy miért hamisak a védelem kiterjesztéséről szóló legendák és veszélyesek a gyengítését célzó elképzelések', *in* Gábor Faludi (ed.), *'Liber amicorum.*

on individual content and increasingly on the flow and enabling of content, where material objects serve less to capture and express a certain creative content (including works, performances) but more to provide a platform for its flow instead.

In this circulation, various works and performances are involved in different ways, according to their essential characteristics (which are also closely related to the creative intent of their creator). The information content of the work/performance, its cultural role, its 'utility', its commercial value, its role in the distribution of information are delicate differences, only part of which can be captured by the law. In this regard, reference is often made to the wording of the Statute of Anne, according to which the original purpose of protection was not for the encouragement of the creation of any work in general, but "for the encouragement of learned men to compose and write useful books."[50] The question of whether a value judgment on the 'usefulness' of a work can serve to determine the threshold for protection was clearly answered in the fight against censorship, just as the adjective 'useful' in the US IP Clause[51] is not employed to filter out 'useless' works.

There are significant differences not only in the 'usefulness' of works/performances, but also in their 'value' in economic terms – the latter factor, however, is already relevant to the appearance of the work/performance on the cultural market and thus also affects the application of copyright, without however influencing its existence.

Thus, while the economic significance of works and, above all, their informational content and cultural significance as characteristics are brought to the foreground in the differentiation of regulation and the application of rules, in a gradually dematerializing world, there has also been a tendency for the application of law to "focus upon creativity in the Abstract, rather than distinguishing between different forms of creativity".[52]

In this context, the importance of the person and the will of the creator has also shifted. This is not to say that the relationship between the work and its creator has closer for all works and similar performances. Moreover, in a number of cases, a greater consideration for the will of the creator shall contribute to making works more freely accessible.

Studia P. Gyertyánfy dedicata. Ünnepi dolgozatok Gyertyánfy Péter tiszteletére', ELTE ÁJK Polgári Jogi Tanszék, Budapest, 2008, p. 225.

50 The Statute of Anne; April 10, 1710, 8 Anne, c. 19 (1710), point I.

51 US Constitution, Article I. Section 8.

52 Jonathan Griffiths, 'Dematerialization, pragmatism and the European copyright revolution', *Oxford Journal of Legal Studies*, Vol. 33, Issue 4, 2013, p. 788.

Today, the central question of copyright is how it relates to a broad and very heterogeneous spectrum of creators, and how creators themselves relate to copyright. Differences between original rightsholders are not only reflected in the types of works and performances and the uses to which they are put (notably that the motivations and interests of a software creator may differ significantly from those of a sculptor), but also in the way rightsholders within each category seek to use the possibilities offered by copyright. While more and more people are becoming receptive to open models for the use of copyright, a line is being drawn between the holders of commercially significant works – created especially for the 'cultural market' – and the creators of other works. The differences between 'typical' and 'atypical', 'professional' and 'hobby' creators, those who use the right of attribution and those who choose to stay anonymous also result in fundamental differences in the application of copyright. A database, a commissioned graphical advertisement, an individual, original ten liner written for Wikipedia, a poem, a sound recording, or a radio broadcast – the motivations behind the creation of different protected works/performances can be quite diverse, and the effect of this on the future application of copyright should not be underestimated. Copyright law can, in principle, deal with these differences. The *opt-out* enabled by the CDSM Directive, according to which creators and other rightsholders can explicitly reserve the use of their works for text and data mining in an appropriate manner, such as through machine-readable means in the case of content made publicly available online, opens up new opportunities for rights holders.[53]

The fact that the author is at the center of copyright law, classically and perhaps even more so in the future, does not mean that the creator is given the means by the legislator to jealously guard the 'tree of knowledge' at the expense of users and the public. The debates on the future of copyright have innocuously confronted the public and the creator, although their relationship is far from hostile even in the digital environment of the 21st century. In copyright law, there is a great need for a strengthening of private autonomy, a return to the author's person to ensure the viability of the chain of access and to support individual, original creative activity in the chaos of mass production. The digital age has indeed 'mined' a new layer of authorship: "questioning the author's originality and ability to create something

---

53 Directive (EU) 2019/790 of the European Parliament and of the Council of 17 April 2019 on copyright and related rights in the Digital Single Market and amending Directives 96/9/EC and 2001/29/EC (CDSM Directive), Article 4(3).

new also means highlighting the creation of texts as a collective work across time and space, and the texts themselves as multi-source, multi-voiced, constantly changing formations."[54] However, the existence of collective creation, the frequent blurring of the lines between creator/recipient, strong interdependence, the short term life of works do not shape the essence of copyright, but rather, its application.[55] In cases where creators are not themselves attached to their work, the main goal is not to artificially maintain that attachment, but to avoid uncertainty. The rightsholders have always been free to allow the use of their work, even without remuneration. It is essential to arrive at a much simpler way of expressing this will, resulting in a transparent framework. If, throughout this process, no dividing line can be drawn between the 'amateur' and the 'professional' creator by means of the law, it is apparent that the various creative groups wish to use the possibilities offered by copyright in different ways. Particularly because the exercise of a private right cannot be made compulsory even if it cannot be waived for otherwise well-founded ethical/philosophical reasons.

As Handke explained, "rights holders would probably gain greater flexibility to adapt the level of protection to their own needs."[56] These are questions that are far from being generated by the AI 'panic', in fact, academics have been ruminating over the issue for decades. Alongside the specific exercise of the right, the extent to which the content of the legal relationship needs to be modified is also of relevance. Common law and civil law copyright approaches take up fundamentally different positions on the treatment of moral rights and the waiver of the same,[57] but their exercise and signifi-

54 Anna Gács, '*Miért nem elég nekünk a könyv: A szerző az értelmezésben, szerzőségkoncepciók a kortárs magyar irodalomban*', Kijárat, Budapest, 2002, p. 32.

55 Despite what the title "The death of the author is the birth of the reader" suggests, the reader and the author are not enemies, and Barthes' critique does not attack the activity of the author, but the authors' determination of the interpretation of texts from a text-theoretical perspective. Roland Barthes, 'A szerző halála', *in* Roland Barthes, *A szöveg öröme, Irodalomelméleti írások*, Osiris, Budapest, 1996. *See in detail* Zoltán Varga, 'Szöveg – mű, olvasás – írás. Roland Barthes szövegelmélete negyven év múltán', *Literatura*, 2013/3.

56 Christian Handke, 'The Economics of Copyright and Digitalisation – A Report on the Literature and the Need for Further Research', 1 May 2010, p. 39.

57 Jonathan Griffiths, 'Moral rights from a copyright perspective', *in* Fabienne Brison *et al.* (eds.), '*Moral rights in the 21st century. The changing role of the moral rights in an era of information overload*', Larcier, Brussels, 2015, p. 83; Antoon Quaedvlieg, 'Introduction. Trying to find a balance', *in* Brison *et al.* (eds.) 2015, p. 93. The Posnerian idea that the abandonment of moral rights can be economically rational for the right holder, and that we must therefore examine the existence of a balance on a case-by-case basis, is expressed in both approaches, with the possibility of abandoning the *exercise* of the right in the

cance are similar. While it is clear that the identity of the creator cannot be 'hermetically separated from the creation', it is also evident that this connection is not always of equal significance.[58]

"The discourse on the protection of intellectual property" is increasingly "moving out of the autonomous author/unique work context",[59] nevertheless, the point of reference will always be the author. It is a further question that, with the gradual eclipse of individual licensing, the mass presence of specific methods of creation and specific types of works, the impact of the particular purposes of creation and use, there is often no social demand either for the identity of the author or for the work's emergence from the digital content. 'Flexibility', as well as the very essence of fairness, is not even a legislative issue. As Boytha warns in relation to the assessment of plagiarism, it is not a question of law, but of fact.[60] The ever-expanding public domain makes it increasingly difficult to meet the threshold of individual originality, particularly in certain fields such as music, and this has a major role to play in the assessment of plagiarism. Indeed, the originality threshold is constantly rising.

3.2. The Threshold Rising, or the 'Margin for Manoeuvre' Narrows?

As Gompel points out, what many of the different national definitions have in common is that they place some form of emphasis on the author's choices that are not primarily constrained by the function of the work, the tools used, or the standards and general practices that apply – in other words, works are based on 'creative choices'.[61]

Therefore, there are significant differences between the works in terms of the scope of creative freedom and, in this context, in the assessment of the

continental solution. Richard A. Posner, '*The Little Book on Plagiarism*', Pantheon Books, New York, 2007, pp. 108–110.

58 As Keserű points out, the works that underlie the design protection of passenger-carrying craft and the topographical protection of microelectronic semiconductors hardly reveal the romantic authorial personality. Barna Arnold Keserű, 'John Locke tulajdonelmélete a szellemi tulajdonjogok nézőpontjából', *in* Barna Arnold Keserű & Ákos Kőhidi (eds.), '*Tanulmányok a 65 éves Lenkovics Barnabás tiszteletére*', Eötvös, Budapest–Győr, 2015, p. 220.

59 Balázs Bodó, '*A szerzői jog kalózai*', Typotex, Budapest, 2011, p. 137.

60 Boytha 1989.

61 Daniel J. Gervais, '*(Re)structuring Copyright. A Comprehensive Path to International Copyright Reform*', Edward Elgar, Cheltenham–Northampton, 2017, p. 95.

originality of expression. The degree of 'margin for manoeuvre' available to the creator to express originality varies from case to case and from genre to genre, and this margin of manoeuvre is very limited particularly in the case of functional works,[62] but it also raises some striking questions about the copyright protection of photographs.[63] Beside the well-known *Painer* case, the CJEU pointed out also in *Funke Medien,* that the starting point is whether the author was able to express his creative abilities in the production of the work by making free and creative choices.[64] This is not a European characteristic, similarly 'formative freedom' is a recognized requirement in the US: just to refer to the much cited *Burrow-Giles Lithographic Company v Sarony,*[65] where the court also discussed the importance of creative choices in relation to photographic images. As Travis reminds, countries in North America and much of Europe require only minimally creative choices to qualify as a work of authorship.[66]

However, we are applying this standard in a context where mass production is rapidly increasing the number of what can now be called 'commonplace solutions', an "unprotected cliché" that belongs to the public domain.[67] "Copyright law does not protect works (or specific elements of works) which are not original, which consist of familiar or expected clichés".[68] Numerous legal disputes and famous cases (concerning *e.g.,* musical chords and melodies)[69] highlight the fact that, through natural processes, the public

62 Paul Torremans, 'The Role of the CJEU's Autonomous Concepts as a Harmonising Element of Copyright Law in the United Kingdom', *Intellectual Property Quarterly,* 2019/4, p. 271.

63 Judgment of 1 December 2011, *Case C-145/10, Painer,* ECLI:EU:C:2011:798. Marian Jankovic, 'How the Two Child Abuse Cases Helped to Shape the Test of Originality of Photographic Works', *Masaryk University Journal of Law and Technology,* Vol. 17, Issue 2, 2023, pp. 197–218.

64 Judgment of 29 July 2019, *Case C-469/17, Funke Medien,* ECLI:EU:C:2019:623.

65 *Burrow-Giles Lithographic Company v Sarony,* 111 U.S. 53 (1884).

66 Hannibal Travis, 'Augmented Creativity in a Harmonized Trans-Atlantic Knowledge Economy', *in* Péter Mezei *et al.* (eds.), *Harmonizing Intellectual Property for a Trans-Atlantic Knowledge Economy,* Brill, Leiden, 2024, p. 76.

67 Gideon Parchomovsky & Alex Stein, 'Originality', *Virginia Law Review,* Vol. 95, Issue 6, 2009, p. 1539.

68 Tyler T. Ochoa, 'Origins and Meaning of the Public Domain', *University Dayton Law Review,* Vol. 28, Issue 2, 2002, cited in Pamela Samuelson, 'Enriching Discourse on Public Domains', *Duke Law Journal,* Vol. 55, Issue 4, 2006, pp. 783–834.

69 *See from early time:* M.D. Calvocoressi, 'Innovation and Cliché in Music', *The Musical Times,* Vol. 64, Issue 959, 1923, pp. 25–27; Changsheng Xu *et al.,* 'Automatic Structure Detection for Popular Music', *IEEE Multimedia,* Vol. 13, Issue 1, 2006, p. 67.

domain is constantly expanding and the scope for creativity is becoming narrower.[70]

In other words, time itself, and the tremendous amount of content that is being produced – supposedly protected or unprotected, but of a similar character – is closing the door to authors. Of course, if the threshold can be raised, that in itself may be a very welcome (side)effect, but it still leaves creators and practitioners in a difficult position to deal with it under the existing regulatory framework. Into this already difficult situation AI brings its own changes. On the one hand, prompting also offers the artist a very narrow margin of manoeuvre, mostly excluding the possibility of creating an original work,[71] but it also has a much wider impact: the existence of creations that are produced at a very fast rhythm, competing with and similar to the author's works, also generally narrows the margin of manoeuvre. Although the concept of copyright protection does not refer to *new* content, the concept of originality does raise the question of whether a similar solution already exists, and somehow we measure the presence of originality to the existing set of works (now more correctly, content). And the more elements there are in the existing set, the harder it is to cross the threshold. In deciding whether something is a 'commonplace' solution, it is obviously relevant if a number of very similar creations are known. "These creative choices can be characterized as those which can be isolated by a method of asking whether two authors would have been likely to produce essentially the same work in comparable circumstances."[72]

The CJEU points out in *Brompton* that in the context of crossing the threshold, the court has to explore whether the conditions are met.[73] In the literature, the use of AI tools as a means of doing so has been suggested. The issue has also been raised by a Member State in the policy questionnaire that the level of originality could be assessed with the assistance of new technol-

70 Aviv H. Gaon, '*The Future of Copyright in the Age of Artificial Intelligence*', Edward Elgar, Cheltenham–Northampton, 2021, p. 232. Referring to Gervais, that if the creation is determined, there is no "room for creativity".

71 Gergely Csősz, 'A prompt szerepe az alkotásban', *Iparjogvédelmi és Szerzői Jogi Szemle*, Vol. 19, Issue 5, 2024, p. 120.

72 Jankovic 2023, p. 207.

73 *Case C-833/18, Brompton Bicycle Ltd,* para. 34. Therefore, in order to establish whether the product concerned falls within the scope of copyright protection, it is for the referring court to determine whether, through that choice of the shape of the product, its author has expressed his creative ability in an original manner by making free and creative choices and has designed the product in such a way that it reflects his personality.

ogies.[74] The capabilities of AI applications developed for certain purposes can also be beneficial in this regard, such as the ability of a method of Microsoft to create a traceable path for greater transparency between the model and users.[75] Another example, that some authors have called for the introduction of 'originality points':

> "In fact, we assume that choices regarding originality reflect normative tradeoffs, which should be decided by social institutions (*e.g.*, courts, regulators, standard-setting bodies) using acceptable procedures. Nevertheless, such choices could now be better informed by evidence. Originality scores could empower policymakers to go beyond ensuring compliance."[76]

This raises another fundamental copyright issue: in copyright doctrine, in theory, parallel creation can lead to parallel protection (even if the scope of works, where there is a realistic chance of this, is limited). Parallel creation, however, becomes practically impossible if, as in the field of industrial property, reference is made to existing protected subject matter.

Until recently, it was possible to tell whether something was a work of art simply by looking at it. Today, the picture has fundamentally changed. It is a good illustration of how far back we have to go in the footprint of digital technologies, and AI in particular, that the questions put to the CJEU in September 2023 in the request for a preliminary ruling in *Mio* go right back to the very basics. After all, it has also become uncertain how to decide whether a subject matter of applied art reflects the author's personality by giving expression to his or her free and creative choices.[77] The first question is particularly relevant to our topic: in the assessment of whether a subject matter of applied art merits the far-reaching protection of copyright as a work, how should the examination be carried out – and which factors must or should be taken into account – in the question of whether the subject matter reflects the author's personality by giving expression to his or her free

74 Member States contributions on the policy Questionnaire on the relationship between generative artificial intelligence and copyright and related rights Prepared by the Hungarian Presidency Brussels, 20 December 2024 (OR. en) 16710/1/24 REV 1.

75 Microsoft Filed Patent Application on Method for Eliminating Artificial Intelligence Hallucinations, at https://natlawreview.com/article/microsoft-filed-patent-application-method-eliminating-artificial-intelligence.

76 Uri Y. Hacohen & Niva Elkin-Koren, 'Copyright Regenerated: Harnessing GenAI to Measure Originality and Copyright Scope', *Harvard Journal of Law & Technology*, Vol. 37, Issue 2, 2024.

77 *Case C-580/23, Mio and others*, pending.

and creative choices? In that regard, the question is in particular whether the examination of originality should focus on factors surrounding the creative process and the author's explanation of the actual choices that he or she made in the creation of the subject matter or on factors relating to the subject matter itself and the end result of the creative process and whether the subject matter itself gives expression to artistic effect.[78] The third question is also highly pertinent: how should the assessment of similarity be carried out and what similarity is required in the examination and in particular whether the examination should focus on whether the work is recognizable in the allegedly infringing subject matter or on whether the allegedly infringing subject matter creates the same overall impression as the work, or what else the examination should focus on.[79]

The theoretical literature has been experimenting for some time with the use of a new originality test, either in general or for specific types of works.[80] While the role of protection is obviously not to ensure the recognition of a few creators 'highlighted' from society, at the same time, it is also a problem to interpret the existence of a 'personal touch' into every piece of content. Gyertyánfy believes that the doubling of the threshold for copyright entry cannot be avoided, arguing for the need to differentially raise the threshold of protection.[81]

However, it is also a question of whether it is possible to create an original work at all, if the creative scope is extremely limited, either because of the functional nature or because of the mass availability of similar works. Is a minimum margin of manoeuvre really enough to reflect personality? The CJEU also requires a reflection of personality in functional works – which does not, however, indicate an increase of the threshold in practice, although such a meaning could be attributed to the maintenance of this requirement.[82] As Advocat General Szpunar underlined in his Opinion delivered on 8 May 2025, "in copyright law, what distinguishes two works is not the overall impression but the details that uniquely personalize them."[83] He

---

78 Id. Question 1.

79 Id. Question 3.

80 *See e.g.* Emma Steel, 'Original sin: reconciling originality in copyright with music as an evolutionary art form', *European Intellectual Property Review,* Vol. 37, Issue 2, 2015.

81 Péter Gyertyánfy, 'A holliwoodi takácsok és a szerzői jog', *Iparjogvédelmi és Szerzői Jogi Szemle,* Vol. 19, Issue 5, 2024, p. 228.

82 Audrey Pope: 'Recovering Personality in Copyright's Originality Inquiry.' *Harvard Law Review,* Vol. 138, Issue 4, 2025, p. 1123.

83 Opinion of Advocate General Szpunar delivered on 8 May 2025, *Case C-580/23, Mio and others,* ECLI:EU:C:2025:330. para. 67.

also warns of two extremes: neither choices dictated by the various constraints that bind the creator are creative, nor those that "although free, do not bear the imprint of the author's personality by giving the subject matter a unique appearance. In particular, the possibility of making free choices, at the time of creation, does not give rise to a presumption that those choices are creative."[84] In the light of this, the CJEU's judgment in *Mio* will be particularly significant, where we can also hope for further guidance on the degree of originality.[85] The questions asked in this case twenty years ago would have seemed completely pointless, however, due to digital mass production, and even recognizability and transparency, they could have a significant impact now also in terms of AI.

4. Chances and Reflections

Answering our first research question (RQ1), we have to evaluate the rise of AI, which has a great impact on creative industries, particularly in the realm of the artistic creations. Algorithms used by AI-programs are becoming ever so subtle. AI-driven art platforms such as DEEPArt, Deep Dream Generator, DALL-E – to only name a few – are capable of generating artistic images based on text prompts, thereby creating unique visual effects. Their advanced deep learning technologies and user-friendly platforms allow users to experiment with AI without the need for extensive programming knowledge.[86]

With the growing popularity of AI among art enthusiasts, the phenomenon raises fundamental questions about the nature of creativity and the threshold of originality. As Marketa Trimble points out in an interesting parallel, Socrates believed that writing would weaken the human memory, as

> "[...]. this invention will produce forgetfulness in the minds of those who learn to use it, because they will not practice their memory. [...]You have invented an elixir not of memory, but of reminding; and you offer your pupils the appearance of wisdom, not true wisdom, for they will read many things without instruction and will therefore seem to know many

84 Id. para. 62.

85 *Case C-580/23, Mio and others,* Question 4(a).

86 Deep Dream Generator Blog: *'AI-Generated Art and the Question of Originality',* at https://deepdreamgenerator.com/blog/ai-art-originality.

things, when they are for the most part ignorant and hard to get along with, since they are not wise, but only appear wise."[87]

The impact of AI models are quite similar, as this new and effortless way to create could potentially effect human creativity negatively.[88] While AI has the potential to accelerate the creation process, it also includes the risk of losing thoughtful human touch and the value of individuality.[89] Creators are no longer forced to use their full potential of creativity and imagination when creating an artwork.

Regarding our first research question (RQ1), we concluded that the very low entry threshold for copyright has already generated a number of side effects, such as the difficulty of treating the diverse genres of works differently, the ambiguous position of orphan works, the issue of grey zones of licensing and free use in mass production. However, AI has added a massive additional dimension by fundamentally shaking up the notion of the work itself, its identification and the proof and examination of originality in relation to content that appears to be creative.[90]

While the basic criterion of originality for copyright protection has been examined in a number of recent studies, it is clear that because of the low threshold for entry also includes works that are questionable for protection, but the discourse tends to move in the direction of whether to protect creative content that appears to have a similar outcome to human creation, or AI-assisted works more generally. Yet we can thank the cutting-edge scientific discourse spawned by AI for making copyright originality 'show its hand'. With rapid technical innovations of AI-models, it is becoming increasingly difficult to distinguish whether a particular work was created by a generative AI, with the assistance of AI, or is it the direct result of human craftsmanship. AI-generated works are appearing in large numbers on the market. We have identified problems with massification *per se,* one of which is that, although individual originality can only be examined on a case-by-case basis, there is neither time nor adequate tools available. The other one

87 Plato, '*The Phaedrus*', Translated by Benjamin Jowett, Dover Publications, 2000. (Original work published circa 370 BCE).

88 Marketa Trimble, 'Artificial Intelligence and Human Intelligence', *GRUR International,* Vol. 72, Issue 1, 2023, pp. 1–2.

89 Michael Machado, 'Preserving Craft in the Era of AI', 2025, at https://devrev.ai/blog/era-of-ai.

90 Francesca Mazzi, 'Authorship in artificial intelligence-generated works: Exploring originality in text prompts and artificial intelligence outputs through philosophical foundations of copyright and collage protection', *Journal of World Intellectual* Property, Vol. 27, Issue 3, 2024, p. 41.

is related to the scope of creative freedom. This is the issue we addressed under our second research question (RQ2).

Several ideas for raising or doubling the low entry threshold, and for the method of assessing originality, have been outlined in the academic literature. Our research has led us to conclude that, on the one hand, there seems to be a shift in the way we look at existing copyright presumptions and the proof of the existence of protection, with a greater emphasis on the comparison with the existing body of work. On the other hand, the scope for creativity is naturally narrowing as a result of massification, which also means a *de facto* increase in the threshold for entry. In addition, by taking seriously the concept of the 'personal touch', *i.e.*, the personality reflected in the work and performances, which is consistently included in the practice of the CJEU and which is also required for functional works, a considerable contribution could be made to clarifying the doctrine of copyright protection and making it more effective.

AI Act and IPR Enforcement

The European Regulatory Framework and Practical Challenges

*György Kovács**

Abstract

The EU's Artificial Intelligence Act seeks to strike a delicate balance between fostering innovation and establishing robust safeguards for legal compliance, including the effective enforcement of IPRs. This study delves into the intricate intersection of the AI Act and IPR, with a focus on the multifaceted challenges related to copyright, patents, data protection, and trade secrets. It examines the implications of the emerging regulations on AI-generated content and the practical difficulties encountered in IPR enforcement within the EU's legal framework. By analyzing the regulatory landscape and its potential shortcomings, this study offers insights into how AI regulation may evolve to better protect intellectual property while nurturing innovation. Furthermore, the study incorporates comparative perspectives, contrasting the EU's approach with those of other significant jurisdictions, and concludes with actionable policy recommendations aimed at harmonizing AI regulation with intellectual property law.

Keywords: Artificial Intelligence, intellectual property rights, IPR Enforcement, AI Act, Digital Single Market

* György Kovács: attorney-at-law; visiting lecturer, Pázmány Péter Catholic University, Budapest; president, Hungarian Fulbright Association, kovacs.gyorgy@jak.ppke.hu.

1. Introduction

The swift advancement of artificial intelligence technologies has heralded a new era brimming with both unprecedented opportunities and intricate legal challenges pertaining to intellectual property rights (hereinafter: IPR). The integration of AI technologies into a wide array of sectors, including healthcare, finance, security, and creative industries, has become increasingly pervasive.[1] Generative AI models, exemplified by OpenAI's GPT-4 and DALL·E, have demonstrated the capacity to produce texts, images, and music that closely emulate human-created works.[2] Similarly, AI-assisted design tools are instrumental in fostering novel inventions and technological breakthroughs.[3] These developments precipitate fundamental inquiries regarding authorship, ownership, and inventorship, thereby challenging the conventional IPR frameworks that were not initially designed to accommodate non-human creators.[4]

The EU's Artificial Intelligence Act (hereinafter: AI Act), initially proposed in 2021, is a pioneering effort to regulate AI within a structured legal framework. This regulation seeks to strike a balance between incentivizing innovation and safeguarding fundamental rights, with a focus on safety, transparency, and accountability.[5] However, the protection of IPRs in AI-generated works or inventions presents unprecedented challenges, particularly when defining ownership, originality, and inventorship.[6] Traditional IP frameworks were not designed to accommodate non-human creators, leading to legal uncertainties and requiring a re-evaluation of existing legal norms.[7]

---

1 Artificial Intelligence, 'Opportunities and Challenges for the internal market and consumer protection', Briefing, *European Parliament,* 2020, p. 2, at https://www.europarl.europa.eu/thinktank/en/document/IPOL_BRI(2020)642352.

2 GPT-4 Technical Report, *OpenAI,* 2023, pp. 10–12, at https://cdn.openai.com/papers/gpt-4.pdf.

3 Spotlight on skills in the age of AI. The impact of emerging technology on skills, training and talent, Report, Autodeks, 2022, pp. 3–4, at https://damassets.autodesk.net/content/dam/autodesk/www/pdfs/adk-24122-skills-in-the-age-of-ai-report-final-012425.pdf.

4 Ryan Benjamin Abbott, 'I Think, Therefore I Invent: Creative Computers and the Future of Patent Law', *Boston College Law Review,* Vol. 57, Issue 4, 2016, pp. 1080–1083.

5 Proposal for a Regulation Laying Down Harmonised Rules on Artificial Intelligence, *European Commission,* 2021, COM(2021) 206 final.

6 Daniel J. Gervais, 'The Machine As Author', *Iowa Law Review,* Vol. 105, 2019, pp. 2053–2106.

7 Josef Drexl *et al.,* 'Artificial Intelligence and Intellectual Property Law – Position Statement of the Max Planck Institute for Innovation and Competition of 9 April 2021 on the Current

The advent of AI technologies necessitates a re-evaluation of the traditional concepts underpinning IPR law. The rise of AI-generated content and AI-assisted inventions has blurred the lines of authorship and inventorship, raising complex questions about who should be entitled to the economic benefits derived from these creations. The AI Act seeks to address some of these concerns, but its effectiveness hinges on the development of clear guidelines and robust enforcement mechanisms that can adapt to the rapidly evolving landscape of AI technology.

This study focuses on analyzing the key provisions of the AI Act related to IPR enforcement, identifying challenges in applying existing intellectual property frameworks to AI-generated outputs, and evaluating its impact on copyright, patent, and trade secret protection. Finally, the study aims to provide policy recommendations for harmonizing AI regulation with intellectual property law to foster innovation while ensuring the protection of IPRs.

The lack of clarity in current legal frameworks risks stifling AI-driven creativity and investment. Without adequate regulation, AI-generated works could either be left unprotected, leading to economic inefficiencies, or improperly assigned, resulting in unfair monopolies.[8] This study will explore how the AI Act, alongside existing IPR regimes, can better address these emerging challenges. Furthermore, it will contribute to the ongoing debate on AI governance and provide practical recommendations for policymakers seeking to navigate the complex intersection of AI and IPRs.

2. Key Provisions of the AI Act Relevant to IPRs

The AI Act adopts a risk-based approach, classifying AI systems into four categories: unacceptable risk, high risk, limited-risk, and minimal-risk systems.[9] High-risk systems must comply with stringent transparency and accountability requirements. This classification significantly impacts how AI systems are regulated and the level of scrutiny they face, which in turn affects IPR enforcement. While the AI Act primarily aims to ensure safety,

---

Debate', *Max Planck Institute for Innovation & Competition Research Paper*, No. 21-10, 2021, pp. 21–25.

8 Peter K. Yu, 'Artificial Intelligence, Intellectual Property, and Sustainable Development', *in* Christophe Geiger (ed.), *Intellectual property, ethical innovation and sustainability: towards a new social contract for the digital economy?*, Edward Elgar, Cheltenham, 2026 (forthcoming), pp. 7–10, at https://ssrn.com/Abstract=5098200.

9 Primarily Articles 5–6 of the Regulation (EU) 2024/1689 of the European Parliament and of the Council of 13 June 2024 on Artificial Intelligence (AI Act).

transparency, and fundamental rights protection, it has significant implications for IPRs, particularly regarding copyright, patents, and trade secrets.

2.1. Risk-Based Classification and Its Impact on IPRs (Articles 5–6)

The AI Act defines AI systems under Article 3(1) as a machine based system that is designed to operate with varying levels of autonomy and that may exhibit adaptiveness after deployment, logic- and knowledge-based approaches, which can generate outputs influencing physical or virtual environments.[10] This broad definition covers generative AI models that produce text, images, or inventions, directly affecting copyright and patent law. The risk classification mechanism raises several concerns regarding IPR enforcement.

Article 5 outlines AI practices that are prohibited due to their unacceptable risk, including manipulative AI techniques. Although these prohibitions are mainly driven by ethical considerations, they may also affect AI applications involved in generating counterfeit or infringing content. Article 6 specifies that AI systems categorized as high-risk under Annex III must adhere to stricter compliance requirements. This applies to AI used in biometric identification, critical infrastructure, and automated decision-making, but it could also encompass AI-generated works and inventions that necessitate IPR enforcement.

The AI Act does not explicitly classify AI systems that generate copyrighted or patentable material as high-risk, creating regulatory gaps and potentially insufficient oversight. Additionally, the lack of direct provisions on IPR enforcement may hinder rights holders' ability to address AI-driven infringement, as the Act primarily focuses on safety and fundamental rights without specific mechanisms for handling IPR violations.

The absence of explicit IPR provisions in the risk classification framework underscores the need for supplementary regulations or guidelines to address the unique challenges posed by AI-generated content and inventions. It also highlights the importance of ongoing monitoring and assessment to ensure that the AI Act remains effective in protecting IPRs in the face of rapidly evolving AI technology.

10 Article 3(1) of the AI Act.

2.2. Transparency and Data Governance (Articles 10–15, 53)

Article 13 of the AI Act mandates transparency for high-risk AI systems, requiring providers to ensure interpretable decision-making.[11] These measures create significant tensions between copyright enforcement and trade secret protection.

For copyright, the Act fails to require explicit disclosure of copyrighted training content. Article 13(3)(vi)'s ambiguous data provenance rules and Article 53(1)'s dataset summaries prove insufficient for infringement verification. Rights holders lack work-by-work audit capabilities, relying on private litigation due to the AI Office's limited oversight[12] [Preamble, Recitals (104)–(109)]. Regulatory exemptions for SMEs/researchers further enable loopholes.

Regarding trade secrets, transparency obligations clash with Directive (EU) 2016/943.[13] While Recitals 88/107/167 and Articles 25(5)/52(6)/53(1)(b)/55(3)/78(1) acknowledge confidentiality needs, they offer no resolution. Supply-chain disclosures [Article 25(5)] and continuous documentation updates [Article 53(1)(b)] risk exposing proprietary data. Cross-border regulatory exchanges under Article 78 lack safeguards for jurisdictions with weak trade secret enforcement, compounded by absent challenge mechanisms.

Ultimately, while the AI Act aims to enhance transparency and accountability in AI development, its framework does not sufficiently safeguard IPRs. The broad disclosure requirements and ambiguous confidentiality protections could discourage innovation and investment in proprietary AI models, particularly for companies relying on exclusive datasets and algorithms as competitive assets. Unless stronger safeguards are implemented, the regulation risks creating an environment where businesses must choose between compliance and the protection of their intellectual property. Balancing transparency with trade secret protection remains a fundamental challenge

---

11 For discussion emphasizing the importance of a proactive stance, *see White & Case EU AI Act Handbook,* 2025, pp. 43–87, at https://www.whitecase.com/sites/default/files/2025-06/wc-eu-ai-act-handbook.pdf.

12 On the considerable practical obstacles to effective monitoring, detection, and enforcement of IPRs in complex AI environments, *see* Bird & Bird, *Study on the AI Act,* 2025, pp. 49–63, at https://www.twobirds.com/-/media/new-website-content/pdfs/capabilities/artificial-intelligence/european-union-artificial-intelligence-act-guide.pdf.

13 Directive (EU) 2016/943 of the European Parliament and of the Council of 8 June 2016 on the protection of undisclosed know-how and business information (trade secrets) against their unlawful acquisition, use and disclosure.

that must be addressed to ensure that AI regulation fosters both innovation and legal certainty.

2.3. Copyright and AI-Generated Content (Articles 50)

Article 50(2) of the AI Act mandates explicit identification of AI-generated texts, images, audio, and video to prevent unauthorized commercial exploitation of protected content. Despite this transparency measure, critical legal uncertainties persist. *(i)* First, it remains unclear whether labelling alone satisfies copyright obligations or requires supplementary licensing. The AI Act provides no explicit guidance, delegating interpretation to national courts. This risks divergent treatments across EU member states, potentially creating regulatory fragmentation. *(ii)* Second, the Act fails to address rights holders' recourse when their works are used in AI training without authorization. Without a clear framework for claiming infringement or compensation, rights holders face significant enforcement gaps. The absence of harmonized IPR enforcement mechanisms exacerbates these issues,[14] fostering legal uncertainty for creators and developers alike. This underscores the urgent need for legislative clarification to balance copyright protection, innovation incentives, and public access to AI-driven outputs.

2.4. Authorship and Inventorship Challenges

Patent law mandates human inventorship, as affirmed by the European Patent Office. The AI Act's silence on AI-generated inventions creates legal uncertainty regarding patentability and developers' rights. This omission necessitates legislative or judicial clarification to resolve questions about AI's role in inventorship.

Without harmonized guidance, inconsistent jurisdictional approaches may emerge. Requiring the disclosure of AI's contribution to inventions and proof of patentability criteria (novelty, inventive step, industrial applicability) could mitigate risks. However, unaddressed inventorship issues threa-

14 For further analysis highlighting the need for standardization, awareness-raising, and a harmonized framework for implementation and enforcement, *see* the EUIPO study on the development of generative artificial intelligence from a copyright perspective, 2025, pp. 63–64, and 262–263, at https://www.euipo.europa.eu/en/news/euipo-releases-study-on-generative-artificial-intelligence-and-copyright.

ten innovation: unpatentable AI-assisted inventions may deter R&D investment, while patentable AI outputs risk monopolization and fairness concerns. Policymakers must balance innovation incentives with patent system integrity.

2.5. Enforcement and Compliance (Articles 72–74, 99)

Articles 72–74 of the AI Act focus on ensuring regulatory compliance, not on directly addressing IPR violations. Article 99 sets significant penalties for non-compliance – imposing fines of up to €35 million or 7 % of annual global turnover for severe breaches – these are aimed at safety and the ethical use of AI, not at safeguarding IPRs. This leaves a gap in the Act's ability to combat AI-driven infringements such as unauthorized data scraping or content generation. Rightsholders lack clear legal avenues under the AI Act to challenge these practices and must often rely on private litigation or the traditional mechanisms of Directive 2004/48/EC (IPRED),[15] which may not be well-suited to the complexities of AI-generated content and its enforcement.

3. Copyright Issues in AI-Generated Content

As stated above, the question of originality and authorship is central to copyright law, yet AI-generated works challenge traditional concepts.[16] While copyright law generally requires human authorship, AI-generated content raises issues concerning ownership and protection. Moreover, the use of copyrighted material in training datasets raises further legal concerns.[17] These challenges require a re-evaluation of the fundamental principles of copyright law and the development of new legal frameworks that can address the unique characteristics of AI-generated content.

---

15 Directive (EU) 2004/48/EC of the European Parliament and of the Council of 29 April 2004 on the Enforcement of IPRs.

16 Jane C. Ginsburg & Luke A. Budiardjo, 'Authors and Machines', *Berkeley Technology Law Journal,* Vol. 34, Issue 2, 2020, pp. 366–445.

17 Jenny Quang, 'Does training AI violate copyright law?', *Berkeley Technology Law Journal,* Vol. 36, Issue 4, 2022, pp. 1408–1435.

3.1. Originality and Authorship

Copyright law protects original works of authorship, which typically requires human creativity and intellectual effort. AI-generated content challenges this principle because it's unclear whether such creations qualify for copyright protection.[18] The level of human intervention required to qualify an AI-generated work for copyright protection remains a contentious issue. For example, if an AI generates a musical piece with minimal human input, it is debatable whether that piece qualifies as an original work under copyright law. The lack of a clear definition of originality in the context of AI-generated content creates uncertainty for creators, users, and those responsible for IPR enforcement.

The concept of authorship is also challenged by AI-generated content. Traditional copyright law assumes that a human author is responsible for the creation of a work, but AI systems can generate content autonomously, without direct human intervention. This raises questions about who should be considered the author of an AI-generated work and who should be entitled to the economic benefits derived from it.

The debate over originality and authorship in AI-generated content has sparked a wide range of opinions among legal scholars, policymakers, and industry stakeholders. Some argue that AI-generated content should not be protected by copyright because it lacks the necessary human creativity and intellectual effort. Others contend that AI-generated content should be protected to incentivize investment in AI technology and promote innovation. Still others propose a *sui generis* system of protection for AI-generated works, which would provide a tailored approach to addressing the unique challenges posed by these creations.[19]

3.2. Training Data and Copyright Infringement

AI models often rely on vast amounts of pre-existing data, raising concerns about potential copyright infringement during the training process.[20] If co-

18 James Grimmelmann, 'Copyright for Literate Robots', *Iowa Law Review*, Vol. 101, Issue 2, 2016, pp. 669–670.

19 Ryan Benjamin Abbott & Elizabeth Rothman, 'Disrupting Creativity: Copyright Law in the Age of Generative Artificial Intelligence', *Florida Law Review*, Vol. 75, Issue 6, 2023, pp. 1195–1200.

20 Samantha Fink Hedrick, 'I "THINK," THEREFORE I CREATE: Claiming Copyright in the Outputs of Algorithms', *NYU Journal of Intellectual Property & Entertainment Law*, Vol. 8, Issue 2, 2019, pp. 46–50.

pyrighted material is used without permission to train AI models, it could constitute copyright infringement. This issue is particularly relevant for large language models and image-generation models that rely on extensive datasets scraped from the internet. The legal doctrine of fair use or fair dealing may provide some defense, but its application to AI training data is not yet well-defined.[21]

The use of copyrighted material in AI training datasets raises complex legal and ethical questions. On the one hand, AI developers need access to large datasets to train their models effectively. On the other hand, copyright holders have a legitimate interest in protecting their IPRs and controlling the use of their works.

The application of fair use or fair dealing to AI training data is a complex legal issue that has not yet been fully resolved by courts. Some argue that the use of copyrighted material in AI training datasets should be considered fair use because it is transformative and does not directly compete with the original works. Others contend that the use of copyrighted material in AI training datasets should not be considered fair use because it is commercial and could harm the market for the original works.

The lack of clear guidance on this issue creates uncertainty for AI developers and copyright holders alike. It also underscores the need for further discussion and analysis to determine the appropriate legal framework for addressing the use of copyrighted material in AI training datasets.

In the EU context, the issue is further complicated by the interplay between the AI Act and the text and data mining (TDM) exceptions under the Copyright in the Digital Single Market (CDSM) Directive.[22] While the AI Act does not directly regulate copyright matters, recital 105 of the AI Act's preamble explicitly acknowledges the relevance of these exceptions by stating that the use of copyrighted materials in the training of AI systems should comply with applicable copyright laws, including limitations and exception for TDM. Under Article 3 and 4 of the CDSM Directive, text and data mining is permitted for research and, under certain conditions for commercial uses, provided that rights holders have not expressly reserved their rights. This means, that in principle, AI developers operating in the EU may rely on the TDM exception – especially for commercial training – only if the rightsholders have not opted out, for instance through machine-readable

21 Pamela Samuelson, 'How to Think About Possible Remedies in the Generative AI Copyright Cases', *Communications of the ACM,* Vol. 67, Issue 7, 2024, pp. 27–30.

22 Directive (EU) 2019/790 of the European Parliament and of the Council of 17 April 2019 on Copyright and Related Rights in the Digital Single Market.

means. However, the enforcement, and awareness of these opt-outs remain inconsistent in practice, and the AI Act does not create new powers in this regard. This gap reinforces the need for closer coordination between sectoral legislation and copyright frameworks, as well as for further guidance on how to operationalize TDM exceptions in the context of AI development.

3.3. Legal Uncertainty and Potential Solutions

The legal uncertainty surrounding copyright in AI-generated content creates challenges for both creators and users of AI technology. Potential solutions include the development of licensing mechanisms for training data, the establishment of clear guidelines for determining originality and authorship in AI-generated works, and the implementation of effective enforcement mechanisms to address copyright infringement.[23] Some scholars suggest a *sui generis* system of protection for AI-generated works, which would provide a tailored approach to addressing the unique challenges posed by these creations.[24]

Licensing mechanisms for training data could provide a way for copyright holders to be compensated for the use of their works in AI training datasets. These mechanisms could also help clarify the legal rights and obligations of AI developers and copyright holders, reducing uncertainty and promoting innovation.

Clear guidelines for determining originality and authorship in AI-generated works could help address the challenges posed by these creations to traditional copyright law. These guidelines could clarify the level of human intervention required for copyright protection and provide guidance on how to determine the author of an AI-generated work.[25]

Effective enforcement mechanisms are essential for protecting copyright in the age of AI. These mechanisms should be able to address AI-driven copyright infringement, including unauthorized data scraping and the use of AI tools to generate infringing content.

---

23 Ariel Katz, 'Debunking the Fair Use vs. Fair Dealing Myth: Have We Had Fair Use All Along?', *in* Shyamkrishna Balganesh *et al.* (eds.), *The Cambridge Handbook of Copyright Limitations and Exceptions,* Cambridge University Press, Cambridge, 2021, pp. 111–139.

24 Bingbin Lu, 'A Theory of 'Authorship Transfer' and Its Application to the Context of Artificial Intelligence Creations', *Queen Mary Journal of Intellectual Property,* Vol. 11, Issue 1, 2021, pp. 4–23.

25 Abbott & Rothman 2023, pp. 1161–1169.

A *sui generis* system of protection for AI-generated works could provide a tailored approach to addressing the unique challenges posed by these creations. This system could be designed to balance the interests of creators, users, and the public, promoting innovation while protecting IPRs.

4. Patent Law and AI-Generated Inventions

The issue of AI-generated inventions has sparked legal debates, particularly regarding inventorship.[26] Patent law requires an identifiable human inventor, which was challenged in cases such as the DABUS dispute, where an AI system was listed as the inventor.[27] These debates have focused on whether AI systems should be recognized as inventors, the role of AI in the inventive process, and the policy implications of different approaches to AI-generated inventions.

4.1. The DABUS Case

The *DABUS* case involved patent applications in multiple jurisdictions listing an AI system as the inventor.[28] Patent offices and courts in the US, Europe, and the UK rejected these applications, reaffirming the requirement of human inventorship.[29] The case highlights the challenges of applying traditional patent law to AI-generated inventions. The legal reasoning behind the rejection typically centers on the definition of an inventor as a natural person. The *DABUS* case has been widely discussed and analyzed by legal scholars and policymakers. Some argue that the rejection of the DABUS patent applications was the correct decision because AI systems are not capable of possessing the necessary legal and moral attributes of an inventor.[30]

26 Timothy Richard Holbrook, 'The Supreme Court's Quiet Revolution in Induced Patent Infringement', *Notre Dame Law Review,* Vol. 91, Issue 3, 2016, pp. 1027–1035.

27 European Patent Office (Legal Board of Appeal), Cases J 8/20 and J 9/20, 21 December 2021.

28 *Thaler v Hirshfeld,* 558 F.Supp.3d 238 (E.D.Va. 2021).

29 Ryan Benjamin Abbott, 'I Think, Therefore I Invent: Creative Computers and the Future of Patent Law', *Boston College Law Review,* Vol. 57, Issue 4, 2016, pp. 1079–1083.

30 Lital Helman & Gideon Parchomovsky, 'Artificial Inventorship', *University of Pennsylvania, Institute for Law & Economics Research Paper,* No. 24-19, 2024, pp. 11–15.

4.2. Inventorship and AI Assistance

While AI cannot be listed as an inventor, AI tools can assist human inventors in the invention process. The extent to which AI can contribute to an invention without disqualifying it from patent protection remains a complex issue.[31] Clear guidelines are needed to determine the level of human intervention required for an invention to be patentable. This includes determining the degree of human involvement necessary for the invention to be considered a product of human ingenuity rather than solely a result of AI processing.

One potential approach is to consider AI as a sophisticated tool that assists human inventors, similar to a computer or a laboratory instrument. In this view, the human inventor would still be the primary driver of the inventive process, using AI to perform tasks such as data analysis, simulation, and optimization. As long as the human inventor contributes a significant inventive step, the invention could be patentable, even if AI played a substantial role in its development. However, this approach raises questions about how to assess the significance of human contribution. What level of human intervention is sufficient to qualify an invention as patentable? How should patent offices and courts evaluate the relative contributions of humans and AI in the inventive process? These are complex questions that require further analysis and clarification.

Another approach is to focus on the technical contribution of AI to the invention. In this view, if AI performs a task that would otherwise require significant human skill and effort, the invention might not be patentable because it lacks an inventive step. This approach could be particularly relevant in cases where AI is used to automate routine tasks or to generate obvious variations of existing technologies.

5. Enforcement Challenges in the Context of the AI Act

The enforcement of IPRs in the context of artificial intelligence presents unique challenges, particularly given the cross-border nature of AI-generated content. The ability of AI systems to produce and disseminate content instantaneously across jurisdictions complicates the application of national

31 Adam B. Jaffe & Josh Lerner, *Innovation and Its Discontents: How Our Broken Patent System Is Endangering Innovation and Progress, and What to Do About It,* Princeton University Press, Princeton, 2006, pp. 27–65.

and international enforcement mechanisms. Moreover, the AI Act's transparency requirements, while designed to promote accountability, may conflict with proprietary interests, creating further obstacles for IPR enforcement. Addressing these complexities requires a multifaceted approach that considers the technical, legal, and policy dimensions of AI governance.

5.1. Cross-Border Infringement

AI-generated content transcends national borders, making traditional enforcement mechanisms less effective in addressing IPR violations. The ease with which AI can generate and distribute infringing material across multiple jurisdictions underscores the need for enhanced international cooperation. Effective enforcement in this context requires harmonization of legal standards, information-sharing frameworks, and coordinated enforcement actions of national authorities.[32]

One approach to mitigating cross-border infringement is the development of international agreements that specifically address the legal complexities associated with AI-generated content. Such agreements could establish uniform standards for copyright protection, patentability, and trademark enforcement, thereby facilitating more consistent enforcement across jurisdictions. Additionally, fostering closer collaboration between law enforcement agencies across different countries could improve enforcement efforts. This could involve intelligence-sharing mechanisms that enable authorities to track and target AI-driven IPR violations more effectively. Establishing dedicated task forces to investigate AI-related infringement could also strengthen international enforcement capabilities.

Technological solutions may further support enforcement efforts. AI-powered detection tools can assist in identifying infringing content, while automated takedown mechanisms could be deployed to remove unauthorized AI-generated works. Additionally, access control technologies, such as geofencing and content filtering, could be employed to restrict the cross-border dissemination of infringing material.

---

32 Gaétan de Rassenfosse *et al.*, 'AI-Generated Inventions: Implications for the Patent System', *Southern California Law Review*, Vol. 96, Issue 6, 2024, pp. 1476–1478.

5.2. Transparency versus Proprietary Interests

The AI Act's emphasis on transparency is intended to promote accountability in AI deployment. However, these requirements may come into tension with the protection of trade secrets and proprietary technologies. Striking a balance between transparency and the preservation of confidential business information is a critical challenge in AI regulation.

One potential solution is the implementation of mechanisms that allow for selective disclosure of AI-related information. For example, AI developers could be required to disclose relevant operational details to regulatory authorities or designated third-party auditors while safeguarding sensitive commercial information from public exposure.[33] This approach would ensure compliance with transparency mandates without unduly compromising competitive interests. Another possibility is limiting transparency obligations to information that is strictly necessary for accountability and public understanding. Disclosure requirements could be confined to key aspects such as training data sources, decision-making algorithms, and risk mitigation strategies, ensuring that stakeholders have access to essential information without jeopardizing proprietary innovations.

A further strategy involves creating incentives for voluntary disclosure. Governments could offer financial or regulatory benefits, such as tax incentives or expedited regulatory approvals, to encourage AI developers to adopt best practices in transparency. This approach would align regulatory objectives with industry incentives, fostering a culture of responsible disclosure while maintaining commercial competitiveness.

5.3. Technical Challenges

Enforcing IPR in the AI era is further complicated by the difficulty of identifying and tracking AI-generated content. AI systems can produce derivative works, deepfakes, and counterfeit products that are indistinguishable from human-created content, making it challenging for rightsholders and regulators to detect and prevent infringement. Addressing these technical challenges requires the adoption of advanced technological enforcement mechanisms. One promising approach is the development of AI-powered

---

33 Frank Pasquale, *The Black Box Society: The Secret Algorithms That Control Money and Information,* Harvard University Press, 2015, pp. 193–217.

detection tools capable of identifying AI-generated content based on distinct patterns and characteristics. These tools could employ machine learning algorithms to recognize anomalies in digital works, distinguishing AI-generated material from human-created content.

Blockchain technology also presents a potential solution for tracking the provenance of AI-generated content. By recording the creation, modification, and ownership history of digital assets on a decentralized ledger, blockchain could enhance traceability and facilitate the authentication of legitimate works. This would assist rightsholders in proving authorship and detecting unauthorized reproductions.[34]

Finally, industry-wide adoption of AI-generated content labeling standards could improve transparency and enforcement. Embedding metadata within AI-generated works to indicate their origin and authorship would enable consumers, platforms, and enforcement agencies to identify and monitor AI-generated material more effectively. Such labeling mechanisms could be mandated through regulatory frameworks or encouraged through industry self-regulation.

6. Conclusion and Recommendations

The intersection of the AI Act and IPR enforcement presents both challenges and opportunities for the EU. While the AI Act provides a comprehensive regulatory framework for AI governance, it does not directly address the complexities of IPR protection in the context of AI-generated content and inventions. The legal uncertainties surrounding authorship, inventorship, and enforcement mechanisms require further fine tuning to ensure that the regulatory framework effectively balances innovation incentives with the protection of intellectual property.

The AI Act offers a structured approach to AI regulation but lacks specific provisions on IPR enforcement, leaving critical questions unanswered. Copyright law faces significant challenges in addressing AI-generated works, particularly in determining originality and human authorship. Patent law, in turn, adheres to the requirement of human inventorship,[35] creating diffi-

34 EUIPO Strategic Plan 2025, at https://euipo.europa.eu/tunnel-web/secure/webdav/guest/document_library/contentPdfs/about_euipo/strategic_plan/SP2025_en.pdf.

35 A. Saravanan & M. Deva Prasad, 'AI as an Inventor Debate under the Patent Law: A Post-DABUS Comparative Analysis', *European Intellectual Property Review*, Vol. 47, Issue 1, 2025, pp. 26–39.

culties in recognizing AI-assisted innovations.[36] Furthermore, IPR enforcement in the AI landscape is complicated by the cross-border nature of AI-generated content and the potential conflict between transparency obligations and proprietary business interests.

To address these challenges, targeted legal reforms are necessary. The AI Act should be amended to include explicit provisions on IPR enforcement, ensuring that copyright, patent, and trade secret protections are effectively applied in AI-related cases. Specific guidelines on originality and authorship must be developed to clarify the extent of human intervention required for copyright protection. Additionally, a licensing framework should be established to regulate the use of copyrighted material in AI training data, ensuring that copyright holders receive appropriate compensation. Patent law should also be adapted to provide clear guidance on the role of AI in the inventive process, outlining the extent to which AI can contribute without undermining the requirement for human inventorship.

Beyond legislative amendments, enhanced international cooperation is crucial for addressing cross-border IPR infringements in the AI domain. Establishing common legal standards, facilitating cross-border enforcement mechanisms, and fostering collaboration among national authorities will be essential in preventing regulatory fragmentation. Moreover, technological advancements should be leveraged to strengthen enforcement efforts. AI-powered detection tools could play a significant role in identifying AI-generated content, tracing its origin, and monitoring potential copyright or patent violations. Transparency requirements within the AI Act should also be carefully calibrated to balance the need for accountability with the protection of trade secrets, ensuring that businesses can safeguard proprietary AI models without undermining regulatory objectives. A continuous dialogue between policymakers, legal experts, and industry stakeholders is necessary to develop best practices and maintain a legal framework that remains responsive to technological advancements.

The legal response to AI must strike a careful balance between fostering innovation and ensuring adequate protection for intellectual property. Without a coherent and adaptive regulatory approach, the rapid advancement of AI could lead to significant legal uncertainty, ultimately undermining both the integrity of the IPR system and broader AI governance objectives. Addressing these challenges through informed legal and policy interven-

---

36 Tim W. Dornis, 'Artificial Intelligence and Innovation: The End of Patent Law As We Know It', *Yale Journal of Law & Technology*, Vol. 23, Fall, 2020, p. 111–113.

tions will be critical in shaping an AI-driven economy that is both innovative and legally sound.

Plagiarism in Higher Education

The Impact of EU-funded Research, Law, and AI on Evolving Academic Norms

*Adrienn Aczél-Partos**

Abstract

What qualifies as plagiarism, and how has its perception evolved over the past decades? Does the rise of digitalization and artificial intelligence redefine the concept of plagiarism, or does it merely introduce new forms of literal copying? The definition and assessment of plagiarism have undergone continuous transformation, particularly with the increasing influence of digital technologies and AI. This raises the question of whether these innovations create novel challenges in identifying and managing plagiarism or simply bring existing problems to the fore in new ways. This paper explores the multifaceted nature of plagiarism definitions, in particular in national copyright and criminal law provisions as well as EU regulations. It examines EU-funded projects conducted between 2010 and 2019 that investigated plagiarism in higher education, paying special attention to differences between faculty and student attitudes. In addition, the present paper analyses the impact of AI-based technologies, which present both new challenges to, and opportunities for detecting and preventing plagiarism. The research aims at mapping how legal and ethical approaches to plagiarism may evolve with the appearance of these technologies and to what extent the findings of past EU projects remain applicable in the current academic landscape.

Keywords: plagiarism, higher education, artificial intelligence, academic integrity, originality

* Adrienn Aczél-Partos: Head of the Legal Informatics Education Group, Pázmány Péter Catholic University, Budapest, aczel-partos.adrienn@jak.ppke.hu.

Adrienn Aczél-Partos

> "If you copy from one author, it's plagiarism.
> If you copy from many, it's research."
>
> (Wilson Mizner)

1. Introduction

Plagiarism is one of the most serious and complex ethical problems in higher education, damaging the integrity and effectiveness of education systems. The phenomenon is not simply a matter of individual student behavior, but also an issue for institutional regulation and social norms. Almost all higher education institutions in Hungary refer to legal norms (typically copyright, sometimes criminal law) in relation to plagiarism, although plagiarism is not a legal category under national law.[1] This paper describes the concepts of usurpation, fraud, theft, infringement of copyright or copyright-related rights, contrasted with the ethical aspects of plagiarism. The main role of higher education institutions is to create and transmit knowledge and to promote the development of critical thinking and ethical research practice.[2] Plagiarism, however, undermines these principles and, in the long term, threatens the role of higher education in society.[3]

Originality and authenticity are the foundations of the scientific community. Plagiarism is a total violation of these two principles, which can ultimately lead to a loss of confidence in the education system. Plagiarism also has a negative impact on the quality of education, as it hinders the development of independent thinking and creative problem solving. In addition, the reputation and international competitiveness of higher education institutions suffers when the fight against plagiarism is ineffective.

1 Barna Mezey, 'A tudományetikai felelősség kérdései a magyar felsőoktatásban: Az egyetemi és tudományos élet etikai szabályozása – az egyetemi etikai kódexek', *Magyar Tudomány*, Vol. 175, Issue 6, 2014, pp. 655–666; István Kollár, 'Plágium, vagy mások eredményeinek összefoglalása? Egy kutató tűnődései', *Magyar Tudomány*, Vol. 177, Issue 1, 2016, p. 93.

2 Act CCIV of 2011 on National Higher Education (hereinafter: NHE Act), Section 1 (1).

3 The preamble of the NHE Act reads as follows: "The National Assembly, aware of its responsibility towards the nation, in accordance with the avowal of the Fundamental Law, agreeing with the need for the spiritual and intellectual renewal of the nation, trusting in the commitment of the young generations becoming university citizens, and expressing its belief that our children and grandchildren will once again raise Hungary by their talent, perseverance and spiritual strength, shall pass a new law to regulate national higher education."

To understand and prevent plagiarism and strengthen academic (scientific) integrity, a number of projects have been launched in the EU between 2010 and 2019. The projects launched at that time aimed to identify the types of plagiarism, analyze the attitudes of students and teachers in higher education, promote scientific ethics and prevent plagiarism. The present paper discusses, among others, the ENAI (European Network for Academic Integrity), IPPHEAE (Improving the Prevention of Plagiarism in Higher Education Across Europe), SEPPHAI (Supporting the Enhancement of Plagiarism Prevention in Higher Education Institutions) and AIRS (Academic Integrity Research Study) projects, their results and recommendations. Together, these projects have contributed to the development of anti-plagiarism policies in European higher education institutions and to the strengthening of academic integrity.

The digital age and the development of artificial intelligence have brought new challenges in the management of plagiarism. While these tools create new opportunities for learning and research, they also raise ethical and practical problems that require a new type of regulation and a change of approach. The huge amount of data available on the Internet and the appearance of large language models (LLMs) in the public domain have made it even more difficult to distinguish between original and copied content. This underlines the responsibility of higher education institutions to develop effective anti-plagiarism strategies in the form of policies. To achieve these objectives, it is essential to raise students' awareness of the principles of academic integrity.[4] Education in ethical behavior, in particular the compulsory teaching of research methodology, would provide significant support in preventing plagiarism. It would enable students to understand the fundamental importance of source criticism, citation and academic responsibility.

The emergence and use of Artificial Intelligence (hereinafter: AI) systems raises quite a few questions in respect of copyright law.[5] There is still no consensus on whether the use of AI systems qualifies as plagiarism or not.[6]

---

4 Eszter Benke & Andrea Szőke, 'Akadémiai kultúra és etikai kódexek: vizsgálat a gazdaságtudományi felsőoktatásban', *Iskolakultúra,* Vol. 34, Issue 9, 2024, pp. 76–95.

5 Anikó Grad-Gyenge & Edit Tomasovszky, 'Az AI és a szerzői jogi kihívás', *in Mesterséges Intelligencia – felelősségteljes fejlesztések,* Wolters Kluwer, forthcoming, at https://real.mtak.hu/210037/1/AzAI%20és%20a%20szerzői%20jogi%20kihívás%20%20.pdf.

6 *See* Anett Pogácsás, 'A plágium új jelentésrétege? A "társszerzőség" útjai és megítélése a mesterséges intelligencia vonatkozásában', *Iparjogvédelmi és Szerzői Jogi Szemle,* Vol. 19, Issue 5, 2024, pp. 139–155.

Overall, the problem of plagiarism goes beyond individual offences, its impact extends to the whole higher education system, including its ethical, economic, psychological and social dimensions.[7] Higher education institutions must develop comprehensive strategies that support the strengthening of a culture of academic integrity at the faculty, student and institutional levels, based on common principles and objectives. It is therefore important to understand that plagiarism is not only a problem at the level of the perpetrator, but it also has a serious impact on the reputation of higher education institutions and the credibility of academic work.

2. *"He Steals Work and Writes his Name on it":*[8] *The Concept, Forms and Dilemmas of Plagiarism*

Authorship, the moral norms associated with authorship, already appeared in antiquity, with creators demanding to have their names recognized in the context of their own work.[9]

The term plagiarism comes from the latin *plagiarius* (kidnapper, soul-snatcher), which originally meant a child snatcher.[10] The abducted children were held as slaves, a metaphor for the theft of intellectual property. In antiquity, book copiers were slaves, many of whom were brought to Rome from Greece. The price of copy slaves, especially if they could read and write in Greek, was considerable. In the early days of Rome, most of the professional educators were slaves of Greek origin.[11]

In antiquity, books were usually copied by someone dictating the text aloud, which the slaves would write down at the same time. Terentius, in his Eunuchus, quotes Luscius Lanuvinus as saying that 'it was a thief, not a poet, who told the tale', referring to the literary passages copied from others. A similar approach can be observed in Martialis, who compares his own poem to a child that has fallen into the hands of a plagiarist. By the eight-

7 Gábor Király *et al.*, 'Csalással az élre? A hallgatói csalás vizsgálata az üzleti felsőoktatásban', *Vezetéstudomány – Budapest Management Review*, Vol. 49, Issue 3, 2018, p. 36.

8 Mihály Vörösmarty, '*A plagiarius*', Pest, 1826.

9 Aurél Benárd & István Tímár (ed.), '*A szerzői jog kézikönyve*', Közgazdasági és Jogi Könyvkiadó, Budapest, 1973, p. 11.

10 Lexiq.com, 'Plágium', at https://lexiq.hu/plagium.

11 Zoltán Gloviczki & László Zsinka, '*Nevelés és iskola az antik és középkori Európában*', PPKE BTK, Piliscsaba, 2014, pp. 72–73.

eenth century, literary plagiarism[12] had also been defined as a legal concept.[13]

The concept of plagiarism is widely known, but its exact meaning is not always clear. As the analysis below shows, the definition of the term is complex. In scientific discourse, it is not an uncommon phenomenon that the definition of certain concepts are challenging and there is often a lack of consensus on their interpretation. The essence of plagiarism can be summarized briefly as the use of another people's intellectual property – be it written text, pictures, diagrams, tables, oral communications, videos, data or music – as one's own, either without permission or proper attribution.

The definition of plagiarism varies in emphasis from source to source, reflecting the historical and linguistic evolution of the concept. The ancient definition originally understood the term plagiarism as kidnapping, which meant the unlawful taking of a free man or slave. By contrast, modern definitions use the term exclusively in relation to intellectual works. The Dictionary of the Hungarian Language, the Dictionary of Legal Terms and the Dictionary of Foreign Words and Expressions all emphasize the aspect of copyright infringement, *i.e.,* the communication of another's work as one's own without proper attribution. The etymological analysis shows that the concept's semantic shift from Latin to French has evolved through the French language. The Code of Ethics of the Hungarian Academy of Sciences approaches the issue in a broader scientific context, as it considers not only the appropriation of texts but also the appropriation of ideas and scientific results as plagiarism. According to the definition of the Oxford English Dictionary, the definition of plagiarism includes the idea as a protected element. The idea is not protected under domestic copyright law.[14] Overall, the different definitions have in common the lack of originality and unauthorized

---

12 The first case of plagiarism in Hungarian literature was the so-called *Íliász-pör.* In this case, the rules for referring to another author are laid down for the first time.

13 In 1740, the Wittenberg professor Augusin von Leyser, developing the Roman legal concept, used the term *plagium litterarium* ('literary plagiarism') to give the author criminal protection. Contrary to the broader moral interpretation, only the knowing and intentional appropriation, in whole or in part, in form or in substance, of works protected by copyright under one's own name constitutes plagiarism in law. It is not plagiarism to make an individual, original adaptation of an idea taken from another work. Benárd & Tímár 1973, p. 12.

14 Act LXXVI of 1999 on Copyright, Section 1(6) Ideas, principles, theories, procedures, operating methods, and mathematical operations are not entitled to receive copyright protection.

misappropriation, but each definition places different emphasis on the ethical, legal and linguistic aspects of the concept.

Plagiarism is a very complex concept, and it is important to separate it from inspiration, idea, coincidental similarity and common knowledge.[15] One form of plagiarism is *ghostwriting,* where a student at a higher education institution submits a piece of writing by another person as his or her own, often in exchange for payment. These works are formally original and properly referenced, yet they constitute a serious breach of academic integrity through misrepresentation of authorship. Plagiarism detection software, such as Turnitin, is usually ineffective, as it primarily looks for text concordance rather than verifying authorship.[16] Online ghostwriting services build professionally on students' insecurities and legitimize unethical use in their advertising.[17] Educators can play a major role in identifying the problem, and, if they are lucky enough to know their students' thinking and writing skills, they may be able to spot this type of abuse. But effective prevention requires a holistic approach: rethinking study tasks, ethical sensitization and targeted teacher support.[18]

Artificial intelligence technologies pose further challenges in the detection and prevention of plagiarism. According to a recent survey,[19] nearly a third of students have already used ChatGPT for their academic assignments, which could lead to new forms of plagiarism. While AI tools can be useful in supporting writing, they also increase uncertainty around academic purity. Plagiarism detection[20] AI tools such as Turnitin AI, DetectGPT and Ghostbuster are already capable of identifying AI-generated content, but their effectiveness is limited. Techniques such as recursive paraphrasing or authorship obfuscation can easily circumvent verification sys-

---

15 Gréta Varga & Edit Sápi, 'Idegen tollakkal ékeskedve – plágium "mintázatok" sajátosságai egyes műtípusoknál', *Miskolci Jogtudó,* 2023/1, p. 95.

16 Shawren Singh & Dan Remenyi, 'Plagiarism and ghostwriting: The rise in academic misconduct', *South African Journal of Science,* Vol. 112, Issue 5–6, 2016, pp. 36–42.

17 Lisa Lines, 'Ghostwriters guaranteeing grades? The quality of online ghostwriting services available to tertiary students in Australia', *Teaching in Higher Education,* Vol. 21, Issue 8, 2016, pp. 889–914.

18 Avodele Morocco-Clarke *et al.,* 'The implications and effects of ChatGPT on academic scholarship and authorship: a death knell for original academic publications?', *Information & Communications Technology Law,* Vol. 33, Issue 1, 2024, pp. 21–41.

19 Héctor Galindo-Domínguez *et al.,* 'Relationship between the use of ChatGPT for academic purposes and plagiarism: the influence of student-related variables on cheating behavior', *Interactive Learning Environments,* 2025, pp. 1–15.

20 Singh & Remenyi 2016.

tems.[21] However, AI can also play a positive role in the teaching of academic writing. Recent developments, such as the Academic Writing System,[22] provide a personalized learning experience and have the potential to shape students' anti-plagiarism awareness, attitudes and behavior.

Overall, technological control alone is not enough to deal with ghostwriting and AI-induced forms of plagiarism. Only education in ethics, awareness-raising among teachers, thoughtfulness in assignments and the development of students' literacy skills can provide a real solution.

3. *Where Is the Border?*

The plagiarist was branded a thief by the Romans, and his act a theft. In Martialis' epigrams[23] the plagiarist appears several times:

52.
Quíntíanus.

I commend my book to you, Quintianus; -
- Maybe I can only claim it as my own, though
Your poet recites it as his own -; [...]
And if you claim to be an author, say,
That it is I, I have set you free,
Shout this in evidence four or five times,
And the plagiarist is ashamed.

53.
The plagiarist.

Fidentinus, pray, there is a page in my poem,
Which is yours, but is also marked with the master's mark,
And your poems are obviously branded as theft. [...]
His varied voice, so hurt by the sarcasm.
My book does not need an accuser, a judge;
Your card itself says in your ear, "You thief!"

21 Yin Zhang *et al.*, 'Enhancing anti-plagiarism literacy practices among undergraduates with AI', *Interactive Learning Environments,* 2025, pp. 1–15.

22 Noriko Kano, 'The Efficiency of the Academic Writing System: Can Prewriting Discussion be Eliminated?' *LET Kanto Journal,* Vol. 5, 2021, pp. 39–57.

23 János Csengery, '*Marcus Valerius Martialis epigrammáinak tizennégy könyve a Látványosságok Könyvével*', MTA, Budapest, 1942, pp. 70 and 75.

The earliest form of copyright infringement is plagiarism, the first meaning of which – as discussed above – is kidnapping, child abduction, soul theft. It does not require a deep and precise semantic analysis, nor a serious psychological background to understand the meaning of these terms and to feel their impact and energy. A negative sentiment is attached to them, since we associate the activity with appropriation. Plagiarists take something that is not theirs; a kidnapper deceives others as if the child he has kidnapped was his own. A soul-scoundrel is a person who, for his own benefit or that of the group he represents, misleads others on matters of ideology, politics or morality, and seeks to influence them to serve a false cause in good faith.[24] Plagiarism has been included in the category of forgery.[25] It existed as a moral norm, the violation of which was punishable by public ostracism and humiliation.

Even in the 1700s, plagiarism was considered one of the greatest sins of scientists, but it was difficult to prove. At that time, plagiarism was understood as a scientific technique of paraphrasing, *i.e.,* taking small passages from a work and inserting them into their own text. It was during this period that the practice of Abstraction (making extracts) became widespread, which was considered to be less for the head than for the hand, and therefore it is difficult to distinguish from plagiarism. This period saw the emergence of historiography as an innovation of the time. It was not simply understood as being without reference, but rather as an intellectual dependence on colleagues in the discipline.[26]

The diagram below clearly shows that plagiarism is at the border between social and legal regulation. As emphasized above, plagiarism is not a legal doctrine and the term is not found in any copyright law. We can speak of plagiarism in cases where the unauthorized use of a work, coupled with a false attribution of authorship, infringes the rights of the original author. Although the two concepts may seem identical to the layman, copyright infringement is a much narrower concept and therefore acts of plagiarism can only constitute copyright infringement in very specific cases.

---

24 Quoting the Hungarian language dictionary.

25 Tamás Nótári, '*A magyar szerzői jog fejlődése*', Lectum, Szeged, 2010, p. 18.

26 Daniel Fulda, 'Plagiieren als wissenschaftliche Innovation? Kritik und Akzeptanz eines vor drei Jahrhunderten skandalisierten Plagiats im Zeitalter der Exzerpierkunst', *Berichte zur Wissenschaftsgeschichte,* Vol. 43, 2020, pp. 218–238.

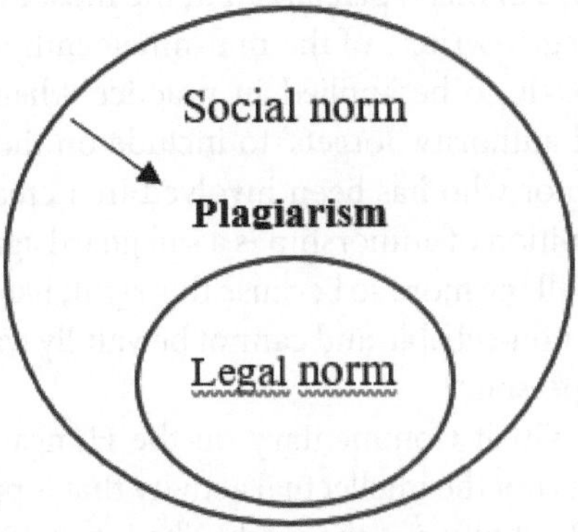

Figure 1. The place of plagiarism in the system of norms

Plagiarism is when someone uses a work created by another author,[27] or parts of it, without attribution to the author, or without the author's permission, as if it were their own. In other words, he presents himself as the author, even though he has taken the ideas contained in the words or sentences from someone else. The right of attribution is a moral right which prohibits a work from being published under another person's name or without the author's permission. Related but not identical[28] to this is the concept of plagiarism, which is the slavish copying of another person's intellectual work[29] and publishing it under their own name or taking extracts or parts of another's work without attribution to the author.[30]

The right to use the name also provides protection in the less common case where the name of a person other than the author appears on the work.

27 Under current domestic and international legislation, we mean the human being, *i.e.*, artificial intelligence systems are not considered authors. *See Thaler v Perlmutter*, No. 22-CV-3 84–1564-BAH, at https://caselaw.findlaw.com/court/us-dis-crt-dis-col/114916944.html.

28 It is important to emphasize that plagiarism is not the same as the right to attribution, as known from copyright law, nor is it the same as quotation.

29 Plagiarism is also called slavish copying under copyright law. Varga & Sápi 2023, p. 95. The present paper will later discuss the place of plagiarism in the legal-ethical normative system, where I take the position that plagiarism is not a legal category, but an ethical, moral one. In the context of higher education, plagiarism is identified as an ethical concept. I do not agree with the authors' lawyers' understanding of slavish copying as plagiarism. In my view, slavish copying is only one type of plagiarism, not a synonym. The act of slavish copying implies intentionality, but is not supported by several international studies (*see e.g.* John Walker, 'Student Plagiarism in Universities: What are we Doing About it?', *Higher Education Research & Development*, Vol. 17, Issue 1, 1998, pp. 89–106) of plagiarism as a careless form of representation.

30 Dénes Legeza (ed.), '*Szerzői jog mindenkinek*', SZTNH, Budapest, 2017, p. 95.

One conceivable form of this is plagiarism in the most extreme sense, or the institution of the 'negro' writers of the mid-nineteenth century. Nowadays, this rule is more likely to be applied in practice when a co-author with greater professional authority 'forgets' to include on the finished work the name of a collaborator who has been involved in a creative way. The personal right to recognition of authorship is a safeguard against such infringements of copyright, all the more so because this right, like all personal rights, is non-transferable, non-sellable and cannot be validly waived by the author in favor of another person.[31]

According to the Great Commentary on the Hungarian Copyright Act LXXVI of 1999,[32] it is not the intellectual activity that is protected by the law, but the *result* of that activity, *i.e.,* the work. The interpretation then clarifies that it is not in fact the work itself that is protected, but rather the rights of the rightsholder in relation to the work, *i.e.* the copyright relationship, which is the subject of copyright law. The indirect object of this legal relationship – an indispensable element – is the copyright work. This is where plagiarism itself really comes into its own, since the work must belong to the author, *i.e.,* the work has a personal link to the author, it is subjectively original, and has not been taken from someone else. It infringes the recognition of authorship if someone presents another person's work as their own. Also important in the context of plagiarism is the individual character of the intellectual activity, which is an original, individual, particular expression of the author that must be reflected in the work. The law emphasizes that intellectual activity can only be related to man, and that a work of authorship can only be a work of human authorship. The individual, original character of the content must be expressed in thought, put into the text, in a precise and clearly perceptible manner. As a minimum, the work must not be a slavish copy of another work. And this brings us to the question of whether plagiarism is a legal or an ethical concept.

An interesting and thought-provoking cross-cultural approach to plagiarism[33] is that the form of reference is unfamiliar and incomprehensible to academics of the Far East, but is extremely important in Western culture and academia. Students in the Far East have been socialized to believe that citing sources can be downright offensive, because it implies that one is not famil-

---

31 Benárd & Tímár 1973, p. 102.

32 Péter Gyertyánfy & Dénes Legeza (eds.), '*Nagykommentár a szerzői jogról szóló 1999. évi LXXVI. törvényhez*', Wolters Kluwer, Budapest, 2021, 1(6).

33 Tamás Bíró, *Plágium a zsidó hagyományban és a felsőoktatásban,* at https://birot.web.elte.hu/files/plagium-BT.pdf.

iar with the sources in question. If they do quote, it is necessary to do so literally, as it is insulting to the quoted author not to quote his words or ideas accurately, but to paraphrase them, which in turn has the effect of correcting the author's words. By contrast, plagiarism is perhaps the greatest scholarly crime in Western academic life. In this community, we rarely find exact, verbatim quotations, and in fact, in academia, exact quotations longer than a few lines are expressly avoided. We prefer to paraphrase the ideas of the author cited in our own words. While in the East, communal knowledge, collectivism is in the foreground, in the West, individual traits and individualism are considered as virtues.

4. The EU Framework on Plagiarism

Almost all studies on plagiarism describe it almost unanimously as the most serious unethical behavior in education. In order to prevent plagiarism and, where appropriate, to reduce its incidence, it is essential to identify and understand the causes of plagiarism. The following summarizes some projects in which the exploration of the possible causes of plagiarism played a significant role.

Higher education institutions have a responsibility to ensure the quality of degrees and academic integrity. Plagiarism undermines this.

Table I. Summary of the European projects about the plagiarism

	ETINED	IPPHEAE	ENAI	SEPPHAI	AIRS
Full name	European Network of Information Exchange on Ethics and Integrity in Education	Impact of Policies for Plagiarism in Higher Education Across Europe	European Network for Academic Integrity	Supporting the Enhancement of Plagiarism Prevention in Higher Education Institutions	Academic Integrity Research Study
Duration	From 2015 to this day	2010–2013	From 2017 to this day	2022–2024	From 2020 to this day
Funding	Council of Europe	European Commis-	European	Erasmus+	University and

	ETINED	IPPHEAE	ENAI	SEPPHAI	AIRS
		sion (Erasmus, Lifelong Learning Programme)	Commission, voluntary membership		research funds
Geographical scope	50 countries (States Parties to the European Cultural Convention)	EU-27 Member States	Global (mainly Europe)	EU Member State	International
Main objective	Promoting academic integrity and fighting corruption in education	Examining the effectiveness of anti-plagiarism policies and making recommendations	Developing academic integrity and building community	Support for preventive measures against plagiarism	Researching and raising awareness of academic integrity
Methodology	Identification and dissemination of good practices, seminars, development of guidelines	Online questionnaires, interviews, case studies	Research, training, recommendations	Development of educational materials and tools	Empirical research, surveys
Main activities	Organizing seminars (*e.g.* on plagiarism), sharing best practices, developing guidelines	Compare plagiarism policies, collect data from students, teachers and managers, make recommendations	International cooperation, conferences, research	Support for teachers and students, awareness-raising campaigns	Examining academic integrity in different countries
Results achieved	Increasing the capacity of higher education institutions to detect plagiarism, promot-	Recommendations to tackle plagiarism, set international	Developing guidelines for academic integrity,	Development of teaching aids, training materials	Publishing data and research on aca-

	ETINED	IPPHEAE	ENAI	SEPPHAI	AIRS
	ing academic integrity	benchmarks, raise awareness of academic integrity	establishing an international network		demic integrity
Key findings	Academic integrity contributes to improving democracy and the quality of education	Plagiarism management varies across the EU, with institutions not always applying the directives consistently	Institutional support is key to ensuring academic integrity	The effectiveness of measures to prevent plagiarism can be increased	Challenges to academic integrity vary globally, influenced by cultural factors
Recommendations	Raising awareness of plagiarism and academic integrity, establishing common standards and procedures	Developing common policies, international cooperation, developing tools to prevent plagiarism	Enhancing institutional cooperation, supporting education	Expanding education programmes, using prevention tools	Continuation of detailed research, global comparative analyses
Applicability of results	Across Europe, to higher education institutions and government bodies	Within the EU at institutional and national level	For the international academic community	Developing educational institutions and policies	International research and education policy

As far as secondary schools are concerned, the Genius (plaGiarism or crEativity: teachiNg Innovation versUs Stealing) project[34] was a program designed mainly for these schools, under the EU's Lifelong Learning Pro-

34 A detailed description of the project can be found here: https://www.fenice-eu.org/genius-en.htm. The project is analyzed in detail here: https://www.sciencedirect.com/science/article/pii/S 1877042814006223.

gramme, in which, alongside the development of digital skills, the issue of plagiarism also played a central role. The project involved seven European countries: Greece, Italy, Portugal, Romania, Spain, Turkey, United Kingdom. Each participating country's higher education institution also supported the above initiative, which was important because it provided participants with reliable information and training on the issue of plagiarism. This could be a very good practice to be followed in the future, so that high school students are already aware of plagiarism, its prevention and the main copyright and ethical principles in general.

5. The Digital Transformation of Plagiarism

The launch of ChatGPT in November 2022 almost immediately triggered a technological panic, primarily due to concerns about the impact of artificial intelligence (AI) on education and research. In the eras of information revolutions, the emergence of new technology has generally caused mass panic; the emergence of the printing press, computers, and the internet followed a similar trajectory.[35] In 2021, Sarah Elaine Eaton argued that technology is leading us into a 'post-plagiarism' era – one in which the co-authorship of humans and technology is fully accepted, and the final product is seen as a hybrid creation of both. In this post-plagiarism era, people use AI applications on a daily basis to enhance and refine creative outputs. Soon, it may become impossible to distinguish where human writing ends and machine-generated text begins, as both forms will intertwine and become indistinguishable. The key issue is that while individuals may delegate full or partial control to AI applications, allowing technology to generate content on their behalf, humans remain ultimately responsible for the output. It is crucial to prepare university students for this reality, which is not a distant future but the present.

Where does the boundary lie between AI-generated content and plagiarism? Is there even a clear boundary, or is AI-generated text just another form of plagiarism? The latest large language models (LLMs) are capable of human-level performance in text generation and modification. However, these models can produce inaccurate information, and users may not always

35 Sarah Elaine Eaton, 'Artificial intelligence and academic integrity, post-plagiarism', *University Word News*, 2023, at: https://www.universityworldnews.com/post.php?story=20230228133041549.

be aware of these limitations. AI-generated texts often either lack proper citations to their sources or produce fabricated references, *i.e.,* the system is 'hallucinating'.

Under the harmonized copyright framework of the European Union, the fundamental requirement for copyright protection is originality. The EU copyright[36] directives succinctly define this principle as 'the author's own intellectual creation', which must express the author's individual creativity and personality. The CJEU has elaborated on the criteria for originality in multiple rulings (*Infopaq,*[37] *Painer,*[38] and *Murphy*[39] cases), stating that a work qualifies for copyright protection if: *(i)* the author is able to express their creative abilities through free and individual choices *(Painer); (ii)* the work reflects the author's personal involvement *(Painer); (iii)* the creative process allows room for the type of artistic freedom protected under copyright law *(Murphy).*

Based on these rulings, most European countries grant copyright protection to works that result from human involvement and where the author has engaged in a substantive creative process. Consequently, works in which AI merely assists human creativity are generally eligible for copyright protection, whereas those entirely generated by AI without human input are typically not. Future legislative developments and court rulings will play a crucial role in determining how AI's expanding role can be accommodated within the copyright framework.[40]

The European Artificial Intelligence Regulation (hereinafter: AI Act), adopted on 21 May 2024, aims to address the risks posed by AI while fostering innovation. The Act entered into force in August 2024 and will be fully applicable by summer 2026. However, certain prohibitions on specific AI applications came into effect in February 2025. The integration of AI into higher education presents numerous opportunities and challenges, particularly in the realm of academic integrity. As AI technologies become more prevalent in the educational environment, it is essential that institutions implement strategies that preserve academic values while taking advantage of

36 P. Bernt Hugenholtz & João Pedro Quintais, 'Copyright and Artificial Creation: Does EU Copyright Law Protect AI-Assisted Output?', *IIC – International Review of Intellectual Property and Competition Law,* Vol. 52, 2021, pp. 1190–1216.

37 Judgment of 16 July 2009, *Case C-5/08, Infopaq,* ECLI:EU:C:2009:465.

38 Judgment of 1 December 2011, *Case C-145/10, Painer,* ECLI:EU:C:2011:798.

39 Judgment of 4 October 2011, *Joined cases C-403/08 and C-429/08, Football Association Premier League and Others,* ECLI:EU:C:2011:631.

40 Eleonora Rosati, *Originality in EU Copyright. Full Harmonization through Case Law,* Edward Elgar, Cheltenham, 2013.

AI's potential. Below, I outline key issues and propose solutions for navigating AI's dual role in academia.[41]

When generating content with AI tools, users must first provide instructions, typically through a prompt.[42] The AI tool interprets this prompt and generates text based on the vast dataset it has been trained on. The AI Act emphasizes transparency regarding the datasets used for training language models. One of the most fundamental issues regarding AI tools is being aware of the sources from which these models derive their content. The determination of whether we are dealing with plagiarism when using AI can only be made based on the answer to the previous question. OpenAI, for example, claims that its various ChatGPT models have been trained on vast amounts of internet-derived data.

The indication of AI application or use in the texts of dissertations prepared by students is the so-called 'accuracy dilemma'. A significant number of domestic higher education institutions use Turnitin software for plagiarism detection. Text-matching analysis plays a crucial role in verifying the authenticity of academic work. However, it is an important question how reliable is it? Generative AI models evolve rapidly, posing challenges for text comparison methods.

Large language models, such as ChatGPT or LaMDA, exhibit significant variations in content quality. Educational institutions must definitely take these facts into account. AI systems often struggle with contextual and semantic understanding, which affects the quality and reliability of their outputs. Opinions vary on whether using AI constitutes academic misconduct or whether improper use is the primary concern – or perhaps the situation may be more nuanced that that. The automatic generation of content as a substitute for independent academic work is perhaps the clearest example of a threat to academic integrity. However, AI can also support academic integrity through advanced plagiarism detection tools, personalized learning experiences, and simulations that promote awareness. Teaching students the ethical use of AI and proper attribution practices is essential.

Researchers identify three main factors driving the increase in plagiarism: the spread of digital technology, the attitudes of newer generations, and cultural backgrounds. Studies indicate that plagiarism is often driven by the desire for higher grades, academic pressure, or differing perceptions of what

41 Thomas Conway, 'AI and Academic Integrity in Higher Education: A Caution on Punitive Approaches', *in* Tracey Bretag (ed.), *Handbook of Academic Integrity,* Springer, 2016.

42 Nuno Sousa e Silva, 'Prompts as code?' *Kluwer Copyright Blog,* 5 November 2024.

constitutes academic dishonesty. Some students do not even realize they are committing plagiarism or do not consider it a serious issue. Institutions that clearly define academic dishonesty and plagiarism, and enforce strict policies, tend to report lower rates of plagiarism. Research by McCabe et al. suggests that ongoing discussions on academic integrity can help reduce plagiarism.[43]

The New York Times[44] has claimed that some of ChatGPT's responses contain near-verbatim excerpts from its articles. If these allegations are accurate, tools like ChatGPT may be plagiarizing the authors of the training dataset by reproducing their words and sentences without proper citation.

6. Is This the End?

A thorough analysis of the concept of plagiarism, along with efforts to uphold academic integrity, demonstrates that plagiarism is primarily an ethical rather than a legal issue, as it endangers the credibility and reputation of the academic community. Legal and ethical approaches to plagiarism, particularly the measures implemented within the framework of EU projects, provide a crucial foundation for preserving academic integrity. European-level guidelines and initiatives, such as researcher ethics codes and anti-plagiarism programs, represent significant progress in reducing and preventing plagiarism. Higher education institutions must combat plagiarism through both legal and ethical means to ensure the authenticity of theses and the integrity of academic writing and research. The projects discussed in this paper play a fundamental role in shaping students' ethical behavior. On the long run, these efforts can help ensure that students fully comprehend the importance of academic integrity and recognize the legal and ethical consequences of plagiarism.

Considering the numerous challenges associated with the interpretation of plagiarism, it is essential to develop a comprehensive action plan that formulates recommendations for addressing plagiarism effectively in the future. These recommendations should, on the one hand, promote a more

43 Katalin Doró, 'Students' perceptions of cheating and plagiarism: An exploratory study among Hungarian EFL undergraduates', *in* Beatrix Fregan (ed.), *Success and challenges in foreign language teaching,* Nemzeti Közszolgálati Egyetem, Budapest, 2014, pp. 43–47.

44 Bobby Allyn, 'The New York Times takes OpenAI to Court', *npr-org.com,* 14 January 2025, the lawsuit is available at https://nytco-assets.nytimes.com/2023/12/NYT_Complaint_Dec2023.pdf.

unified approach and, on the other hand, emphasize the necessity of recognizing the different forms of plagiarism interpretation and imposing corresponding sanctions accordingly. To achieve a more standardized approach, the European Code of Conduct for Research Integrity[45] could serve as a model for all higher education institutions within the EU. Furthermore, it is important to strengthen cross-border cooperation, which is key to the exchange of legal enforcement experiences related to plagiarism. The coordinated protection against plagiarism (primarily software that examines text similarity) fills a crucial gap. It is of paramount importance to distinguish between intentional and unintentional plagiarism, with appropriate differentiation in the application of sanctions. Additionally, the rules and penalties concerning plagiarism must be defined with precision and detail, particularly in relation to students. Moreover, higher education institutions should make research methodology training mandatory, focusing on the practical development of writing skills and creative thinking to provide a solid foundation for academic integrity.

Ultimately, the effective fight against plagiarism will be successful only if the appropriate combination of ethical standards, legal regulations, and education is achieved. The future academic community can function effectively and credibly only if ethical research conduct and anti-plagiarism practices are prioritized in both education and research.

45 *See* at https://allea.org/code-of-conduct/.

Part II
– Developments in international law

Revisiting the Notion of '*Combat Action*' in the Context of the War Crime of Attack against Protected Historical Monuments and Buildings

*Péter Kovács**

Abstract

A temple is the 'house of God 'and monuments are a very important part of the cultural, historical and national identity of the local population. UNESCO established the World Heritage List inventorying natural and man-made sites that are of paramount importance for mankind. The so called The Hague law and Geneva law related to the conduct of hostilities or to the protection of victims of armed conflicts contain special provision protecting these items from attack except when they are already being used for military purposes and contribute considerably to the military efforts of belligerents. The Rome Statute also contains special rules criminalizing the attack against such objects. However, the International Criminal Court (ICC) was confronted with challenges in those cases where the charge was brought for a crime that represented or contained inter alia the attack against this type of protected object. The paper seeks to shed light on the legal background of the doctrinal and jurisprudential controversy and endeavors to suggest an adequate solution.

Keywords: combat action, ICC, war crime, protected historical monuments, Rome Statute

1. *William A. Schabas about the interpretation of 'attack' in the Al Mahdi judgment*

Shortly after the delivery of the *Al Mahdi* judgment, Professor William A. Schabas, one of the best specialists of the legal system of the International Criminal Court established by the Rome Statute, published an article with

---

* Péter Kovács: professor of law, Pázmány Péter Catholic University, Budapest; judge of the International Criminal Court (2015–2024), profpeterkovacs@hotmail.com. This contribution was written in my personal capacity. The thoughts expressed therein cannot be attributed to the ICC.

a shocking title: 'Al Mahdi Has Been Convicted of a Crime He Did Not Commit'.[1]

Schabas's article pointed out that the charge formulated under Article 8(2)(e)(iv) *i.e.,* "intentionally directing attacks against [...] historic monuments"[2] and admitted under guilty plea by Al Mahdi, whose liability was established by the trial chamber does not seem to correspond to the specific facts of the destruction of the mausoleums and other historic monuments of Timbuktu upon the order of the leaders of fundamentalist forces called *AlQueda du Magreb Islamique* (hereinafter: AQMI) and Ansar Dine when they took over the city and ruled it cruelly in 2012/2013. It is without any doubt that Al Mahdi – as appointed leader of the Hesbah, the 'moral police', one of three police forces established by the ruling 'islamic council' – executed the order through people under his authority. However, Schabas questioned the qualification of the destruction as an 'attack' *stricto sensu* because the destruction did not occur during the military takeover and the incursion of the AQMI and Ansar Dine into the city left without defense by the Malian army units. Instead, the attack took place a couple of weeks later, when Timbuktu lived under the cruel fundamentalist regime without being the area of an actual military operation.

Schabas cited the explanation given in the *Elements of crimes* and pointed out that whenever 'attack' as a war crime is mentioned in the Rome Statute or in the *Elements of crimes,* it should have the same content according to a well known principle of international law.[3] Following a deep analysis of the *travaux préparatoires* of the Rome Statute,[4] he concluded that upon the proposal of the US delegation, the drafters had agreed[5] to follow the formulation contained in the 4th Convention[6] of The Hague peace conference (1907) and its annex –commonly referred to as The Hague Regulation[7] –

1 William Schabas, 'Al Mahdi Has Been Convicted of a Crime He Did Not Commit', *Case Western Reserve Journal of International Law,* Vol. 49, Issue 1, 2017, pp. 75–102.

2 Full text of Article 8 (2)(e)(iv): "Intentionally directing attacks against buildings dedicated to religion, education, art, science or charitable purposes, historic monuments, hospitals and places where the sick and wounded are collected, provided they are not military objectives."

3 Schabas 2017, pp. 78–79.

4 Id. pp. 84–88.

5 Id. pp. 86 and 88.

6 Convention (IV) respecting the Laws and Customs of War on Land and its annex: Regulations concerning the Laws and Customs of War on Land, at https://ihl-databases.icrc.org/assets/treaties/195-IHL-19-EN.pdf

7 Annex to the Convention. Regulations respecting the laws and customs of war on land.

and in particular that of Article 27[8] of the annex, disregarding however the formulation of Article 56[9] of the same annex. Although none of these articles contain the word 'attack', Article 27 indubitably refers to active military operations while Article 56 leaves the timing of destruction open. The agreed formula was inserted into the subsequent reports of the negotiations without real changes *in merito*.[10]

Schabas also examined the analysis of the notion of attack in the 1st additional protocol (1977) to the 1949 Geneva Conventions, and pointed out that according to the commentary to the protocol an attack means 'combat action'.[11]

In the light of the above considerations, Schabas concludes that as the destruction did not occur in 'combat action', but at a moment that cannot be considered as the time of active hostilities according to the Geneva law terms, one important element is missing from the criteria required by the *Elements of crimes*.

He also considered whether the 1954 The Hague Convention for the protection of cultural property in the event of armed conflict could be invoked to better fulfill the necessary criteria of Article 8(2)(e)(iv).[12] Schabas clearly condemns the destruction and enumerates several other crimes that could have been chosen by the prosecutor in the Rome Statute and in which the word 'attack' is not present, *e.g.*, Article 8(2)(e)(xii) on destroying the property of the adversary;[13] it is true, however, that in this case, other problems could emerge regarding the compatibility of the article with the given facts.[14]

8 Article 27: "In sieges and bombardments all necessary steps must be taken to spare, as far as possible, buildings dedicated to religion, art, science, or charitable purposes, historic monuments, hospitals, and places where the sick and wounded are collected, provided they are not being used at the time for military purposes."

9 Article 56: "The property of municipalities, that of institutions dedicated to religion, charity and education, the arts and sciences, even when State property, shall be treated as private property. All seizure of, destruction or wilful damage done to institutions of this character, historic monuments, works of art and science, is forbidden, and should be made the subject of legal proceedings."

10 Schabas 2017, p. 87.

11 Id. pp. 79–80.

12 Id. pp. 91–92.

13 Full text in the Rome Statute: "Destroying or seizing the property of an adversary unless such destruction or seizure be imperatively demanded by the necessities of the conflict;"

14 Schabas 2017, pp. 90–91.

2. *The Appeals Chamber and Article 8(2)(e)(iv) in Ntaganda*

Given the guilty plea, the Appeals chamber of the ICC did not need to pronounce on the issue of the interpretation of 'attack' in the context of the destruction of historical monuments in *Al Mahdi.* The issue resurfaced, however, in *Prosecutor v Bosco Ntaganda,* where both parties appealed different parts of the judgment of condemnation. The Office of the Prosecutor (hereinafter: OTP) was not satisfied that Ntaganda's criminal responsibility had not been established concerning the destruction of the church of Sayo in the Ituri region of the DRC, as the trial judgment did not consider this event as having occurred during an attack.[15] The Appeals Chamber approved the decision of the trial judgment by majority and several separate or partly dissenting opinions tried to clarify the meaning of the word 'attack' in the context of Article 8(2)(e)(iv).

The common separate opinion[16] written by judge Morrison and judge Hofmański was based on the in-depth analysis of the *travaux préparatoires* and the judges' conclusion was more or less the same as that of Schabas: in the context of war crimes, the word 'attack' should always have the same meaning[17] and destruction falling under Article 8(2)(e)(iv) presupposes 'combat action.'[18] Like Schabas, the judges also examined the impact of the

15 "1136. As set out above, the term 'attack' is to be understood as an 'act of violence against the adversary, whether in offence or defence'. As with the war crime of attacking civilians, the crime of attacking protected objects belongs to the category of offences committed during the actual conduct of hostilities. Article 8(2)(e)(iv) only requires the perpetrator to have launched an attack against a protected object and it need not be established that the attack caused any damage or destruction to the object in question." "1142. In addition, given that the attack on the church in Sayo took place sometime after the assault, and therefore not during the actual conduct of hostilities, the Chamber finds that the first element of Article 8(2)(e)(iv) of the Statute is not met. This incident is therefore also not further considered." ICC-01/04-02/06-2359 08-07-2019, pp. 502 and 504.

16 Separate opinion of Judge Howard Morrison and Judge Piotr Hofmański on the Prosecutor's appeal , ICC-01/04-02/06-2666-Anx1 30-03-2021, (hereinafter: Morrison-Hofmański).

17 "8. We are of the view that, unless the Statute contains an indication to the contrary, such as in the above-mentioned Article 7, which includes a specific definition of the term in the context of crimes against humanity, a term appearing therein may be expected to have the same meaning each time it is used, in particular if it appears in the same provision. In all the above-quoted instances of the use of the term 'attacks' in Article 8, it should thus be presumed to have the same meaning, in particular since all the instances in which the term appears in that provision concern the definition of the various war crimes over which the Court has jurisdiction." Morrison-Hofmański, pp. 3-4.

18 "43. We find that, viewed in the light of the established framework of international law of armed conflict and the drafting history of the Statute, Article 8(2)(e)(iv) of the Statute

1954 The Hague Convention for the protection of cultural property in the event of an armed conflict and whether it could be invoked to support the necessary criteria of Article 8(2)(e)(iv). However, they concluded that the text of the 1954 Convention refers only to properties 'of great importance to the cultural heritage of every people', and the small church of Sayo did not fall under this category.[19]

Although in her separate opinion Judge Solomy Bossa[20] was *in abstracto* open to accepting a more elastic interpretation of the attack in the context of the destruction of monuments and religious buildings, but *in concreto,* and taking into account the lack of precision regarding the timeframe of the given 'attack', she was inclined to follow the principle *in dubio pro reo.*[21]

In her dissenting points inserted into the judgment, Judge Luz Ibáñez Carranza advocated against the "narrow interpretation of the attack" emphasizing that in the light of the object and the purpose of the Rome Statute, the proper interpretation of this notion should cover "combat action and immediate aftermath thereof".[22]

---

is based on Article 27 rather than on Article 56 of the 1907 Hague Regulations. The choice of the word 'attacks', rather than 'acts of hostility' or 'seizure of, destruction of or wilful damage done to', shows the drafters' intention to apply a narrow definition of that word. In that sense, the term 'attack' must be understood in the same way as it is defined in article 49(1) of Additional Protocol I: it is an 'act of violence against the adversary, whether in offence or in defence'. It is narrower than the term 'acts of hostilities' used in, among other provisions, article 16 of Additional Protocol I. It follows that the term 'attack' means 'combat action', or, if used as a verb, 'to set upon with hostile action'." Morrison–Hofmański, p. 13.

19 Morrison–Hofmański, pp. 11–12.

20 Separate Opinion of Judge Solomy Balungi Bossa on the Prosecutor's Appeal, ICC-01/04-02/06-2666-Anx4 30-03-2021 (hereinafter: Bossa).

21 "2. For the reasons that follow, I agree with Judges Eboe-Osuji and Ibáñez, who consider that the interpretation assigned by the Trial Chamber to the meaning of the word "attack" is narrow, in the particular circumstances of this case. (...) However, for the same reasons as Judge Eboe-Osuji [...] I also agree that the appellant should be acquitted on the count relating to the attack on the church in Sayo for the same reasons. [...] 14. Regarding the church in Sayo, it was attacked by UPC/FLPC soldiers sometime after the initial assault. The Trial Chamber accepted that the church was actually damaged, its doors were broken and furniture strewn all over the place, after being taken over by soldiers and turned into a kitchen. However, it was not possible for the Trial Chamber to situate the attack in time, except that it occurred sometime after the initial assault. Since it was not possible from the evidence to situate the attack in time, it is not possible to say whether it took place during the ratissage operation. I would therefore resolve this uncertainty in favor of the appellant and acquit him of the charge of attacking protected objects as a war crime, against the church in Sayo." Bossa, pp. 2 and 5.

22 "1167. In the view of Judge Ibáñez Carranza, the narrow interpretation of attack adopted by the Trial Chamber is contrary to the object of the provision, namely to prevent attacks

Judge Chile Eboe-Osuji referred to different English Legal Dictionaries, scholarly works and international jurisprudence, as well as the similarities between crimes against humanity and war crimes within the Rome Statute in order to substantiate why he is unable to accept the Trial Chamber's reasoning that "the actions of the UPC/FPLC troops against the Mongbwalu hospital and the church in Sayo do not amount to 'attacks' for purposes of Article 8(2)(e)(iv), merely because they occurred after actual combat operations to capture those locations and 'not during the actual conduct of hostilities."[23]

3. *The Decision on the Confirmation of Charges and the First Instance Judgment in Al Hassan*

The Pre-Trial Chamber and the Trial Chamber acting in the case of *Prosecutor v Al Hassan* – former deputy leader of the Islamic Police, *i.e.*, another police force established by the AQMI/Ansar Dine power – had to deal with the question of an attack against historical monuments and buildings. The Prosecutor charged Al Hassan as co-perpetrator of the destruction, since several members of the Islamic Police could be seen on the video footages capturing the events where they had to secure the site during the destruction.

The Pre-Trial Chamber[24] indicated that it was aware of the doctrinal debate launched by Schabas's criticism[25] and studied the first instance judg-

---

against protected buildings in the context of non-international armed conflicts. Such interpretation is also at odds with the object and purpose of the Rome Statute to put an end to impunity for the perpetrators of the most serious crimes of concern to the international community as a whole, including for acts that are undoubtedly serious violations of international humanitarian law. Finally, the interpretation proposed would not be in line with the 'established framework of international law' as stipulated in the chapeau of article 8(2)(e) of the Statute. 1168. In line with the above considerations, Judge Ibáñez Carranza is of the view that the term 'attack' includes the preparation, the carrying out of combat action and the immediate aftermath thereof, including criminal acts committed during ratissage operations carried out in the aftermath of combat action." Judgment on the appeals of Mr Bosco Ntaganda and the Prosecutor against the decision of Trial Chamber VI of 8 July 2019 entitled 'Judgment', ICC-01/04-02/06–2666-Red 30-03-2021, pp. 424–425.

23 Partly concurring opinion of Judge Chile Eboe-Osuji, ICC-01/04-02/06–2666-Anx5 30-03-2021, para. 132, p. 53.

24 *Corrected Version of "Décision relative à la confirmation des charges portées contre Al Hassan Ag Abdoul Aziz Ag Mohamed Ag Mahmoud"*, ICC-01/12-01/18–461-Corr-Red-tENG 03–05-2024, date of the original decision: 30 September 2019 (hereinafter: Al Hassan confirmation decision).

25 "518. The Chamber refers to the definition of the crime of "attacking protected objects" as set out in Article 8(2)(e)(iv) of the Statute and in the Elements of Crimes. The Prose-

ment delivered in *Ntaganda*[26] as well. Nevertheless, it decided to follow the *Al Mahdi* approach.[27]

The Trial Chamber condemned Al Hassan, but not on all charges. After presenting the chain of the events and the respective roles of the three police formations (Hesbah, Islamic Police and Security Battalion),[28] the judges – relying on the principle *in dubio pro reo* – acquitted him *inter alia* from the charge of attack against historical monuments and buildings.[29] The Trial Chamber did not enter into the analysis of the notion of 'combat action'.

---

cutor seeks confirmation of the charge relating to the demolition of the mausoleums (count 7) under the legal characterization provided for in Article 8(2)(e)(iv) of the Statute. 1399 The Chamber nonetheless notes that the suitability of this characterization is a matter of dispute between the parties. 1400" (Then, in the rather long paras. 519 and 520, the standpoints of the prosecution and defence are recapitulated also with the use of citations.) Footnote 1400 says: "DCC, paras. 687–715; Prosecutor's Final Written Submissions, paras. 143–155; Defence Written Submissions, paras. 136–137; Defence Final Written Submissions, paras. 37–44. See also: William Schabas, Al Mahdi Has Been Convicted of a Crime He Did Not Commit, Case Western Reserve Journal of International Law 49 (2017)." *Al Hassan confirmation decision,* para. 518, p. 244.

26 "521. The category of attacking protected objects (Article 8(2)(e)(iv) of the Statute) was chosen in *Al Mahdi,* first by this Chamber in its previous composition1411 and later by Trial Chamber VIII. In Ntaganda, Trial Chamber VI recalled that the crime of attacking protected objects belonged to the category of offences committed during the actual conduct of hostilities but noted that this interpretation did not find application in cases where protected cultural objects enjoying a special status were the object of the attack." *Al Hassan confirmation decision,* para. 521, p. 246.

27 "522. The Chamber subscribes to the analysis of Trial Chamber VIII in *Al Mahdi,* which held that "the element of 'direct[ing] an attack' encompasses any acts of violence against protected objects" and that no distinction need be made as to whether these acts "w[ere] carried out in the conduct of hostilities or after the object had fallen under the control of an armed group". Trial Chamber VIII highlighted that "[t]his reflect[ed] the special status of religious, cultural, historical and similar objects" and, recalling that the Statute made no such distinction, it considered that "the Chamber should not change this status by making distinctions not found in the language of the Statute." *Al Hassan confirmation decision,* para. 522, p. 246.

28 *The Prosecutor v Al Jassan Ag Abdoul Aziz Ag Mohamed Ag Mahmoud,* Trial Judgment, ICC-01/12-01/18-2594-Red 26-06-2024 (hereinafter: Al Hassan trial judgment), paras. 1030–1055, pp. 505–525.

29 "1053. Having regard to the aforementioned considerations and further noting that the heavy security deployment applied only to the first cemetery at which demolitions occurred and that it was Talha and the Security Battalion which undertook these measures, the Chamber cannot infer from Mr Al Hassan general role in relation to the security of the city, the patrols, and the assignment of Police members for these tasks, that he managed the security in relation to the demolition of the mausoleums. Taking all of the foregoing factors into account, the Chamber also cannot infer that Mr Al Hassan 'would have been responsible' for tasking specific members of the Police to participate in the demolition operations." [...] "1055. In light of the foregoing, the Chamber finds that there is in-

4. The View of the Office of the Prosecutor

Apparently, there is no difference between Fatou Bensouda and her successor Karim Khan concerning the legal perception of the attack against protected monuments. In a policy paper issued in 2021, duly taking into account the analysis by Schabas and referring to the considerations of judges Morrison and Hofmański in the footnotes, the prosecutor confirmed that

> "the ICTY's recognition that customary international law prohibits intentional harm to specially protected objects – regardless of the degree to which they are controlled by a party to the conflict – is consistent with the approach of the Court in *Al Mahdi*. This took the view that "attack" under Articles 8(2)(b)(ix) and 8(2)(e)(iv) had a special meaning, including acts directed against protected objects under the control of a party to the conflict, and not merely those under the control of the adverse party. In this way, it would seem that "attack" for the purpose of Articles 8(2)(b)(ix) and 8(2)(e)(iv) may be defined differently from other 'conduct of hostilities' offences in Articles 8(2)(b) and (e). While the Ntaganda Trial Chamber declined to follow *Al Mahdi* on this point, and this led to a wide-ranging judicial discussion among members of the Ntaganda Appeals Chamber, the Appeal Judgment ultimately contains no majority overturning the legal principles recognised in *Al Mahdi*. While respectful of the judicial opinions which have been rendered, the Office therefore remains of the view that *Al Mahdi* was correctly decided. In the ordinary exercise of its mandate, and subject to judicial guidance, it will seek to clarify the law further in this respect."[30]

---

sufficient evidence to establish that Mr Al Hassan took any particular action or had a specific role in relation to the demolition of the mausoleums. Therefore, in the absence of any factual findings on Mr Al Hassan's involvement, the Chamber considers it unnecessary to undertake any legal characterisation of the charged crime under Count 7 or the related criminal responsibility of Mr Al Hassan under Article 25(3)(d) of the Statute." [...] "1181. In light of the Chamber's factual findings made above in which it found that the link between Mr Al Hassan's conduct and the demolition of the mausoleums has not been established to the required standard, the Chamber will not set out the applicable law for the war crime of attacking protected objects under Article 8(2)(e)(iv) of the Statute." *Al Hassan trial judgment,* paras. 1053, 1055 and 1181, pp. 524–525 and 580–581.

30 Office of the Prosecutor, Policy on Cultural Heritage, June 2021, para. 45, p. 16 (footnotes omitted).

5. The Notion of 'Combat Action' as a Problem to Overcome – Some Scholarly Reflections

The ideas voiced by Schabas sparked considerable debate in academia. The result of the reconstruction of the *travaux préparatoires* and the 'attack' = 'combat action' approach was not contested. However, those who were advocating for an enhanced protection of historical and cultural monuments tried, nevertheless, to attribute a special meaning[31] to the word 'attack' when directed against these artifacts *(lex specialis),* or they chose the *de lege ferenda* approach, *i.e.,* the need to add a special clause[32] to the crimes against humanity in Article 7 of the Rome Statute.

6. The Need to Add Subtleties to the Historical Interpretation on the Basis of the Travaux Préparatoires

The interpretative rule that 'a technical word should always have the same meaning in the same legal document' is certainly correct and logical. *In Abstracto,* it cannot be contested. However, if we do not only take the English version of the Rome Statute but also consider the equally authentic French text of the *Elements of crimes,* we might conclude that *in concreto,* the statement that the notion 'attack' is always used in the same way must be given some nuance. Minor as they may be, there are still differences, which are nevertheless embarrassing.

Among the enlisted war crimes, '*directing attacks*' is consistently translated as *'diriger [...] des attaques'* in the French version of the Rome Statu-

31 Emma A. O'Connell, 'Criminal Liability for the Destruction of Cultural Property: The Prosecutor v. Bosco Ntaganda', *DePaul Journal for Social Justice,* Vol. 15, Issue 1, 2022, pp. 54, 62–63; Samira Mathias, 'Prosecuting Crimes Against Culture: The Contributions of the Al Mahdi and Ntaganda Cases to the ICC Approach to Cultural Property Protections', *Emory International Law Review,* Vol. 35, 2021, pp. 64, 74–75; Mark A. Drumbl, 'From Timbuktu to The Hague and Beyond: The War Crime of Intentionally Attacking Cultural Property', *Journal of International Criminal Justice,* Vol. 17, 2019, pp. 86, 92, 95; Juan Pablo Pérez-León-Acevedo &Thiago Felipe Alves Pinto, 'Enforcing Freedom of Religion or Belief in Cases Involving Attacks Against Buildings Dedicated to Religion: The Al Mahdi Case at the International Criminal Court', *Berkeley Journal of International Law,* Vol. 37, Issue 3, 2020, pp. 463–464.

32 Peta-Louise Bagott, 'How to solve a problem like Al Mahdi: proposal for a new crime of 'attacks against cultural heritage', *in* Julie Fraser & Brianne McGonigle Leyh (eds.), *Intersections of Law and Culture at the International Criminal Court,* Edward Elgar, Cheltenham, 2020, pp. 42, 53.

te.[33] However, the only mention of *'launching an attack'* is also translated as *'diriger [...] des attaques'*.[34] As far as the Elements of crimes is concerned, *'directed an attack'* is generally translated as *'a dirigé une attaque'*[35] but sometimes as *'a lancé une attaque'*.[36] *'Launched an attack'* also becomes *'a lancé une attaque'*.[37]

'Attacking' is *'attaquer'*[38] in the French text of the Statute and the Elements of crimes explains it with *'attacked'* the equivalent of which in the French version of this document is: *'a attaqué'*.[39] The Elements of crimes sometimes uses *'attacked'* / *'a attaqué'* also to explain the *'directing attacks'*/ *'diriger des attaques'* expressions in the Statute.[40]

Concerning crimes against humanity, the French version of the Elements of crimes almost exclusively uses *'attaque dirigée'* for *'attack directed'*[41] with the notable exception of the crime of persecution when *'attack directed'* becomes a *'campagne [...] dirigée'*.[42]

I sought advice from two highly qualified colleagues here at the ICC, a native French speaker on the one hand and a native English speaker on the other. The two constructions are nearly the same in both languages, however in French, *'lancer une attaque'* puts the emphasis on 'starting' the action while *'diriger une attaque'* suggests authority or a commanding position.

In the English text, *'to launch an attack'* could imply setting something into motion, starting an action. In that case the emphasis would be more on the 'starting'/ 'prompting' of the activity. To *'direct an attack'* could imply that the attack is 'directed against/towards' something. In that case the emphasis would be more on what is the 'object' (in a general sense of the word), *i.e.* the 'direction', of the activity. (See also the *Oxford English Dictionary* about *'to launch'*[43] and *'to direct'*[44] and the *Larousse Dictionnaire de Français*

33 *See* Articles 8(2)(b)(i), 8(2)(b)(ii), 8(2)(b)(iii), 8(2)(b)(ix), 8(2)(b)(xxiv), 8(2)(e)(i), 8(2)(e)(ii), 8(2)(e)(iii), 8(2)(e)(iv).
34 *See* Article 8(2)(iv).
35 *See* Article 8(2)(b)(i), 8(2)(b)(ii), 8(2)(e)(i).
36 *See* Article 8(2)(b)(ix), 8(2)e)(i), 8(2)(e)(iii), 8(2)(e)(iv).
37 *See* Article 8(2)(b)(iv).
38 *See* Article 8(2)(b)(v).
39 *See* Article 8(2)(b)(v).
40 *See* Article 8(2)(b)(xxiv), 8(2)(e)(ii).
41 *See* Article 7(1)(a), 7(1)(b), 7(1)(c), 7(1)(d), 7(1)(e), 7(1)(f), 7(1)(g), 7(1)(i), 7(1)(j), 7(1)(k).
42 *See* Article 7(1)(h).
43 *See* at https://www.oed.com/dictionary/launch_v?tab=meaning_and_use&tl=true#39805609.
44 *See* at https://www.oed.com/dictionary/direct_v?tab=meaning_and_use#6630372.

or the *Robert – Dictionnaire de la langue française* about '*lancer*'[45] and '*diriger*'.[46])

What I can gather from all this – as a scholar whose mother tongue is neither English, nor French – is that when '*to launch an attack*' appears as '*lancer une attaque*', the two constructions are truly identical (and the same can be said about '*to direct an attack*' and '*diriger une attaque*'), however when '*directed an attack*' *is* '*a lancé une attaque*' as it occurs in the case of Article 8(2)(b)(ix) and Article 8(2)(e)(iv) concerning the attacks against protected objects and monuments, the English and French meanings are slightly different.

We can see that these differences – shown also in the annex appended to my article – appear far more frequently in the *Elements of crimes* than in the Rome Statute, and it is reasonable to suppose that they can be partly explained by the expressions used in the English and French versions of the conventions that prohibit certain war methods and serve the protection of victims or other humanitarian purposes.

Nevertheless, the above overview helps us to go further in the analysis. It is clear that the reconstruction of the genesis of the crime falling under Article 8(2)(e)(iv) was very professionally done by Schabas and when judges Morrison and Hofmański revisited it, their research led to the same conclusion concerning the will expressed by governmental experts during the negotiations and the drafting. They are also right as to the impact of the submitted US proposal.

Nevertheless, the latter[47] is worth revisiting. The submitted document concerned not only the destruction of monuments, hospitals *etc.*, but a whole series of war crimes. Apparently, it was conceived as a counter-proposal against the use of the Draft Code of Crimes against the Peace and Security of Mankind prepared by the International Law Commission.[48] It can be recognized *prima vista* that the war crimes listed by the ILC contain war crimes according to the 1907 The Hague Conventions, the 1949 Geneva Conventions and the 1977 Additional protocols. This is, by the way, clearly explained in the commentary of the draft.[49]

45 *See* at https://www.larousse.fr/dictionnaires/francais/lancer/46124; *see also* https://dictionnaire.lerobert.com/definition/lancer#google_vignette.

46 *See* at https://www.larousse.fr/dictionnaires/francais/diriger/25796; *see also* https://dictionnaire.lerobert.com/definition/diriger.

47 War Crimes: Proposal Submitted by the United States, 14 February 1997, A/AC.249/1997/WG.1/DP.1, pp. 2–3; (hereinafter: War Crimes: Proposal Submitted by the U.S.).

48 *See* at https://legal.un.org/ilc/texts/instruments/english/draft_articles/7_4_1996.pdf.

49 *See* at https://legal.un.org/ilc/texts/instruments/english/commentaries/7_4_1996.pdf, paras. 4, 11, 14, 15, pp. 54–56.

It is widely known, however, that the US is a signatory but not a contracting party to the 1977 Additional protocols. That is why, in a very logical way, and aiming to avoid that the 1977 novelties could enter through the backdoor, the US delegation put the ILC Draft Code on the table and wherever they discovered elements taken from the Additional protocols, they meticulously tried to find their equivalents in the 1907 The Hague regulation. As a result, the ILC draft was structurally and mostly *in merito* followed, nevertheless it was still reformulated into *The Hague style* where necessary. Some minor aesthetic changes were also introduced, such as the use of capital letters first, followed by small letters in the numbering (A. was followed by a, b, c, *etc.* instead of an a. followed by i, ii, iii, *etc.*).

In this way, the A. point of the US proposal contains the same eight grave breaches of the 1949 Geneva Conventions, as did the ILC draft (although there was no mention in the main text that they were taken from the Geneva Convention).

The B. point of the US proposal under the subtitle 'other serious violations of the laws and customs applicable in international armed conflict within the established framework of international law, namely:' enumerates war crimes mostly taken *verbatim* from The Hague Regulations, although the original *to kill, to wound, to declare etc.* became *killing, wounding, declaring, etc.* Among the eighteen subpoints, as I try to show in the footnotes, eleven[50] were clearly taken from the 1907 The Hague Regulation, two[51] from the 1949 Geneva Conventions, four[52] from other conventions (in which the US is a contracting party) prohibiting the use of some types of weapons. There is also one[53] (but only one) which exhibits clear textual similarity with the 1977 Additional protocol. This can be explained by the fact that the crime of "intentionally directing an attack against civilians" can be considered as being an evident customary law rule.

It should be emphasized that the US proposal concerning cultural monuments brought slight changes to The Hague formula and the criminalization of "intentionally directing attacks" is definitely much stricter than the

50 *See* i = 1907, Article 23/ b; ii = 1907, Article 23/ c; iii = 1907, Article 23/d; iv = 1907, Article 23/f; v = 1907, Article 23/g; vi = 1907, Article 23/h first part; vii = 1907, Article 23/h second part; viii = 1907, Article 25; ix = 1907, Article 28; x = 1907, Article 28; xv = 1907, Article 27.

51 *See* xvii = 1949/IV/Article 27; xviii = 1949/IV/Article 28.

52 *See* xi = 1925 Geneva Gas Protocol; xii = 1980 CCW; xiii = 1972 BWC; xiv = 1993 CWC.

53 *See* xvi = *grosso modo* 1977 Geneva I/Article 51(2) + Article 48.

original introductory formulation reading "[i]n sieges and bombardments all necessary steps must be taken to spare, as far as possible [...]".

Point C. of the US proposal deals with serious breaches of Article 3 common to the four 1949 Geneva Conventions and reproduces their text.[54]

In a document of the Prep. Com's working group on the definition of crimes issued a week later[55] than the US proposal, we can see that although the borrowing of several formulas of the 1977 Additional protocol resulted in a considerable modification of the text submitted by the US delegation, the formula of the protection of cultural monuments is still there. A longer alternative had also been presented preceding the proposal of the US delegation. The new elements of this alternative are seemingly from Additional protocol I (and the 1954 The Hague Convention for the protection of cultural property in the event of armed conflict) and they read as follows: "[...] cannot be object of attack [...]".

At later stages of the diplomatic negotiations, plenty of addenda and reformulation proposals were put on the table and the finally adopted text of the crimes in the Rome Statute is very different from the original US proposal. However, as Schabas[56] and later Morrison and Hofmański[57] convincingly argue, only slight stylistic changes occurred concerning the crime of the destruction of historical and cultural monuments and the governments agreed that the same short text should be introduced in the list of war crimes committed in an international armed conflict and in a non-international armed conflict.

This is the reason why in a – at first glance – surprising way, the interpretation of the rules of humanitarian law applicable in an international armed conflict played such an important role in the assessment of the destruction in *Al Mahdi* and later in *Bosco Ntaganda.* Schabas,[58] Morrison and Hofmański[59] refer to the notion of 'attack' as defined by the 1977 Additional Protocol I. Although both Additional Protocol I and II use the word 'attack' several times,[60] only Protocol I gives an Abstract definition of the notion. It is to be emphasized that those articles in the protocols that cover – in very

54 *See* i = 1949/I/3/a ; ii = 1949/I/3/b ; iii 1949/I/3/c ; iv = 1949/I/3/d.

55 A/AC.249/1997/WG.1/CRP.2., 20 March 1997, p. 4. *See also* A/AC.249/1997/WG.1/L.5, 12 March 1997, pp. 8–9.

56 Schabas 2017, pp. 86–88.

57 Morrison–Hofmański, pp. 6–8.

58 Schabas 2017, p. 80.

59 Morrison–Hofmański, pp. 8–9.

60 Protocol I: Articles 12, 27, 31, 39, 41, 42, 44, 49, 51, 52, 56, 57, 58, 59, 85. Protocol II: Articles 11, 13, 14, 15.

similar terms – the protection of cultural monuments, do not contain the word 'attack'.

Taking into account the text of the definition of attack in Article 49 of Additional protocol I, Schabas,[61] Morrison and Hofmański[62] turned to the ICRC Commentary and they highlight the formula that "the term 'attack' means 'combat action'".

It is worth noting that the commentary[63] uses this expression first and foremost in order to emphasize that both sides of the armed conflict (*i.e.*, to put it simply: both the 'aggressor' or 'first shooter' and the 'defender') all under the same rules.[64] Moreover, it gives an example (*i.e.*, 'placing of mines') showing that 'attack' as a 'combat action' does not necessarily and exclusively mean a human 'face to face' exercise of force or a long distance action with heavy artillery, bombing or rocketing.[65]

Although it is clear that 'attack' cannot be equated either with 'hostilities' or with 'military operation', which are generally conceived as a broader term than 'attack' in Protocol I, it is still obvious that the proper interpretation of

---

61 Schabas 2017, pp. 79–80.

62 Morrison–Hofmański, p. 9.

63 "1880 The definition given by the Protocol has a wider scope since it – justifiably – covers defensive acts (particularly "counter-attacks") as well as offensive acts, as both can affect the civilian population. It is for this reason that the final choice was a broad definition. In other words, the term "attack" means "combat action". This should be taken into account in the instruction of armed forces who should clearly understand that the restrictions imposed by humanitarian law on the use of force should be observed both by troops defending themselves and by those who are engaged in an assault or taking the offensive." *See* at https://ihl-databases.icrc.org/en/ihl-treaties/api-1977/article-49/commentary/1987?activeTab=.

64 "1882. Finally, it is appropriate to note that in the sense of the Protocol an attack is unrelated to the concept of aggression or the first use of armed force; (6) it refers simply to the use of armed force to carry out a military operation at the beginning or during the course of armed conflict. Questions relating to the responsibility for unleashing the conflict are of a completely different nature." *See* at https://ihl-databases.icrc.org/en/ihl-treaties/api-1977/article-49/commentary/1987?activeTab=.

65 "1881 During the above-mentioned enquiry the question arose whether the placing of mines constituted an attack. The general feeling was that there is an attack whenever a person is directly endangered by a mine laid." *See* at https://ihl-databases.icrc.org/en/ihl-treaties/api-1977/article-49/commentary/1987?activeTab=. The reference to the 'enquiry' concerns the background documents of the III committee during the 1974–1977 diplomatic conference. "1879. [...] The questions that were raised included one relating to this question of terminology. In general, the replies indicated that the meaning given by the Protocol to the word "attacks" did not give rise to any major problems, even though military instruction manuals in many countries define an attack as an offensive act aimed at destroying enemy forces and gaining ground." *See* at https://ihl-databases.icrc.org/en/ihl-treaties/api-1977/article-49/commentary/1987?activeTab=.

'combat action' largely depends on the degree to which the example of *mines* in the ICRC commentary is taken into consideration. In my view, the ICRC reference to the use of landmines (*i.e.,* emplacing, laying or hiding mines) – also emphasized by Marco Sassoli[66] in this context – is particularly important and interesting, because it presupposes a relative inactivity on the battlefield or in the occupied territory.

Looking back on history, we will find several examples of destruction committed much later than the seizure of a territory either for vengeance purposes or in order to humiliate the local population or to erase its artistic or religious presence. See *e.g.,* the destruction of the great synagogues of Strasbourg (1940), Riga (1941) and Vilna (1941) or the deliberate destruction of Warsaw by the troops of the Hitlerian Germany from October 1944 to January 1945 after the surrender of the July-September 1944 uprising of the Home Army *(Armia Krajowa)* resistance movement.

In this sense, taking into account the huge impact of the Geneva Conventions and the Additional protocols on the genesis of the Rome Statute and the declared will of governments as expressed by their representatives during the Rome Diplomatic conference, the question is not whether the war crimes of 'attacks against [...] historic monuments'[67] or 'attacks against civilian objects'[68] or 'attacks against civilian population'[69] or 'attacks against [...] material [...] involved in a humanitarian assistance'[70] or an attack caus-

66 The definition in Article 49(1) "[...] however does not correspond to the normal use of the term 'attack' in military language (nor is it related to the separation of *jus in bello* from *jus ad bellum:* both a State fighting in self-defence and an aggressor may be conducting attacks) but rather to the uncontroversial idea that, for instance, laying mines and returning fire must also comply with the rules on distinction, proportionality and precautions." Marco Sassoli, *International Humanitarian Law. Rules, Controversies, and Solutions to Problems Arising from Warfare,* Edward Elgar, Cheltenham, 2024, note No. 8.300, p. 375.

67 Rome Statute, same texts in Articles 8(2)(b)(ix) and 8(2)(e)(iv): "Intentionally directing attacks against buildings dedicated to religion, education, art, science or charitable purposes, historic monuments, hospitals and places where the sick and wounded are collected, provided they are not military objectives."

68 Rome Statute, Article 8(2)(b)(ii): "Intentionally directing attacks against civilian objects, that is, objects which are not military objectives;".

69 Rome Statute, same texts in Articles 8(2)(b)(i) and 8(2)(e)(iv): "Intentionally directing attacks against the civilian population as such or against individual civilians not taking direct part in hostilities;".

70 Rome Statute, same texts in Articles 8(2)(b)(iii) and 8(2)(e)(iii): "Intentionally directing attacks against personnel, installations, material, units or vehicles involved in a humanitarian assistance or peacekeeping mission in accordance with the Charter of the United Nations, as long as they are entitled to the protection given to civilians or civilian objects under the international law of armed conflict;".

ing disproportional collateral damages[71] *etc.* – where 'attack' is a composite element of the given crime – can be perpetrated outside of 'combat action', but whether it is legitimate to use a restrictive interpretation of 'combat action'?

Is the notion of 'combat action' explained by Schabas as a 'battlefield'[72] provision only a face-to-face struggle, a seizure, a 'Sturm', a shelling from howitzers and guns, bombings and/or rocketing? In other words: what is a 'combat action'? The ICRC Commentary[73] to the Additional protocols dates back to 1987. It seems that the International Committee of the Red Cross has since been engaged since in a serious reflection about the need for a more elastic interpretation of 'combat action', especially concerning the impact of cyber-attacks in armed conflicts whether perpetrated by soldiers of the army or by civilians. As an ICRC position paper notes,

> "[i]f the *notion of attack is interpreted as only referring to operations that cause death, injury or physical damage,* a cyber operation that is directed at making a civilian network (such as electricity, banking, or communications) dysfunctional, or is expected to cause such effect incidentally, might not be covered by essential IHL rules protecting the civilian population and civilian objects. *Such an overly restrictive understanding of the notion of attack would be difficult to reconcile with the object and purpose of the IHL rules on the conduct of hostilities.* It is therefore essential that States find a common understanding in order to adequately protect the civilian population against the effects of cyber operations."[74] *(emphasis added)*

---

71 Rome Statute, Article 8(2)(b)(iv): "Intentionally launching an attack in the knowledge that such attack will cause incidental loss of life or injury to civilians or damage to civilian objects or widespread, long-term and severe damage to the natural environment which would be clearly excessive in relation to the concrete and direct overall military advantage anticipated;".

72 "Thus, case law of the Court has made a very clear distinction between the war crimes associated with "battlefield attacks," of which article 8(2)(e)(iv) is a species, and those that are associated with the conflict but that take place after a civilian population has "fallen into the hands" of the party charged with violating the laws and customs of war. The situation in "occupied" Timbuktu belongs to this second category." Schabas 2017, p. 83, *see also* on pp. 82, 86, 94.

73 Sandoz *et al.* (eds.), *Commentary on the Additional Protocols of 8 June 1977 to the Geneva Conventions of 12 August 1949,* International Committee of the Red Cross, Martinus Nijhoff, Geneva, 1987.

74 Cyber warfare: Eight rules for "civilian hackers" during war, and four obligations for states to restrain them International Humanitarian Law and Cyber Operations during Armed Conflicts. ICRC position paper Submitted to the 'Open-Ended Working Group

Knut Dörmann, whom Schabas cited concerning the relationship between 'attack' and 'combat action',[75] notes in another article that the notion of 'armed attack' is not completely the same when used in the context of international humanitarian law and in case of recourse to legitimate self-defense. He also refers to governmental positions in the perception of cyber warfare.[76] He confirms that the ICRC is clearly in favor of considering that type of cyber operation as an 'attack'.[77] In another article Dörmann mentions other examples as well.[78] In the chapter written in the 4th edition of the Commentary of the Rome Statute, Dörmann emphasizes – in the context of cyber warfare – that

---

on Developments in the Field of Information and Telecommunications in the Context of International Security' and the 'Group of Governmental Experts on Advancing Responsible State Behaviour in Cyberspace in the Context of International Security'. November 2019, p. 8.

75 Schabas 2017, p. 80. (Schabas refers to the text about Article 8 of the Rome Statute in the 3rd edition of the Triffterer Commentary: Otto Triffterer & Kai Ambos (eds.), *The Rome Statute of the International Criminal Court: A Commentary, Third Edition,* C.H. Beck–Hart–Nomos, München–Oxford–Baden-Baden, 2016, p. 342.

76 Laurent Gisel *et al.*, 'Twenty years on: International humanitarian law and the protection of civilians against the effects of cyber operations during armed conflicts', *International Review of the Red Cross,* Vol. 102, Issue 913, 2020, pp. 307–308.

77 "The question of whether or not an operation amounts to an "attack" as defined in IHL is essential for the application of many of the rules deriving from the principles of distinction, proportionality and precaution, which afford critical protection to civilians and civilian objects. For many years, the ICRC has taken the position that an operation designed to disable a computer or a computer network during an armed conflict constitutes an attack as defined in IHL whether the object is disabled through destruction or in any other way. This view is also reflected in the positions of a number of States." Gisel *et al.* 2020, p. 333.

78 "Bothe/Partsch/Solf in their commentary to AP I point out that the term "acts of violence" denotes physical force. Thus, the concept of "attacks" excludes dissemination of propaganda, embargoes or other non-physical means of psychological, political or economic warfare. Based on that understanding and distinction, CNA through viruses, worms, logic bombs etc. that result in physical damage to persons, or damage to objects that goes beyond the computer program or data attacked can be qualified as "acts of violence" and thus as an attack in the sense of IHL. Given that elsewhere in the same section of AP I, namely in the definition of a military objective, reference is made to neutralization of an object as a possible result of an attack, one may conclude that the mere disabling of an object, such as shutting down of the electricity grid, without destroying it should be qualified as an attack as well. It is also helpful to look at how the concept of attack is applied to other means and methods of warfare. There is general agreement that, for example, the employment of biological or chemical agents that does not cause a physical explosion, such as the use of asphyxiating or poisonous gases, would constitute an attack." Knut Dörmann, *Applicability of the Additional Protocols to Computer Network Attacks,* at https://www.icrc.org/sites/default/files/external/doc/en/assets/files/other/applicabilityofihltocna.pdf, p. 4.

> "[s]uch attacks could be for example the opening of a floodgate of a dam which leads to the death of persons in the flooded areas – it can't mean a difference whether such casualties are caused by a bomb or by means of a cyber attack. What defines an attack is not the violence of the means – as it is uncontroversial that the use of biological, chemical or radiological agents would constitute an attack –, but the violence of the effects or consequences, even if indirect."[79]

Cyber-attacks against health institutions may also fall into this category. In his comprehensive overview about the applicability of international humanitarian law on cyber warfare, citing the so-called Tallin Manual,[80] Marco Sassoli posits that "[t]he intended effects of a cyber operation therefore determine whether it can be qualified as an attack."[81]

As ICRC experts Kubo Mačák, Laurent Gisel, Tilman Rodenhäuser argue that "a cyber attack may qualify as a war crime provided certain specific conditions are fulfilled [...]. For example, the war crime of directing an attack against a medical facility under the *Rome Statute* of the International Criminal Court provided for in Articles 8(2)(b)(xxiv) and (e)(ii), could conceivably be committed using cyber-means."[82]

It is worth adding that the attacks against hospitals also fall under Articles 8(2)(b)(ix) and 8(2)(e)(iv), *i.e.,* the same articles where attacks against historical monuments are penalized.

Following this line of arguments and taking into account the creativity and technical skills of robotic and drone producing military engineers, one can easily imagine operations where a neighborhood is targeted to annihilate the given object or when a hidden device emplaced earlier is activated from a distance, or a planned avalanche or flooding caused by an explosion

---

79 Knut Dörmann, 'B2 Para. 2(a): Meaning of 'war crimes' – Grave breaches', *in* Kai Ambos (ed.), *Rome Statute of the International Criminal Court, Article-by-Article Commentary, Fourth edition,* Beck–Hart–Nomos, München–Baden-Baden–Oxford, 2022, pp. 362–410, cited text on p. 369.

80 The cyber-attack is "a cyber operation, whether offensive or defensive, that is reasonably expected to cause injury or death to persons or damage or destruction to objects. [...] it is the use of violence against a target that distinguishes attacks from other operations [...] non-violent operations, such as psychological operations or cyber espionage, do not qualify as attacks." Michael N. Schmitt (ed.), *Tallinn Manual 2.0 on the International Law Applicable to Cyber Operations,* Cambridge University Press, Cambridge, 2017, Note No. 255, p. 415.

81 Sassoli 2024, Note No. 10.121, p. 580.

82 Kubo Mačák *et al., Cyber attacks against hospitals and the COVID-19 pandemic: How strong are international law protections?,* at https://blogs.icrc.org/law-and-policy/2020/04/02/cyber-attacks-hospitals-covid-19/.

destroys the envisaged target. I am convinced that such an operation can be lawfully considered an 'attack' and apparently, it is such a 'combat action' where the military units of the respective parties are present at different times.

Instead of submitting other possible examples of military actions thought up in an ivory tower, I'd rather return to the example of the 'placement of mines' contained in the explanation of 'attack' in the Commentary of the additional Protocols. In my view, this example cannot be disregarded when the meaning of 'combat action' is construed. Dörman notes that

> "[t]he term 'acts of violence' denotes physical force. It covers the use of weapons, but such as disseminating propaganda, embargos or non-physical forms of psychological, political or economic warfare would not fall under the notion of attack. However, there is no reason to believe the 'attack' is limited to kinetic means and methods of warfare."[83]

Recently, the 34th International Conference of the Red Cross and Red Crescent, *i.e.*, a regular meeting of governments and of national red cross societies included this issue in a resolution stating that the conference

> "[…] 8. urges States and parties to armed conflicts to protect civilian populations and other protected persons and objects, including historic monuments, works of art or places of worship which constitute the cultural or spiritual heritage of peoples, in accordance with their international legal obligations, including with regard to ICT activities;".[84]

7. Conclusions

To conclude, in my view, the notion of 'combat action' does not only cover loud and ferocious man-to-man, weapon-to-weapon type devastating direct confrontations. Instead, an 'attack' embraces other *hostile action(s)* if planned with the purpose of causing harm to the opponent in the armed conflict, irrespective of whether it is directed against human beings or material or immaterial property.

83 Dörmann 2022, p. 399.

84 *See* at https://rcrcconference.org/app/uploads/2024/10/34IC_R2-ICT-EN.pdf. *See also* Kubo Mačák, 'The First Humanitarian ICT Resolution: Ambitions and Limitations', *EJIL Talk,* 25 November 2024.

With regard to individual crimes, the fulfillment of the factual and legal criteria specified in the *Elements of crimes* determines whether the conduct in question constitutes a crime punishable under the Rome Statute.

The International Legal Mechanism of Humanitarian Aid

Activities during Martial Law in Ukraine

*Ielyzaveta Lvova – Volodymyr Dryshliuk**

Abstract

This paper contributes to the definition of the evolving, separate field of international legal mechanisms for humanitarian aid. Moreover, the paper's aim is to introduce and examine the practice of humanitarian cooperation in Ukraine, with special regard to the role of the EU. The research relies on a survey of the relevant literature and interviews conducted with representatives of humanitarian organizations working in Ukraine. With this paper we aim to contribute not only to the shaping of this field of international law, but to the formation of its separate elements with the ambition of improving the efficiency of international legal mechanisms for humanitarian policy.

Keywords: humanitarian aid, Ukraine, International Red Cross Society, martial law, war

1. Introduction

In February 2022, the unprecedented full-scale Russian military aggression in Ukraine caused innumerable damages and catastrophic humanitarian crises with socio-economic, environmental and cultural challenges affecting Ukrainian statehood. After the ceasefire millions of Ukrainians suffered physical pain, mental harm, stress and other traumas that forever changed their lives. Understanding the impact of war, international humanitarian organizations fulfill the crucial task of fostering cooperation within states for the protection of humans in areas within and outside the control of Ukraine. Meanwhile, the responsibility of the international community for improving the existing system of humanitarian aid is becoming increasingly urgent.

---

* Ielyzaveta Lvova: professor of law, Odessa State University of Internal Affairs. ORCID: 0000–0002-3391-318, lvovaliza@outlook.com.
Volodymyr Dryshliuk: associate professor of law, Odessa State University of Internal Affairs, ORCID 0000–0002-2274-441X, drishliuk@gmail.com.

In this context the international legal mechanism of humanitarian aid governs a civilizational choice to observe to the principles of human safety and environmental conservation, focusing on the activities of local non-governmental organizations. While the international legal mechanism for providing humanitarian aid as an independent field of public international law is still being formed, the threat of new wars strongly contributes to the reinforcement of control measures over the provision of humanitarian aid not only in Ukraine, but also abroad.

Under the above mentioned conditions, the international legal mechanism of humanitarian aid is a multidisciplinary phenomenon and ensuring: *(i)* control over cash and commodity flows; *(ii)* assessment of prospects and efficiency of use; *(iii)* analysis of the interaction between civil society and the authorities; *(iv)* monitoring of compliance with the principle of neutrality, fairness, and control over the distribution of funds by civil society, *etc.*

The article examines theoretical and legal approaches to the definition of humanitarian aid, equipping the reader with the current prerequisites and prospects for the formation of (inter)national legislation on humanitarian aid. The article draws on the international statements and interviews conducted with the representatives of the International Red Cross Society (hereinafter: ICRS) in Ukraine and non-governmental humanitarian organizations. It uses statistic data published in open sources and telegram channels to explore the significance of international humanitarian aid and assistance to Ukraine. The purpose of this article is to review the relevant literature to suggest some possible directions for future research in the context of the formation of an international legal mechanism of humanitarian aid. The findings resulting from the analysis of international legislation on the provision of international humanitarian aid and assistance show a fragmentation and lack of conceptual principles and norms to solve existing problems (*e.g.*, humanitarian access and humanitarian logistics). For an effective solution, the system of forecasting, planning, and coordination of international humanitarian support in Ukraine must be improved. In addition, there is a need for a reliable system to monitor the volume of the support provided. Ukraine implements the elements of EU humanitarian policy within the framework European trade policy. Such engagement helps provide international governments and non-governmental humanitarian organizations with relevant information on the level social and economic security in Ukraine. This article reflects is attempt to build the theory underpinning the international legal mechanisms for humanitarian aid with the ambition to contribute to the development of international public law scholarship. It develops a taxonomy of methods, used in the international and national law governing humanitarian aid, also pointing out which of these methods work best.

2. General Remarks on the International Mechanism of International Humanitarian Aid

It is well known that under the conditions of international armed conflicts, states are obliged to provide humanitarian assistance and facilitate its receipt by persons affected. This is to be done in accordance with their needs, however, it is worth emphasizing that the theory of public international law does not contain a well-developed doctrine and cannot live up to the above-mentioned expectations. Moreover, the relevant international law does not entail international criminal liability for states, are these responsibilities detailed in the provisions of the sources of international humanitarian law.

As a matter of principle, international humanitarian aid during armed conflicts is provided directly to the victims of catastrophe. Moreover, international assistance mostly includes services that facilitate protection (*e.g.*, consultation, training, work to prevent harm to the environment from explosive remnants of war). So, precluding international humanitarian aid can be understood as a crime against humanity.

Humanitarian aid is a form of charitable assistance. More specifically, in Ukraine, recipients of humanitarian aid are legal entities, as well as accredited representative offices of foreign states, international and foreign humanitarian organizations in Ukraine (without creating a legal entity), determined in accordance with the procedure established by the Cabinet of Ministers of Ukraine as recipients of humanitarian aid. For the period of martial law and within three months after its termination or cancellation, persons who may be recipients of humanitarian aid in accordance with this law shall be recognized as such regardless of their inclusion in the Unified Register of Recipients of Humanitarian Aid. Humanitarian aid donors are legal entities established and registered in accordance with the legislation of Ukraine or a foreign state, and individuals located in Ukraine or abroad who voluntarily provide humanitarian aid to recipients of humanitarian aid in Ukraine or abroad.

Humanitarian aid provided in cash by a state is managed by the central executive body that ensures the formation and implementation of foreign policy, realized through transferring funds in foreign currency to the bank account of a foreign state. The transfer of funds is carried out in accordance with the procedure established by law. Humanitarian assistance in the form of involving civil defense forces in carrying out emergency rescue and other urgent work, extinguishing fires, providing life support to victims, *etc.* is provided by the central executive body responsible for civil defense, and/or another authorized central executive body to which such forces are subordinate. Humanitarian assistance in the form of involving disaster relief and medical units to provide assistance to victims in the event of emergencies is provided by the central executive body responsible for the field of health care, jointly with the central executive body that implements state policy in the field of civil protection.[1]

It is clear that the task of the international community to improve the existing system of institutions for providing humanitarian aid is becoming more urgent. Taking into account the unattainable effect of recognizing the problems of providing humanitarian aid from the point of view of a revisionist approach (from the Latin *revisio* – review), we note the need to revise the established doctrine of providing humanitarian aid by law enforcement agencies. The legal mechanisms for international humanitarian aid are operated based on the principles of humanitarian logistics. Rojas Trejos *et al.* argue that

> "Decisions in humanitarian logistics can be divided into four key phases: mitigation, preparedness, response and recovery. [...] [O]ne of the challenges of humanitarian aid distribution logistics with accessibility constraints is to redistribute relief goods to avoid severe shortages in some nodes and excess inventory in others. Likewise, it is important to work on alternative transport mechanisms such as drones for infrastructure network assessment and humanitarian aid delivery and their possibility of integration with networks and modes of transportation used in each particular area. It is also necessary to explore new supply systems, such as shared vehicles, whose structure allows an easy and safe sharing of different types of goods, or hybrid delivery vehicles, which are viable under various social, economic and infrastructure constraints. The study of collaborative environments in inventory management, transportation, storage, location of facilities and stakeholder's coordination is relevant. Given that the distribution of aid may jointly involve decisions associated with

1 On humanitarian aid, *see* Law of Ukraine vid 22 October 1999, № 1192-XIV. Vidomosti Verkhovnoi Rady Ukrainy, 1999 r., № 51, st. 451 iz nastupnymy zminamy [Law of Ukraine on humanitarian aid, № 1192-XIV] (in Ukrainian).

> the evacuation of victims, it may be an interesting research opportunity to analyze issues on coordination of these two processes. It is also necessary to generate maturity models for humanitarian distribution chains or networks, which allow the selection and evaluation of logistics suppliers that contribute to obtain inputs, supplies, and equipment in an effective manner."[2]

The principles of charitable assistance are enshrined under clause 3.1. Decision of the Constitutional Court of Ukraine dated 28 October 2009, No. 28-rp/2009, which enumerates the following principles: *(i) selflessness* – indicating the provision of assistance for others without any own benefit; *(ii) voluntariness* – the activity carried out by one's own will and motivations upon a moral and ethical basis, without any coercion and interference from other persons and subjects of authority; *(iii) targeted orientation* – the presence of a specific goal served through the provision assistance to those who need it, within the areas and under the procedure defined by the law.[3] Pedro Arcos González and Rick Kye Gan rightfully observe that

> "Humanitarian aid raises ethical dilemmas of a different nature that have worsened in recent decades. The reasons for this are the deterioration of the international economic and geopolitical context, international relations based on states' return to unilateralism and protectionism, and the loss of the capacity of multilateral organizations to guarantee respect for international humanitarian law. These ethical dilemmas affect essential elements of humanitarian aid, such as an adequate selection of crises to which to provide aid and a selection of beneficiaries based on needs and not political or geostrategic criteria; neutrality against the aggressor or collaboration with governments that do not respect human rights; the allocation of resources and prioritization when they are limited; the safety and protection of aid recipients; cultural and political sensitivity and the recognition of local knowledge, skills, and capacities in responding to crises; the appropriateness, sustainability, and long-term impact of actions; security risks for aid personnel; transparency and accountability; the duty to report and civil activism in the face of the violation of human rights and the deterioration of respect for international humanitarian

---

2 Rojas Trejos *et al.*, 'Humanitarian aid distribution logistics with accessibility constraints: a systematic literature review', *Journal of Humanitarian Logistics and Supply Chain Management,* Vol. 13, 2023, Issue 1, pp. 26–41.

3 Decision of the Constitutional Court of Ukraine dated 28 October 2009, No. 28-rp/2009, at https://zakon.rada.gov.ua/laws/show/v028p710-09#Text.

> law; and the rights of affected groups and local communities in humanitarian decision-making and implementation."[4]

Ukrainian Professor V. Krikun examined the theoretical and semantic content, as well as the legal bases for the protection of *national interests,* mentioning that

> "the analysis of the use of the term 'security' shows that there is no security separated from human life, and the category of security is determined by all objective and subjective factors of human life, society and the state. It was concluded that the national interest determines the essence of both the domestic and foreign policy of any state, as it orients its priority goals in the system of international coexistence, which is determined primarily by the level of socio-economic development and the type of political system of the country, as well as historical traditions, mentality, the degree of security of one's sovereign rights through the system of national or collective security and its geographical location. It is in the national interests of Ukraine at this historical stage to do everything possible to become an active subject of regional politics and join the discussion of European security issues. And, in the end, all of the above will not make sense if the national interests of Ukraine do not include a significant, rapid and tangible increase in the standard of living of the country's citizens. This point is the most difficult to fulfill, because it involves the presence in politics of people with high personal qualities, who are able to put the interests of society above their own interests."[5]

In general, international organizations actively working in the field of humanitarian assistance in Ukraine are: *(i)* the UN Office for the Coordination of Humanitarian Affairs (OCHA): Humanitarian Coordinator in Ukraine[6] – the government's leading partner in coordinating actions with the international humanitarian community; the National Working Group on Humanitarian Issues. *(ii)* The International Red Cross Society (ICRS) in Ukraine. *(iii)* The World Health Organization (WHO) in Ukraine. *(iv)* The North Atlantic Treaty Organization (NATO) – one of the main areas of ac-

---

4 Pedro Arcos González & Rick Kye Gan, 'The Evolution of Humanitarian Aid in Disasters: Ethical Implications and Future Challenges', *Philosophies,* Vol. 9, Issue 3, 2024, p. 62.

5 Viacheslav Krikun, 'Legal principles of protection of national interests as the basis of ensuring national security of the state', *Actualni problem vitchiznjanoi jurisprudencii,* 2023/1, pp. 16–17.

6 *Ukraine: Summary for the humanitarian needs and response plan and regional refugee response plan,* UN Office for the Coordination of Humanitarian Affairs, January 2025.

tivity is the provision of humanitarian assistance to countries affected by natural and man-made disasters. *(v)* The Committee on Humanitarian Aid and Food Aid (COHAFA) is the main forum in the EU for discussing humanitarian aid policy, focusing on issues of implementation, effectiveness and coordination. *(vi)* The UNICEF Global, UNICEF Ukraine for every child – the organization protects and advocates for the rights and interests of Ukrainian children. *(vii)* The Office of the UN High Commissioner for Refugees in Ukraine (UNHCR) – provides support to the government and civil society organizations that meet the needs of IDPs through the provision of legal, material and social assistance. *(viii)* The USAID's Bureau of Humanitarian Assistance (BHA) – which provides life-saving humanitarian assistance, including the provision of food, water, shelter, emergency medical care, sanitation and hygiene, and essential nutrition services to the world's most vulnerable and hardest-to-reach the people. *(ix)* The EU – it initiates new programmes of humanitarian aid for Ukrainian citizens and refugees. (*e.g.*, EU4Ukraine,[7] the Horizon Europe Office in Ukraine is the result cooperation between the Directorate of the National Research Foundation of Ukraine, the Government of Ukraine and the European Commission).

3. The Humanitarian Aid Activities of the International Red Cross Society (ICRS) in Ukraine

In general, humanitarian organizations that provide humanitarian assistance can be categorized according to certain criteria, depending on their competence in protection and assistance. Based on these criteria, they can be grouped into organizations that have as their mission the international protection of affected persons and have the competence to analyze the situation in the country, state policies and procedures to protect the fundamental rights of citizens within the framework of international humanitarian law.

In 2024, over 660[8] humanitarian organizations provided assistance to 8.4 million people in Ukraine under the 2024 Humanitarian Needs and Response Plan, OCHA, which was 73% funded. By the end of January 2025, nearly 980 people had received assistance under the Autumn-Winter Re-

7 *See* at https://eu4ukraine.eu/.
8 *See* at https://response.reliefweb.int/ukraine/operatyvne-zvedennia.

sponse Plan, including support for heating needs and other non-food items specifically provided for winter.[9]

An important condition for ensuring the effectiveness of the international legal mechanism of humanitarian aid at the current stage is to optimize the legislation prescribing humanitarian principles under martial law in Ukraine. For example, Article 70 of the Protocol Additional to the Geneva Conventions[10] relating to the Protection of Victims of International Armed Conflicts sets forth the specifics of implementing an assistance operation, namely: *(i)* If the civilian population of any territory under the control of a Party to the conflict, other than occupied territory, is not adequately provided with the supplies mentioned in Article 69,[11] relief actions which are humanitarian and impartial in character and conducted without any adverse distinction shall be undertaken, subject to the agreement of the Parties concerned in such relief actions. Offers of such relief shall not be regarded as interference in the armed conflict or as unfriendly acts. In the distribution of relief consignments, priority shall be given to those persons, such as children, expectant mothers, maternity cases and nursing mothers, who, under the Fourth Convention or under this Protocol, are to be accorded privileged treatment or special protection. *(ii)* The Parties to the conflict and each High Contracting Party shall allow and facilitate rapid and unimpeded passage of all relief consignments, equipment and personnel provided in accordance with this Section, even if such assistance is destined for the civilian population of the adverse Party. *(iii)* The Parties to the conflict and each High Contracting Party which allow the passage of relief consignments, equipment and personnel in accordance with paragraph 2: *a)* shall have the right to prescribe the technical arrangements, including search, under which such passage is permitted; *b)* may make such permission conditional on the distribution of this assistance being made under the local supervision of a Protecting Power; *c)* shall, in no way whatsoever, divert relief consignments from the purpose for which they are intended nor delay their forwarding, except in cases of urgent necessity in the interest of the civilian population concerned. *(iv)* The Parties to the conflict shall ensure the protection of relief supplies and shall facilitate their rapid distribution. *(v)* The Parties to the

9 *Ukraine Winter Response Plan, October 2024 – March 2025,* UN Office for the Coordination of Humanitarian Affairs, July 2024.

10 Convention for the Amelioration of the Condition of the Wounded in Armies in the Field. Geneva, 22 August 1864, at https://ihl-databases.icrc.org/en/ihl-treaties/gc-1864/state-parties.

11 *See* at https://ihl-databases.icrc.org/en/ihl-treaties/api-1977/article-69.

conflict and each High Contracting Party concerned shall encourage and facilitate effective international coordination of relief operations referred to in paragraph 1.[12]

In Ukraine the ICRC provides international aid and international assistance to the vulnerable population of Ukraine, to prisoners of war, to missing persons, and others. According to official information provided by the Ukrainian Red Cross, the activities of the Ukrainian Red Cross Society (URCS) are based on Geneva Conventions of 12 August 1949 and three Protocols Additional thereto: Protocols I and II of 8 June 1977 and Protocol III of 8 December 2005. The URCS activities are regulated by the Law of Ukraine "On the Ukrainian Red Cross Society" of 2014, Law of Ukraine "On Emblems of the Red Cross, Red Crescent, and Red Crystal in Ukraine" of 2010, Decree of the President of Ukraine No 548/92 "On the Ukrainian Red Cross Society" of 28 October 1992, as well as the Charter of the Red Cross of Ukraine. The Society was recognized by the ICRC on 29 September 1993 as well as by the Decision of the IX session of the General Assembly of the International Federation of Red Cross and Red Crescent Societies, adopted by the collective membership of the International Federation of Red Cross and Red Crescent Societies. The Society's activities are carried out with the support and cooperation of state authorities and local self-government bodies, public organizations, corporate sector, as well as partners within the international movement: International Committee of the Red Cross (ICRC), International Federation of Red Cross and Red Crescent Societies (IFRC) and other National Societies.[13]

Exploring fundamental principles of the Red Cross and Red Crescent Movement, Varga noted the constraints of cooperation between a national society and authorities, providing the following example:

> "Access by authorities to documents of national societies or to personal information managed by them may be a sensitive issue, especially if these are related to persons who went missing during the war and the search for whom was initiated with the national societies, because in view of their independence and the sensitivity of the activity they are carrying out, tracing service documents are confidential, but at the same time national societies have to cooperate with their own authorities. In such cases states often accept the fact that the humanitarian mission served by the

12 The Geneva Conventions and their Commentaries, at https://www.icrc.org/en/law-and-policy/geneva-conventions-and-their-commentaries.
13 *See* at https://redcross.org.ua/en/about-urcs/mission/.

> tracing service is more important that the state's right of access, with the exception of certain priority cases like *e.g.*, criminal procedures [...] The fundamental principles thus serve the victim-centered, efficient operation of humanitarian organizations [...] We can say that the Movement and especially ICRC's practiced serve as guidance for many humanitarian organizations, even though they often divert from that practice."[14]

Since the start of the full-scale war, the Ukrainian Red Cross sent to the regions of Ukraine over 12,947,402 food and hygiene kits. Every day the staff and volunteers in logistical centers receive, sort, assemble, and send to the regions hundreds of tons of cargo containing food, hygienic products, medicines, water, bed linen and other essentials. 13,000,000 people received assistance from Ukrainian Red Cross Society, in the form of 12,974,402 humanitarian aid delivered to all regions of Ukraine, 326,000 people received assistance in the evacuation, 308,000 people learned how to provide first aid.[15]

In 2024, 174,366 medical and technical items were donated to support humanitarian demining activities across Ukraine. In 2024, 21 hospitals regularly received support in the form of medical equipment and medicines. 16,524 people received either cash assistance or agricultural equipment to conduct agricultural activities or livestock breeding to obtain a new source of income.

Due to the international armed conflict, hundreds of thousands of people face difficulties in accessing water in Ukraine. In 2024, access to essential services (water, heating, electricity and sanitation) was restored or improved for over 27 million people thanks to the ICRC's support to municipal enterprises. In December 2024, the ICRC provided 1,300 tons of solid fuel materials to medical institutions in Odessa, Mykolaiv and Kherson regions. On 7 January 2025, with the donation of the International Committee of the Red Cross, the Odessa region received a shipment of 40 tons of medicines and consumables delivered to 132 health care institutions, a modern laboratory, which will become the basis for the training of students who will be Ukraine's future prosthetists and orthotists.

URCS maintains a close relationship with the EU. In March 2023, Budapest hosted a two-day kick-off meeting for the #EU4Health programme par-

---

14 Reka Varga, 'International Red Cross and Red Crescent Movement and Humanitarian Activities for Migrants', *Hungarian Yearbook of International Law and European Law*, Vol. 4, Issue 1, 2016, p. 375.

15 *See* at https://redcross.org.ua/en/.

ticipants, focused on "Providing Quality and Timely Psychological First Aid (PFA) to the Population Affected by the Crisis in Ukraine". During the meeting, Anna Didenko, the Head of the Mental Health and Psychosocial Support Unit of the Ukrainian Red Cross Society (URCS) presented the key achievements in this area.

The main objectives of the EU4Health programme are: *(i)* providing quality and timely PFA to the affected population through the possibility of contacting the URCS information center; *(ii)* conducting webinars and psychoeducational sessions (providing information on how to overcome stress in conditions of uncertainty); *(iii)* offering psychosocial support to the URCS staff and volunteers, including training sessions to raise awareness of PFA and meetings to ensure the well-being of the entire team; *(iv)* cooperation with the public sector, communities, and representatives of organizations involved in emergency response.

With these goals in mind, the URCS implements related activities with the support of the European Commission. Countries participating in the programme include Denmark, the Czech Republic, Hungary, Poland, Romania, Slovakia, Bulgaria, Croatia, Germany, Switzerland, Iceland, and others.[16] The outstanding value of this project comes from restoring family links, from the first aid training in response to emergencies of mines and explosive remnants of war, mental health aid and psychological support, blood donation, social services and home care, humanitarian education, health promotion and disease prevention, advocacy and mobilization of the public, to name just a few.

4. The Stance of EU Member States towards the Humanitarian Situation in Ukraine

International aid provided by the EU to Ukraine is a mutually beneficial affair, and the EU stands firmly within a policy of granting military and humanitarian aid to Ukraine.[17] The interaction between entities implementing humanitarian aid and the coordination of their activities is important, and so is the development of new international norms to ensure control the implementation and effectiveness of international law in this area.

---

16 *See* at https://redcross.org.ua/en/uncategorized/2023/03/83259/.

17 *See e.g.* Humanitarian aid and civil protection, at https://eur-lex.europa.eu/summary/chapter/04.html.

For example, at the level of the EU, humanitarian aid and civil protection are part of the EU's external action enshrined in the Article 21 TEU in the context of the EU's values, rules and principles. Article 214 TFEU provides the basis for EU humanitarian aid operations and the establishment of the European Voluntary Humanitarian Aid Corps. According to Article 21(2)(g) TEU, the EU shall seek to assist populations, countries and regions affected by natural or man-made disasters. The competence for civil protection is based on Article 196 TFEU and is governed by Decision No 1313/2013/EU establishing a Union Civil Protection Mechanism. The European Commission's Directorate-General for Civil Protection and Humanitarian Aid Operations (ECHO) is not only a humanitarian aid donor, but is also responsible for coordinating civil protection operations at the EU level.

The rules for providing humanitarian aid, including its financing instruments, are set out in Council Regulation (EC) No 1257/96 (Humanitarian Aid Regulation). Humanitarian action, based on the fundamental humanitarian principles of humanity, neutrality, impartiality and independence, aims to provide special assistance, relief and protection to people in non-EU countries affected by natural or man-made disasters.

Based on data provided by EU Neighbors East, almost €1.1 billion has been made available in humanitarian aid projects to help civilians affected by the war in Ukraine. EU humanitarian assistance includes support for shelter, cash support, healthcare, food assistance, education, water and sanitation. The EU is also providing large-scale support to Ukraine itself to help overcome the crisis, including emergency macro-financial assistance of up to €25.2 billion in the form of loans, and an additional €620 million to Ukraine in budget support.[18]

From among the directives ensuring product quality, the following may be mentioned: Directive 85/347/EEC on liability for defective products, as amended by Directive 1999/34/EC,[19] as well as Directive 2001/95/EC on general product safety.[20] The general framework of humanitarian aid policy and its principles are set out in the European Consensus on Humanitarian

18 EU Neighbours East. What about humanitarian support? *See* at https://euneighbourseast.eu/news/explainers/eu-support-for-ukraine-from-sanctions-to-military-and-humanitarian-aid-how-is-the-eu-helping/.

19 Council Directive 85/374/EEC of 25 July 1985 on the approximation of the laws, regulations and administrative provisions of the Member States concerning liability for defective products.

20 Directive 2001/95/EC of the European Parliament and of the Council of 3 December 2001 on general product safety.

Aid Council Regulation (EC) No 1257/96[21] of 20 June 1996 concerning humanitarian aid (2007).[22]

Ukraine, as a welfare state, is signatory to the ICESCR and has recognized the right of everyone to an adequate standard of living for himself and his family, including adequate food, clothing and housing, and to the continuous improvement of living conditions. Together with the States parties to the ICESCR, it shall take appropriate measures to ensure the realization of this right, recognizing the importance of international cooperation based on free consent. Also, the States Parties, recognizing the fundamental right of everyone to freedom from hunger, take the necessary measures, individually and through international cooperation, including the implementation of specific programs, in order to: *(i)* to improve methods of production, storage and distribution of food through the wide use of technical and scientific knowledge, the dissemination of knowledge of the principles of nutrition and the improvement or reform of agricultural systems so as to achieve the most efficient development and use of natural resources, *(ii)* to ensure an equitable distribution of world food supplies according to the needs and taking into account the problems of countries, both importing and exporting products.

In 2024, the humanitarian community, with the participation of donor countries, including Denmark, provided assistance to at least 7.2 million Ukrainians. In 2024, Denmark allocated 6 million euros to restore Ukraine's energy infrastructure damaged by Russian attacks. As part of the response plan for the autumn-winter period 2024–2025, Denmark contributed to funding measures to support 1.8 million people in need of assistance during the winter. This includes providing heat, temporary housing and other necessary resources.

According to public sources, as of May 2024, the United 24 programme raised $650 million from donors in 110 countries. In December 2024, the platform reported its highest monthly fundraising total in its history, over 160 million US dollars, which was half of its annual fundraising for that year. In February 2025, the total amount of donations exceeded 1 billion US dollars, but this already includes data for January 2025. Thus, for 2024, it can be assumed that the platform raised about 800–850 million US dollars, taking into account the increase until the end of the year.

---

21 European Consensus on Humanitarian Aid, at https://civil-protection-humanitarian-aid.ec.europa.eu/who/european-consensus_en.

22 *See e.g.* https://civil-protection-humanitarian-aid.ec.europa.eu/what/humanitarian-aid_en.

The charitable project 'United 24' funds were directed to key needs: *(i)* medical assistance (*e.g.*, the purchase of armored ambulances 'Gurkha'); *(ii)* reconstruction of infrastructure, in particular bridges (in October 2023, the reconstruction of the 19th bridge in the Mykolaiv region was completed, with the process continuing in 2024); *(iii)* support for the Armed Forces of Ukraine, in particular the purchase of equipment and technology.

As of the end of 2024, about 150,000 declarations of goods recognized as humanitarian aid had been registered, covering approximately 123.2 million units of goods (according to data published in early 2025). The majority of the shipments were delivered by charitable organizations (63.94% of the total volume).[23]

The international legal mechanism for providing humanitarian aid can be defined through the following approaches: *(i)* in the axiomatic sense, humanitarian aid is a legal phenomenon that, according to the classification of values, has a special subjective element; *(ii)* in the praxeological sense, humanitarian aid is of human nature, promoting the development of human potential; *(iii)* in practical and functional terms – this is the daily activities of competent persons with the aim of creating decent conditions for people finding themselves in emergency circumstances.[24] The complementary nature of the humanitarian aid should also be emphasized. This character is well reflected in its interdisciplinary nature and the fact that it is an institution connected with several branches of law: international humanitarian law, international human rights law and EU law.

5. Concluding Remarks

In conclusion, humanitarian aid activities in Ukraine are connected to the sphere of activity of non-governmental organizations. Their activity is implemented at different levels (international, national and local), and under different legal regimes of civil-military cooperation – the legal regime during wartime (for states participating in armed conflicts) and in peacetime (for foreign donors). Ukraine does not have the ability to independently dispose over a budget to restore the damaged infrastructure of the regions. In-

23 *See e.g.* https://unity.gov.ua/2023/08/15/gumanitarne-reaguvannya-v-ukrayini-pidsumky-pershogo-pivrichchya-2023-roku/.

24 Ielyzaveta Lvova, 'International-legal mechanism of humanitarian aid as an interdisciplinary instrument for the protection of human rights', *Bulletin of Mariupol State University*, 2024/28, pp. 79–86.

deed, the scale of efforts that must be made to restore such infrastructure requires joint financing and other activities.

An analysis of international legislation on the provision of international humanitarian aid and assistance indicates its fragmentation and the lack of conceptual principles and norms to solve existing problems (*e.g.*, humanitarian access and humanitarian logistics). To solve these problems, it is crucial to improve the system of forecasting (foresight), planning, and coordination of international humanitarian aid; in this particular case, the support provided in Ukraine. In addition, there is a need for a reliable system of monitoring the volume of the provided support. Harmonizing the legal regulation of international humanitarian aid with humanitarian logistical standards is considered as a challenge for future integration of Ukraine to the EU. Nevertheless, Ukraine implements the elements of EU humanitarian policy in balance with European trade policy. Such engagement help provide governments and non-governmental humanitarian organizations with relevant information on the socio-economic situation and security in Ukraine.

Part III
– Developments in European law

The 'Price' of the Rule of Law

Financial Issues Arising from the Change in Higher Education Models in Hungary in the Proceedings of the CJEU

*Laura Gyeney – Maja Szabó**

Abstract

On 15 December 2022, the Council of the European Union adopted Implementing Decision 2022/2506, setting out measures to protect the EU budget against breaches of the rule of law in Hungary. Perhaps the most notable aspect of this Implementing Decision is the prohibition on the Commission entering into legal commitments with Hungarian public interest asset management foundations (known as "KEKVAs") and legal entities maintained by them. As a direct consequence of this sanction, Hungarian higher education institutions that have changed their model and are maintained by KEKVAs have been excluded from EU mobility (Erasmus+) and research (Horizon Europe) programmes. Six Hungarian higher education institutions have filed annulment actions against the Implementing Decision with the General Court. This study examines the well-foundedness of the legal arguments presented in these actions and their likely chances of success, based on the case law of the CJEU.

Keywords: Conditionality Regulation, KEKVA, model changing, higher education, rule of law

---

* Laura Gyeney: associate professor of law, Pázmány Péter Catholic University, Budapest, gyeney.laura@jak.ppke.hu.
Maja Szabó: law student, Pázmány Péter Catholic University, Budapest, majera12@gmail.com.

1. Introduction

On 15 December 2022, the Council of the EU adopted Implementing Decision 2022/2506, setting out measures to protect the EU budget against breaches of the rule of law in Hungary[1] (hereinafter: Implementing Decision). This decision has significant political and economic consequences for several Hungarian higher education institutions. Due to concerns raised by certain EU institutions regarding Hungary's compliance with the fundamental principles of the rule of law, the Implementing Decision has suspended a number of EU funds allocated to Hungary.[2] According to Article 2(2) of the Implementing Decision, the Commission shall not enter into legal commitments with any public interest asset management foundation (hereinafter: KEKVA) established under Hungarian Act IX of 2021[3] (hereinafter: KEKVA Act) or any legal entity maintained by such a KEKVA. As a direct consequence of this sanction, Hungarian higher education institutions that have changed their model and are maintained by KEKVAs have been excluded from EU mobility (Erasmus+) and research (Horizon Europe) cooperation. The Implementing Decision affects a significant number of Hungarian higher education institutions, including their lecturers, researchers and students, and its indirect consequences negatively impact the Hungarian higher education sector as a whole. Six Hungarian higher education institutions subsequently initiated proceedings before the General Court to annul the Implementing Decision; these proceedings are ongoing at the time of finalizing this manuscript.

This paper examines the potential legal consequences of these actions and other possible legal solutions.[4]

1 Council Implementing Decision (EU) 2022/2506 of 15 December 2022 on measures for the protection of the Union budget against breaches of the principles of the rule of law in Hungary.

2 Implementing Decision, Article 2(1).

3 Act IX of 2021 on public interest asset management foundations performing public duty (hereinafter: KEKVA Act).

4 This study is a shortened, edited and revised version of Maja Szabó's OTDK (National Scientific Competition for Law Students) thesis, which was presented in March 2025, and awarded first place. The OTDK thesis was supervised by Laura Gyeney.

2. Background to the Adoption of the Implementing Decision

2.1. A Brief Overview of the Model Change

To date, 21 higher education institutions (the majority of the Hungarian universities and colleges) in Hungary have changed their operational models.[5] The Hungarian Government's stated aim is to increase the competitiveness of higher education by making the management framework more flexible. The government's vision is to provide high-quality education and help young people in higher education to find employment more easily upon graduating.[6]

In contrast to the approach of the previous constitution (was in force until 2012), the Fundamental Law distinguishes between management autonomy and the autonomy granted to higher education institutions.[7] According to Article X(3) of the Fundamental Law, "The Government shall, within the framework of the Acts, lay down the rules governing the management of public institutes of higher education and shall supervise their management." However, the (constitutional) legal basis for the model change is not Article X(3), but rather Article 38(6) of the Fundamental Law, which came into force with the Ninth Amendment to the Fundamental Law (2020) and established constitutional protection for the KEKVA. Higher education institutions that have undergone a model change under the provisions of the KEKVA Act are no longer considered "state institutions" and are therefore excluded from the scope of Article X(3) of the Fundamental Law.

According to the relevant provisions of the KEKVA Act,[8] "a board of trustees comprising not more than five natural persons shall be responsible for the management of the foundation."[9] According to the text of the Act in force at the time of its adoption, "board of trustees and supervisory board mem-

5 Although the Budapest University of Technology (*Budapesti Műszaki és Gazdaságtudományi Egyetem*, BME) is formally a model-changing university, it continues to operate as a company (under the aegis of BME Fenntartó Zrt.) rather than a foundation.

6 Norbert Kis, 'Esszé a magyar felsőoktatási modellváltás kockázatairól és mellékhatásairól', *in* Attila Barna & Péter Krisztián Zachar (eds.), '*Titkos cikkek az örök békéhez: Ünnepi tanulmányok a 70 éves Fülöp Mihály tiszteletére*', Ludovika Egyetemi Kiadó, Budapest, 2023, p. 207.

7 *"Egyetemi demokrácia" – Jogi háttértanulmány*, Eötvös Károly Intézet, Budapest, n.d., p. 6,

8 For more details, *see* Gergely Cseh-Zelina & Zsófia Kincső Varga, '*A felsőoktatási modellváltás, valamint az újonnan létrejövő közérdekű vagyonkezelő alapítványok főbb aspektusai.*' Publicationes Universitatis Miskolcinensis, Sectio Juridica et Politica, 2022/2, pp. 77–95.

9 Section 6(1) of the KEKVA Act.

bership shall not be incompatible with any further employment relationship, or employment-related relationship and any other position or office under an other Act."[10] The KEKVA Act also enabled the boards of trustees (and supervisory boards) to decide on the recall of members and the filling of vacancies for whatever reason; this power was not granted to the Government, but to the boards of trustees themselves.[11]

2.2. The Path to the Adoption of the Implementing Decision

Article 2 TEU enshrines the rule of law as a value of the EU. This article forms the basis for Regulation 2092/2020, also known as the Rule of Law Conditionality Regulation (hereinafter: Conditionality Regulation).[12] The Conditionality Regulation explicitly permits the application of financial penalties, including the suspension of payments or financial corrections▪, for breaches of the rule of law in a Member State. These penalties are applied when it is established that the breach affects, or poses a sufficiently direct risk of affecting, the sound financial management of the EU budget or the protection of the Union's financial interests.[13]

On 24 November 2021, the Commission sent Hungary a request for information based on Article 6(4) of the Conditionality Regulation. One of the issues concerned public interest asset management foundations.[14] The Commission was concerned that the rules on public procurement and conflict of interest rules were not being applied and that there was a "lack of transparency regarding the management of funds by these foundations."[15] Following the Commission's observations, Hungary amended Section 5(1) of Act CXLIII of 2015 on Public Procurement by Act XXIX of 2022, clarifying that KEKVAs are also subject to public procurement procedures.[16] The dispute between the Commission and Hungary has since mainly concerned and still concerns the conflict of interest rules for the boards of trus-

10 Id. Section 15(1).
11 Id. Section 7(4).
12 Regulation (EU, Euratom) 2020/2092 of the European Parliament and of the Council of 16 December 2020 on a general regime of conditionality for the protection of the Union budget.
13 Conditionality Regulation, Article 4(1).
14 Implementing Decision, Recitals (1) and (2).
15 Id. Recital (11).
16 Act CXLIII of 2015, Section 5(1)(f).

tees of public interest trusts.[17] For this reason (and, according to the wording of the Implementing Decision, *solely* for this reason), a general prohibition of legal commitments with public interest trusts was declared in accordance with Article 2(2) of the Implementing Decision.[18]

Prior to the adoption of the Implementing Decision, the Hungarian Government replaced the previously cited Section 15(1) of the KEKVA Act, which contains the conflict of interest rules, with a new Section 15(3). The new Section clearly states that

> "a person who cannot, or can only to a limited extent, perform their tasks in an impartial, objective and unbiased manner due to an economic or other personal interest or circumstance (including family, emotional, political or national reasons), shall refrain from any activity that could be contrary to the interests of the foundation, its members or donors."[19]

Anyone with a conflict of interest shall not participate in the decision-making process. Act XXIX of 2022 does not introduce additional conflict of interest rules under the KEKVA Act. Instead, members of the board of trustees of public interest trusts that are subject to the KEKVA Act are excluded from participating in decision-making processes that give rise to a conflict of interest under the laws governing the legal status of certain Hungarian state institutions.[20] This means that, while the Commission deemed it necessary to declare a conflict of interest based on legal status, the Government opted for a case-by-case approach. This also means that the Government and the Parliament did not formally comply with the Commission's requirements. In terms of substance, however, it is questionable whether the adopted amendments appropriately address the Commission's concerns regarding conflict of interest and, if not, whether the complete prohibition of legal commitments to public interest trusts and legal entities maintained by them under the KEKVA Act can be considered a necessary and proportionate measure.

---

17 Implementing Decision, Recital (43).

18 Id. Recital (62).

19 Established by Section 20 of Act XXIX of 2022, in force from 13 October 2022.

20 *See* Section 225(2a) of Act CXXV of 2018 on Government Administration and Section 51(10a) of Act CVII of 2019 on Bodies of Special Legal Status and on the Legal Status of their Employees.

2.3. EU Powers in the Field of Education

As the EU can only act within the limits of the powers conferred on it by the Member States,[21] the existence of these powers must be considered when examining all EU acts. The EU has only limited competence in the area of education policy. In the field of education, "the Union shall have competence to carry out actions to support, coordinate or supplement the actions of the Member States."[22] Article 165(1) TFEU states that the EU shall contribute to the development of quality education by encouraging cooperation between Member States and, if necessary, by supporting and supplementing their actions. This shall be done while fully respecting "the responsibility of the Member States for the content of teaching and the organization of education systems and their cultural and linguistic diversity."

Accordingly, specific education policy issues fall under the competence of Member States. However, the exercise of these competences necessarily impacts other areas of EU competence,[23] as illustrated by the *lex CEU* case.[24] According to the facts of the case, Hungary amended Act CCIV of 2011 on National Higher Education (hereinafter: Higher Education Act) by Act XXV of 2017 (the so-called *lex CEU*), by introducing a licensing system for the foreign higher education institutions operating in Hungary.[25] Although the amendment formally covered all foreign higher education institutions operating in Hungary, the Government did not conceal the fact that it aimed to review the operation of the Central European University (CEU).[26] Although the law ostensibly regulated matters relating to the 'organization' of individual higher education institutions, the CJEU ruled that national rules gover-

21 We interpret "conferred powers" in a broad sense, including all powers derived directly or indirectly from the Treaties, such as the external powers included therein. For more information, *see* László Knapp, 'A beleértett külső hatáskörök doktrínájának kodifikálása és az EU-Szingapúr szabadkereskedelmi megállapodás.' *Jog-Állam-Politika,* 2019/1, pp. 79–100.

22 Article 6 TFEU.

23 In the context of the right to free movement, *see* Ildikó Bartha, *Felsőoktatás az Európai Unióban: tagállami szabályozás és integrációs kötelezettségek,* Debreceni Egyetemi Kiadó, Debrecen, 2019, pp. 75–98.

24 Judgment of 6 October 2020, *Case C-66/18, Commission v Hungary,* ECLI:EU:C:2020:792.

25 Dóra Lovas, 'Lex CEU, avagy a szabad oktatáshoz való jog kérdése.' *Közjavak,* 2017/1, pp. 5–9.

26 László Valki, 'A lex CEU és a nemzetközi jog normái', *in* Attila Menyhárd & István Varga (eds.), *350 éves az Eötvös Loránd Tudományegyetem Állam- és Jogtudományi Kara: a jubileumi év konferenciasorozatának tanulmányai.* ELTE Eötvös, Budapest, 2018, pp. 1215–1224.

ning the operation of such institutions fall within the scope of the freedom of establishment under Article 49 TFEU, in so far as "that requirement applies to a higher education institution that has its seat in a Member State other than Hungary and offers education or training for remuneration in Hungary."[27] According to the settled case law of the CJEU, "any measure which prohibits, impedes or renders less attractive the exercise of the freedom of establishment must be regarded as a restriction on that freedom."[28] This also means that, where a matter falling within a Member State's competence in education policy also falls within the EU's exclusive or shared competence, the compatibility of legislation with EU law will not be assessed within the framework of the education policy competence. The CJEU also found that the Charter of Fundamental Rights could be invoked, since the legislation concerned freedom of establishment.

However, the *lex CEU* infringement proceedings were specific due to its *cross-border* element; therefore, we could not speak of a purely internal situation. In the case of the KEKVA Act, however, no such cross-border element can be identified.

3. *Framework for Proceedings before the General Court*

3.1. General Characteristics of Actions for Annulment Challenging the Implementing Decision

Following the adoption of the Implementing Decision, *Debreceni Egyetem* (University of Debrecen) initiated annulment proceedings before the General Court under Article 263 TFEU on 2 March 2023. A few days later, on 13 March 2023, five other universities – the *Állatorvostudományi Egyetem* (University of Veterinary Medicine), the *Dunaújvárosi Egyetem* (University of Dunaújváros), the *Miskolci Egyetem* (University of Miskolc), the *Óbudai Egyetem* (University of Óbuda), and the *Semmelweis Egyetem* (Semmelweis University) – did the same. These six cases can be divided into three groups based on their main features.

27 *Case C-66/18, Commission v Hungary,* para. 163.
28 Id. para. 167.

No.	Case number	Applicant	Defendant(s)	The contested (legal) act	Interim measure
1	T-115/23	*Debreceni Egyetem*	Council	Article 2(2)	yes
2	T-132/23	*Óbudai Egyetem*	Council and Commission	Article 2(2) in part + additional acts	not
	T-133/23	*Állatorvostudományi Egyetem*			
	T-139/23	*Miskolci Egyetem*			
	T-140/23	*Dunaújvárosi Egyetem*			
3	T-138/23	*Semmelweis Egyetem*	Council	Article 2(2)	not

Edited by the authors based on the information on the CJEU's website.

For the analysis of each procedure, we have used documents published on the Court's and Semmelweis University's website (in English), which were made public by the applicant.[29] The actions seek the annulment of Article 2(2) of the Implementing Decision, its entirety or in part (*i.e.,* the phrase "any legal entity maintained by such public interest trust"). Nevertheless, these applications have an equivalent impact on the applicants' legal position.[30]

3.2. Request for Interim Measures

Only the *Debreceni Egyetem,* one of the six higher education institutions, submitted a request for interim measures, asking for the Implementing Decision to be suspended. The university justified its claim of serious and irreparable damage by stating that it would lose funding for EU projects and be prohibited from participating in them. This would affect its reputation, academic prestige, and financial situation.[31] However, the President of the General Court dismissed the application for interim measures, considering

29 The relevant documents are available at https://semmelweis.hu/english/2023/03/application-for-partial-annulment-in-respect-of-council-implementing-decision-eu-2022–2506/.

30 Debreceni Egyetem has requested total annulment; Állatorvostudományi Egyetem, Dunaújvárosi Egyetem, Miskolci Egyetem and Óbudai Egyetem have requested partial annulment; and Semmelweis Egyetem has requested partial and total annulment in part or in whole.

31 Order of the President of the General Court of 1 June 2023, Case T-115/23 R, Debreceni Egyetem v Council of the European Union.

that the damage claimed by the University was essentially financial and could be remedied subsequently in the absence of exceptional circumstances.[32] Furthermore, the University did not claim that the Implementing Decision would engender its existence.[33] The President of the General Court dismissed the University's further arguments regarding non-material damage rather cynically. He argued that the Implementing Decision does not prohibit or restrict the University's academic activities,[34] and that an institution's involvement in a research proposal is not solely dependent on EU funding; consortium partners also consider other aspects.[35]

The findings of the order are undoubtedly correct in form and are in line with the case law of the CJEU. Following a successful action for annulment, there is also no doubt that the applicant institutions can claim compensation for the material damage they suffered due to the Implementing Decision. However, by calling into question the direct causal link between academic performance and the research proposals, as well as the prohibition imposed by the Implementing Decision, the order also highlights the applicants' potential difficulties in proving their case in a possible future action for damages. It is important to note that it is no longer sufficient to prove elements of damage and a causal link, as was the case with the interim measure.

In this context, it is interesting to note that after submitting the actions, the Hungarian Academy of Sciences conducted a thorough questionnaire survey to assess the impact of the Implementing Decision on the Hungarian scientific and research community, as well as the situation arising from the suspension.[36] The survey reveals that the leaders of foreign consortia in EU research tenders view Hungarian universities and research institutions with uncertainty. Perhaps the most interesting finding of the survey is that the Implementing Decision has also made things more difficult for non-model-changing higher education institutions, as there is a public perception within the EU that contracting with 'Hungarian' universities is banned.[37]

32 Id. para. 23.
33 Id. para. 25.
34 Id. para. 30.
35 Id. para. 32.
36 Júlia Koltay *et al.*, '*A fiatal kutatóknak káros az európai uniós forrásokból történő kizárás.*' Fiatal Kutatók Akadémiája, 2024, at https://fka.mta.hu/wp-content/uploads/EU_suspension_report_HUN_final_0610.pdf.
37 Id. p. 3.

4. *Assessment of the Arguments Raised in the Proceedings before the General Court*

The applicant model-changing higher education institutions set forth several legal arguments explaining how the Implementing Decision is flawed in form and substance. While only *Semmelweis Egyetem* made its detailed legal reasoning publicly available, summaries of the other applicant's actions are also available on the Court's website.

4.1. Formal (Procedural) Arguments

In our point of view, formal arguments are those that do not require an examination of the substance of the Implementing Decision; they relate solely to its adoption or the existence of its mandatory elements.

4.1.1. Lack of Adequate Reasoning

According to Article 6(9) of the Conditionality Regulation, when proposing an implementing decision, the proposal "shall set out the specific grounds and evidence on which the Commission based its findings". According to Article 4(1), an implementing decision may be adopted if "breaches of the principles of the rule of law in a Member State affect or seriously risk affecting the sound financial management of the Union budget or the protection of the financial interests of the Union in a sufficiently direct way". Consequently, the Implementing Decision should have included a statement of reasons explaining why the sound financial management of the Union budget or the financial interests of the Union are affected in the case of legal persons covered by the KEKVA Act. This is particularly pertinent given that the Government had already responded to the Commission's comments on public procurement procedures and amended Hungarian legislation in line with the Commission's legal expectations. In the context of higher education institutions changing their operational model, the only legal issue debated was conflicts of interest among the members of the boards of trustees. Notably, at the time the Implementing Decision was adopted, the KEKVA Act already stipulated the exclusion of individuals with conflicts of interest from decision-making processes (rather than a general exclusion, as the Commission had suggested).

According to the case law of the CJEU, the obligation to provide reasons goes beyond merely checking whether the EU act in question is reasoned. Rather, the statement of reasons must be detailed enough to withstand judicial review. In other words, it must be able "to produce and set out clearly and unequivocally the basic facts which had to be taken into account as the basis of the contested measures of the act and on which the exercise of their discretion depended."[38]

In the present case, the Implementing Decision concludes that Hungary has not met the Commission's expectations regarding conflicts of interest and therefore "a serious risk for the Union budget remains and can best be addressed by a prohibition on entering into new legal commitments with any public interest trust and any entity maintained by them under any programme under direct or indirect management."[39] The Implementing Decision does not explain why the serious risk to the EU budget remains unchanged despite Hungary's compliance with the Commission's recommendations on public procurement and the tightening of conflict of interest rules on trusteeship. Nor does it explain why this risk justifies a total ban on contracting with organizations covered by the KEKVA Act. However, as the Implementing Decision contains a statement of reasons for sanctioning the entities covered by the KEKVA Act which is open to judicial review, it is more likely that the General Court will ultimately reject the applicants' argument.

4.1.2. Misuse of Powers

Semmelweis Egyetem's action highlights power abuse as a separate issue.[40] According to the action, the sanctioning of universities subject to the KEKVA Act is merely a way for Hungary to relinquish its position in the dispute with EU institutions over the rule of law.[41]

From a purely formal point of view, we do not consider that there was a misuse of powers in this case. The Commission had already made the Government aware of the issues relating to public interest trusts in its writ-

38 Judgment of 8 December 2020, *Case C-620/18, Hungary v Parliament,* ECLI:EU:C:2020:1001, para. 116.
39 Implementing Decision, Recital (62).
40 Article 263 TFEU.
41 Action brought on 13 March 2023, *Case T-138/23, Semmelweis Egyetem v Council,* pp. 47–49, para. 172.

ten notification of 27 April 2022.[42] Therefore, the debate on the legal status of universities covered by the KEKVA Act formed an integral part of the process from the outset. The combination of personal (conflict of interest) and financial (procurement) issues undoubtedly increases the risk of damage to the Union's financial interests. While the partial resolution of the legal issues identified by the Commission in Hungary may render the direct threat to the Union's financial interests debatable, it does not negate the potential threat to higher education institutions covered by the KEKVA Act.

4.1.3. Failure to Involve Higher Education Institutions Undergoing Model Change in the Process

At first glance, one of the strongest formal arguments put forward by higher education institutions is that the Commission (and the Council) failed to consult them when adopting the Implementing Decision. This argument features in all of the universities' applications. *Semmelweis Egyetem* cites it as a breach of the right to be heard and the right to defense,[43] the *Debreceni Egyetem* cites it as a failure to consult,[44] the *Állatorvostudományi Egyetem,* the *Dunaújvárosi Egyetem,* the *Miskolci Egyetem* and the *Óbudai Egyetem* cite it as a (presumably) violation of essential procedural requirements.

In *Front Polisario,*[45] the General Court ruled that the right to be heard before the adoption of individual measures that adversely affect an individual, as outlined in Article 41(1)(a) of the Charter of Fundamental Rights, applies only to such measures. Therefore, the General Court must determine whether the Implementing Decision can be considered a general or individual measure. When rejecting the Council's objections regarding admissibility, the General Court held that the Implementing Decision "has general effect since it applies to all the economic operators concerned."[46] This statement suggests that, when deciding the cases' merits, the General Court will probably treat the Implementing Decision as a source of law with gene-

42 Implementing Decision, Recital (2).
43 Action brought on 13 March 2023, *Case T-138/23, Semmelweis Egyetem v Council,* paras. 118, 140, and 147.
44 Action brought on 2 March 2023, *Case T-115/23, Debreceni Egyetem v Council,* sixth plea in law.
45 Judgment of 10 December 2015, *Case T-512/12, Front Polisario,* ECLI:EU:T:2015:953, para. 132.
46 Order of the General Court of 4 April 2024, *Case T-115/23, Debreceni Egyetem,* ECLI: EU:T:2024:208, para. 36.

ral effect. Consequently, the General Court will probably conclude that the procedure for adopting the Implementing Decision did not legally require the involvement of public interest foundations (trusts) under the KEKVA Act. This is true even though the Implementing Decision in this case defines the relevant persons in a taxative manner. However, this definition is not in the Implementing Decision itself, but in the Hungarian law – specifically, Annex 1 to the KEKVA Act. The Implementing Decision is a source of law with general effect because, under the Conditionality Regulation, implementing decisions are always addressed to a Member State. Designating a Member State as the addressee necessarily gives the act general scope.

However, for the sake of completeness, it should be noted that, while the applicant universities' legal argument is morally understandable; it is common knowledge that the change in the higher education model affected the legal status of higher education institutions. Nevertheless, the KEKVA Act names the maintainers of the applicants (*i.e.,* the public interest foundations themselves), not the applicant universities. In our view, this distinction is so vital that, for procedural reasons, the General Court will probably not need to address the infringement of the applicants' "right to be heard."[47]

4.1.4. Arguments on Lack of Competence

In its application, *Debreceni Egyetem* set out several arguments to demonstrate that the Implementing Decision's provision relating to the KEKVA Act falls outside the EU's area of competence.

(i) Firstly, "the tasks of guaranteeing the functioning of higher-education establishments and designing the framework in which they operate – fall within the exclusive competence of the Member States."[48] This means that the EU does not have the power to define it.[49] *Debreceni Egyetem* essentially repeats this argument when it claims that "the TFEU did not confer on the

---

47 If the General Court were to conclude that the Implementing Decision is not of general application, the failure to include the individually concerned public interest trusts in the proceedings would lead to the annulment of the Implementing Decision. This would be the case if the KEKVAs had initiated the proceedings. Judgment of 3 July 2014, *Joined Cases C-129/12 and C-130/13, Kamino International,* ECLI:EU:C:2014:2041, paras. 28–31.

48 Action brought on 2 March 2023, *Case T-115/23, Debreceni Egyetem v Council,* second plea of law.

49 Tamás Kende *et al., 'Európai közjog és politika',* Wolters Kluwer, Budapest, 2018, p. 222.

European Union, in the area of policy relating to education and scientific research"[50] and asserts that the article on freedom of scientific research in the Charter of Fundamental Rights is infringed.[51] *(ii)* On the other hand, *Debreceni Egyetem* claims that the contested element of the Implementing Decision does not contribute the high level of education and training; rather, it explicitly contradicts this goal,[52] and fails to contribute to the development of quality education.[53] *(iii)* Finally, *Debreceni Egyetem* also claims that the Implementing Decision (indirectly) attacks Hungary's (different) autonomous legal system and legal traditions.[54]

With regard to competences in education policy, the aforementioned *lex CEU* case clearly shows that if a matter falls within the competence of the EU and concerns other matters within the scope of supporting (complementary) competence, the "stronger" competence framework rule will prevail. Regarding the substantive arguments of *Debreceni Egyetem,* the General Court is likely to conclude that the Implementing Decision does not address the substance of education and training in any way, nor its financial aspects: it only regulates issues relating to the eligibility of specific EU funds. The argument concerning Hungary's different legal tradition does not seem convincing. This is not only because the existence of the KEKVA system can hardly be considered part of Hungary's national identity or historical constitution (as it is a legal institution of only a few years' standing without precedent), but also because the CJEU only accepts similar references by Member States in exceptional cases.[55]

4.1.5. Specific Case of Misuse of Powers: Only the CJEU Has the Power to Declare an Infringement

Finally, the question of why the Implementing Decision was adopted can be considered a formal argument, as it is also an argument found in the univer-

50 Action brought on 2 March 2023, *Case T-115/23, Debreceni Egyetem v Council,* seventh plea of law.
51 Id. fifteenth plea of law.
52 Id. eighth plea of law.
53 Id. thirteenth plea of law.
54 Id. tenth plea of law.
55 Marcel Szabó, 'Összenő, ami összetartozik? A tagállami állampolgárság és az uniós polgárság viszonyának jövője', *in* Laura Gyeney & Marcel Szabó (eds.) '*Az uniós polgárság jelene és jövője: úton az egységes európai állampolgárság felé?*', ORAC, Budapest, 2023, p. 186.

sities' application.[56] "The purpose of the Conditionality Regulation is to protect the Union budget from the effects of breaches of the rule of law in a Member State in a sufficiently direct way",[57] and not to penalize such breaches.[58] Breaches of the rule of law are governed by separate procedures, particularly those under Article 7 TEU.[59] By contrast, the Implementing Decision establishes a breach of the rule of law and therefore imposes legal consequences. This is due to the fact that it is based on a finding of a breach, rather than a presumption of one, in order to protect financial interests.[60] In this context, one could argue that the Implementing Decision exceeds the scope of the Conditionality Regulation as enabling legislation.

In our view, the wording of the Implementing Decision suggests that the Council found a breach of the rule of law by Hungary based on the Commission's proposal. However, the Conditionality Regulation does not empower the Council to make such a finding. While it is undoubtedly true that the 'finding' of a breach is indeed contained only in the preamble to the Implementing Decision, the purpose of the preamble in EU law is not merely symbolic; rather, it demonstrates that the act in question was adopted through the proper application of powers.

However, the General Court's decision in favor of the applicants could easily be interpreted as meaning that Hungary did not violate the rule of law. Therefore, it seems unlikely that the General Court will base a favorable decision on this argument.

---

56 Action brought on 2 March 2023, *Case T-115/23, Debreceni Egyetem v Council,* Nineteenth plea of law; Állatorvostudományi Egyetem, Dunaújvárosi Egyetem, Miskolci Egyetem and Óbudai Egyetem, first plea of law. This plea is not raised in the action brought by Semmelweis Egyetem.

57 *Case C-156/21, Hungary v Parliament and Council,* para. 119.

58 Conditionality Regulation, Article 3.

59 Erzsébet Szalayné Sándor, 'Az Európai Unióról szóló Szerződés 7. cikke Nizza előtt és után – az Ausztriával szembeni szankciók háttere és következményei.' *Európai Jog,* 2001/3, pp. 3–8.

60 Implementing Decision, in particular Recital (22) as regards KEKVAs. Recital (60) is even clearer.

4.2. Substantive Arguments

4.2.1. Lack of Factual Basis

In their applications, both *Semmelweis Egyetem*[61] and *Debreceni Egyetem*[62] referred to the fact that no serious risk to the financial interests of the Union could be identified with regard to the KEKVA Act. Under Article 5(1)(a) of the Conditionality Regulation, the adoption of implementing decisions may explicitly refer to "governmental entities". However, under Article 2(b), a governmental entity is defined as including not only national authorities, but also Member States organizations within the meaning of Article 2(42) of Regulation (EC) No 1605/2002 of the European Parliament and of the Council (Financial Regulation) 2018/1046,[63] which includes the KEKVAs. This means that the Implementing Decision was correct in designating Hungary as the addressee of the legal prohibition of legal commitments for KEKVAs under the KEKVA Act, while remaining within the legal borders of the Conditionality Regulation. Conversely, if the public interest foundations under the KEKVA Act are considered to be 'governmental bodies' (as the Implementing Decision does following the Conditionality Regulation), it is at least difficult to see why government-linked political actors' involvement in these KEKVAs operations poses a legal problem. However, as the Implementing Decision remains within the framework of the enabling legislation, it is unlikely to be invalid for this reason. The question of the invalidity of the Conditionality Regulation could still be raised, though.[64]

Both *Semmelweis Egyetem*[65] and *Debreceni Egyetem*[66] also argued that none of their public interest foundations have any individuals on their

61 Action brought on 13 March 2023, *Case T-138/23, Semmelweis Egyetem v Council*, para. 112.

62 The sixteenth and nineteenth pleas in law relied on by Debreceni Egyetem in its action.

63 "Member State organisation means an entity established in a Member State as a public law body, or as a body governed by private law entrusted with a public service mission and provided with adequate financial guarantees from the Member State." Recital (42).

64 Although Állatorvostudományi Egyetem, Dunaújvárosi Egyetem, Miskolci Egyetem and Óbudai Egyetem have raised plea of illegality against the Conditionality Regulation, they have done so because the Conditionality Regulation does not allow for individual exemptions to be granted.

65 Action brought on 13 March 2023, *Case T-138/23, Semmelweis Egyetem v Council*, paras. 108–109.

66 Action brought on 2 March 2023, *Case T-115/23, Debreceni Egyetem v Council*, Sixteenth plea of law.

boards of trustees who would be affected by a dispute over a conflict of interest.[67]

Under Article 3 of the Conditionality Regulation, a breach of the rule of law is defined as "failure to ensure the absence of conflicts of interests". However, it must also be demonstrated that this breach "affects or seriously risks affecting the sound financial management of the Union budget or the protection of the financial interests of the Union in a sufficiently direct way"[68] It is also noteworthy that the Implementing Decision does not identify a single case in which a conflict of interest on the part of the KEKVAs' board of trustees directly affected the protection of the Union budget or financial interests. Nevertheless, the Council considers the conflict of interest to be systemic.[69]

The 'systemic' nature of a problem means an individual assessment is not necessary. However, in this case, the Implementing Decision does not clearly explain why the conflict of interest reported by the Commission constitutes a 'systemic' problem, particularly given the resignation of all senior political leaders in 2023 under the KEKVA Act. In these circumstances, the factual soundness of the Implementing Decision seems questionable at best.

4.2.2. Violation of the Principle of Proportionality

The principle of proportionality, which underlies all actions, may be the strongest argument of the applicants.[70] According to Article 5(3) of the Regulation, which sets out the criteria for proportionality, "the nature, duration, gravity and scope of the breaches of the principles of the rule of law shall be duly taken into account. The measures shall, insofar as possible, target the Union actions affected by the breaches". In the proceedings for the annulment of the Conditionality Regulation, the CJEU specifically mentioned the importance of the principle of proportionality. Accordingly,

---

67 However, the boards of trustees of the public interest foundations of the other four applicant universities were or are made up of individuals who may be affected by the conflict of interest.

68 Conditionality Regulation, Article 4(1).

69 Statement of Defence lodged by the Council of the European Union on 21 May 2023, *Case T-138/23, Semmelweis Egyetem v Council,* para.17.

70 Debreceni Egyetem's action also mentions a breach of the proportionality principle in relation to the subsidiarity principle. However, it is difficult to establish a breach of the subsidiarity principle in the context of the Implementing Decision. Action brought on 2 March 2023, *Case T-115/23, Debreceni Egyetem v Council,* third plea in law.

> "Those various requirements thus entail an objective and diligent analysis of each situation which is the subject of a procedure under the contested regulation, as well as the appropriate measures necessitated, as the case may be, by that situation, in strict compliance with the principle of proportionality, to protect the Union budget and the financial interests of the Union effectively against the effects of breaches of the principles of the rule of law, while respecting the principle of equality of the Member States before the Treaties."[71]

The requirement of proportionality is met if *(i)* the acts of the EU institutions are "appropriate for attaining the legitimate objectives pursued by the legislation at issue" and *(ii)* "do not exceed the limits of what is necessary to achieve those objectives; when there is a choice between several appropriate measures, recourse must be had to the least onerous, and the disadvantages caused must not be disproportionate to the aims pursued".[72] However, the Implementing Decision merely states that a total ban on contracting with foundations covered by the KEKVA Act is necessary and proportionate.[73] It does not explain the criteria on which the Council (and the Commission) based their conclusion in accordance with Article 5(3) of the Conditionality Regulation. In the context of proportionality, it is also noteworthy that, in its defence, the Council pointed out that the measure in question is suitable for protecting the financial interests of the Union because it does not authorize any payments,[74] which, in our view, is likely to constitute a severe breach of the principle of proportionality in itself.[75]

In the context of the proportionality test, it should be noted that the Horizon Europe programme is a long-term research project spanning several years. Therefore, the legal consequences of the Implementing Decision will persist for many years, clearly exceeding the proportionality requirement in terms of time. Another aspect of the proportionality principle is that the boards of trustees of the foundations have no real influence over the allocation and expenditure of funds under the Horizon Europe programmes. The groups awarded the grants manage and control these funds, so even if con-

---

71 *Case C-156/21, Hungary v Parliament and Council,* para. 317.

72 Judgment of 4 May 2016, *Case C-358/14, Poland v Parliament and Council,* ECLI: EU:C:2016:323, para. 78.

73 Implementing Decision, Recital (62).

74 Statement of defence lodged by the Council of the European Union on 21 May 2023, *Case T-138/23, Semmelweis Egyetem v Council,* para. 50.

75 This legal reasoning is akin to arguing in a criminal trial that the death penalty is an appropriate punishment because it precludes the possibility of reoffending.

flicts of interest were present, there would be no real risk of harm to specific EU financial interests.[76] In this context, the Council should also consider which rules apply to the use of specific EU funds. Are they directly part of the higher education institutions' budget, or are they only formally part of the KEKVA as a kind of 'separate fund' with specific financial rules? The latter applies to ERASMUS+ and Horizon Europe.

For all these reasons, it can rightly be argued that the Implementing Decision fails to meet the proportionality requirement, for several reasons. *(i)* Firstly, the Council did not consider the possible alternative measures, partly because the prohibition imposed on undertakings applies automatically to all KEKVAs without any examination of their individual situations, and partly because the effects of the measure are felt over time. *(ii)* The Council did not consider the substantive weight of the contracting prohibition (*i.e.,* that it applies equally to all funds, regardless of the differences in the rules governing their use) or the temporal nature of the measure (research proposals cover several years). *(iii)* Finally, in the context of the proportionality principle, the Council failed to consider the impact of the measure on academics and researchers. This is interesting because, when there was a realistic possibility that the UK would leave the EU without an agreement, the Commission drafted a regulation specifically to ensure the smooth continuation of the Erasmus programme for states leaving the EU, taking into account the proportionality principle.[77] Therefore, while the Commission would have considered the termination of the Erasmus programme to be disproportionate for one state, the possibility that the adoption of the decision would adversely affect Hungarian lecturers, researchers and students was not raised in the proportionality test for another state, as set out in the Implementing Decision. Nevertheless, the Conditionality Regulation explicitly states that, "When considering the adoption of measures, the Commission should consider their potential impact on final recipients and beneficiaries."[78]

---

76 Action brought on 13 March 2023, *Case T-138/23, Semmelweis Egyetem v Council,* paras. 122–124.

77 *See* at https://data.consilium.europa.eu/doc/document/PE-55–2019-INIT/hu/pdf.

78 Conditionality Regulation, Recital (19).

4.2.3. Arguments on the Impact on the Education Market

The universities also argue that the Implementing Decision distorts the education market, placing them at a competitive disadvantage against other universities within the same market.

The competition provisions of the TFEU (in particular Articles 101–108) essentially concern the effects of state aid and measures in Member States. Therefore, an EU measure cannot, in principle, result in a breach of EU competition law. Commitments entered into with the KEKVA, which may provide EU funds, cannot be considered a "subject matter right", such as area-based subsidies under the Common Agricultural Policy. Therefore, applicants cannot argue that the Implementing Decision has diverted funds intended for them to other higher education institutions. Paradoxically, it is precisely the "non-model-changing" higher education institutions that can continue to apply for student mobility and research funds without considering the KEKVAs as competitors when submitting their applications, putting the applicants at a legal disadvantage. In other words, the KEKVAs in Hungary are disadvantaged by the fact that Hungary did not lose all mobility and research funds (even temporarily) by adopting the Implementing Decision. Therefore, it can be assumed that the General Court will not accept this argument.

5. Concluding Thoughts

In our view, the legal arguments put forward by the higher education institutions may provide a sufficient basis for annulling the Implementing Decision. Therefore, the General Court would be acting in accordance with the letter and spirit of EU law by annulling the Implementing Decision. However, given the highly politicized nature of this issue, it cannot be assumed that the General Court will not consider 'non-legal' arguments when reaching its decision.

Therefore, it is interesting to review the other legal options available (or that were available) against the Implementing Decision. *(i)* On the one hand, Hungary could have brought an action for annulment against the Council itself, but did not do so. This was presumably because Hungary had previously challenged the Conditionality Regulation unsuccessfully before the ECJ. The action brought by the applicant universities is not before the ECJ but before the General Court. This possibility is no longer available due to the deadline for taking legal action having passed. However, according to press reports, in February 2025, Hungary filed an action for annulment against the Commission's decision of 16 December 2024 not to initiate an amendment of the Implementing Decision. At the time of finalizing this study in April 2025, this action was not listed on the CJEU's website. Even if the annulment procedure were successful, however, the consequence would only be that the Commission would have to reassess the justification for maintaining or amending the Implementing Decision under the Conditionality Regulation (and not lift the standstill obligation). *(ii)* In principle, some academics or students could have brought an action for annulment before the General Court. However, in this case, it would have been almost impossible for them to satisfy the requirement of "direct and personal" involvement, since they would have needed a tender to be awarded to them. Nevertheless, it cannot be excluded that an interest group, such as the National Conference of Student Self-Governments (hereinafter: HÖOK), could successfully challenge the Implementing Decision before the General Court. The reason for this is that the HÖOK is the collective representative of students' interests under Article 60(1) of the Higher Education Act, and the General Court has already recognized in *Growth Energy* that if an organization entrusted with defending the collective interests of its members is expressly conferred a right of action by national law, this may give it standing to bring a legal action.[79] *(iii)* In principle, there is also no legal barrier to bringing a damages claim against the Hungarian State in Hungary. In such a case, it may even be possible to initiate a preliminary ruling procedure under Article 267 TFEU. *(iv)* Finally, depending on the General Court's decision, the model-changing universities can claim damages against either the Council or the Hungarian State.

On the other hand, in the case of the Erasmus and Horizon Europe programmes, much of the real damage is in terms of lost mobility and research cooperation, which cannot easily be compensated for financially. This is due not only to the various (often procedural) difficulties related to the aforementioned procedures, but also to the specific nature of mobility and research cooperation. In this sense, even if the General Court ultimately rules in their favor, universities, students and lecturers who have opted for the model will lose out.

---

79 Judgment of 9 June 2016, *Case T-276/13, Growth Energy,* ECLI:EU:T:2016:340, para. 45.

Can We Still Afford the Consequences of Failing Forward?

The Ineffective Attempts of Reforming the EU Asylum System from a Hungarian Perspective

*Ágnes Töttős**

Abstract

The study guides the reader through the idea, negotiations and main pillars of solidarity and responsibility under the new European Pact on Asylum and Migration. It highlights its anomalies, pointing out the signs that render the Pact yet another incomplete step in the series of failing forward cycles, therefore raising the question whether we can still afford to fail forward in the area of asylum and migration. The study also intends to shed light on the reasons why Hungary failed to channel its own practical experiences effectively during the negotiations of the Pact. It is also discussed what practical tests of the regulatory frameworks Hungary had carried out that led to its total rejection of the Pact with the focus of providing a more refined interpretation of the country's rejecting position in European negotiations. Finally, the paper introduces the latest initiatives in innovative solutions and identifies hindering factors that posed major obstacles in achieving meaningful reforms, continuously resulting in the phenomenon of failing forward in the field of European asylum and migration policy.

Keywords: Common European Asylum System, CEAS, migration, Hungary, New Pact on Asylum and Migration

* Ágnes Töttős: visiting lecturer, Károli Gáspár University of the Reformed Church, Budapest; chief government counsellor, Ministry of EU Affairs of Hungary, Budapest, agnes.tottos@eum.gov.hu.

1. Introduction

In his memoirs, Jean Monnet famously stated that "Europe will be forged in crises and will be the sum of the solutions adopted for those crises."[1] Over the past years the world has been affected by a cluster of related crises with compounding effects, such that the overall impact exceeds the sum of each part, also described as a state of 'polycrisis'.[2] The combined action of the interwoven crises influences the migration outlook in a unique way as on the one hand, it creates multifaceted drivers that shape people's aspirations for migration, and on the other hand, the polycrisis challenges the capacity of existing migration policy instruments and key stakeholders to provide adequate responses to unforeseen situations.

Hungary, being under a significant migratory pressure at the EU's external borders by illegally arriving migrants on the Western Balkan route, has experienced the effects of these various crises that interact with increasing speed and severe impact.[3] Consequently, Hungary has also been a country of early reaction and in the meantime, a country that took the courage to draw honest conclusions about the effectiveness of each new initiative and to make further changes to its regulatory concept for the sake of efficiency. Apart from national innovative solutions Hungary has been active in channeling its own crisis management experiences into the negotiations on the reforms of the European asylum and migration policy.

The aim of this study is to discuss what practical test of the regulatory frameworks has been carried out by Hungary that led to its total rejection of the EU's New Pact on Asylum and Migration with the focus of providing a more refined interpretation of the country's rejecting position in European negotiations. The study also intends to shed light on the reasons of why Hungary failed to channel its own practical experiences effectively during the negotiations of the Pact. Consequently, the idea and the main elements of the reforms are also discussed from the critical viewpoint of a transit country, also drawing conclusions from a pan-European approach.

The study employs the concept of failing forward in order to examine the outcome of the negotiations of the new European Pact. "By advancing integration through incomplete agreements, the EU has created the very condi-

1 Jean Monnet, *Memoirs*, Doubleday and Company, 1978, p. 417.

2 World Economic Forum, *The Global Risks Report 2023*, 18th Edition, 2023, at https://www3.weforum.org/docs/WEF_Global_Risks_Report_2023.pdf.

3 *See e.g.* Nikolett Pénzváltó, 'A nyugat-balkáni útvonal – migrációs trendek magyar szemszögből', *Nemzet és Biztonság*, Vol. 15, Issue 1, 2022, pp. 4–16.

tions for the emergence of crises, and this has, in turn, spurred on further agreements to deepen integration."[4] This EU policy-making pattern where EU institutions address crises with temporary, often incomplete, solutions, which, while not fully resolving the underlying issues, push the EU towards further integration, constitutes the concept of failing forward.[5] Therefore, we must always be able to provide an adequate solution to the existing and upcoming migration challenges as legislation cannot operate in a vacuum, notwithstanding what many legislators imagine. Employing this theoretical lens, the study also raises the question whether we can still afford the consequences of failing forward as we look with concern at the security situation in Europe, taking into consideration global migration trends. The study guides the reader through the Pact's proposal, negotiation and adoption, highlighting its anomalies and pointing out the signs that make the Pact yet another incomplete step in the series of failing forward cycles, therefore raising the question whether we can still afford to fail forward in the area of asylum and migration.

2. Hungary Going Clear on to the End... and Beyond

At present, there are three layers of rules regulating asylum procedure in Hungary based on which refugee status or subsidiarity protection could be gained. Although the main rules of procedure have been set out by transposing the applicable EU asylum acquis, there are two other special sets of rules applicable under particular circumstances.

A "state of crisis due to mass migration" was introduced into Hungarian law in September 2015, and as a result, from 28 March 2017 until 26 May 2020 (but in practice until March 2020), asylum applications could only be submitted in the transit zones, with the exception of those applicants staying lawfully in the country. All asylum seekers, excluding unaccompanied children below the age of 14, had to stay in the transit zones for the whole duration of their asylum procedure. Nevertheless, judgment *C-808/18* rendered in an infringement procedure the CJEU declared[6] that Hungary had failed

4 Marco Scipioni, 'Failing forward in EU migration policy? EU integration after the 2015 asylum and migration crisis', *Journal of European Public Policy,* Vol. 25, Issue 9, 2018, pp. 1357–1375.

5 Erik Jones *et al.*, 'Failing forward? Crises and patterns of European integration', *Journal of European Public Policy,* Vol. 28, Issue 10, 2021, pp. 1519–1536.

6 Judgment of 17 December 2020, *Case C-808/18, Commission v Hungary,* ECLI:EU:C:2020:1029.

to fulfil its obligations deriving from certain elements of EU migration and asylum acquis.[7]

Since 26 May 2020, another set of special conditions are applicable to submitting an asylum application, deviating from the general rules.[8] This second set of special procedural provisions was first implemented in view of the emergency situation caused by the COVID-19 pandemic. Currently, the armed conflict and humanitarian disaster in Ukraine, and the prevention and management of their consequences in Hungary provide the factual basis[9] for their implementation. As a result, in the present state of emergency, the regular procedure can be used only by those who carry out a special procedure before entering the country.[10] It is also important to note that, according to Hungarian legislation, if one enters Hungary without a legal title authorizing the entry and stay, authorities may stop them and remove them from Hungarian territory through the border fence with Serbia. Nevertheless, it also needs to be stated that on 22 June 2023, the CJEU found that not allowing people to seek asylum on the territory of Hungary violates EU law.[11]

However, it is worth getting to know more about the processes that led to the emergence of these regulatory layers within the Hungarian system, which also greatly influenced the position Hungary takes regarding EU reform initiatives in the field of asylum and migration.

---

7 *See* Ágnes Töttős, 'The Possibility of Using Article 72 TFEU as a Conflict-of-Law Rule, Hungary Seeking Derogation from EU Asylum Law', *Hungarian Yearbook of International Law and European Law*, Vol. 9, 2021, pp. 212–232.

8 Based on Act LVIII of 2020 and Government Decree No. 292/2020. (VI. 17.).

9 Government Decree No. 424/2022. (X. 28.)

10 If one is outside Hungary, they shall first submit a so-called "declaration of intent" to the Hungarian embassy in Belgrade (Serbia) or Kyiv (Ukraine). To do this, one needs to make an appointment at the relevant embassy. They may be summoned to the embassy for an interview. If the Hungarian authorities approve the declaration of intent, one will receive a one-time travel document with which they can travel to Hungary and apply for asylum. If the person is already in Hungary, they do not need to submit a declaration of intent to the embassy if they belong to any of the following groups: *(i)* Recognized beneficiaries of subsidiary protection staying in Hungary (and he/she would like to be recognized as a refugee); *(ii)* Family members of recognized refugees or beneficiaries of subsidiary protection staying in Hungary; *(iii)* Any person who is in detention, custody or imprisoned, except for those who have crossed the state border of Hungary in an irregular manner. In these cases, one can apply for asylum by visiting any of the National Directorate-General for Aliens Policing client offices in person and expressing their wish to do so.

11 Judgment of 22 June 2023, *Case C-823/21, Commission v Hungary,* ECLI:EU:C:2023:504.

2.1. Extraordinary Situations, Extraordinary Solutions – Take One!

The border procedure applicable till 2017 was tested before the ECtHR as a result of which the ECtHR declared that Hungary violated Article 3 ECHR by failing to conduct an efficient and adequate assessment when applying the safe third country clause to Serbia.[12] After 28 March 2017, extraordinary rules applied regarding the asylum procedure. The aim of the so-called reinforced legal border closure was to prevent migrants with an unclear status from moving freely within the country or the EU, thereby reducing the security risk of migration. Within this special legal framework, the procedures in the transit zones in Hungary were no longer special procedures, since the asylum authority examined the applications according to the general rules by first assessing the admissibility of the application, and in case of an application being admissible, assessed it on its merit. Another major amendment of the rules meant that the applicants were accommodated in the transit zone for the whole duration of the asylum procedure, however the possibility of leaving the transit zone through the exit gate to Serbia was still an option.

In the infringement procedure *C-808/18*[13] the CJEU however identified four aspects of Hungary's asylum system's non-compliance with EU law.[14] *(i)* Firstly, in providing that applications for international protection from third-country nationals or stateless persons who, arriving from Serbia, wish to access, in its territory, the international protection procedure, may be made only in the transit zones of Röszke and Tompa, while adopting a consistent and generalized administrative practice drastically limiting the number of applicants authorized to enter those transit zones daily. *(ii)* Secondly, in establishing a system of systematic detention of applicants for international protection in the transit zones, without observing the guarantees provided for in the Asylum Procedures Directive and the Reception Conditions Directive. *(iii)* Thirdly, in allowing the removal of all third-country nation-

12 Ágnes Töttős, 'The ECtHR's Grand Chamber Judgment in Ilias and Ahmed versus Hungary: A Practical and Realistic Approach. Can This Paradigm Shift Lead the Reform of the Common European Asylum System?', *Hungarian Yearbook of International Law and European Law*, Vol. 8, 2020, pp. 169–191.

13 Directive 2013/33/EU of the European Parliament and of the Council of 26 June 2013 laying down standards for the reception of applicants for international protection (recast) (hereinafter: Reception Conditions Directive).

14 *See* Ágnes Töttős, 'The Possibility of Using Article 72 TFEU as a Conflict-of-Law Rule, Hungary Seeking Derogation from EU Asylum Law', *Hungarian Yearbook of International Law and European Law*, Vol. 9, 2021, pp. 212–232.

als staying illegally in its territory, with the exception of those who are suspected of having committed a criminal offence, without observing the procedures and safeguards laid down in the Return Directive. *(iv)* Finally, in making the exercise by applicants for international protection who fall within the scope of the Asylum Procedures Directive of their right to remain in its territory subject to conditions contrary to EU law.[15] Even before this judgement, the CJEU examined the legal nature of the placement in the transit zone and in a preliminary ruling on the *joined cases C-924/19 and C-925/19 PPU*[16] and found that given the circumstances (length, security tools, space, contacts, *etc.*) the placing of applicants for international protection in the transit zones is no different from a detention regime applied in an unlawful manner, which actually led to the immediate closure of the transit zones by the Hungarian authorities in May 2020.[17]

2.2. Extraordinary Situations, Extraordinary Solutions – Take Two!

In 2020, following the outbreak of the COVID-19 pandemic, Hungary adopted a new law requiring those who wish to seek asylum in Hungary and are outside Hungary to first submit a so-called statement of intent at the embassy of Hungary in Belgrade (Serbia) or in Kyiv (Ukraine). After examining that statement, the Hungarian authorities can decide whether or not to grant a travel document allowing entering into Hungary for the submission of the actual application for international protection. The European Commission considered that by adopting these provisions, Hungary failed to fulfil its obligations under EU law, in particular, the directive on common

---

15 The CJEU declared that Hungary had failed to fulfil its obligations under Articles 5, 6(1), 12(1) and 13(1) of Directive 2008/115/EC of the European Parliament and of the Council of 16 December 2008 on common standards and procedures in Member States for returning illegally staying third-country nationals (hereinafter: Return Directive or RD), under Articles 6, 24(3), 43 and 46(5) of Directive 2013/32/EU of the European Parliament and of the Council of 26 June 2013 on common procedures for granting and withdrawing international protection (hereinafter: Asylum Procedures Directive or APD), and under Articles 8, 9 and 11 of Directive 2013/33/EU of the European Parliament and of the Council of 26 June 2013 laying down standards for the reception of applicants for international protection (hereinafter: Reception Conditions Directive or RCD).

16 Judgment of 14 May 2020, *Joined Cases C-924/19 PPU and C-925/19 PPU, Országos Idegenrendészeti Főigazgatóság Dél-alföldi Regionális Igazgatóság and Országos Idegenrendészeti Főigazgatóság*, ECLI:EU:C:2020:367.

17 *See* at https://hu.euronews.com/2020/05/21/mar-az-ejjel-elszallitottak-a-tranzitzonak bol-a-menedekkeroket.

procedures for granting and withdrawing international protection and initiated an infringement procedure against Hungary.

In its judgment of 22 June 2023, the CJEU held that by requiring the prior submission of a declaration of intent at a Hungarian[18] embassy situated in a third country and the grant of a travel document, Hungary has failed to fulfil its obligations under the Asylum Procedure Directive. The Court found that the condition relating to the prior submission of a declaration of intent was not laid down by the directive and was contrary to its objective of ensuring effective, easy and rapid access to the procedure for granting international protection. In addition, according to the Court, that legislation deprived the third-country nationals or stateless persons concerned of the effective enjoyment of their right to seek asylum from Hungary, as enshrined in the Charter of Fundamental Rights. The Court also considered that the restriction laid down could not be justified by the objective of public health protection, and, more specifically, the fight against the spread of COVID-19, as argued by Hungary. Moreover, the procedure implemented by Hungary constituted a manifestly disproportionate interference with the right of persons seeking international protection to make an application for international protection upon their arrival at a Hungarian border.

3. The Path to a New Pact on Asylum and Migration

3.1. First Initiatives and Instructions on the Way Forward

The Commission in its 2016 Communication "Towards a reform of the Common European Asylum System and enhancing legal avenues to Europe"[19] considered that the Common European Asylum System (CEAS) needs to be made more crisis proof in the future and presented two packages of altogether seven reform proposals in 2016. However, the negotiations ran aground as "Member States remained unwilling to leave their entrenched positions, which were firmly anchored to their respective roles in the EU migration system":[20] the first group being the frontline Member States (MED5), the second group the destination countries in North-West Europe

18 *Case C-823/21, Commission v Hungary.*

19 Communication from the Commission to the European Parliament and the Council, Towards a reform of the Common European Asylum System and enhancing legal avenues to Europe, COM(2016) 197 final.

20 *See* at https://www.tandfonline.com/doi/full/10.1080/07036337.2023.2209273.

and the transit states on the Eastern part of the EU, including the V4,[21] many having extensive external border sections. Negotiations among these three blocks were heavily politicized and led to a stalemate as both the Mediterranean states and the eastern states thought the reform elements cannot be separated from each other, they must be accepted as a package, on the other hand, the Western Member States would have been willing to conclude the negotiation of the seven legislative files even individually.

The European Council also drew its conclusions in two respects with regard to migration and asylum reforms. It set out in its June 2018 conclusions that "a precondition for a functioning EU policy relies on a comprehensive approach to migration which combines more effective control of the EU's external borders, increased external action and the internal aspects."[22]

In 2019 the leaders reconfirmed their dedication in this regard when setting out the New Strategic Agenda 2019–2024.[23] The European Council Conclusions adopted in December 2023 and March 2024 equally reaffirmed the EU's commitment to continue pursuing a comprehensive approach to migration. Therefore, it was not enough to proceed further on internal asylum reforms, if amidst the constant inflow of migrants the external borders were not protected or the third-country nationals found to be illegally staying could not be effectively returned to their countries of origin.

Furthermore, the European Council also gave policy directions as regards the procedure of adopting the reforms, especially when negotiations began to drag on: it set out a plan on returning to the policy discussions on the reform and emphasized that they "will seek to reach a consensus during the first half of 2018."[24] The necessity of finding a consensus on the Dublin Regulation was later reiterated in June 2018 by the leaders.[25] Finally, the New Strategic Agenda 2019–2024 also contained the very same instructions: "A consensus needs to be found on the Dublin Regulation to reform it based on a balance of responsibility and solidarity, taking into account the persons disembarked following Search and Rescue operations."

21 *See* more: Ágnes Töttős, 'European Asylum Policy and its Reforms from a Central and Eastern European Perspective', *in* András Osztovits & János Bóka (eds.), *The Policies of the European Union from a Central European Perspective,* Central European Academic Publishing, Miskolc–Budapest, 2023, pp. 217–237.

22 European Council, 28 June 2018, para. 1.

23 European Council meeting (20 June 2019) – Conclusions, Annex: A New Strategic Agenda 2019–2024.

24 *See* at http://www.consilium.europa.eu/media/21620/19-euco-final-conclusions-en.pdf.

25 European Council, 28 June 2018, para. 12.

Consensus was not inevitably required by the Treaties as ordinary legislative procedure and qualified majority voting in the Council was extended to this policy area by the Lisbon Treaty.[26] A clear consequence of the new rules on legislation was that because of the new qualified majority voting rule in the Council medium-sized and smaller Member States had less weight in the institution, while larger Member States were seen as the main beneficiaries of the change.[27] Consequently, the realization that finding consensus was necessary followed among others from the failure of implementing the 2015 relocation decisions, in the knowledge that unless all the Member States are on board with the main pillars of the reforms, effective implementation cannot be guaranteed. Hungary and its allies also aimed at determining the main directions and elements of the asylum and migration reforms at the highest level with consensus.

3.2. Neither New, Nor a Pact

"Asylum and migration are amongst the most significant challenges the EU has faced in recent years. Along with security, they rank high among the priorities and concerns of many Europeans. They will inevitably remain at the center of our politics during the next mandate."[28]

The new commissioner for Home Affairs, Ylva Johansson, was entrusted by Commission President von der Leyen with the task of finding the common ground and a fresh start on migration and asylum by developing the New Pact on Migration and Asylum. This was to involve a comprehensive approach looking at external borders, systems for asylum and return, the Schengen area and working with partner countries outside the EU. The New Pact was initiated in a Commission Communication[29] on 23 September 2020, with another set of ideas and legislative proposals. While in 2020, the Commission supported a quick adoption of the proposals, or at least those that have advanced well during the negotiations, the only reform element in

26 Article 78(2) TFEU.

27 Changed rules for qualified majority voting in the Council of the EU, December 2014, p. 1, at http://www.europarl.europa.eu/RegData/etudes/ATAG/2014/545697/EPRS_ATA%282014%29545697_REV1_EN.pdf.

28 Ursula Von der Leyen, Mission letter sent by to Ylva Johansson, the Commissioner for Home Affairs, 2019, p. 4.

29 Communication from the Commission to the European Parliament, the Council, the Economic and Social Committee and the Committee of the Regions on a New Pact on Migration and Asylum, COM/2020/609 final.

which the co-legislators could reach an agreement was to turn EASO into a fully-fledged EU asylum agency.[30]

Although the newest reform proposals were prepared through rounds of consultations with the capitals, and they aimed at balancing the various interests of the different groups of like-minded countries, what was proposed was a strange mixture of already existing elements of migration and asylum policy that have a questionable effect on their own, and when seemingly arranged into one set of rules, they do not necessarily create a fully operable system that is capable of resisting crises. There was a clear element it was missing, namely impact assessment. And this was already the second big legislative package that was proposed by the Commission without impact assessment – it was already lacking from the proposals launched in 2016. What the Commission instead did was a *tour des capitales,* so mapping the position of the governments in order to search for a compromise instead of a workable solution. The measure of success is the appropriate compromise and not efficiency; this seems to underline that EU reforms in the area of asylum and migration are predestined to continue on the path of failing forward.

The New Pact of the von der Leyen Commission was meant to resolve the stalemate. Nevertheless, the so-called New Pact was neither new, nor a pact. Many Member States were surprised to see that the solidarity measures of the reforms focused once again on compulsory relocation, while this element was one of the most unacceptable in the previous proposal to several Member States. As for the designation as a Pact, which is supposed to indicate a formal agreement between parties, no such agreement preceded the issuance of the pact, even though the European Council gave clear guidance on the need to find consensus on the major elements of the reforms. Instead, complex legislation was presented that was in no way based on the political consensus of EU leaders. The Pact was formally a Commission Communication issued with a number of new proposals, a number of modified proposals, maintaining a number of the proposals issued in 2016.

While the Communication on the Pact was based on a comprehensive approach, the different areas got different emphasis as the Commission pushed forward internal reforms by legislative proposals while expending less energy on the external dimension. It was also obvious that while new challenges arose, the negotiations on the legislative reforms were pushed further, while the need for a paradigm shift was clear. Nevertheless, it would

30 Regulation (EU) 2021/2303.

have meant allowing leaders to have a meaningful discussion on the way forward. Instead, what we saw was that

> "The external dimension was characterized by heavy political (EUCO) involvement, which was meant to steer the Commission and Council for instance, on issues of instrumentalization, hybrid threats and returns. This EUCO involvement was generally perceived as a nuisance by insiders, who felt that it politicized discussions and interfered with technical level work. This would explain why seemingly limited progress has been made in the area of returns and readmissions, action plans, and partnerships with third countries. The internal dimension saw little to no EUCO involvement [...]. Drawing lessons from the previous round of CEAS reform the institutional actors have been united in their attempts to keep the file away from their leaders. However, this 'technical' approach has also not been very effective."[31]

4. The Reforms of the Pact

The reforms of the Pact were to create a legal framework that balances solidarity and responsibility between the Member States, in a comprehensive approach to managing migration effectively and fairly. Following a political agreement on 20 December 2023, 10 legal acts[32] were adopted by the European Parliament on 10 April 2024, and later by the Council on 14 May. The legal instruments of the Pact, including some which had been already proposed in 2016, entered into force on 11 June 2024 and will enter into application after two years, as of 12 June 2026; except for the Union Resettlement and Humanitarian Admission Framework Regulation, which is already applicable today.

On 12 June 2024, the European Commission adopted a Common Implementation Plan for the Pact on Migration and Asylum.[33] This plan sets out

---

31 *See* at https://www.tandfonline.com/doi/full/10.1080/07036337.2023.2209273.

32 Eurodac regulation, Asylum procedure regulation, Regulation establishing a return border procedure, Regulation establishing a resettlement and humanitarian admission framework, Regulation addressing situations of crisis and force majeure, Screening regulation, Asylum and migration management regulation, Regulation on consistency amendments related to screening, Reception conditions directive, Qualification regulation.

33 Communication from the Commission to the European Parliament, the Council, the Economic and Social Committee and the Committee of the Regions, Common Implementation Plan for the Pact on Migration and Asylum, COM/2024/251 final.

the key actions required to translate the new rules on migration into practice. To do so, it brings all EU countries together, launching the necessary preparations that will allow the new system to become a well-functioning reality by the end of a two-year transition period. Guided by the Common Implementation Plan, the next step was for EU countries to prepare their respective national implementation plans by December 2024 as work must be started to translate the large and complex set of legislative acts into operational reality. On 16 April 2025, the Commission also proposed accelerating the implementation of certain aspects of the Pact on Migration and Asylum by frontloading two key elements of the Asylum Procedure Regulation with the aim of supporting Member States in processing asylum claims faster and more efficiently for applicants whose claims are likely to be unfounded.[34]

4.1. The Sweaty Balance between the Principles of Responsibility and Solidarity

The negotiations based on the new Pact brought to the surface all the previous differences between the positions of the three groups of Member States. The different legislative proposals outlined a very complex reform with several elements, but the main driver of the dynamics of the discussion was how to create a balance between solidarity and responsibility that formed the two main pillars of the reform ideas.

4.1.1. The Pillar of Responsibility

In case of the pillar of responsibility, the aim of the relevant provisions is to select as soon as possible those who are entitled to international protection and those who do not have any right of residence from among the migrants arriving illegally to the territory of the EU. The central elements of achieving this goal are the introduction of a compulsory screening in case of those crossing the border illegally and the reform of the currently optional rules of the border procedure. According to the new regulations, once migrants reach the borders of the EU, only a five-day screening procedure is envisioned, and only a part of the migrants would be kept at the border for car-

34 *See* at https://ec.europa.eu/commission/presscorner/detail/en/ip_25_1070.

rying out compulsory asylum and/or return border procedures. Most asylum seekers would need to be provided access to the territory of the EU. Even if certain groups of migrants would be kept at the external borders for specific asylum and/or return procedures, the time of applying such procedures with the legal fiction of non-entry would be very limited (12 weeks for each procedure to be concluded completely, with the possibility of extending it to 16 weeks). Consequently, even those most likely to be expelled from the EU would need to be provided entry to the territory of the EU after a certain period, yet the ratio of effective return of these migrants is still very low.

Pursuant to Articles 46 and 47 of the new Asylum Procedures Regulation[35] the adequate capacity for border procedures at Union level shall be considered to be 30,000, and it is necessary to calculate and set up the adequate capacity of each Member State and the maximum number of applications for international protection each Member State is required to examine in the border procedure per year. The Commission shall, by means of implementing acts, calculate the number that corresponds to the adequate capacity of each Member State by using a specific formula, thereby setting out a new type of quota.[36] According to the first such implementing act[37] Hungary alone needs to provide for the 25.7% of the total common capacity that is 7716 places at its external borders, and it is only Italy (26.7%, 8016) that needs to set up a slightly bigger capacity for border procedures. While the purpose of the border procedure for asylum and return should be to quickly assess in principle at the external borders whether applications are unfounded or inadmissible and to swiftly return those with no right of stay, the specific provisions of the Asylum Procedures Regulation not only create an

35 Regulation (EU) 2024/1348 of the European Parliament and of the Council of 14 May 2024 establishing a common procedure for international protection in the Union and repealing Directive 2013/32/EU.

36 The number shall be calculated by multiplying the number set out in Article 46 by the sum of irregular crossings of the external border, arrivals following search and rescue operations and refusals of entry at the external border in the Member State concerned during the previous three years and dividing the result thereby obtained by the sum of irregular crossings of the external border, arrivals following search and rescue operations and refusals of entry at the external border in the Union as a whole during the same period according to the latest available Frontex and Eurostat data.

37 Commission Implementing Decision (EU) 2024/2150 of 5 August 2024 laying down rules for the application of Regulation (EU) 2024/1348 of the European Parliament and of the Council, as regards the adequate capacity of Member States and the maximum number of applications to be examined by a Member State in the border procedure per year.

unreasonable burden for two particular states, but also contradict the main aim of selecting different groups of migrants as early as possible on their route to the EU. Interestingly, none of the Member States located on an earlier part of the Balkan route is obliged to have such big capacities.

4.1.2. The Pillar of Solidarity

As regards the pillar of solidarity, the goal is that Member States need not collect the necessary assistance when affected by migration pressure on an ad-hoc basis, but rather have a solidarity pool of these solidarity offers that can be mobilized at any time, which makes the response faster and more predictable. To achieve this, forecasting is also essential, so that the assets to be provided can be planned to some extent. That is why the Asylum and Migration Management Regulation,[38] which replaces the Dublin Regulation, creates a solidarity mechanism based on an annual migration management cycle. Furthermore, the crisis management regulation[39] also establishes additional solidarity tasks beyond the annual solidarity mechanism.

In preparation for the annual solidarity cycle, the Commission prepares its report on the expected migration and asylum trends and needs for the following year by 15 October of the previous year. In addition, the Commission also proposes the creation of a Solidarity Pool to manage the expected migration challenges in the coming year, in response to the identified potential migration pressure and the potential needs of the Member States expected to be affected. With regard to this stock of solidarity measures, the Commission will also propose a pan-European target number of not less than 30,000 relocations, or EUR 600 million (*i.e.,* the relocation of one person has been equated with EUR 20,000 by the Commission). The Commission's proposal also determines for each Member State how much the indicative contribution (fair share) per Member State is; the formula used for this is the same as that used in the 2015 relocation decisions (50–50 % consideration of GDP and population). Member States can make three types of offers to the solidarity pool: *(i)* relocation (asylum seekers or even recognized at

38 Regulation (EU) 2024/1351 of the European Parliament and of the Council of 14 May 2024 on asylum and migration management, amending Regulations (EU) 2021/1147 and (EU) 2021/1060 and repealing Regulation (EU) No 604/2013.

39 Regulation (EU) 2024/1359 of the European Parliament and of the Council of 14 May 2024 addressing situations of crisis and force majeure in the field of migration and asylum and amending Regulation (EU) 2021/1147.

the request of the beneficiary Member State); *(ii)* financial contribution (paid to the Union, from which the beneficiary Member State benefits, or a project implemented by the beneficiary Member State, which is implemented with a third country directly related to the given migration pressure); *(iii)* alternative measures (*e.g.* operational contribution, provision of personnel or equipment based on the needs of the beneficiary Member State).

Although the Member States are theoretically free to decide what type of offer they make and to what extent, at the same time, their room for maneuver is limited in several respects: financing projects implemented with third countries can only be done through the beneficiary Member State; agencies, especially Frontex, have priority as providers of operational assistance in relation to the offers of personnel or equipment for border protection, the offer provided through Frontex is not considered an additional solidarity offer; a Member State's own border protection expenditure does not qualify as an offering through the solidarity mechanism; in the case of all alternative offers, the offeror and recipient Member State must also agree on the method and the value of the given offer.

The finalized solidarity pool, compiled and adjusted through consultation by the Member States, is adopted by the Council in an executive act with a qualified majority, the provisions of which are binding. Based on the above, although the Member States have room for maneuver both in terms of the instruments to be offered and the amount of the offer, the fact that the Council adopts this implementing act with a qualified majority entails the risk that the Council establishes an obligation different from that offered by the particular Member State should there be a need for more or different type of offers. The Member States' contributions stipulated in the solidarity pool should not be fulfilled immediately, but at the request of a Member State facing migration pressure, to the extent necessary to respond to the given situation.

4.2. Hungary's Position

Central European countries many times functioned as an 'early warning region' voicing their concerns regarding the inoperability of the present acquis. Nevertheless, their position has been constantly disregarded. Throughout the negotiations Hungary remained firmly convinced of the need to develop a Common European Asylum System which aims at tackling the root causes of illegal migration, minimizes and ultimately eliminates the incentives for illegal migration and discourages persons who wish to abuse the asylum system, and includes the possibility for examining asylum applications in third countries. Consequently, solely fine-tuning the existing system, such as extending border procedures from 4 to 12 weeks, or cementing expensive experimentations with non-effective relocation, would not be effective.

Furthermore, Hungary was clear in advocating not for a compromise measured with mathematical precision, but instead reforms that serve the purpose of deterring migrants that only claim asylum for economic purposes, stemming illegal migration at the earliest possible point on their route to the EU, and even those eligible for asylum would be provided protection closest to their country of origin instead of incentivizing migration using criminal organizations to reach the EU. The fact that all the efforts dedicated to border protection at the external borders could still be overridden by masses of people submitting unfounded claims for asylum, and even more capacities must be developed for the purpose of temporarily holding back such people whose identity is often times unknown, contradicts the country's expectations.

As regards solidarity contributions, they are expected without taking into account measures carried out on the country's own territory even where the borders on which border protection and asylum management efforts are carried out are also the external borders of the Schengen area. Consequently, Hungary has persistently advocated that resources from national budgets spent on the protection of the external borders of the EU should be regarded as a means of solidarity. Instead, it was presented with a compromise of a solidarity mechanism that would not represent a viable solution for dealing with migratory crises, inter alia as it aims to solve the crisis situations primarily through *de facto* and *de jure* mandatory relocation, while doing so would only lead to an exponential increase in the migratory flows, which will consequently deepen the crises and increase solidarity needs.

In line with the repeated call of the European Council, Hungary remained firm on the need to find consensus on the main building blocks of an effective migration and asylum policy. Later, as the impact of mass illegal migration deepened and had a severe effect on the functioning of the Schengen area, Hungary also called for a Schengen summit to be established, based on the model of Eurosummit, convened regularly, involving the heads of state and government of the Schengen Area.

5. *Failing Forward: Not Effective and Not Enough*

While the Commission communicated that the closure of the reform process was a huge success and called for an early start of implementation, already on the day following the adoption of the Pact, fifteen Member States[40] pleaded with the European Commission to go beyond the new reforms aiming for more innovative solutions.[41] The European Council in its Conclusions adopted in October 2024[42] not only called on "the Council, the Member States and the Commission to strengthen work on all strands of action in the comprehensive approach to migration", but specified two particular areas, where it practically declared that the reforms of the Pact cannot effectively handle the arising challenges or that the reforms are minor compared to the nature and extent of the migratory pressure. Although the Commission called the adoption of the Pact a "historic agreement",[43] already in October 2024 the European Council concluded that new ways to prevent and counter irregular migration should be considered.

First of all, it declared that "Russia and Belarus, or any other country, cannot be allowed to abuse our values, including the right to asylum, and to undermine our democracies. [...] Exceptional situations require appropriate measures. The European Council recalls its determination to ensure effective control of the Union's external borders through all available means [...]."[44] "In addition, new ways to prevent and counter irregular migration should be considered, in line with EU and international law."[45] A possible area where new, innovative solutions are sought for is returning illegally staying migrants. In this regard the European Council also called for "determined action at all levels to facilitate, increase and speed up returns from the European Union, using all relevant EU policies, instruments and tools, including diplomacy, development, trade and visas. It invites the Commission to submit a new legislative proposal, as a matter of urgency".[46]

---

40 Austria, Bulgaria, Cyprus, the Czech Republic, Denmark, Finland, Estonia, Greece, Italy, Latvia, Lithuania, Malta, the Netherlands, Poland and Romania

41 *See* at https://www.euronews.com/my-europe/2024/05/16/15-eu-countries-call-for-the-outsourcing-of-migration-and-asylum-policy.

42 European Council Conclusions, 17 October 2017.

43 *See* at https://ec.europa.eu/commission/presscorner/detail/en/ip_24_3161.

44 European Council Conclusions, 17 October 2017, para. 38.

45 Id. para. 39.

46 Id. para. 37.

5.1. The Instrumentalization of Migration

In 2021a highly worrying phenomenon was observed as the Belarusian regime started to artificially create and facilitate illegal migration, using migratory flows as a tool for political purposes, to destabilize the EU and its Member States. The European Council Conclusions of October 2021 underlined that the EU would "not accept of any attempt by third countries to instrumentalize migrants for political purposes" and it condemned all hybrid attacks at the EU's borders.[47] The leaders also invited the Commission to propose any necessary changes to the EU's legal framework and concrete measures underpinned by adequate financial support to ensure an immediate and appropriate response.[48] On 23 November 2021, the Commission, after already raising the phenomenon in the renewed EU action plan against migrant smuggling (2021–2025), adopted a Communication summarizing the measures taken to address the immediate situation as well as additional ones underway to create a more permanent toolbox to address future attempts to destabilize the EU through the instrumentalization of migrants.[49]

On 1 December 2021, as part of these measures, the Commission adopted a proposal for a Council Decision based on Article 78(3) TFEU aimed at supporting Latvia, Lithuania and Poland by providing for the measures and operational support needed to manage in an orderly and dignified manner the arrival of persons being instrumentalized by Belarus, in full respect of fundamental rights.[50] Accompanying the proposal for an amendment of the Schengen Borders Code, this proposal addressed the instrumentalization situation from the migration, asylum and return perspective. The objective of this proposal was to support the Member State facing a situation of instrumentalization of migrants by setting up a specific emergency migration and asylum management procedure, and, where necessary, providing for support and solidarity measures. The proposed options were to complement and reinforce the proposals under the New Pact on Migration and Asylum, setting out specific, limited derogations in such special situations.[51]

47 European Council conclusions, 21–22 October 2021, para. 19.

48 Id. para. 20.

49 Joint communication to the European Parliament, the Council, the European Economic and Social Committee and the Committee of Regions, Responding to state-sponsored instrumentalisation of migrants at the EU external border, JOIN/2021/32 final.

50 Proposal for a Council decision on provisional emergency measures for the benefit of Latvia, Lithuania and Poland, Brussels, 1.12.2021, COM(2021) 752 final.

51 Derogations proposed were as follows: possibility for the Member State concerned to register an asylum application and offer the possibility for its effective lodging only at

As a result of the negotiations, some elements of this proposal have been incorporated in the Crisis and Force Majeure Regulation[52] adopted within the Pact (including the definition of instrumentalization of migration),[53] and in the revision of the Schengen Borders Code.[54] Yet, the Commission announced in its Annual Work Program in February 2025, that it will withdraw the 2021 proposal for a Regulation addressing situations of instrumentalization, as it had not advanced in the interinstitutional negotiations since 2022.

Various measures were taken within the EU to manage the situation, and there have been some successful steps in the external dimension of migration, namely, strengthening cooperation with key countries of origin along the Eastern Land Route (particularly in the Horn of Africa, Middle East and Silk Route countries), and the main transit countries (especially Türkiye, United Arab Emirates, Egypt). Nevertheless, progress in stabilizing the situation with the overall aim of preventing undesired migration-related political pressures could not be achieved, in particular, since another State actor, Russia joined Belarus in weaponizing migration. On 7 June 2024, as a joint initiative on EU level to effectively address instrumentalization of migration, 8 countries (Denmark, Estonia, Latvia, Lithuania, Norway, Poland, Finland, Sweden) signed a letter to the Commission, in which they concluded that EU acquis does not enable the Member States to effectively counter this type of interference with their sovereignty and national security. They

> "therefore propose that in such situations Member States should be allowed to temporarily derogate from EU law based on national security.

---

specific registration points located in the proximity of the border including the border crossing points designated for that purpose; possibility to extend the registration deadline to up to four weeks; possibility to apply the asylum border procedure to all applications and possibility to extend its duration.

52 Regulation (EU) 2024/1359 of the European Parliament and of the Council of 14 May 2024 addressing situations of crisis and force majeure in the field of migration and asylum and amending Regulation (EU) 2021/1147.

53 Article 1(4)b): "For the purposes of this Regulation, a situation of crisis means: [...] *b)* a situation of instrumentalisation where a third country or a hostile non-state actor encourages or facilitates the movement of third-country nationals or stateless persons to the external borders or to a Member State, with the aim of destabilizing the Union or a Member State, and where such actions are liable to put at risk essential functions of a Member State, including the maintenance of law and order or the safeguard of its national security."

54 Regulation (EU) 2024/1717 of the European Parliament and of the Council of 13 June 2024 amending Regulation (EU) 2016/399 on a Union Code on the rules governing the movement of persons across borders.

> We should increase the possibilities for Member States to address instrumentalization of migration under their national legislation. This requires derogations based on national security, which could, if necessary, include changes to the future APR and Crisis Regulation and to the Schengen Borders Code."[55]

They based their claim on Article 72 TFEU (law and order, and internal security), which, read together with Article 4(2) TEU (national security exclusion), is considered to allow for a derogation from EU secondary legislation, but must be interpreted restrictively. They were of the viewpoint that the CJEU has not yet addressed a situation similar to the ongoing hybrid attack at the Eastern borders, and so the Court has also not taken a position on whether, in such a situation, a derogation from EU secondary legislation under Article 72 TFEU would be possible for protecting public policy and internal security for a limited period of time.

Consequently, the European Council called for firm steps in this regard in its October 2024 Conclusions, and the need for a firm act on behalf of the EU was also discussed at a like-minded meeting of 11 leaders before that meeting.[56] In December 2024 the Commission issued a Communication on countering hybrid threats from the weaponization of migration and strengthening security at the EU's external borders.[57] In this document[58] the Commission essentially legitimizes the disregard of EU secondary law on asylum and migration, *i.e.* the closure of borders and the suspension of the reception of asylum applications, citing the need to exercise Member State competences related to the maintenance of public order and internal security, based on the same Treaty articles that Hungary also invoked in its infringement proceedings over the quota. According to the Commission, migrants arriving illegally under pressure from Russia and Belarus not only

55 *See* at https://www.regjeringen.no/globalassets/departementene/jd/dokumenter/brev-og-kunngjoringer/eu-level-approach-to-effectively-address-instrumentalisation-of-migration.pdf.

56 *See* at https://www.bloomberg.com/news/articles/2024-10-15/meloni-to-gather-eu-like-minded-counterparts-seeking-tougher-migration-rules.

57 Communication from the Commission to the European Parliament and the Council on countering hybrid threats from the weaponisation of migration and strengthening security at the EU's external borders (December 2024) COM(2024) 570.

58 Furthermore, in December 2024, given the new security landscape, including hybrid threats at the EU external borders, the Commission made available through a specific action under the BMVI Thematic Facility, EUR 170 million to EU Member States and Schengen Associated Countries that have borders with Russia and Belarus to strengthen further their border surveillance capabilities.

pose a threat to national security and Member State sovereignty, but also endanger the integrity of the Schengen area and the security of the entire EU. Thus, if the action is sufficiently justified, proportionate, necessary, and appropriate to the aim, the Member States concerned may temporarily take measures beyond EU asylum and migration law.[59] Although the Commission refers to the responsibility of the Member State to decide and prove whether the given situation and measure meet the listed conditions, and the CJEU may ultimately rule on their legality. At the same time – given that the Commission assesses the processes taking place on the EU's Eastern borders as a special situation – it is not expected that the issue of the compatibility of any Member State action on the Eastern borders with EU law would be brought before the CJEU.

5.2. New, Innovative Ways – The 'Fearful' Externalization

After the 15 Member States' joint letter expressing their commitment to developing new solutions to address illegal migration, the Hungarian Presidency of the Council initiated a series of discussions on potential innovative approaches in the area of migration. At the same time, there had already been some initiatives, the outcome of which Member States needed to take into account. EU documents, including the Conclusions of the European Council, do not ignore the call of leaders to ensure that all steps shall be in line with EU and international law. However, we experience that government measures fail in practice owing to the human rights-centered approach of these legal frameworks. This was palpable in three recent attempts to introduce innovative solutions.

(i) Firstly, Hungary's transit zone system, which established a legal border closure and allowed only those with legally recognized status to enter the EU, was found to be contrary to EU law by the CJEU, as was the system of rules requiring a prior declarations of intent submitted from outside the EU. The focus of criticism of these sets of rules was the lack of access to the asylum procedure and the violation of the principle of non-refoulement. *(ii)* Secondly, the implementation of the Rwanda model, which was intended to be implemented by the previous UK government, was first blocked by an

59 Poland, Finland and the Baltic states have already introduced temporary rules that restrict the possibility of submitting asylum applications at border sections affected by instrumentalization.

interim order issued by the ECtHR in June 2022.[60] This found that the deportation violated the human rights of the migrants concerned. Subsequently, the UK Supreme Court, in its judgment of 15 November 2023,[61] found that the UK Rwanda Agreement was unlawful because the transfer of applicants to Rwanda would expose the asylum seekers to a real risk of ill-treatment through possible return to their country of origin since they could not expect an adequate asylum procedure in Rwanda, which could therefore not be considered a safe third country for the asylum seekers concerned. *(iii)* Thirdly, the first application of the agreement between Italy and Albania failed after an Italian court ruled on 18 October that the transfer of Bangladeshi and Egyptian men to Albania after their rescue in international waters was unlawful, as their country of origin was not considered sufficiently safe. The Italian judges referred to a ruling rendered by the CJEU of 4 October 2024[62] which states that a non-EU country can only be considered safe if its entire territory is considered safe. This innovative solution is undergoing another judicial review as the CJEU was called to give an answer to preliminary questions referred by Italian courts in November 2024 on the compatibility with EU law of the Italy-Albania Protocol on asylum applications and return procedures.[63]

5.2.1. Innovative Return Policy

Although there are various reasons why returns may fail to be executed, but one of the main underlying problems is the lack of willingness to readmit migrants on behalf of countries of origin. Even before the European Council gave a very strong push for further initiatives in the field of return policy, the Hungarian Presidency initiated various exchanges of views between the Member States, where many raised the idea of 'return hubs' as one of the

---

60 *N.S.K. v the United Kingdom,* no. 28774/22, formerly K.N.v. the United Kingdom, urgent interim measure.

61 *R (on the application of AAA and others) (Respondents/Cross Appellants) v Secretary of State for the Home Department (Appellant/Cross Respondent),* UKSC/2023/0093.

62 Judgment of the Court (Grand Chamber) of 4 October 2024, *Case C-406/22, CV,* ECLI:EU:C:2024:841.

63 The Tribunale ordinario di Roma and the Tribunale di Palermo in Italy have referred multiple preliminary rulings to the CJEU regarding the designation of safe countries of origin under EU asylum law: *Cases C-758/24 (Alace), C-759/24 (Canpelli), C-763/24 (Mibone), and C-764/24 (Capurteli)* concern the compatibility of national legislative measures with Directive 2013/32/EU on common procedures for granting and withdrawing international protection.

potential innovative solutions that should be further explored. A ministerial working lunch debate[64] in October 2024 confirmed that the review of the current legal framework for returns should enable possible innovative solutions such as 'return hubs'. An agreed and jointly shared understanding of 'return hubs' may not yet exist, but the main principle of a "return hub" is that once a third country national has been issued a return decision but the third-country national in question cannot be promptly returned to their country of origin (*e.g.,* due to lack of documentation or the lack of cooperation by the country of origin or for other reasons), the individual could be transferred to a 'return hub' in a third country where they will remain until their return is carried out, or from where they decide to return voluntarily.

Although legal and practical challenges may arise when developing the concept and performing the practical management of 'return hubs', in March 2025 the Commission presented a proposal for a new legislative framework in the Return Regulation,[65] including a new Common European System for Returns to increase the efficiency of the return process with clear, simplified and uniform rules. The proposal not only turned the previous Directive into a Regulation, but also introduces the idea of 'return hubs', the possibility to return third-country nationals who have been issued a return decision to a third country with which there is an agreement or arrangement for return. According to the draft regulation, an agreement or arrangement can only be concluded with a third country where international human rights standards and principles in accordance with international law – including the principle of non-refoulement – are respected, and the agreement shall be accompanied with a monitoring mechanism to assess implementation and take into account any changing circumstances in the third country. Furthermore, unaccompanied minors and families with minors would be excluded from this scheme.

5.2.2. Reforming the Safe Third Country Concept

EU law imposes both substantive and procedural obligations for the application of the safe third country concept. In line with Article 38 of the cur-

64 *See* at https://www.consilium.europa.eu/en/meetings/jha/2024/10/10/.

65 Proposal for a regulation of the European Parliament and of the Council establishing a common system for the return of third-country nationals staying illegally in the Union, and repealing Directive 2008/115/EC of the European Parliament and the Council, Council Directive 2001/40/EC and Council Decision 2004/191/EC, COM/2025/101 final.

rently applicable Asylum Procedures Directive[66] Member States may apply the safe third country concept only where the competent authorities are satisfied that a person seeking international protection will be treated in accordance with the a number of principles in the third country concerned, such as the safety of life and liberty, the lack of risk of serious harm, and there is a possibility to request asylum. In addition to the general requirements for a given third country, it should also be examined in the individual case of the applicant whether there is a connection between the applicant and the third country concerned, based on which it seems reasonable for this applicant to go to this country, and moreover, if the third country does not allow the applicant to enter its territory despite the fulfilment of the conditions, the Member State must ensure that the applicant has the opportunity to initiate the procedure on the merits.

The conditions of the safe third country principle have not been relaxed by the Asylum Procedure Regulation applicable under the Pact from June 2026, as it only stipulates that the Commission will review the safe third country concept by 12 June 2025 and, where appropriate, propose targeted amendments. In preparation for this, the Hungarian Presidency initiated a discussion at COREPER level, where it became clear that the majority of Member States would like to see a major amendment, despite the Commission's position, and some Member States are also proposing to delete the connection criterion. This would result in the possibility to send an asylum seeker back to a country outside the EU in order for the asylum procedure to take place there as the migrant did not seek protection in the safe country nearest to their country of origin.

6. Conclusions

It is clear that new legislation is adopted by compromise, but the question is whether new legislation also equals meaningful reforms as the concessions we make in the area of asylum and migration policy have a direct effect on the security of our countries. Reh argues that "the EU – a divided, multilevel and functionally restricted polity – is highly dependent on the legitimizing force of 'inclusive compromise', which is characterized by the recognition of

66 Directive 2013/32/EU of the European Parliament and of the Council of 26 June 2013 on common procedures for granting and withdrawing international protection (recast).

difference."[67] Consequently, without proper inclusiveness of the experiences and positions of various Member States, resulting in low legitimacy of the act, proper implementation will also be lacking. Furthermore, in an area as interdependent as the Schengen area, what one country considers to be favorable from its own perspective, cannot result in a favorable situation at the European level if it leaves it to other Member States to resolve alone.

Can we still afford the consequences of failing forward? It is not only the time, money and energy spent on trying to manage the mixed flows of migrants, whose movements are practically organized by international criminal groups of human smugglers. The Hungarian Government found it extremely important that at the October 2024 European Council meeting Member States took increasingly convergent positions and that they were finally on the right track, a track that Hungary had always advocated for. According to the Hungarian position, there is a determination not only to effectively protect the external borders of the EU, but also a determination to effectively address recurrent and new challenges in a way that is significantly different from what the EU has been pushing for so far. Therefore, Hungary found it essential to continue the dynamism of the October 2024 summit. The European Council should therefore recall the importance of continuing the work in new ways to prevent and counter irregular migration, especially by further developing the concept of return hubs and the externalization of asylum procedures. It is also welcomed that the Commission had finally recognized that Member States have the right to adopt exceptional rules for the sake of security and sovereignty, and that these are legitimate steps. Member Staes are well aware of the fact that international networks of criminal organizations are responsible for managing the illegal inflow of migrants, and it is not only state actors that can create serious situations of instrumentalization. The need may arise to allow for deterrent EU rules in such situations.

I have identified two hindering factors that posed major obstacles to achieving meaningful reforms that continuously result in the phenomenon of failing forward in the field of asylum and migration. One factor is the method of agreement. The search for a compromise is coded in the legislative processes and the institutional setup of the EU. The Commission is primarily interested in successfully concluding a comprehensive reform during its own five-year term, but implementation is primarily the responsibility of

67 Christine Reh, 'European Integration as Compromise: Recognition, Concessions and the Limits of Cooperation', *Government and Opposition*, Vol. 47, Issue 3, 2012, pp. 414–440.

the Member States, as are the consequences of the system's failure. The co-legislative function of the Council and the European Parliament also lead to a patchwork of provisions that are more mathematically composed rather than a practically workable, functional system.

> "Ministers in the Council and their representatives might hold the expertise, but they lack the authority to agree on a fundamental overhaul. The EUCO needs to mandate a search for extraordinary solutions. It might have to do these multiple times, but if the machinery gets stuck, the EUCO needs to provide new input and a new sense of direction."[68]

Although occasionally the European Council mandated ministers to seek consensus to give voice and weight to every Member State's situations and experiences, this was not strictly followed. "The EUCO essentially provides the 'organized hypocrisy' part of failing forward, it allows the system to separate the big political talk from the nitty gritty search for solutions. Political grandstanding at the height of the EU crisis has often been perceived as a nuisance."[69] Failing forward therefore necessarily involved affording a superficial role to the European Council, consequently, a vital ingredient of breaking the failing forward cycle would be to have the main building blocks of the reforms agreed at the highest level, otherwise migration and asylum reforms will not only lack legitimacy, but will also result once again in a low level of implementation.

The other problem lies in the legal framework that defines the proposed solutions. Innovative solutions are starting to emerge not only in individual countries, but it is finally on the agenda of the EU. Yet, what we experience is that regardless of the creative and innovative nature of these schemes, when governments try to make them operational, their efforts fail. They fail because the international and European legislative regimes solely acknowledge the rights of migrants and do not take into account the rights of our citizens to safety as the mass influx of people without proper identification raises numerous security concerns. Therefore there is a need not only be innovative in setting out new regimes and new ways of cooperation, but also to find a solution on how to make the interest of our own citizens be the focus of human rights protection. And it is no longer a heretic idea in the EU, as a meeting of 12 Member States that took part on the margins of the March 2025 European Council concluded that discussions should be held

---

68 *See* at https://www.tandfonline.com/doi/full/10.1080/07036337.2023.2209273.
69 Id.

on the possibility to change European Conventions related to migration to reflect today's realities. During the meeting Maltese Prime Minister Abela proposed that this crucial discussion take place during Malta's presidency of the Council of Europe which starts in May 2025.[70]

70 *See* at https://www.independent.com.mt/articles/2025-03-20/local-news/Migration-PM-speaks-of-reform-to-European-Conventions-to-reflect-changes-6736268723.

The CJEU's Infringement Procedure and Its Enforcement Mechanism

*Endre Orbán – Katalin Gombos**

Abstract

The enforcement of EU law takes place at two levels: at the level of the Union in a centralized manner, through direct proceedings before the CJEU, and at the level of the Member States – in a decentralized manner, through the national courts. In the first case, infringement proceedings initiated by the Commission play a central role, whereby the CJEU's responsibility is essentially judicial review: it examines whether a piece of national legislation complies with the requirements of EU law. Therefore, the present study focuses on the infringement procedure, describing its prominent types, features, and rules. In addition, it presents the relevant jurisprudence of the CJEU, with particular reference to the financial sanctions that the CJEU may apply together with a few novelties concerning Hungary.

Keywords: infringement procedure, CJEU, penalty payments, financial penalties, Hungary

1. Introduction

According to the 1973 *Les Verts* case, judicial review must be available for all acts having legal effects in the EU.[1] As the decision reads, "the European Economic Community is a community of law in so far as neither the Member States nor the institutions are exempt from reviewing the conformity of their acts with the fundamental constitutional charter, namely the

* Endre Orbán: senior lecturer, Ludovika University of Public Service, Budapest. ORCID: 0000–0001-5714–8565, orban.endre@uni-nke.hu
Katalin Gombos: professor of law, Ludovika University of Public Service, Budapest. ORCID: 0000–0002-1014-0547, simonne.gombos.katalin@uni-nke.hu.

1 The *ERTA* case can be seen as a precedent for this finding: Judgment of 31 March 1971, *Case C-22/70, Commission v Council,* ECLI:EU:C:1971:32, para. 42.

Treaty."[2] As the quote indicates, the rule of law requires that both EU legal acts and acts of the Member States comply with the founding Treaties.

To ensure such compliance, "[the] Treaty [...] has established a complete system of legal remedies and procedures."[3] The comprehensive system that providing for the examination and enforcement of EU law takes place at two levels: at the level of the Union in a centralized manner, through direct proceedings before the CJEU, and at the level of the Member States in a decentralized manner, through the national courts. This symbiosis is reflected in Article 19(1) TEU, which determines the constitutional role of the CJEU, according to which the CJEU "shall ensure that the law is respected in the interpretation and application of the Treaties", and since the Lisbon Treaty, dedicates a specific paragraph to national courts. According to the latter, "the Member States shall provide for such means of redress as are necessary to ensure effective judicial protection in the areas governed by Union law."

In line with this dual approach, the founding treaties ensure the legal conformity of national acts with EU law at two levels. In a fully centralized approach, the infringement procedure is the direct mechanism before the CJEU. To reinforce this trajectory, Member States have even institutionalized the possibility of imposing fines in the Maastricht Treaty for the enforcement of judgments. This feature can be considered a 'revolutionary' innovation among the powers of international judicial organizations.[4] In addition, there is also an indirect mechanism, the preliminary ruling procedure initiated for the interpretation of EU law, which provides an opportunity to review national rules, as de Witte has noted.[5] The latter procedure has a strongly decentralized character as it requires the cooperation of national courts. This mechanism, which ensures both the enforcement of EU law and at the same time, the implicit normative control of national rules, has substantial advantages over the infringement procedure. On the one hand, its use is not dependent on the Commission's resources[6] or the out-

2 Judgment of 23 April 1986, *Case C-294/83, Les Verts,* ECLI:EU:C:1986:166, para. 23.

3 Id.

4 Vassilios Skouris, 'The Position of the European Court of Justice in the EU Legal Order and Its Relationship with National Constitutional Courts', *Zeitschrift für öffentliches Recht,* 2005/3, p. 324.

5 Bruno de Witte, 'The Preliminary Ruling Dialogue: Three Types of Questions Posed by National Courts', *in* Bruno de Witte *et al.* (eds.), *National Courts and EU Law: New Issues, Theories and Methods,* Edward Elgar, Cheltenham, 2016, pp. 16–17.

6 The number of preliminary ruling procedures overtook the number of infringement procedures in the early 1970s and has been the Court's standard procedure ever since. Renaud

come of the political negotiations between the Commission and the Member State. On the other hand, the enforcement of EU law is more likely to be achieved through the preliminary ruling procedure, as national judges themselves must make the final decision on the instant case. Thus, the CJEU does not have to confront the Member State, and if the Member State government does not wish to comply with the Court's ruling, it will ultimately find itself in a situation where it is condemned by the national court.[7]

Nevertheless, whether the CJEU acts directly in the context of infringement proceedings initiated by the Commission or indirectly through questions referred by national courts, the CJEU's task is essentially judicial review: it examines whether a piece of national legislation complies with the requirements of EU law. Because of this function, the CJEU is considered by many authors to be a quasi-constitutional court,[8] which pursues an Abstract judicial review in infringement procedures and a concrete judicial review in the preliminary ruling procedure. Furthermore, the *quasi* constitutional court position is reinforced by other essential powers: not only can the CJEU review national acts but it also safeguards the legality of the exercise of power in the EU, as well as ensuring the conformity of EU sources of law with the Treaty.[9] The latter is the purpose of the annulment procedure, the preliminary ruling procedure aims at examining the validity of EU legal acts, and the plea of illegality provided for in Article 277 TFEU.[10]

Against this backdrop, the present study will focus on the infringement procedure: it describes the procedure's main types, features, and rules. It presents the relevant jurisprudence of the CJEU, with particular reference

Dehousse, *The European Court of Justice: The Politics of Judicial Integration,* Palgrave Macmillan, 1998, pp. 51–52.

7 Joseph H.H. Weiler, 'The Transformation of Europe', *The Yale Journal,* Vol. 100, Issue 8, 1991, pp. 2420–2421.

8 Monica Claes, The National Courts' Mandate in the European Constitution, Hart, Portland, 2006, p. 391.

9 The constitutional nature of the Treaties was also recognized by the case law of the CJEU in *Les Verts,* which referred to the founding Treaties as a 'basic constitutional charter': *Case C-294/83, Les Verts,* para. 23. The concept has also been used in other cases: Opinion of 14 December 1991, *Opinion no 1/91,* ECLI:EU:C:1991:490, para. 21; Judgment of 3 September 2008, *Joined Cases C-402/05 P and C-415/05 P, Kadi and Al Barakaat,* ECLI:EU:C:2008:461, para. 281; Opinion of 18 December 2014, *Opinion no 2/13,* ECLI:EU:C:2014:2454, para. 163.

10 Article 277 TFEU provides an exceptional legal remedy in the EU legal system. Under this Article, a party can challenge the application of a Union act of general application in a specific case on the grounds that it is unlawful. If the court finds an infringement, the act in question is not applied in the case, but EU law is not repealed either.

to the financial sanctions that the Court may apply in case of infringement together with some new developments concerning Hungary.

2. Two Types of Infringement Proceedings

According to Article 258 TFEU, if the Commission considers that a Member State has failed to fulfill an obligation under the Treaties, it shall deliver a reasoned opinion on the matter after giving the State concerned the opportunity to submit its observations. This is the *first type* of infringement proceedings that is essential for enforcing EU law: the European Commission, as 'the guardian of the Treaties', may launch such a procedure under Article 258 TFEU. Whether the European Commission launches such a procedure is at the discretion of the European Commission. It involves a consultation with the Member State concerned and possibly an agreement between them. However, it is clear that the Commission has no legal obligation to initiate or conduct proceedings.[11] In this respect, the Commission's procedure has had a 'black box' character from the outset: it is not accessible to external parties what criteria the Commission considers when it initiates proceedings in some cases and not in others. In any case, it may be an important consideration that the Commission's capacity is also finite, so it certainly cannot investigate all infringements of EU law.

However, as the Commission is the 'guardian of the Treaties', the recent proliferation of litigation regarding the values of the EU as enshrined in Article 2 TEU[12] has led to a growing number of critical voices in the literature stressing that the Commission should play a more significant role in defending EU values and be more active in bringing substantive infringement proceedings.[13]

The *second type* of infringement procedure, which is relatively rarely used, is litigation between the contracting parties, *i.e.,* the Member States themselves. If a Member State considers that another Member State has failed to fulfil an obligation under the Treaty, it may bring the matter before the CJEU. Before doing so, the Member State must refer the matter to the

11 Judgment of 14 February 1989, *Case C-247/87, Star Fruit,* ECLI:EU:C:1989:58, para. 11.

12 Luke Dimitrios Spieker, *EU Values Before the Court of Justice: Foundations, Potential, Risks,* Oxford Studies in European Law, Oxford, 2023, pp. 87–106.

13 Petra Bárd *et al.*, 'Treaty changes for a better protection of EU values in the Member States', *European Law Journal,* Vol. 30, Issue 4, 2024, pp. 1–16. András Jakab: 'Three misconceptions about the EU rule of law crisis', *Verfassungsblog,* 17 October 2022.

Commission and provide the possibility for the Commission, as the 'guardian of the Treaties', to initiate infringement proceedings in the same matter. If the Commission does not do so within three months, the Member State may bring the action before the CJEU. The legal basis of this procedure is Article 259 TFEU, and its rationale can be traced back to Article 344 TFEU, under which the Member States have undertaken to settle disputes concerning the interpretation or application of the Treaties exclusively by way of the procedures provided for in the Treaties. In light of this, the second type of infringement procedure reflects the *par excellence* characteristics of an international court. The Treaty 'softens' this international judicial character by entrusting the resolution of disputes between Member States primarily to the Commission, by requiring a Member State to communicate the legal issue to the 'guardian of the Treaties' first and ask it to represent its position in the first type of infringement procedure.[14] If the Commission does not agree with the existence of an infringement, the Member State is given the option to refer the dispute between the two Member States to the CJEU as an international court to resolve it.

3. Two Types of Infringements

Infringements can be divided into two broad categories. The first category is the so-called *substantive infringement procedure,* which occurs when a Member State fails to fulfil an obligation under EU law. This may be through national legislation that infringes EU law or through the application or failure to apply EU law in practice.[15] In addition, the second broad category of infringement proceedings relates to the obligation to implement directives. This is the so-called *non-notification infringement procedure* that is more technical. Its additional rules are laid down in Article 260(3) TFEU. The Commission can launch this procedure when a Member State fails to fulfil

14 According to Lenaerts, the infringement procedure that can be initiated by the Commission is an important feature distinguishing EU law from international law: in this procedure, contrary to Article 60 of the Treaty on the Law of Treaties, signed in Vienna on 23 May 1969, Member States cannot rely on the argument of non-reciprocity, *i.e.* the fact that another Member State has also infringed a particular provision of EU law, as a defence on the basis of EU law. *See* Koen Lenaerts, 'The Rule of Law and the Coherence of the Judicial System of the European Union', *Common Market Law Review,* Vol. 44, Issue 6, 2007, p. 1639.

15 Judgment of 9 December 1997, *Case C-265/95, Commission v France,* ECLI:EU:C:1997:595.

its so-called 'notification obligation', *i.e.*, when it does not notify the Commission of the measures adopted to transpose a directive.

The rationale behind the latter procedure is the requirement of legal certainty; the doctrinal starting point is that the provisions of a directive must be implemented with indisputable binding force and with the necessary degree of specificity, precision, and clarity. According to settled case law, it is essential that national law effectively ensure the complete application of the directive. It is also necessary that the resulting legal situation under national law be sufficiently precise and clear, so that individuals know the full extent of their rights to be able to rely on them before the national courts.[16]

Nevertheless, the jurisprudence of the CJEU on the incorrect transposition of directives by the Member States has made it clear that directives don't need to be implemented by legislation. Accordingly, the CJEU has held that "the existence of general principles of constitutional law or administrative law"[17] or "an existing legal framework"[18] may be sufficient to implement the directive without further legislative measures by Member States, provided that they comply with these minimum requirements. However, the CJEU has also held that the simple existence of administrative practice[19] that complies with a directive, or the possibility for courts to interpret national law in conformity with a directive,[20] does not relieve a Member State of the obligation to adopt appropriate binding implementing measures. The CJEU has also established that any Member State implementation that may even in theory jeopardize the implementation of a directive, is prohibited, notwithstanding the fact that the actual implementation itself had not resulted in any detrimental effects.[21] A simple administrative practice that the administration can change at will and which is not sufficiently known cannot be regarded as a valid implementation of the obligations incumbent on

16 Judgment of 9 September 2004, *Case C-70/03, Commission v Spain,* ECLI:EU:C:2004:505, para. 15, and the case law cited.

17 Judgment of 23 May 1985, *Case C-29/84, Commission v Germany,* ECLI:EU:C:1985:229, para. 23.

18 Judgment of 20 May 1992, *Case C-190/90, Commission v Netherlands,* ECLI:EU:C:1992:225, para. 17.

19 Judgment of 15 March 1990, *Case C-339/87, Commission v Netherlands,* ECLI:EU:C:1990:119, para. 36.

20 Judgment of 27 October 1993, *Case C-338/91, Steenhorst-Neerings,* ECLI:EU:C:1993:857, paras. 32–34.

21 Judgment of 9 April 1987, *Case C-363/85, Commission v Italy,* ECLI:EU:C:1987:196, paras. 10 and 12.

Member States in the context of transposing a directive because of the lack of compliance with the minimum requirements.[22]

Furthermore, not only the failure to implement a directive but also other reasons can lead to an action for infringement. The CJEU has ruled on several occasions that the Commission may seek a declaration of failure to fulfil an obligation because the given directive's objective has not been achieved.[23] For instance, the CJEU has held that an action may be justified even if the applicable national legislation is in itself compatible with EU law when the administrative practice violates EU law and constitutes a breach of legal obligations.[24]

Both categories of infringements are channeled into the same procedure at the end of the day. However, two crucial differences between the two types of infringement should be highlighted. On the one hand, substantive infringement proceedings are more sensitive, as they represent a more significant challenge to the EU legal order and are, therefore, the ones that are usually reported in the news.[25]

On the other hand, in non-notification infringement proceedings, since the entry into force of the Lisbon Treaty that introduced Article 260(3) TFEU, the Commission may also seek to impose a financial penalty on the Member State already in its petition under Article 258 TFEU procedure for failure to notify measures transposing a directive. Unlike in substantive infringement proceedings, if the CJEU finds that an infringement has indeed taken place, it may order the Member State to pay a lump sum or penalty payment not exceeding an amount determined by the Commission. Importantly, this financial sanction can also be imposed if the Member State complies with its transposition obligations at the time of the court proceedings, because the existence of an infringement must be assessed in any event based on the situation in which the Member State in question was when the time-limit set in the reasoned opinion expired, and the CJEU may not take

22 Judgment of 12 July 2007, *Case C-507/04, Commission v Austria,* ECLI:EU:C:2007:427, para. 162, and the case law cited; Judgment of 19 December 2013, *Case C-281/11, Commission v Poland,* ECLIEU:C:2013:855, para. 105.

23 Judgment of 10 April 2003, *Joined Cases C-20/01 and C-28/01, Commission v Germany,* ECLI:EU:C:2003:220, para. 30; Judgment of 14 April 2005, *Case C-157/03, Commission v Spain,* ECLI:EU:C:2005:225, para. 44.

24 Judgment of 12 May 2005, *Case C-278/03, Commission v Italy,* ECLI:EU:C:2005:281, para. 13.

25 Statistics on infringement proceedings are available on the following website: https://commission.europa.eu/law/application-eu-law/implementing-eu-law/infringement-procedure/2022-annual-report-monitoring-application-eu-law_en.

into consideration any changes that have occurred since then.[26] Here, the aim is to ensure that the Member States transpose and notify their legislation in time and avoid court proceedings altogether.

4. Steps of the Infringement Procedure

To initiate proceedings, the EU infringement alleged by the Commission must be committed by a Member State, *i.e.*, the infringement must be attributable to the Member State's action in a broad sense. Thus, a Member State may be brought before the CJEU if the infringement in question is committed by the Member State's legislature, government, or judiciary[27] or if the acts of certain persons are closely connected with the functioning of the State and are therefore attributable to it.[28]

If the Commission considers that a Member State did not comply with its obligations under EU law, it may first open a non-public consultation with the Member State's government; this is the so-called pilot procedure.[29] If the consultation with the government does not dispel the doubts raised, the procedure enters the formal phase by the Commission's letter of formal notice. If the Member State's response to the letter of formal notice (or the measures adopted by the Member State in the meantime) do not resolve the infringement, the European Commission will issue a reasoned opinion, setting a deadline for the Member State to correct the infringement.

The correct conduct of the pre-litigation procedure is significant in the infringement procedure. The pre-litigation procedures determine the subject matter of an action for infringement.[30] Therefore, the action cannot be examined on its merits if any of the guarantees of the pre-litigation procedure are missing. Accordingly, the CJEU will examine the pleas in law raised

---

26 Judgment of 5 February 2015, *Case C-317/14, Commission v Belgium,* ECLI:EU:C:2015:63, para. 34; Judgment of 18 December 2014, *Case C-640/13, Commission v United Kingdom,* ECLI:EU:C:2014:2457, para. 42, and the case law cited.

27 Judgment of 4 October 2018, *Case C-416/17, Commission v France,* ECLI:EU:C:2018:811.

28 Judgment of 24 November 1982, *Case C-249/81, Commission v Ireland,* ECLI:EU:C:1982:402.

29 Ernő Várnay, 'Discretion in the Articles 258 and 260(2) TFEU Procedures', *Maastricht Journal of European and Comparative Law,* Vol. 22, Issue 6, 2015, p. 856; EU law: Better results through better application. Communication from the Commission, 2017/C 18/02.

30 Judgment of 10 May 2001, *Case C-152/98, Commission v Netherlands,* ECLI:EU:C:2001:255, para. 23; Judgment of 15 January 2002, *Case C-439/99, Commission v Italy,* ECLI:EU:C:2002:14, para. 11; Judgment of 16 June 2005, *Case C-456/03, Commission v Italy,* ECLI:EU:C:2005:388, para. 35.

by the Member States in the context of admissibility. If such a procedural plea is successful, the CJEU will dismiss the action without examining the substantive merits of the case.[31]

Therefore, the *letter of formal notice and reasoned opinion* sent by the Commission play a key role. The letter of formal notice summarizes the alleged infringement, but it can also help understand the reasoned opinion. However, the most relevant legal effects are linked to the reasoned opinion, where the Commission must clearly identify the conduct it considers to be in breach of EU legal obligations. In other words, the reasoned opinion must contain a coherent and detailed statement of those reasons that have led the Commission to believe that the Member State concerned has failed to fulfil its obligation under the Treaty.[32] This ensures that the Member State concerned knows precisely which obligation the Commission considers to have been infringed by the Member State before it takes legal action before the CJEU, so that the Member State concerned can eliminate the infringement or present its defence.[33]

As a corollary, the Member States are expected to provide clear and precise replies to the formal notice. For example, in the case of an obligation to implement a directive, the Member State concerned must clearly indicate the legislative, regulatory, and administrative measures by which it considers that it has complied with its obligations under the directive. In the absence of this information, the Commission will not be in a position to verify whether the Member State has actually and fully implemented the obligation to implement the directive. Failure by a Member State to fulfil this obligation, either by failing to provide all necessary information or by failing to provide sufficiently clear and precise information, may in itself justify the opening of infringement proceedings.[34]

If the Member State fails to remedy the situation satisfactorily within the deadline set in the reasoned opinion, the European Commission may start the judicial phase of the infringement procedure by bringing an action before the CJEU. A critical procedural aspect is that the Commission, as the applicant, may only raise those grounds against the Member State in its action before the CJEU that it has already put forward in its reasoned opin-

---

31 Judgment of 16 March 2023, *Case C-174/21, Commission v Bulgaria,* ECLI:EU:C:2023:210, para. 22.

32 Judgment of 24 June 2004, *Case C-350/02, Commission v the Netherlands,* ECLI:EU:C:2004:389, para. 20.

33 Id. para. 21.

34 *Case C-456/03, Commission v Italy,* para. 27.

ion.[35] This has a guarantee function since the purpose of the pre-litigation procedure is to enable the Member State concerned to comply with its obligations under Community law and to ensure its right of defence against Commission's legal objections.[36] As the reasoned opinion and the application must be based on the same grounds and pleas, the CJEU cannot examine an objection not raised in the reasoned opinion.[37] Consequently, if an objection has not been formulated in the reasoned opinion, it will be inadmissible at the stage of the proceedings before the CJEU.[38]

Nevertheless, according to the practice of the CJEU, this requirement is not applied n a mechanical way. The requirement that the subject matter of the action must be defined in the pre-action procedure cannot mean that the wording of the objection must be absolutely identical in the letter of formal notice, the operative part of the reasoned opinion, and the application. Following the principle of *a maiore ad minus* deduction,[39] it is possible to reduce the subject matter of the dispute. However, the doctrine of *a minore ad maius* is a strict limitation that does not allow the subject matter of the dispute to be extended, modified, or enlarged.[40]

If the CJEU does not declare the action inadmissible on formal grounds, the case will proceed to the substance of the action. Member States may rely on several pleas in law in the proceedings to defend themselves against the action. Typical Member State arguments that the CJEU has not accepted are references to provisions of national law, the length of legislative procedures, or other difficulties encountered by Member States. Indeed, the CJEU does not accept assertions that the legislative work to bring national legislation

---

35 Judgment of 17 February 1970, *Case C-31/69, Commission v Italy,* ECLI:EU:C:1970:10; Judgment of 9 February 2006, *Case C-305/03, Commission v the United Kingdom,* ECLI:EU:C:2006:90, paras. 22–23; Judgment of 20 March 1997, *Case C-96/95, Commission v Germany,* ECLI:EU:C:1997:165, para. 23; *Case C-439/99, Commission v Italy,* para. 11; Judgment of 20 June 2002, *Case C-287/00, Commission v Germany,* ECLI:EU:C:2002:388, para. 18.

36 *Case C-456/03, Commission v Italy,* paras. 35–37; Judgment of 21 September 1999, *Case C-392/96, Commission v Ireland,* ECLI:EU:C:1999:431, para. 51, Judgment of 29 April 2004, *Case C-117/02, Commission v Portugal,* ECLI:EU:C:2004:266, para. 53.

37 Judgment of 27 April 2006, *Case C-441/02, Commission v Germany,* ECLI:EU:C:2006:253, para. 60; Judgment of 11 May 1989, *Case C-76/86, Commission v Germany,* ECLI:EU:C:1989:184, para. 8.

38 *Case C-439/99, Commission v Italy,* para. 11.

39 *Case C-305/03, Commission v the United Kingdom,* paras. 22–23; Judgment of 1 February 2005, *Case C-203/03, Commission v Austria,* ECLI:EU:C:2005:76, para. 29.

40 *Case C-456/03, Commission v Italy,* para. 39; Judgment of 16 September 1997, *Case C-279/94, Commission v Italy,* ECLI:EU:C:1997:396, para. 25; and Judgment of 11 July 2002, *Case C-139/00, Commission v Spain,* ECLI:EU:C:2002:438, para. 19.

into conformity with EU legal requirements has already been started but has not yet been completed because of the lengthy and complex procedures that must be followed. According to the settled case law of the CJEU, a Member State may not justify non-compliance with obligations under EU law based on provisions of its national legal system, including constitutional provisions.[41] Similarly, a Member State cannot rely on the direct effect of directives as a defence against a claim that it has failed to wholly and correctly implement a directive.[42]

However, a borderline case of inadmissibility and dismissal on the merits is when the CJEU accepts the Member State's argument that the legal effects have ceased, *i.e.*, that the impact of the infringement has essentially been eliminated. In such a case, the CJEU dismisses the action for infringement as inadmissible, considering that the Member State's plea that the alleged violation could no longer produce legal effects following the expiry of the time limit set in the reasoned opinion was well-founded.[43]

5. Enforcing the CJEU's Judgments

The CJEU's rulings are declaratory: they determine whether the Member State concerned has infringed EU law. Should the CJEU find an infringement, the Member State must enforce the judgment, *i.e.*, to end the situation that infringes EU law. This voluntary enforcement is based on the loyalty clause set out abstractly in Article 4(3) TEU and fleshed out more concretely in Article 260(1) TFEU.

Whether the Member State is sued by the Commission or by another Member State, the Member State will appear as a single entity in the proceedings, and the Court's rulings will be declaratory in its direction: the Court will not have direct access to the national legal system, but the Member State will have to remedy the breach of law. In other words, the CJEU only establishes the infringement but does not (may not) determine the measures necessary to comply with its judgment. This means that the

---

41 Judgment of 8 April 2014, *Case C-288/12, Commission v Hungary,* ECLI:EU:C:2014:237, para. 35, and the case law cited.

42 Judgment of 6 May 1980, *Case C-102/79, Commission v Belgium,* ECLI:EU:C:1980:120, para. 12; Judgment of 25 July 1992, *Case C-208/90, Emmott,* ECLI:EU:C:1991:333, para. 20; *Case C-96/95, Commission v Germany,* para. 37.

43 Judgment of 18 May 2006, *Case C-221/04, Commission v Spain,* ECLI:EU:C:2006:329, paras. 25–26; Judgment of 7 April 2011, *Case C-20/09, Commission v Portugal,* ECLI:EU:C:2011:214, para. 33.

measures needed to comply with the judgment finding an infringement are not the subject of the judgment;[44] the choice of the form and nature of the measures remain a matter for the Member State to choose. The enforcement of decisions of the CJEU is not optional but obligatory for the Member State under the principle of *pacta sunt servanda* and the loyalty clause derived from the Treaties. In this regard, Article 4(3) TEU lays down a positive and a negative obligation. On the one hand, Member States must take appropriate measures, whether general or particular, to ensure fulfilment of obligations arising from the Treaties or resulting from action taken by the institutions of the Union, and must assist the Union in the performance of its tasks. On the other hand, Member States must refrain from any measure which could jeopardize the attainment of the Union's objectives. The principle of loyalty is concretized in Article 260(1) TFEU,[45] according to which if the CJEU finds that a Member State has failed to fulfil an obligation under the Treaties, the State shall be required to take the necessary measures to comply with the judgment of the Court. While Article 260(1) TFEU does not specify the time limit by which the judgment must be executed, the CJEU has consistently held that the interest of the immediate and uniform application of EU law requires compliance to begin immediately and to be completed as soon as possible.[46]

6. Financial Penalties

As a safeguard for the enforcement of CJEU judgments, Member States introduced pecuniary sanctions in the Maastricht Treaty. In case of non-notification infringements, such sanctions may be requested already in the procedure under Article 258 TFEU. However, in case of substantive infringement procedures, the Commission is empowered to initiate a second procedure under Article 260(2) TFEU for enforcing CJEU judgments with the prospect of a financial penalty.

Under the latter provision, if the European Commission considers that the Member State concerned has not complied with the CJEU's judgment,

44 *Case C-288/12, Commission v Hungary,* para. 33.

45 Claes 2006, p. 400.

46 Judgment of 14 December 2023, *Case C-109/22, Commission v Romania,* ECLI:EU:C:2023:991, para. 67, and the case law cited; Judgment of 6 November 1985, *Case C-131/84, Commission v Italy,* ECLI:EU:C:1985:447, para. 7; Judgment of 12 November 2019, *Case C-261/18, Commission v Ireland,* ECLI:EU:C:2019:955, para. 123, and the case law cited.

i.e., has not fulfilled its obligations under the CJEU's judgment, the Commission may refer the Member State back to the CJEU after allowing the Member State to submit its observations.[47] This means that – unlike in the non-notification infringement proceedings – in case of substantive infringement proceedings, there is a second procedure before the CJEU where financial penalties might be applied.[48] In this regard, it seems to be appropriate to use the terminology of first and second judgments on failure to fulfil obligations: failure to comply with the first CJEU judgment's finding may result in the Member State being ordered to pay a penalty or a lump sum in the second infringement procedure.[49]

Several similarities can be established between the first proceedings concerning the breach of EU legal obligations and the second, subsequent proceedings for failure to enforce a CJEU judgment. First, the date of the violation of obligations is of primary importance in the case law of the CJEU which is defined as the date of reference. The reference date for assessing the existence of a failure to fulfil an obligation within the meaning of Article 260(2) TFEU (*i.e.*, the breach of the obligation to take the necessary measures to comply with the judgment of the CJEU) is the expiry of the period laid down in the letter of formal notice issued under Article 260(2) TFEU.[50] This date is of similar importance and effect to the time limit set in the reasoned opinion sent out in the first, pre-litigation procedure.[51] Second, the requirement of legal certainty applies equally as under Article 258 TFEU; accordingly, the issuance of a letter of formal notice under Article 260(2) TFEU has significant legal consequences. In the course of the pre-litigation procedure, the Commission must examine whether the first judgment finding an infringement has been enforced. As a first step, the Commission requests information from the Member State, with an information letter on the measures taken to comply with the first judgment. If the Commission is not satisfied with the Member State's reply, it sends a formal notice setting out the deadline for compliance. Here, the Commission must clearly state that the first infringement judgment has not yet been complied

47 *Case C-174/21, Commission v Bulgaria,* para. 22.

48 Judgment of 12 July 2005, *Case C-304/02, Commission v France,* ECLI:EU:C:2005:444, para. 80; *Case C-174/21, Commission v Bulgaria,* para. 22.

49 Judgment of 4 July 2000, *Case C-387/97, Commission v Greece,* ECLI:EU:C:2000:356, para. 42.

50 *Case C-174/21, Commission v Bulgaria,* para. 24; Judgment of 11 December 2012, *Case C-610/10, Commission v Spain,* ECLI:EU:C:2012:781, para. 67.

51 Judgment of 14 March 2006, *Case C-177/04, Commission v France,* ECLI:EU:C:2006:173, para. 20; *Case C-304/02, Commission v France,* para. 30.

with. Accordingly, in the event of a legal action, the CJEU will examine whether the Commission has established *prima facie* that the judgment's requirements have not yet been fulfilled by the reference date.[52]

If the CJEU finds in the second infringement procedure that the first infringement judgment has not been enforced, it will impose a financial penalty to the infringing Member State. However, the two types of infringements are essentially different when it comes to financial penalties. Whereas in the case of non-notification infringement proceedings, the CJEU is bound by the amounts requested by the Commission in its application, no such limit applies in the case of substantive infringement proceedings, and the Commission's proposal for the level of the financial penalty is merely a helpful reference point. This means that the CJEU has discretion to determine the amount of the fine in a way it deems appropriate under the circumstances. In determining the financial sanction, the following criteria must be taken into account: the seriousness of the infringement, its duration and the deterrent effect of the financial sanction, the need to avoid a repetition of the infringement,[53] and its proportionality both to the infringement established and to the ability of the Member State concerned to pay.[54]

To ensure transparency and equal treatment, the Commission has published several communications[55] since 1996, setting out its policy and methodology for calculating financial penalties. The most recent amendment of the current 2023 Communication of the Commission took place in 2025.[56]

---

52 *Case C-174/21, Commission v Bulgaria,* para. 27; Judgment of 5 December 2019, *Case C-642/18, Commission v Spain,* ECLI:EU:C:2019:1051, paras. 17, 18, 26, and the case law cited.

53 *Case C-387/97, Commission v Greece,* para. 92; Judgment of 25 February 2021, *Case C-658/19, Commission v Spain,* ECLI:EU:C:2021:138, paras. 63 and 73; Judgment of 16 July 2020, *Case C-550/18, Commission v Ireland,* ECLI:EU:C:2020:564, para. 81.

54 Judgment of 25 November 2003, *Case C-278/01, Commission v Spain,* ECLI:EU:C:2003:635.

55 In 1996, the Commission published a memorandum on applying Article 171 of the EC treaty, followed in 1997 by its first communication on the method of calculating the penalty payments provided for pursuant to Article 171 of the EC Treaty. In 2001, the Commission adopted an internal Commission Decision on the method of the calculation of fines, followed in 2005 by a Communication on the implementation of Article 228 of the EC Treaty. In 2010, the Commission adopted a Communication on the implementation of Article 260(3) TFEU, following the amendments introduced by the Lisbon Treaty. The current Communication was issued in 2023, updated in 2024 and amended in 2025.

56 Modification of the method of calculation of financial penalties proposed by the Commission in infringement proceedings before the Court of Justice of the European Union, C/2025/1481.

Initially,[57] the Commission introduced a method for calculating the Member State's ability to pay based on the gross domestic product (GDP) of the Member State (weighted 2/3) and the population of the Member State concerned (weighted 1/3). However, in its judgment of 25 April 2024 in *Case C-147/23*,[58] the CJEU ruled that there is no absolute link between the population of a Member State and its capacity to pay. Therefore, the demographic criteria cannot be considered when determining the Member States' ability to pay. Thus, the Communication currently in use follows a different method for determining the Member State's ability to pay ('coefficient n'). The new method of calculation does not apply the demographic criteria. The so-called 'coefficient n' is defined as the ratio of the given Member State's GDP to the Member State's average GDP, which is the ability to pay of the Member State concerned in relation to other Member States. The Communication contains precise calculation methods for calculating the lump sum and penalty payment, including daily, minimum, and reference amounts. The new value of the 'coefficient n' for each Member State is also available in a table in the Annex to the revised Communication.

There are two types of financial penalties. If the CJEU finds that the Member State concerned has not complied with its judgment, it may order it to pay a lump sum or penalty payment. Nevertheless, the CJEU may simultaneously apply both types of penalties, particularly where the infringement has been committed over a long period and is likely to be persistent.[59]

6.1. The Lump Sum Penalty

The lump sum is proportional to the past infringement and ensures that it is remedied. According to the case law of the CJEU, the lump sum must be determined in each case based on all the relevant factors relating to the characteristics of the infringement established and the conduct of the Member State concerned in the proceedings initiated under Article 260 TFEU. This provision gives the CJEU broad discretion[60] to decide whether or not to impose such a sanction. The discretionary criteria include whether the effective prevention of a repetition of a similar breach of EU law in the future

57 Commission Notice 2023/C 2/01 – Financial penalties in infringement proceedings.

58 Judgment of 25 April 2024, *Case C-147/23, Commission v Poland*, ECLI:EU:C:2024:346, paras. 84–86.

59 *Case C-304/02, Commission v France*, para. 81.

60 *Case C-109/22, Commission v Romania*, para. 78, and the case law cited.

justifies the application of a dissuasive measure.[61] The lump sum should be proportionate to the infringement committed.[62] Other criteria to be considered are the seriousness and duration of the infringements found, and the solvency of the Member State concerned.[63]

6.2. Periodic Penalty Payments

In contrast with the lump sum payment, the penalty payment is prospective. It is payable daily until the infringement is remedied, thus incentivizing the Member State to comply with the CJEU's judgment as soon as possible. Accordingly, the imposition of a periodic penalty payment is justified only if the infringement based on non-compliance with the previous judgment persists at the time of the evaluation by the CJEU.[64] The purpose of a periodic penalty payment is to end the infringement complained of, and the CJEU must set it in such a way as to be both appropriate under the circumstances and to the infringement found, including the Member State's ability to pay.[65]

In the case of a periodic penalty payment, the Commission's proposals on the fine amount cannot bind the CJEU, but only serve as a helpful reference point.[66] According to the CJEU, the essential criteria to be taken into account for determining the amount of a periodic penalty payment to ensure that it is coercive for the uniform and effective application of EU law are the following: the gravity of the infringement, the duration of the infringement and the ability of the Member State concerned to pay. In applying those criteria, the CJEU must take into account, in particular, the consequences for private and public interests of non-compliance with the judgment and the

---

61 Judgment of 13 June 2024, *Case C-123/22, Commission v Hungary,* ECLI:EU:C:2024:493, para. 99.

62 *Case C-109/22, Commission v Romania,* para. 80, and the case law cited.

63 *Case C-123/22, Commission v Hungary,* para. 101; *Case C-109/22, Commission v Romania,* para. 81, and the case law cited.

64 *Case C-123/22, Commission v Hungary,* para. 137; *Case C-109/22, Commission v Romania,* para. 52, and the case law cited.

65 Importantly, on 20 November 2017, the CJEU held that it has power under Article 279 TFEU procedure as well, empowering the CJEU to prescribe any necessary interim measures in any cases before it, to impose a periodic penalty payment on a Member State, if the Member State fails to comply with the interim measures ordered. Judgment of 17 April 2018, *Case C-441/17, Commission v Poland,* ECLI:EU:C:2017:877, para. 102.

66 *Case C-123/22, Commission v Hungary,* para. 140; *Case C-109/22, Commission v Romania,* para. 58, and the case law cited.

urgency with which the Member State concerned must comply with its obligations.[67]

6.3. Hungary-related Developments

Recently, Hungary provided examples for both types of infringements that resulted in sanctions.

Concerning the *non-notification type of infringement,* Member States had to implement the whistleblowers directive until 17 December 2021.[68] The European Commission had to be informed by this deadline. Still, five Member States – Germany, Luxembourg, the Czech Republic, Estonia, and Hungary – have not taken the necessary measures and have not fulfilled their obligations under the directive. Therefore, the Commission launched infringement procedures under Article 260(3) TFEU and the CJEU in cases *C-149/23 Commission v Germany, C-150/23 Commission v Luxembourg, C-152/23 Commission v Czech Republic, C-154/23 Commission v Estonia and C-155/23 Commission v Hungary* ordered all five Member States to pay financial penalties. The CJEU fixed the lump sum from the date of the infringement until the date the infringement has been eliminated, or failing that, the date on which the CJEU's judgment is delivered, and a daily penalty thereafter to be paid until the necessary legal provisions are adopted. Accordingly, in the case of Hungary, a lump sum has been requested for the period starting from December 2021, together with a periodic penalty payment of €13,650 per day from the date of the judgment. However, in the meantime, Hungary eliminated the unlawful situation on 24 July 2023, with the entry into force of Law No XXV of 2023 and Government Decree No 225/2023; therefore, it was condemned only to pay a lump sum of EUR 1,750,000.[69]

Concerning the *substantive infringement procedure,* it must be recalled that the European Commission launched infringement proceedings against Hungary due to its asylum rules, including the transit zones established in the country. The matter has reached the court phase, where Hungary lost the case in December 2020. In its first judgment of 17 December

67 *Case C-123/22, Commission v Hungary,* para. 141.

68 Directive (EU) 2019/1937 of the European Parliament and of the Council of 23 October 2019 on the protection of persons who report breaches of Union law.

69 Judgment of 6 March 2025, *Case C-155/23, Commission v Hungary,* ECLI:EU:C:2025:151.

2020,[70] the CJEU found that Hungary had failed to fulfil its obligations by not complying with EU law governing, in particular, the granting of international protection and the return of illegally staying third-country nationals. This infringement consists of restricting access to procedures for international protection, unlawfully detaining persons seeking such protection in transit zones, and violating the right of such individuals to remain in Hungary until a final decision has been taken on their appeal against the rejection of their application, and the removal of illegally staying third-country nationals. Following the decision, the Commission launched the second infringement procedure for non-compliance with the CJEU's judgment on 21 February 2022, requesting financial penalties, after finding that Hungary (apart from closing the transit zones, which it had already done before the judgment was delivered) had failed to comply with the 2020 judgment. In its second judgment,[71] the CJEU holds that Hungary has not taken the measures necessary to comply with the 2020 judgment as regards access to the international protection procedure, the right of applicants for international protection to remain in Hungary pending a final decision on their appeal against the rejection of their application and the removal of illegally staying third-country nationals. By doing so, Hungary has deliberately withdrawn from the entire common EU policy on international protection and from the application of the rules on the removal of illegally staying third-country nationals, in breach of the principle of loyal cooperation. This conduct significantly jeopardizes the unity of EU law, which has a very serious impact on both private interests, including the interests of asylum seekers, and the public interest. Hungary has failed to fulfil its obligations, which, among other things, has financial implications, shifting the responsibility for receiving applicants for international protection, assessing their applications, and returning illegally staying third-country nationals, which seriously undermines the principle of solidarity and fair sharing of responsibility among Member States.

In this procedure, the Commission requested the CJEU to order Hungary to pay a daily lump sum of EUR 5468.45, amounting in total to at least EUR 1,044,000, for the period from the date on which the judgment in the 2020 *Commission v Hungary* judgment was delivered until the date on which the defendant complies with that judgment or the date of delivery of

---

70 Judgment of 17 December 2020, *Case C-808/18, Commission v Hungary,* ECLI:EU:C:2020:1029.

71 Judgment of 13 June 2024, Case C-123/22, *Commission v Hungary,* ECLI:EU:C:2024:493.

the second infringement procedure's judgment, together with a daily penalty payment of EUR 16,393.16 in case Hungary has not yet complied with the first judgment. Nevertheless, the CJEU – "in the light of [...] the exceptional seriousness of the infringements at issue and Hungary's failure to cooperate in good faith in order to bring them to an end"[72] – increased the penalty payments and condemned Hungary to pay a lump sum of €200 million with an additional €1 million daily penalty payment until the government implements a migration law-related ruling of the CJEU.

7. Concluding Thoughts

Infringement proceedings are central to ensuring Member State compliance with EU law. Regarding both types of infringements, *i.e.,* non-notification and substantive infringements, the European Commission plays a vital role as the guardian of the Treaties. The Member States have recognized the proceedings' importance and sought to make the judicial review and the judicial enforcement of EU law as complete as possible in the founding treaties.[73] This is well illustrated by the legal bases empowering EU institutions to request and impose financial penalties in the Maastricht Treaty, serving as a guarantee for the horizontal relations of the 'High Contracting Parties'.

The two types of financial penalties are a lump sum and a penalty payment. Both the lump sum and the penalty payment have the same purpose: to encourage the Member State in breach to comply with the judgment establishing the infringement. In particular, the imposition of a penalty payment seems appropriate to incentivize the Member State to bring the infringement to an end as soon as possible. The imposition of a lump sum is based more on an assessment of the consequences of the infringement for the private and public interests of the Member State concerned, in particular where the infringement has persisted for an extended period since the judgment had established it. In addition, the CJEU has interpreted Article 260(2) TFEU as meaning that the application of a 'cumulative' sanction cannot be excluded because of the different objectives pursued, in particular where the breach of obligations has been of long duration and is of a persistent nature.[74] We may conclude that there is extensive case law on the application

72 *Case C-123/22, Commission v Hungary,* ECLI:EU:C:2024:493, para. 132.

73 Anthony Arnull, 'The European Court and Judicial Objectivity: A Reply to Professor Hartley', *Law Quarterly Review,* Vol. 112, July 1996, p. 416.

74 *Case C-304/02, Commission v France,* paras. 80–83.

of this system of sanctions and on the mechanism for enforcing judgments of the CJEU,[75] and recently, the cases involving Hungary have also contributed to the clarification of the penalties' mechanisms.

75 Id. para. 92; *Case C-174/21, Commission v Bulgaria,* para. 23.

Remuneration in Crypto?

The Digital Reality Ahead of Legislation

*Zsolt Halász**

Abstract

Besides the advancement of digitalization and the increasing use of crypto assets, several issues emerge in our daily lives that may appear surprising at first, but when analyzed in detail, do not seem impossible to implement in practice. This paper explores the creation of a regulatory framework which allows for remuneration for work in crypto assets. The topic is multilayered. On the one hand, it involves the consideration of not only national legislation, but also the relevant international and EU law. This is to identify the various solutions for different solutions that can be used for the various forms of remuneration in crypto assets, to identify solutions that the current regulatory framework allows, and to determine which aspects should be taken into account in a new regulatory environment in light of technological developments.

Keywords: crypto legislation, crypto assets, remunerations of employees, labor law, blockchain

1. Introduction – Aim of the Research

In our changing world, technological development brings about many new tools, methods, and opportunities in various areas of life. The impact of technological progress on the legislative framework is often significant, as it raises questions that are not adequately addressed by current legal provisions. This paper examines the most important international and certain

* Zsolt Halász: associate professor of law, Pázmány Péter Catholic University, Budapest, halasz.zsolt@jak.ppke.hu.

national rules governing remuneration for work related to the payment of certain elements of compensation in crypto assets. The examples shown illustrate how widely different the approaches to the same topic can be in different states, in terms of both legislation and law implementation. As will be demonstrated below, due, *inter alia,* to the relative novelty of crypto assets, most of the applicable legal provisions simply do not address this issue, nor do the relevant provisions promote this method of remuneration. This paper goes beyond a mere analysis of labor law rules, also providing an overview of the relevant financial and fiscal terminology and legal provisions.

Potential users and legislators were first confronted with crypto assets and the challenges they pose in 2009 when bitcoin appeared. In terms of numbers, while in the summer of 2019, there were only 2250 different crypto assets (not a negligible increase in terms of the number of units in just a decade), today their number is over 20,000, of which 8–10,000 may be effectively operational. While the market value of crypto assets was less than USD 500 billion in the autumn of 2020, by February 2025 it had exceeded USD 3,200 billion[1] (equivalent to around 16 times Hungary's GDP in 2023).

2. Methodology

First, I consider why remuneration in an employment relationship should be paid in the form of a crypto asset rather than traditional currency, and what specific characteristics can be identified in the regulation of such (crypto asset) remuneration. Next, I used the comparative method to examine the relationship between international labor law (in particular the provisions of the *ILO conventions* on the protection of wages), the EU regulatory framework, and certain national labor laws to determine the demand and possibility for remuneration in crypto-currencies. In the course of the research, I also examined the extent to which concepts of labor law and financial law can be applied together and whether further conceptual clarification may be necessary.

3. The Possible Benefits and Risks of Remuneration in Crypto Assets

There can be several reasons behind an employee's demand or an employer's intention to provide remuneration in cryptocurrencies. One of these subjec-

1 Source: CoinMarketCap (www.coinmarketcap.com).

tive aspects may be the hype, the fashion, and the acceptance of crypto assets by a particular group of employees and employers.

The blockchain technology behind crypto assets brings transparency to the operation of remuneration schemes, as records are available in the public ledger, and transactions on the blockchain can be tracked by users without identifying their person. The use of crypto assets, in particular certain crypto assets, can be a safe alternative to secure payments in countries with less developed banking systems.

In the case of multinational employers operating globally or at least in several countries, accounting in the same asset may also be crucial from a cost-efficiency perspective. In this case, however, the diversity of crypto regulations in different countries is a challenge for employers. For example, where an employer's national legislation supports cryptocurrency remuneration but the employee's jurisdiction restricts or prohibits the same, the employer may put employees at risk because they may not be able to access their salary or may find it difficult to do so. In addition, countries that restrict crypto markets have lower trading volumes and employees may not be able to, or experience difficulty in accessing such markets.[2]

In the case of the use of crypto assets, the legal risks, including tax risks, and, in the case of multinational users and employers, the risks arising from different national regulations, are not negligible. From a fiscal point of view, the possibility of avoiding income taxes in some countries and the elimination of taxes on financial transactions may be important factors. In some countries, such as Hungary, this would even mean avoiding a significant financial burden (*e.g.*, in Hungary, the financial transaction tax on money exchange together with cash withdrawal in 2025 will result in a total tax burden of 1.8 %). In the case of countries struggling with high levels of inflation (*e.g.*, Turkey, Venezuela), cryptocurrencies – especially stablecoins – also represent a significant financial stability and value-preservation advantage compared to the official currency of the country.[3]

Although easy access to remuneration (currency) and its convertibility (in traditional terms) may be important criteria for employees when working internationally, there is a clear risk of exchange rate volatility in the use of crypto assets, and thus fluctuations in their value, which may be mitigated

2 *Cf.* Bharti Pandya & Priya Rao, 'Viability of compensating employees in cryptocurrency – An exploratory study', *Transnational Marketing Journal,* Vol. 10, Issue 2, 2022, pp. 277–293.

3 *Cf.* Julian Posada, 'Deeply Embedded Wages: Navigating Digital Payments in Data Work', *Big Data & Society,* Vol. 11, Issue 2, 2024.

by the use of stable crypto assets *(stable coins)*. A closely related risk is the actual usability of the crypto asset paid in remuneration (the actual range of recipients). It is therefore important to guarantee the value of the crypto asset received by the employee.

Due to the inherent nature of blockchain technology, all users, including employees, face the risk of irreversible transactions in the event of a wrong transfer, as well as the risk of losing access to their crypto assets in the event of the loss of the private key to their crypto wallet or the death of the person concerned.

4. Legislative Background

4.1. EU Legislation

Although the free movement of persons (employees) is one of the fundamental freedoms in EU law, no general and detailed set of labor law rules exist in EU legislation. In matters relating to employment and employment relationships, the EU has competence regarding remuneration for work only as regards the principle of equal opportunities and equal treatment of men and women, including in particular the principle of equal pay for equal work or work of equal value.

This competence is based on Article 157 TFEU, which lays down a definition of *'pay'* in the context of the provision requiring equal pay for men and women for equal work or work of equal value. According to this provision, 'pay' means the ordinary basic or minimum wage or salary and any other consideration, whether in cash or in kind, which the worker receives directly or indirectly, in respect of his employment, from his employer. However, the Treaty does not, by definition, regulate specific details such as the method and means of payment of wages.

In EU legislation, the issue of wages is, in addition to the above, addressed in the much-debated[4] European Minimum Wage Directive,[5] but neither does this directive contain a definition of, or rules on wages relevant to our topic.

4 *Case C-19/23, Denmark v Parliament and Council,* pending, action for annulment of Directive (EU) 2022/2041 on adequate minimum wages in the EU.

5 Directive (EU) 2022/2041 of the European Parliament and of the Council of 19 October 2022 on adequate minimum wages in the European Union.

4.2. ILO Legislation

At the international level, issues relating to the payment of wages are governed by the *International Labor Organization* (ILO) Convention No. 95, which sets out the rules for the protection of wages.[6] Article 1 of the Convention defines the term wages, as

> "remuneration or earnings, however designated or calculated, capable of being expressed in terms of money and fixed by mutual agreement or by national laws or regulations, which are payable in virtue of a written or unwritten contract of employment by an employer to an employed person for work done or to be done or for services rendered or to be rendered."

Concerning the payment of wages, Article 3 of the Convention stipulates that wages payable in money shall be paid only in legal tender. Payment in the form of promissory notes, vouchers, or coupons, or in any other form alleged to represent legal tender, shall be prohibited. As an exception to this provision, the Convention mentions the possibility of payment of wages by bank cheque, postal order, or money order, subject to special authorization or regulation by the authorities, in cases in which such payment is customary or is necessary because of special circumstances, or where a collective agreement or arbitration award so provides, or, in the absence of such provisions, with the consent of the worker concerned. The Convention does not contain any interpretative provision on which country's legal tender the payment of wages must be made, it merely provides that payment must be made in legal tender.

As a further exception, Article 4 of the Convention mentions that national legislation, collective agreements, or arbitral awards may permit, subject to the fulfillment of further detailed conditions laid down in the Convention, partial payment in kind of wages in those industries or professions where this method of payment is customary in practice or desirable because of the nature of the industry or profession in question.

6 Protection of Wages Convention, 1949 (ILO Convention No. 95).

4.3. National Regulatory Examples

In the following, I will present examples of relevant legislation in a few states, which in some cases have fundamentally different approaches to the issue of remuneration in crypto assets.

4.3.1. Hungary

In Hungary, remuneration from employment is regulated by the Hungarian Labor Code.[7] The essence of an employment contract is that remuneration, *i.e.*, wages, is paid for the work done. The Labor Code does not define the term 'wages' in general, but it does provide a definition of wages among the provisions on the prohibition of discriminatory remuneration. According to this definition, wages include all remuneration in cash or in kind provided directly or indirectly based on the employment relationship [Labor Code, Section 12(2)].[8]

According to the scholarly definition of the term 'wages', wages are defined as any payment in the form of remuneration in kind which is due to the employee under the employment relationship, granted by the employer based on a statutory provision, collective agreement, employment contract or unilateral undertaking by the employer, and which is proportional to the quantity and quality of the work performed.[9] From this definition, it can be derived that wages can always be understood as benefits received concerning employment but are not necessarily always conditional on work, *i.e.*, there are certain cases where the employee becomes entitled to such benefits even in the absence of work.[10] It is apparent from the previous points that wages are an essential element of the employment contract or employment relationship, to which the employee acquires a substantive right, as mentioned above.

The determination of wages is a matter of free agreement due to the legal status of the parties and the contractual nature of the employment relationship, but this freedom is subject to certain limitations. One of the restrictions

7 Act I of 2012 on the Labor Code.

8 Tamás Gyulavári (ed.), *Munkajog*, ELTE Eötvös, Budapest, 2012, p. 304.

9 *See* in detail: Nikolett Hős,' Munkabér', *in* Tamás Gyulavári (ed.), *Munkajog*, ELTE Eötvös, Budapest, 2024, pp. 297–323.

10 György Nádas *et al.*, A *Munka Törvénykönyvéről szóló 2012. évi törvény kommentárja a munkajogi kódexek összehasonlító táblázatával*, OPTEN, Budapest, 2016, p. 178.

on this freedom is the mandatory minimum wage.[11] The Labor Code sets out the basic forms to determine wages, as well as the rules on the minimum wage. The base wage under Section 136 of the Labor Code, the wage based on performance under Section 137, the wage supplements under Sections 139 to 144, and the supplementary rate under Section 145 are all based on the legal provisions of the Labor Code which are mandatory and allow for derogations only in favor of the employee. Base wages must be paid in all cases and, if the legal conditions are met, the employer must also pay the employee a wage supplement. A derogation is possible to the extent that the employee may be paid more than the amount provided for under the Labor Code or may be paid in the form of a supplementary allowance by contractual agreement with the employee.

For all payments, the Labor Code stipulates as a rule that wages must be determined and paid in Hungarian forints, unless otherwise provided by law or when working abroad, and may not be paid in the form of a voucher or other form of substitute for a means of payment (Section 154 of the Labor Code). Wages may be paid either by bank transfer or in cash (Section 158 of the Labor Code). Wages may not be paid in the form of a voucher or other form of substitute for a means of payment. These rules are mandatory and cannot be derogated from either by agreement between the parties or by collective agreement.[12] The purpose of the prohibition on payment by voucher is to prevent the employer from providing goods produced by him instead of money. Although Hungarian labor law practice recognizes the concept of payments in kind, the legislation allows its use only in a very limited range of cases, for payments that do not qualify as wages (*e.g.*, in the context of cafeteria benefits).[13] In the case of these other payments, the employee's entitlement to benefits is not based on the implied statutory provisions of the Labor Code, but on a unilateral commitment by the employer or a separate agreement between the parties (such as bonuses, rewards, or any other similar payments). Although the implied provisions of the Labor Code do not limit these payments in substance, the basic principles must be applied here (good faith, fairness, equal treatment, *etc.*).

---

11 Id. p. 167.

12 Ildikó Rátkai, 'A munkabérrel kapcsolatos feladatok; levonás a munkabérből', *Munkaügyi tanácsadó*, 2013/10, p. 8.

13 *Cf.* Gyulavári 2012, p. 304.

4.3.2. Spain

In Spain, the basic rules on pay for work are laid down in the Workers' Statute (hereinafter: Statute).[14] Section 26.1 of the Statute defines '*wages*' as the remuneration, in cash or in kind, received by an employee for the professional provision of employment services. According to the same provision, remuneration in kind may in no case exceed thirty percent of the employee's remuneration. According to Section 29.4 of the Statute, the employer may pay wages and social security benefits by cheque or other similar means of payment in legal tender through a credit institution, after informing the works council or the staff representatives. According to the correct interpretation of that statutory provision, the language of that provision prohibits the payment of wages by cryptocurrency, since it is not considered by Spanish law to be legal tender in Spain and cannot be considered a 'similar form of payment', since it is not guaranteed by a credit institution. It should be noted, however, that the Statute is not clear as to what exactly it means by legal tender: solely the legal tender of Spain (the euro) or also the legal tender of any other country? If it's the latter, this raises further questions, for example in the case of payments in *bitcoin* – the reasons and details of which are set out below.

Furthermore, as Spanish labor law gives broad permission for remuneration in kind, the question arises whether payouts in crypto assets are in line with the legislation, for example, in the analogy of the internationally widespread stock option schemes for executive remuneration. Spanish legal provisions do not yet provide a clear answer to this question.

4.3.3. India

In India, the payment of wages is regulated by a specific law. The interpretative provisions of the Payment of Wages Act[15] define *wages* as any remuneration (whether in the form of salary, gratuity, or otherwise), whether in monetary or other form, which, if the expressed or implied conditions of employment were fulfilled, would be payable to an employee because of his or her work performed in such employment, including remuneration for overtime, holidays, bonuses (whatever their designation) and payments upon termination of employment.

14 Real Decreto Legislativo 2/2015, de 23 de octubre, por el que se aprueba el texto refundido de la Ley del Estatuto de los Trabajadores.

15 The Payment of Wages Act, 1936.

However, the law does not consider as part of wages the value of any bonus that is not part of the remuneration payable under the employment relationship, the value of house accommodation, supply of lighting, water, medical services, or other services, including those excluded by law from the calculation of wages; any contributions paid by the employer into any pension or provident fund and any interest accrued thereon; the value of any travel allowance or any travel concession; any amount paid to cover special expenses incurred by the employee in connection with the nature of his employment; or any allowance paid upon termination of employment in specified cases.

Under Section 6 of the Act, all wages must be paid in current coins or bank notes, by cheque, or by crediting to the employee's bank account, but in 2017 by amendment of the law, the Government was also entitled by law to limit the method of payment of wages to cheques and bank transfers in certain cases. Similar provisions are included in the 2019 law on wages.[16] Contrary to the above, India's Equal Remuneration Act[17] defines remuneration as the basic salary and any additional remuneration paid in cash or in kind to the person employed based on the work performed in the course of employment.

The Minimum Wage Act[18] considers as wages all monetary benefits which, if the conditions of the employment contract are fulfilled, are due to the employed person for the employment relationship or the work performed in such employment relationship. It also defines payments that are not included in the definition of wages, such as housing, electricity, water, medical care and travel allowances, pension insurance contributions, and severance payments upon termination of employment. The minimum wage shall be paid in cash, except where it is the local practice to pay all or part of the wage in kind, in which case the government of the competent constituent state shall authorize payment of all or part of the minimum wage in kind.[19]

Based on the legal provisions on wages described above, it can be concluded that the concept of wages is interpreted quite broadly in Indian law, which allows wages to be paid either in cash or in a claim for cash (cheque or bank account) as a general rule. Indian law does allow payment in kind

16 The Code on Wages, 2019.

17 The Equal Remuneration Act, 1976.

18 The Minimum Wages Act, 1948.

19 Arundhati Kale, 'Cryptocurrency as Wages and Salary', *Indian Journal of Integrated Research in Law*, Vol 2, Issue 2, 2022, pp. 708–715.

on an exceptional basis, but only within the scope of the minimum wage rules and with special government permission if local custom so justifies. Under this regime, there may be a limited possibility for remuneration in crypto assets if crypto assets are considered as benefits in kind, but the legislation is far from providing for a general and unlimited possibility in this respect.

4.3.4. United Arab Emirates

The United Arab Emirates (hereinafter: UAE) is one of the fastest growing business hubs of the world, and the growing crypto markets and crypto services are an important part of its development. While the regulatory framework[20] in the UAE is designed to support this development, recent court decisions are of particular relevance, especially in light of the ambiguity under Islamic sharia law as to whether crypto assets are considered to be prohibited *(haram)* or permitted *(halal)*.[21]

The courts in the UAE are more frequently confronted with labor disputes concerning the applicability of remuneration in cryptos than in other countries. This issue arises particularly because there is a growing local demand for the inclusion of crypto assets in the remuneration of employees, especially in the technology and fintech industries, where the inclusion of bonuses or partial payments in crypto assets is already the practice. The Payment Token Service Regulation[22] of the UAE strictly restricts the acceptance of payment tokens in commercial transactions (for the sale of goods and the provision of services), but this restriction only applies to merchants and commercial transactions and does not apply to remuneration in the context of employment relationships.

The starting point of the regulation is that, according to Section 22 of the UAE's Labor Law,[23] wages must be paid in the local currency, the *dirham*

---

20 For the details of the regulatory framework *cf.* Moatasem El-Gheriani & Adham Hashish, 'Harnessing the crypto-horse. Factors affecting a friendly regulator of the crypto-industry: Dubai as a test case', *Information & Communications Technology Law,* February 2025, pp. 1–21.

21 Mervan Selcuk & Suleyman Kaya, 'A Critical Analysis of Cryptocurrencies from an Islamic Jurisprudence Perspective', *Turkish Journal of Islamic Economics,* Vol. 8 Issue 1, 2021, pp. 137–152.

22 Payment Token Services Regulation of 2024, (United Arab Emirates) Section 2(7).

23 Federal Decree by Law No. (33) of 2021 Regulating Labor Relations (United Arab Emirates).

(AED), but can be paid in other currencies if the parties agree to this in the employment contract. In the first lawsuit in 2023, the Dubai Court of First Instance (hereinafter: DCFI) had to rule on an employment dispute concerning the payment of wages in tokens, namely EcoWatt project tokens.[24] Although the court acknowledged that the employment contract included these tokens, it ultimately rejected the legality of the employee's claim. The basis for the rejection was that the claimant employee could not demonstrate a clear method for calculating the value of the crypto asset in fiat currency. In this decision, the court underlined the need for precise and tangible evidence in determining financial obligations, especially in the case of non-traditional payments such as crypto assets. One year later, another judgment of the DCFI,[25] contrary to the previous judgment, confirmed the legality of paying wages in crypto assets – again in EcoWatt tokens – under employment contracts without conversion into fiat currency, based on an employment contract where the employee was entitled to wages in fiat currency and the tokens. This decision marked a significant change of direction in the UAE court's approach to crypto assets.

However, the judgment confirmed that in the case of remuneration in crypto assets *(i)* the agreement must specify the crypto-currency used for remuneration; *(ii)* the agreement must set out a clear valuation method for expressing the value of the crypto asset in fiat currency; *(iii)* in the event of the possibility of significant exchange rate volatility, appropriate safeguards should be in place.

5. Can Crypto Assets Be Considered as Money for the Purposes of Employment Remuneration?

As demonstrated above, for reasons of the particular importance of the guarantee of the payment of wages, several national and international provisions require payment in money (official currency) and, although there are differences between countries, these provisions limit the possibility for the employer to pay wages in kind. In this context, it is also necessary to address the question of to what extent and under what conditions crypto assets can be considered as money?

24 Dubai Court of First Instance, Case DCFI No. 6947/2023.

25 Dubai Court of First Instance, Case DCFI No. 1739/2024 of 17 July 2024, at https://www.lexismiddleeast.com/case/Dubai/DCFI_2024_1739_2024/.

The deficiencies in the legal definition of money and securities, and the differences in definition do not make it easy to distinguish crypto assets from their conventional counterparts.

As a starting point, it is important to underline that crypto assets are not just an alternative to fiat money, but a much broader category of assets. Among the main types of crypto assets we can identify: *(i) payment tokens,* also known as virtual/cryptocurrencies, which act as a medium of exchange or store of value (*e.g.,* bitcoin was originally created for this purpose); *(ii) asset/security (investment) tokens,* which represent a form of debt or equity (*e.g.,* EGX); *(iii) utility tokens,* which provide access to a product or service (*e.g.,* Filecoin, VET); and *(iv) hybrid tokens,* which can fall into multiple categories (*e.g.,* ETH).

Given the fact that there are thousands of different crypto assets that can be classified into different token categories, while each crypto asset is more or less different from the others, we can see a very colorful picture, where by analyzing different tokens it is worth focusing on the similarities and differences between payment tokens and traditional money, and it is necessary to look at the similarities of each payment token to fiat money individually. Consequently, the fact that a single selected crypto asset may be found to be monetized for remuneration purposes does not imply that this finding can be automatically extended to any other crypto asset.

It is important to emphasize that the situation is not made any easier by the fact that there is no general legal definition of money. Each country defines its official currency and stipulates that payments to fulfill financial obligations made in its official currency must be accepted by all. However, in many cases the relevant legal provisions allow parties in civil law relationships to deviate from this in the performance of their obligations.

As regards the distinction between traditional money – issued by states or central banks – and payment tokens, it is appropriate to have a look at the phenomena of the legal theories of money (state and social theory of money), which are in principle mutually exclusive, but in fact coexist. We can see that, according to the social theory of money, any scarce, homogeneous, and easily recognizable instrument can in practice function as money if it is accepted and used as such by society. (The question of whether any of the payment tokens actually perform all the economic functions of money does not affect the legal approach).

The state theory of money, on the other hand, emphasizes that only an instrument declared by state regulation as such can be considered money. However, state regulations do not simply determine the monetary character of any asset, but all states of the world regulate what is their currency,[26] and the states of the world permit or prohibit the use of official currencies of other states as a means of payment for obligations. From the notion of official currency, we can logically deduce that what is considered official currency is also necessarily money, but it is not logically necessary that only an official currency of a country can be regarded as money.[27] Based on the economic functions of money, the currently existing payment tokens cannot be regarded as money on a normative basis, since they can only perform some but not all of the functions of money. Meanwhile, it can be argued in a functionalist sense that they can be used for certain purposes in a similar way to conventional money.

Each state may decide to issue its official currency or to recognize as such the official currency of any other state, owing to its financial sovereignty. There is no legal obstacle to a state recognizing as official currency an instrument/asset that no other state has issued. This happened in 2021 in *El Salvador* and 2022 in the *Central African Republic,* when these countries declared *bitcoin* as their official currency. Making any payment token – in these cases the historically best known and most widely used one – the official currency in these two countries, necessarily means that Bitcoin became money in these countries. Although this decision is so far the decision and regulation of only two and less dominant states in the world economy, but its legal implications could go far beyond the borders of these small countries, given that the recognition as official currency removes the objection that the crypto asset in question is not official currency anywhere.

6. Can Bitcoin Be Legally Regarded as Money?

Based on the above-mentioned fact that *bitcoin* is now recognized as an official currency by two countries, one might draw the simple logical conclu-

26 *See e.g.* Article K) of the Fundamental Law of Hungary; Article L111-1 of the *Code monétaire et financier* of France. It should be noted that the vast majority of the world's states use their own currency, but there are groups of countries that operate a common monetary system (the most famous examples are the Economic and Monetary Union, the Eurozone in Europe and the group of Central African countries that use the CFA Franc). There are some states that use the official currency of another state as their own (*e.g.* Montenegro), and in certain coutries more than one different official currency exist, even if geographically separated (*e.g.* the *yuan (remninbi),* the *Hong Kong dollar* and the *Macanese pataca* in case of China).

27 On the theory of private money *cf.* Friedrich August von Hayek, *Denationalisation of Money,* Institute of Economic Affairs, London, 1976.

sion that bitcoin should be considered as money in general. bitcoin operates as money in the functionalistic sense, at least in jurisdictions where it is already officially recognized as a currency. However, as it is not recognized as a currency in the rest of the world, it could be argued that bitcoin is not recognized as money under the state theory of money.[28] On further reflection, there is no obligation under international law for any state to recognize the official currency of any other state as a universal monetary instrument.

It is therefore appropriate to consider the legal monetary nature of bitcoin in the light of the law of those countries where the question of bitcoin as money arises. For the time being, apart from the two above-mentioned countries, neither bitcoin nor any other crypto asset is recognized as money by the legal provisions in force. However, the situation is not so clear-cut when looking at court cases.

To date, the CJEU has only dealt with the legal status of a crypto asset in one case. The core issue in *Hedquist* (2015) was the interpretation of the VAT exemption for the conversion of bitcoin into fiat money. In its judgment, the CJEU underlined that "the 'bitcoin' virtual currency with bidirectional flow, which will be exchanged for traditional currencies in the context of exchange transactions, cannot be characterized as 'tangible property' [...], given that [...] virtual currency has no purpose other than to be a means of payment." The CJEU has added in its ruling, that "the 'bitcoin' virtual currency, being a contractual means of payment, cannot be regarded as a current account or a deposit account, a payment or a transfer. Moreover, unlike a debt, cheques and other negotiable instruments [...] the 'bitcoin' virtual currency is a direct means of payment between the operators that accept it."[29]

In the grounds for US court rulings, we also see findings in favor of bitcoin being used as money. In *SEC v Shavers*[30] (2013) the US District Court in Sherman, Texas highlighted:

> "It is clear that bitcoin can be used as money. It can be used to purchase goods or services, and as Shavers stated, used to pay for individual living expenses. The only limitation of bitcoin is that it is limited to those places that accept it as currency. However, it can also be exchanged for conven-

28 Asya Passinsky, 'Should Bitcoin Be Classified as Money?', *Journal of Social Ontology* Vol. 6, Issue 2, 2020, pp. 281–292.

29 Judgement of 22 October 2015, *Case C-264/14, Hedqvist*, ECLI:EU:C:2015:718, paras. 24 and 42.

30 *Securities and Exchange Commission v Trendon T. Shavers and Bitcoin Savings and Trust*, Case No. 4:13-CV-416.

tional currencies, such as the U.S. dollar, euro, yen, and yuan. Therefore, bitcoin is a currency or form of money."

In *U.S. v Ulbricht (Silk Road)*[31] (2014) the U.S. District Court, S.D. New York added, that "bitcoins carry value – that is their purpose and function – and acts as a medium of exchange. bitcoins may be exchanged for legal tender, be it U.S. dollars, euros, or some other currency. Accordingly, this argument (that bitcoin is not money) fails."

7. Conclusions

The demand for remuneration in crypto assets in the framework of employment relations has now emerged and is spreading globally. The elements of international labor law and, in line with this, many national labor laws governing the protection of wages and salaries severely restrict the possibility of crypto remuneration, mainly by relegating it to the sphere of fringe benefits in kind (cafeteria elements). However, it is also important to consider that these rules were adopted well before the emergence and spreading of crypto assets. The rules governing the protection of wages do not exclude the payment in crypto assets of non-wage benefits provided unilaterally or by agreement.

It is apparent that there is a lack of consistency between legislation and court practices in the legal recognition of crypto assets, and Bitcoin in particular, as money. The courts in Europe, the US, and the Middle East are much more flexible on this issue than the legislator.

There are huge differences between crypto assets in terms of their purpose and basic characteristics. Not all of them were created to be a means of payment and therefore not all of them can be considered as an alternative to money. It is therefore important to bear in mind that any conclusions should be specific to the crypto asset under consideration and should not be generalized. The recognition of a particular crypto asset as an official currency by certain states raises additional issues for countries that do not consider any crypto asset to be money.

31 *U.S. v Ulbricht*. 2014. 31 F. Supp. 3d 540 (S.D.N.Y. 2014).

“Digital Only” in Administrative Procedures and Fundamental Rights

A German Perspective

*Elias Wirth**

Abstract

In Germany, the digital transformation of public administration has sparked a debate about the compatibility of ‘digital-only’ administrative procedures with fundamental rights. As far as can be seen, there is no discussion about whether the EU Charter of Fundamental Rights (CFR) includes a ‘fundamental right to analogue life’, nor about the fundamental rights limits of mandatory e-government. This is surprising, given that European fundamental rights will have a significant impact on the digitalization of Member State administrations and that digitalization of administration will, of course, also occur at the European level. The paper distinguishes between three scenarios: (i) complete digitalization; (ii) partial digital-only services; and (iii) incentivized (nudge-based) digital engagement between citizens and companies affected by mandatory digital administration. The current status of the digitalization of administrations and the relevant secondary legislation is presented. The findings suggest that full digitalization without analogue alternatives or hardship provisions for citizens is incompatible with the CFR. In addition, reform ideas for a fundamental right to analogous life are presented and critically evaluated.

Keywords: analogous life, digital administration, Germany, e-government, digitalization

* Elias Wirth: professor of law, Hesse University of Applied Sciences for Public Management and Security, elias.wirth@gmx.at. The article is based on a lecture given at the Pázmány Péter Catholic University in Budapest in the summer of 2024. The lecture format has been retained.

1. Introduction

In the EU, administrative services are increasingly being digitalized. This means that all procedural steps of an administrative procedure can be carried out electronically. In particular, applications and documents can be submitted to authorities, communication can be handled and a decision by the authority can be delivered electronically. This can be achieved through communication by email, app and/or via an account created for this purpose. Digital procedures exclude verbal or written interaction with the administrative authorities, also referred to below as analogue communication.

Exclusively digital communication could be a logical next step. This is because the efficiency of the administration will not be increased and costs will not be reduced if analogue and digital channels are kept open in parallel.[1] So far, there has been little discussion as to whether not offering an analogue alternative would be compatible with European fundamental rights and which limits demanded by fundamental rights would have to be drawn. The CFR does not contain a specific "fundamental right to analogous life" or a right of defence against e-government. As far as can be seen, there is no relevant case law from EU courts or the ECtHR.[2]

In this paper, first of all, the status quo with regard to the digitalization of administrative services is portrayed. This is necessary to find out which constellations must be examined for their compatibility with fundamental rights. The EU law is implemented by the Member States to a significant extent. Therefore, the current status of administrative digitalization in one Member State, namely Germany, is studied. From this it can be deduced how far digitalization has progressed (Section 2). It must then be assessed whether the identified constellations are compatible with the fundamental rights guarantees of the CFR (Section 3). In order to obtain regulatory impulses, regulations that already exist and have been put forward in the sphere of legal policy are then examined to determine whether they are suitable as a blueprint for a fundamental rights norm (Section 4). Finally, a conclusion is drawn (Section 5).

1 Sönke E. Schulz, 'Der elektronische Zugang zur Verwaltung', *Recht Digital,* 2021, p. 378.

2 Dariusz Kloza, 'It's All About Choice', *Völkerrechtsblog,* 29 November 2021.

2. The Development of the Digitalization of the Administration

2.1. EU Law

EU law does not yet contain any provisions on the mandatory use of digital communication channels for citizens to access administrative services. However, there are general objectives set at Union level for the Member States to achieve as part of the 'Digital Decade' proclaimed by the Commission from 2020 to 2030. The Member States must provide essential public services in digital form according to Article 4(1) no. 4 lit. a) Decision 2022/2481.[3] At the same time, the use of digital form is to be voluntary.[4] Indeed, the European Parliament points out that analogue alternatives must always be offered.[5]

In recent years, the legislative framework has been created at European level to digitalize administrative services. First of all, natural or legal persons must be able to provide clear proof of their identity for their digital interaction with public authorities. To this end, the EU took action in 2014 and adopted the eIDAS Regulation.[6] However, initially not all member states established electronic identification options.[7] In 2021, the Commission presented the draft of an amended regulation,[8] which was significantly amended during the legislative process and adopted by the European Parliament in February 2024.[9] In particular, the amended eIDAS Regulation

---

3 Decision (EU) 2022/2481 of the European Parliament and of the Council of 14 December 2022 establishing the Digital Decade Policy Programme 2030.

4 Id. Recital (18).

5 Digitalisation and Administrative Law, European Parliament resolution of 22 November 2023 with recommendations to the Commission on Digitalisation and Administrative Law, 2021/2161(INL), Annex, Recommendation No. 2, 2.iii.

6 Regulation (EU) No 910/2014 of the European Parliament and of the Council of 23 July 2014 on electronic identification and trust services for electronic transactions in the internal market and repealing Directive 1999/93/EC. 'eIDAS' stands for Electronic IDentification, Authentication and trust Services.

7 Commission Staff Working Document, Accompanying the document Report from the Commission to the European Parliament and the Council on the evaluation of Regulation (EU) No 910/2014 on electronic identification and trust services for electronic transactions in the internal market (eIDAS), SWD(2021) 130 final, pp. 14 *et seq.*

8 Proposal for a Regulation of the European Parliament and of the Council amending Regulation (EU) No 910/2014 as regards establishing a framework for a European Digital Identity, COM(2021) 281 final.

9 European Parliament, legislative resolution of 29 February 2024 on the proposal for a regulation of the European Parliament and of the Council amending Regulation (EU) No 910/2014 as regards establishing a framework for a European Digital Identity, COM(2021) 0281 – C9-0200/2021 – 2021/0136(COD).

contains a European wallet for digital identity (Article 5a *et seq.* eIDAS Regulation), which the Member States must provide by the fall of 2026. Citizens can use the wallet to identify themselves and store digital evidence. However, its use is voluntary [Article 5a(15) sentence 1 eIDAS Regulation].

In addition, Regulation 2018/1724 (SDG Regulation)[10] requires the Commission and the Member States to set up a single digital gateway. Digital access to information (Article 4 *et seq.* SDG Regulation), full online access to procedures (Article 6 SDG Regulation) and access to assistance and problem-solving services in accordance with Article 7 SDG Regulation must be guaranteed. The material scope is codified in the three annexes, and the procedures covered are enshrined in Annex II. The material scope is limited by Article 6(3) of the SDG Regulation. According to this, Member States may require personal presence for administrative services relating to public safety, public health and combating abusive behavior if the public interest so requires. Even more significant, however, is the restriction to areas with a potential cross-border dimension (21 in total), as these are the only areas in which the Union has competence (see *e.g.,* recitals 4 and 6 of the SDG Regulation). In the information areas listed in Annex I, an explicit reference to the EU is made (*e.g.,* travel within the Union or work and retirement within the Union). There are no such clear references in Annex II, but the life events mentioned there imply an (at least potential) cross-border element.[11] Thus, with the SDG Regulation the legislator does not want to harmonize the administrative procedures of the Member States (and is not allowed to do so for reasons of competence), but to create a uniform digital access gateway.

The Union framework is therefore generally rather restrictive. However, the Member States may extend the single digital gateway to domestic matters. This is because nationals could otherwise be discriminated against compared to EU citizens and because the technical infrastructure exists anyway.[12] Digital identity is a prerequisite for the provision of e-government services and its establishment makes it easier for Member States to offer more administrative services digitally.

10 Regulation (EU) 2018/1724 of the European Parliament and of the Council of 2 October 2018 establishing a single digital gateway to provide access to information, to procedures and to assistance and problem-solving services and amending Regulation (EU) No 1024/2012.

11 Thorsten Siegel, 'Der Europäische Portalverbund – Frischer Digitalisierungswind durch das einheitliche digitale Zugangstor ("Single Digital Gateway")', *Neue Zeitschrift für Verwaltungsrecht,* 2019, p. 908.

12 Id. pp. 908 *et seq.*

Union law therefore does not impose a general obligation to use digital administrative services. The situation is different in certain sectors, where companies in particular must use a digital gateway. For example, online use is largely mandatory in public procurement law.[13] As far as can be seen, there was no discussion in the legislative process about whether such mandatory electronic use violates fundamental rights. These specific areas also show that the legislative framework created is sufficient to offer at least some administrative services only in digital form.

2.2. Germany as an Example of the Development of Digital Administrative Services

The following section outlines the development of digital administration in Germany. The overview serves as an example of the current status of the Member States and how this may develop in the near future. This is important for the assessment of fundamental rights because the Member States implement Union law within the meaning of Article 51(1) sentence 1 CFR. The compatibility of national law with the national constitutional law, in particular with national fundamental rights, is not considered in this article.

In Germany, the federal states implement the majority of laws and have their own administrative procedural laws that govern their administrative activities. However, these often largely refer to the Administrative Procedure Act ("*Verwaltungsverfahrensgesetz*"; VwVfG) of the federal government. An important first step towards digital administration was the recognition of electronic form in Sections 3a; 37(2) VwVfG. Furthermore, Section 35a VwVfG (as well as Section 31a of the Tenth Book of the German Social Code ("*Sozialgesetzbuch X*") and Section 155(IV) of the Fiscal Code ("*Abgabenordnung*"; AO) provides for the possibility of issuing an administrative act completely automatically under certain conditions. In addition to this, the federal government has enacted the E-Government Act ("*E-Government-Gesetz*"; EGovG), which enables electronic payment (Section 4 EGovG) and provides for electronic file management (Section 6a EGovG). The federal states also created their own e-government laws.[14] In September 2017, Ger-

13 Thorsten Siegel, 'Elektronisierung des Vergabeverfahrens', *Landes- und Kommunalverwaltung*, 2017, pp. 387 *et seq.*, 391.

14 Wissenschaftliche Dienste des Deutschen Bundestags, *Sachstand: E-Government in Deutschland*, WD 3 – 3000 – 134/19, 2019, at https://www.bundestag.de/resource/blob/655082/32a17c3834d5c5c5d6f5a7232f0491c0/wd-3-134-19-pdf-data.pdf, pp. 9 *et seq.*

many was the first EU member state to notify an eID system to the Commission.[15]

These voluntary procedural options have been used only in a few areas.[16] For this reason, the federal legislator passed the Online Access Act ("*Onlinezugangsgesetz*"; OZG), which came into force in 2017 and obliged the federal and state governments to offer certain administrative services digitally via an administrative portal by the end of 2022 (Section 1 OZG). This interconnected concept is also reflected in the SDG Regulation. The plan was to create online access to 575 service bundles. However, administrative services that were not suitable for legal, economic or factual reasons were excluded, such as waste disposal[17] or preventive police measures. The coronavirus pandemic was another catalyst for digital administration. However, it must be noted that the objectives pursued with the OZG were not achieved. Of the planned services,[18] only a fraction had been digitalized by the deadline.[19] Some of the federal states are more successful than others in the transformation towards digital administration. In Bavaria, for example, according to Article 20(1) of the Bavarian Digital Act ("*Bayerisches Digitalgesetz*"; BayDiG), administrative procedures are generally to be carried out digitally.

At the same time, there is no general obligation to communicate electronically or to issue electronic administrative acts at either federal or state level. Meanwhile, electronic communication is already a basic principle in some areas in which companies operate, for example when awarding public contracts.[20] The basic obligation to submit an advance VAT return to the tax office electronically by remote data transmission was deemed constitutional by the Federal Fiscal Court,[21] which was justified by the hardship rule. A

15 European Commission, SWD(2021) 130 final, p. 14.

16 Bettina Spilker, 'E-Government – Anforderungen an das Verwaltungsverfahren', *Neue Zeitschrift für Verwaltungsrecht*, 2022, pp. 681 and 685.

17 Siegel 2019, p. 907; Thorsten Siegel, 'Auf dem Weg zum Portalverbund – Das neue Onlinezugangsgesetz', *Die Öffentliche Verwaltung*, 2018, p. 188.

18 *See* at https://www.it-planungsrat.de/fileadmin/beschluesse/2018/Beschluss2018-22_TOP2_Anlage_OZGUmsetzungskatalog.pdf.

19 Jonas Botta, '"Digital First" und "Digital Only" in der öffentlichen Verwaltung', *Neue Zeitschrift für Verwaltungsrecht*, 2022, p. 1247 with further references.

20 *See* Section 97(5) Act against Restraints of Competition ("*Gesetz gegen Wettbewerbsbeschränkungen*"); Section 9(1) "*Vergabeverordnung*"; VgV]. Furthermore, EU-wide announcements are also made using standard electronic forms (*see* Section 10a VgV). In addition, certain tax returns, for example, must be submitted electronically, *see* Section 150(1) AO and Section 18(1) Value Added Tax Act ("*Umsatzsteuergesetz*"; UStG). An exception from this can be granted upon request in cases of hardship [Section 150(8) AO; Section 18(1) UStG].

21 Ruling from 14.3.2012 – XI R 33/09; ruling from 14 February 2017 – VIII B 43/16.

case of hardship exists in particular if taxpayers are unable or only able to use electronic access to a limited extent due to their personal capabilities [Section 150(8) AO]. The provision of information for the census must also be carried out electronically in accordance with Section 23(1) Census Act 2022 ("*Zensusgesetz 2022*"), although exemptions are available in cases of hardship.

Section 1a(1) OZG also stipulates that company-related administrative services are to be offered exclusively in digital form ("digital only") five years after the Act came into force in the summer of 2024. However, exemption may be granted if the user can show a legitimate interest. Therefore, in individual cases where it is justified, analogue access to the administration is still possible for companies.

In some cases, however, there is an obligation for citizens without hardship regulations to communicate digitally with administrative authorities. This applies, for example, to the implementation of the Student Energy Price Allowance Act ("*Studierenden-Energiepreispauschalengesetz*"; EPPSG). According to Section 1 EPPSG, students enrolled at German universities on a specific cut-off date received a one-off payment of 200 euros upon application. This allowance was granted in response to rising energy prices. The federal states implemented this law. The state of Saxony-Anhalt created an Internet portal through which applications could be submitted. This portal, in turn, mandated the use of the federal government's online account ("*BundID*") to submit an application. There was no other way to receive the energy price allowance. Applying digitally was therefore made mandatory; there was no other way for applicants to receive the money, even if they met the statutory requirements. This is a violation of Section 2(5) OZG, which foresees that the use of user accounts is voluntary. Furthermore, the system was also considered to be contrary to fundamental rights. The mandatory processing of personal data was not necessary and there was no corresponding legal basis, meaning that Article 8(1)-(2) CFR and the right to informational self-determination derived from Articles 1(1) and 2(1) of the German Constitution were violated.[22]

---

22 Landesbeauftragter für den Datenschutz Sachsen-Anhalt (State Commissioner for Data Protection in Saxony-Anhalt), '*Digitalisierung ja, aber nicht zwangsweise*', press release dated 27 June 2024, at https://datenschutz.sachsen-anhalt.de/landesbeauftragte/pressemitteilungen/pm-lfd-27062024; Datenschutzkonferenz (Data Protection Conference), Statement by the Conference of Independent Data Protection Supervisory Authorities of the Federal and State Governments dated 3 February 2023, pp. 4 *et seq.*

The application for Corona emergency aid for freelance artists in the Free State of Bavaria was also only possible digitally. This was deemed lawful by administrative courts.[23] The Administrative Court of Würzburg did not consider the "digital discrimination" within the meaning of Article 3(1) GG invoked by the plaintiff to be arbitrary because it made administrative work more effective and a distribution can be made promptly in the event of short-term liquidity bottlenecks.

Some university applications for degree courses are also only possible digitally. Furthermore, in some municipalities, appointments can only be made digitally and bank transfers also.[24] Finally, public administration only allows for the electronic transmission of application documents in some cases.[25] This means that in certain areas in Germany, an obligation to use administrative services digitally already exists.

2.3. Nudges to Use the Digital Access to Administration

As there is currently no general obligation to use digital administration at either European or national level, the question arises as to how citizens and companies can be encouraged to use digital services voluntarily. To this end, legislators can provide incentives, *i.e.,* favor the digital use of administrative services digitally over analogue use (so-called nudges). Such advantages would be, for example, the charging of reduced administrative fees for online applications, the extension of deadlines, pre-filled electronic application forms or prioritized processing of online administrative procedures.[26] Of course, this does not change the voluntary nature of digital administration, but such incentive systems must also be put to the test in terms of fundamental rights.

The obligation to activate the eID function, which is being discussed (at least in Germany), is not entirely relevant to this topic, but should also be

23 Verwaltungsgericht Würzburg (Administrative Court of Würzburg), judgment of 18 January 2021 – W 8 K 20.814; *see also* Bayerischer Verwaltungsgerichtshof (Bavarian Administrative Court), decision of 5.8.2020 – 6 CE 20.1677.

24 Destatis, *Knapp 6% der Bevölkerung im Alter von 16 bis 75 Jahren in Deutschland sind offline,* at https://www.destatis.de/DE/Presse/Pressemitteilungen/Zahl-der-Woche/2023/PD23_15_p002.html#:~:text=Knapp%206%20%25%20der%20Menschen%20im,Bundesamt%20(Destatis)%20weiter%20mitteilt.

25 Meinhard Schröder, 'Rahmenbedingungen der Digitalisierung der Verwaltung', *Verwaltungsarchiv,* 2019, p. 336.

26 Martin Eifert, *Electronic Government,* Nomos, Baden-Baden, 2006, p. 40; Spilker 2017, p. 683.

addressed here. This does not expressly mean an obligation to use it, but rather that all citizens would have to activate the function. This is based on the consideration that the biggest hurdle is the effort involved in activation, which is disproportionate to the added value for citizens. Furthermore, few people are aware of the possibility of digital administration and users are dissatisfied. However, if citizens were obliged to activate it, at least some of the hurdles would be removed and they would also use the administrative services digitally.[27] As far as can be seen, an obligation to activate has not been discussed at EU level in the context of the regulatory procedure for the eIDAS Regulation. However, this would also be a viable path towards greater administrative digitalization.

2.4. Interim Conclusion

Mandatory e-Government is not being sought at either European or German level. Precise specifications for mandatory e-Government at Union level for the implementation of Union law are likely to be ruled out for reasons of competence alone; rather, this would be the responsibility of the Member States within their procedural autonomy. For administrative procedures carried out at European level, there is also no obligation for citizens to communicate digitally. Nevertheless, the respective developments reveal that on the one hand – particularly at European level – the conditions for a purely digital administration are gradually being created. At a national level, it is observable in Germany that purely digital access to administrative services is already possible in some cases.

This is likely to increase, because resources can be saved through digital administration. This applies in particular to benefit administration and specifically to legal claims, *i.e.*, when there is no discretion or scope for assessment.[28] The authorities can save on personnel resources in this context because only the infrastructure needs to be created and then automated decision-making systems check eligibility requirements. Digitalized administrative services in this area are likely to increase.[29] EU secondary legisla-

27 Mario Martini, 'Transformation der Verwaltung durch Digitalisierung', *Die Öffentliche Verwaltung,* 2017, pp. 449 *et seq.*

28 *See* Section 35a VwVfG; Section 31a SGB X.

29 Nadja Braun Binder, 'Vollautomatisierte Verwaltungsverfahren im allgemeinen Verwaltungsverfahrensrecht?', *Neue Zeitschrift für Verwaltungsrecht,* 2016, p. 963; Annette Guckelberger, 'Automatisierte Verwaltungsentscheidungen: Stand und Perspektiven', *Die Öffentliche Verwaltung,* 2021, p. 570.

tion in particular, which provides for a lot of benefit administration, for example in the area of the common agricultural policy,[30] is likely to be well suited to being offered purely digitally for reasons of efficiency. However, a digital obligation can of course also be considered in the context of administrative intervention, for example regarding communication with the respective authority. Here too, digital data enables faster processing.

Consequently, three constellations must be examined for their compatibility with the fundamental rights of the CFR. All of them can apply to companies or citizens. *(i)* Firstly, the compatibility of a situation – admittedly unlikely in the near future – in which all digitizable administrative services are only available in digital form needs to be examined. *(ii)* It should then be examined whether individual administrative services can be offered completely digitally, which is particularly suitable for simply structured mass procedures. Of course, the assessment of fundamental rights in individual cases will depend on the administrative service offered digitally. However, such a case-by-case assessment cannot be made; rather, the conflicts with fundamental rights should only be outlined as guidelines. In both cases, a distinction must be made as to whether there are hardship provisions. A hardship provision is a rule that provides for an exemption from the digitalization obligation on request if its application is personally unreasonable. If this is the case, there should be no official discretion. However, unreasonableness must be examined by the authorities. Grounds for this may be digital illiteracy or the lack of electronic devices. *(iii)* Finally, it needs to be discussed whether there are fundamental rights limits to nudges towards the use of digital government services.

3. Compatibility with Fundamental Rights

First of all, the applicability of the CFR is determined by Article 51(1) CFR; the first half of the first sentence states that it applies to the institutions, bodies, offices and agencies of the Union. Although the (executive) agencies of the EU, among others, perform independent administrative tasks, the Member State administrations bear the main burden for the implementation of Union law. According to the second half of the first sentence, the Member States are obliged to respect fundamental rights when they implement Union law. This refers to primary law, in particular the fundamental freedoms,

30 *Cf.* Article 38 *et seq.* TFEU.

and secondary law, with the legislative implementation of directives and the administrative enforcement of regulations being particularly relevant. Data protection issues must be measured against the CFR on the basis of the GDPR[31] and Directive 2016/680.[32] Finally, there is an obligation to observe the CFR in relation to tertiary law. The Member States are also bound when they have discretion in implementing EU law.[33]

3.1. Compatibility with Human Dignity

The possible legislative measures outlined in the previous chapter may violate human dignity (Article 1 CFR). The absolute limits of the permissible use of technology can be found in human dignity. The entire personality of a person cannot be forcibly registered and catalogued by state authorities.[34] Even if all digitally possible administrative services would only be available digitally, this would not deprive citizens of their subject quality. Consequently, human dignity does not include a right of defence against compulsory e-Government in one of the three forms described above.[35]

However, it is worth considering whether the *status positivus* of human dignity may be affected by the digitalization of administrative services without a hardship clause. That means the dimension as the individual's right to demand an action from the state.[36] The *status positivus* has a particular impact on social benefits law. According to a CJEU ruling, human dignity can

31 Regulation (EU) 2016/679 of the European Parliament and of the Council of 27 April 2016 on the protection of natural persons with regard to the processing of personal data and on the free movement of such data, and repealing Directive 95/46/EC (General Data Protection Regulation).

32 Directive (EU) 2016/680 of the European Parliament and of the Council of 27 April 2016 on the protection of natural persons with regard to the processing of personal data by competent authorities for the purposes of the prevention, investigation, detection or prosecution of criminal offences or the execution of criminal penalties, and on the free movement of such data, and repealing Council Framework Decision 2008/977/JHA. *See* Botta 2022, p. 1249.

33 Hans D. Jarass, *Charta der Grundrechte der Europäischen Union, 4th edition,* C.H. Beck, München, 2021, Art. 51, margin no. 26 with further references.

34 *Cf.* BVerfGE 27, 1 (6); Sebastian J. Golla, 'In Würde vor Ampel und Algorithmus – Verfassungsrecht im technologischen Wandel', *Die Öffentliche Verwaltung,* 2019, pp. 675 *et seq.*

35 *Cf.* Botta 2022, p. 1250.

36 Just to name one source: Walter Frenz, *in* Matthias Pechstein *et al.* (eds.), *Frankfurter Kommentar EUV/GRC/AEUV, 2nd edition,* Mohr Siebeck, Tübingen, 2023, Art. 1 CFR, para. 41 *et seq.*

be relied on to derive a fundamental right of asylum seekers to receive the minimum benefits provided for in secondary legislation after lodging an asylum application and before being transferred to the responsible Member State.[37] In particular, this means that the State must create appropriate conditions in order not to violate human dignity.

If these conditions, such as accommodation, could only be applied for in digital form, the question arises as to whether this would already be a violation of human dignity. The fact that the majority of asylum seekers have access to digital services is an argument against this. Internet cafés or public Wi-Fi hotspots could be used if necessary. Furthermore, human dignity in its *status-positivus* dimension could be understood in such a way that it includes only a substantive entitlement, but requirements regarding procedural implementation cannot be derived from human dignity. However, the fact that a mandatory online application can *de facto* prevent access to benefits that are intended for living a dignified life substantiates a violation of human dignity. This is all the more true as some asylum seekers are (digitally) illiterate and would therefore be unable to claim the benefits. However, this is a problem of equality law. It is therefore not possible to derive from human dignity an obligation to provide for such exceptions from mandatory e-government in the area of those (social) benefits provided for under EU law that enable a dignified life.

The same applies to the European Pillar of Social Rights proclaimed by the European Parliament, Council and European Commission. Paragraph 20 states that everyone should have the right of access to essential services. It is unclear whether this includes analogue access. However, this provision is in any case not legally binding.[38]

3.2. Access to Services of General Economic Interest (Article 36 CFR)

A different result could arise with regard to Article 36 CFR. This is because the Union "recognizes and respects access to services of general economic interest as provided for in national laws [...]." However, according to prevailing opinion, this article does not include a subjective right, especially in

37 Judgment of 27 September 2012, *Case C-179/11, Cimade and GISTI,* ECLI:EU:C:2012:594, para. 56; *see also* Judgment of 27 February 2014, *Case C-79/13, Saciri and others,* ECLI:EU:C:2014:103, para. 35; Judgment of 2 December 2014, *Case C-148/13, A and others,* ECLI:EU:C:2014:2406, para. 72.

38 *Cf.* nos. 17 *et seq.* of the preamble to the Proclamation.

view of the wording.[39] It is also unclear whether the norm only addresses the Union or also the Member States.[40]

3.3. Compatibility with the Fundamental Right Personal Data Protection

In what follows, I will analyze prescriptions addressed to individual regarding digital administration in the form of the fundamental rights restriction test.

(i) Interference. Article 8(1) CFR protects personal data, *i.e.,* all information relating to an identified or identifiable natural person. The authorities interfere with the scope of protection when they process data, *i.e.,* in particular when they store, use, disclose or erase it.[41] The respect for private life guaranteed in Article 7 CFR is closely related to this; the two fundamental rights guarantee a uniform substance.[42]

Nudges to use administrative services digitally indirectly ensure that personal data is processed. However, the mere incentive does not constitute an interference with Article 8(1) CFR; rather, it raises tensions in terms of equality law (*see* Section 3.4.). In contrast, any obligation to use digital communication channels with the state interferes with the fundamental right because it obliges the individual to disclose data. This also applies to the analogue use of administrative services, especially because the transmitted data via an analogue channel may be digitalized. However, the obligation to transmit data electronically is an additional obligation, as the (automated) data processing possibilities are different.[43] Moreover, the digital transmission process also generates more data, for example about the type of device used.[44] The interference is also independent of the existence of a hardship clause. This is because the requirements of the provision have to be met and the citizen has to apply for it.

---

39 Johanna Wolff & Kristin Rohleder, *in* Jürgen Meyer & Sven Holscheidt (eds.), *Charta der Grundrechte der Europäischen Union, 6th edition,* Nomos, Baden-Baden, 2024, Art. 36 para. 12 *et seq.* with further literature; other view: Bernd Lorenz, 'Das Recht auf ein analoges Leben', *Zeitschrift für das Recht der Digitalisierung, Datenwirtschaft und IT,* 2022, pp. 936 *et seq.*

40 Id.

41 Jarass 2021, Art. 8, para. 9.

42 *See e.g.* Judgment of 6 October 2020, *Cases C-511/18, C-512/18 and C-520/18, La Quadrature du Net and others,* ECLI:EU:C:2020:791.

43 Botta 2022, p. 1250.

44 Thilo Weichert, 'Gegen Digitalzwang – ein Recht auf eine analoge Alternative', *Neue Juristische Online-Zeitschrift,* 2024, p. 1540.

(ii) Justification. The fundamental right to personal data is not guaranteed without restriction: any interference with it can be justified. However, this only applies if it does not interfere with the essence of the right [Article 52(1) CFR]. The CJEU has not yet defined the essence of the right to personal data. However, an interference with this is subject to stringent requirements and would only be considered in the case of a comprehensive surveillance program, for example.[45] Even the complete digitalization of all digitizable administrative services without a hardship clause would not constitute such an interference.

The legitimate aim of the total or partial obligation to communicate digitally with authorities is to make administration more effective.[46] Of course, in each individual case a distinction would have to be made and the digitalized administrative activity would have to be examined in detail. Digitalization pursues different objectives. Firstly, administrative services become more cost-effective and less personnel-intensive, since the (partially) automated processing leads to relief effects (*see* already under Section 2). This is ultimately based on the principle of sound financial management, which is also codified in the TFEU,[47] according to which the most favorable balance between the use of funds and the achievement of objectives must be achieved. Second, administrative services are usually provided more rapidly, although there may be exceptions. Finally, the quality of the administrative services can also be improved; however, this also varies from case to case. It is questionable whether a legal interest can be found behind the last two dimensions mentioned in EU primary law. The right to good administration under Article 41(1) TFEU comes into consideration here. It explicitly states that the matter must be dealt with within a reasonable period of time. The standard only addresses institutions, bodies, offices and agencies of the Union. But it is also a general principle of EU law.[48] Furthermore, digitalized administration enables the state to make its relationship with its companies and citizens more transparent and interactive.[49] Finally, digitalized administration can also reduce costs for citizens and businesses. Overall, these are legitimate objectives.

45 Jürgen Kühling, *in* Frankfurter Kommentar 2023, Art. 8 para. 41.

46 *See also* Digitalisation and Administrative Law, European Parliament resolution of 22 November 2023 with recommendations to the Commission on Digitalisation and Administrative Law, 2021/2161(INL), p. 6.

47 Articles 310(5) and 317(1) TFEU.

48 Judgment of 8 May 2014, *Case C-604/12, N,* ECLI:EU:C:2014:302, paras. 49 *et seq.*

49 EU eGovernment Action Plan 2016–2020. Accelerating the digital transformation of government, COM(2016) 179 final, p 4.

The mandatory digital use of administrative services is also in line with the necessity principle. It is true that more administrative staff could be employed to achieve the objectives. However, there is legislative discretion in this respect. This is all the more true since the speed of automated decision-making simply cannot be achieved by humans.

However, it is questionable whether the legitimate objectives are proportionate to the interference with fundamental rights that this causes. In this respect, a distinction must be made between the quality and quantity of the data that must be submitted digitally. The more sensitive the data and the more data that must be submitted digitally, the greater is the interference. Nevertheless, no right of defence against digital administration can be derived from the fundamental right to personal data. This is because Article 7 *et seq.* CFR primarily protect how the data is stored and processed. If, in individual cases, a data protection-compliant organization of further administrative action is ensured, the obligation to use digital administrative access does not violate this fundamental right.[50]

3.4. Unequal Treatment

3.4.1. "Digital Only" for Some or All Administrative Services

(i) Unequal treatment. Firstly, exclusively digital administrative access discriminates against those who do not have the appropriate hardware and/or software. This may be for financial reasons or due to the technical scepticism of those concerned.[51] The latter is probably particularly high in Germany due to the collective consciousness resulting from two totalitarian regimes.

Those who lack digital literacy are also at a disadvantage. This particularly includes those with a low level of formal education and older people. The latter, who are also often visually impaired, are not discriminated against directly, but indirectly.[52] There is therefore unequal treatment within the meaning of Article 21(1) CFR. According to the provision, no one may be

50 *Cf.* Botta 2022, p. 1250.

51 Id. p. 1251; Weichert 2024, p. 1538.

52 Dirk Heckmann, 'Grundrecht auf IT-Abwehr? – Freiheitsrechte als Abwehrrechte gegen aufgedrängtes E-Government', *Zeitschrift für das Recht der Digitalisierung, Datenwirtschaft und IT*, 2006, pp. 6 *et seq.*; Schulz 2021, p. 382; Weichert 2024, p. 1538.

treated unequally. In this context, this means that a lack of financial resources to purchase hardware or software may also lead to unequal treatment. The same applies to people with disabilities.[53]

Finally, forcing businesses to use only digital access, as is the case in Germany (*see* Section 2.2), puts them at a disadvantage compared to citizens. In addition, and this should only be mentioned in passing, it interferes with the freedom to conduct a business and, where applicable, the freedom to choose an occupation (Articles 15 *et seq.* CFR).

(ii) Justification. The unequal treatment of those who do not (or do not wish to) have digital access weighs little against the legitimate aims outlined above. Those treated unequally are likely to be a small group. For example, 95% of households in Germany used the internet in 2024.[54] Moreover, they can gain access in other ways, such as through internet cafés or by using public Wi-Fi hotspots.[55]

However, indirect unequal treatment based on age, lack of financial assets or disability weighs heavily. This affects a great number of people. The ease of technical access to administrative services must also be taken into account. The more technical skills are required, the fewer citizens possess them and the greater the intensity of unequal treatment. If "digital only" were applied to all services that could be digitalized, the majority of administrative services would no longer be available to citizens. Complete switchover therefore constitutes unjustified discriminations.

If some services can only be accessed digitally, it would be necessary to consider which services would be covered. This will depend on the importance of the digitalized administrative service and the target audience. What is clear is that digital-only access to essential services violates the CFR. Compulsory use of technology could negatively affect social services on which socially disadvantaged citizens depend. Unequal treatment in this area would be difficult to justify. This may be different, for example, in the case of digital-only applications to universities. The crucial factor here is that the applicants concerned are usually young and therefore digitally savvy and have a high level of education.

It would be possible to mitigate the intensity of the interference, if authorities would provide digital access options at their branches[56] and, if neces-

53 *Cf.* Weichert 2024, p. 1542.

54 Statista, Share of internet users in Germany in the years 1997 to 2024.

55 Verwaltungsgericht Würzburg (Administrative Court of Würzburg), decision of 13 July 2020 – 8 E 20.815, para. 32.

56 Botta 2022, p. 1251.

sary, also offer assistance there.[57] Also, hardship clauses would have a mitigating effect. With them, it would be possible to receive administrative services in analogue form for citizens, who do not have the necessary digital skills and/or the technology. With such hardship regulations, digital-only administrative services would also comply with fundamental rights.

The need for hardship clauses may change in the foreseeable future. The higher the level of digital literacy and the more widespread the hardware in the groups mentioned, the lower the intensity of the interference.[58] Nevertheless, there will always be a group, albeit a small one, that is excluded by exclusively digital offerings.[59] It would also be necessary to examine the degree of technical sophistication required for the digital access in question. The easier the digital access, the lower the intensity of interference.

The unequal treatment of businesses can be justified. This is because, as participants in business transactions, they are already technically equipped and have the know-how to transmit data electronically. The digital transformation is so far advanced that a hardship clause is not necessary.[60] However, for reasons of proportionality, the possibility of analogue access must be granted at least in emergencies, *i.e.*, in particular in the event of an Internet breakdown, cyber-attacks or similar.[61] Finally, it would be worth considering hardship clauses for micro-enterprises.

3.4.2. Nudges for the Use of Digital Communication Channels

It should also be discussed whether incentives for citizens to use digital channels also violate equality rights. Such regulations treat citizens unequally, depending on whether they use analogue or digital services. This particularly affects older citizens, see above. Various forms of unequal treatment are conceivable, such as reduced fees or faster processing, *see* Section 2.4.

The legitimate purposes of the incentive to use digital procedures are again those mentioned above, in particular the costs. In addition, the indi-

57 *Cf.* Heckmann 2006, p. 7.

58 Id. p. 6.

59 *Cf.* Weichert 2024, p. 1538.

60 *Cf.* Jonas Botta, Stellungnahme zum Entwurf eines OZG-Änderungsgesetzes (OZG-ÄndG), BT-Drs. 20(4)303 C, p. 9.

61 *Cf.* Annette Guckelberger, 'Gutachterliche Stellungnahme für den Ausschuss für Inneres und Heimat des Deutsches Bundestages' (sic!), Sachverständigen-Anhörung am 9. Oktober 2023 zum Entwurf eines Gesetzes zur Änderung des Onlinzugangsgesetzes, BT-Drs. 20(4)303 J, p. 7.

rect aim is also to ensure that more digital administrative services are used. These purposes also predominate, as both the order of processing and the costs are likely to correlate in principle with the processing effort involved.[62] Consequently, fundamental rights limits are only to be drawn where the unequal treatment is particularly pronounced, for example if the fee for an analogue administrative service is a several times greater than that the for digital administrative service.

3.5. Interim Result

As a preliminary conclusion, it can be stated that digital-only access for citizens to all administrative services that can be digitalized is compatible with fundamental rights only if there is a hardship clause. In the case of individual administrative services that can only be accessed digitally, the specific nature of the service must be taken into account. The more essential the service, the less likely it is to be compatible with the CFR without a hardship clause. On the other hand, a digital only obligation could be introduced for companies, provided that there is a hardship clause for technical problems. The mere privileging of the digital procedure is unproblematic from the perspective of equality law.

4. Ideas for Reform

In the legal policy debate, various ideas for reform need to be addressed, some of which have already been implemented and some of which have been formulated as demands. Firstly, there is a proposal at European level in a legislative resolution of the European Parliament on European administrative procedural law. The European Parliament recommends that "analogue alternatives to digital services should always be provided and offered clearly to citizens and companies, and a human contact point should be physically and remotely available to support citizens [...]."[63] This goes beyond what is required by fundamental rights, see above. As far as can be seen, however, the Commission has not yet submitted a proposal.

62 *Cf.* Martini 2017, p. 450.

63 Digitalisation and Administrative Law, European Parliament resolution of 22 November 2023 with recommendations to the Commission on Digitalisation and Administrative Law, 2021/2161(INL), p. 9.

At national level, legislation already exists that prevents a digital-only access to administrative services, for example in France[64] Also, in Germany at state level different regulations exist. For example, the constitution of Schleswig-Holstein provides in Article 14(2): "Within the scope of its powers, the state shall ensure personal, written and electronic access to its authorities and courts. No one may be disadvantaged because of the type of access" (own translation). The first sentence of this provision is a state objective provision and not a fundamental right. Accordingly, multi-channel access to the state authorities and courts must be created, with scope for implementation.[65] According to the wording, this should also apply to companies. By contrast, sentence 2 contains a subjective right in the form of a requirement for equal treatment. It is argued that incentives intended to make the use of digital alternatives attractive to citizens or companies are therefore excluded because they constitute discrimination.[66] On the other hand, however, it should be noted that this requirement of equal treatment can be weighed against other legitimate objectives.[67] Overall, the added value of this provision is therefore low. The Free State of Bavaria has taken a different approach. Pursuant to Article 20(2) BayDIG, at least a hardship provision must be provided for when implementing digital administrative procedures.

There are also reform ideas at civil society level. Recently, an association published a petition for a life without digital restrictions.[68] In addition, an initiative led by the "Zeit-Stiftung" has published a proposal for a CFR.[69] Article 3(2) of this Charter states that no one may be denied access to goods and services or be excluded from participation in public life through the use of automated processes. This does not necessarily include purely digital access to administrative services, as an automated process does not have to take place.

It is clear that regulation would only be necessary for those aspects that are not already excluded by fundamental rights. Three possible regulations

64 Weichert 2024, p. 1540.

65 Christian Hoffmann & Sönke E. Schulz, 'Schleswig-Holsteins digitale Verfassung – Digitale Basisdienste, elektronischer Zugang zu Behörden und Gerichten und digitale Privatsphäre in der Schleswig-Holsteinischen Landesverfassung', *Zeitschrift für Öffentliches Recht in Norddeutschland,* 2016, pp. 392 *et seq.*

66 Id. pp. 394 *et seq.*

67 Botta 2022, p. 1252.

68 Digitalcourage, Petition gegen Digitalzwang, at https://digitalcourage.de/blog/2024/petition-fuer-recht-auf-ein-leben-ohne-digitalzwang-gestartet.

69 *See* at https://digitalcharta.eu/wp-content/uploads/DigitalCharter-English-2019-Final.pdf.

are conceivable. Either a regulation that provides for an analogue access to all administrative services that can be digitalized. This is the direction taken by the regulation proposed by the European Parliament. Alternatively, a regulation is perceivable, which, similarly to the BayDIG, at least provides for hardship cases for all digitalized administrative services. Finally, a provision inspired by the constitution of the state of Schleswig-Holstein, which excludes incentives for the use of digital access alone, is conceivable.

5. Conclusion and Outlook

European law creates the conditions for offering exclusively digital administrative services in the Member States and does not contain a general right of defence against this, at least not yet. In Germany, some administrative services are already offered exclusively in digital form, although this is still the absolute exception for citizens. By contrast, digital-only services for businesses are common in some areas, although there are hardship regulations. Finally, there can be incentives that privilege digital access.

The digital-only provision of essential administrative services to citizens is not compatible with the CFR. However, the situation is different if there are hardship clauses. Finally, digital access may be privileged from a fundamental rights perspective.

Existing legislation could be used as a blueprint for a regulation to be created in the future. However, it is still unclear how extensive the protection against compulsory digitalization should be. If the European legislator wishes to provide for a guarantee of analogous administrative access in the implementation of Union law, this would have to be explicitly included in the CFR or in secondary law. The parallel provision of analogue and digital access would conflict with the goal of rendering administration more effective. At the end of the day, it is conceivable that digital administration could prevail without any obligation, simply because it is easier to use and faster.

Part IV
– Case notes

The Recent Fight Over Usufruct Rights in Hungary

What Insights Does the CJEU's Judgment in Nemzeti Földügyi Központ (C-419/23) Offer?

*Hajnalka Szinek Csütörtöki**

Abstract

Recent developments in land acquisition rules have been increasingly shaped by international and European law, with the EU playing a central role in influencing national land law regulations, including those of Hungary. The country's land law has gradually evolved into a more structured system, driven mainly by the requirements of EU law. However, the regulation of usufruct rights over agricultural land, inter alia, remains a recurring point of legal contention. This is precisely what resurfaced in the recent judgment of the CJEU in Nemzeti Földügyi Központ (C-419/23), where the Court addressed the reinstatement of usufruct rights over agricultural land in Hungary. Furthermore, this case also brings some 'innovations' when compared to the CJEU's earlier jurisprudence, including in SEGRO and Horváth, Commission v Hungary, and Grossmania.

Keywords: land law, national land law, usufruct, arable land, agricultural land

1. Introduction

To begin with, it is essential to note that while Hungarian land law had undergone dynamic changes until the end of the 20th century, it nevertheless remained under-regulated in certain aspects. To address these 'gaps', the Hungarian legislator undertook significant reforms, including re-regulating Act LV of 1994 on Arable Land. Simultaneously, a parallel land restitution process was undertaken to resolve historical land ownership issues. While these measures addressed many concerns, they also created new chal-

* Hajnalka Szinek Csütörtöki: senior research fellow, Central European Academy, Budapest; Ph.D. Candidate, Ferenc Deák Doctoral School of Law, University of Miskolc, hajnalka.szinek.csutortoki@centraleuropeanacademy.hu.

lenges.[1] Additionally, Hungary's accession to the EU marked a significant turning point, bringing substantial changes to, *inter alia,* its land law.[2]

As part of the largest enlargement round in the EU's history, Hungary and other Member States were required to harmonize their national legislation with EU law. A specific feature of the 'enlargement process' is that the issue of agricultural land acquisition has consistently been a priority in Accession Treaties.[3] In this context, Hungary enacted several acts to ensure compliance with EU law – including Act CXXII of 2013 on the Transfer of Agricultural and Forest Land (commonly known as the Land Transfer Act). This legislative framework, supplemented by additional legislation, was designed to implement EU law while simultaneously safeguarding property rights and protecting agricultural land[4] – a national asset of vital importance and a natural resource enshrined in the Fundamental Law of Hungary.[5]

Newly joined Member States, including Hungary, were given derogation to maintain national restrictions on the acquisition of agricultural and forestry land for a transitional period[6] under their Accession Treaties.[7] While

1 János Ede Szilágyi, 'Hungary: Strict Agricultural Land and Holding Regulations for Sustainable and Traditional Rural Communities', *in* János Ede Szilágyi (ed.), *Acquisition of Agricultural Lands: Cross-border Issues from a Central European Perspective,* Central European Academic Publishing, Miskolc-Budapest, 2022, p. 336.

2 János Ede Szilágyi & Hajnalka Szinek Csütörtöki, 'The Past, Present, and the Future of Hungarian Land Law in the Context of EU Law', *Hungarian Yearbook of International Law and European Law,* Vol. 11, Issue 1, 2023, pp. 318–334.

3 Unlike 'older' EU members, countries that joined in 2004 or later had agricultural land acquisition explicitly addressed in their Accession Treaties, making it a key part of their legislative frameworks. For further details on this topic, *see* János Ede Szilágyi, 'European legislation and Hungarian law regime of transfer of agricultural and forestry lands', *Journal of Agricultural and Environmental Law,* Vol. 12, Issue 23, 2017, p. 151.

4 Tamás Prugberger, 'Földvédelem és környezethez való jog', *in* József Szalma (ed.), *A Magyar Tudomány Napja a Délvidéken 2016: A vidék népességmegtartó erejének fokozását elősegítő társadalmi, jogi és természeti tényezők,* Dialóg Campus, Budapest, 2016, pp. 69–106.

5 The Fundamental Law of Hungary uses the term arable land. Hungarian land law has undergone significant reforms, especially in regulating agricultural holdings and land. Act LXXI of 2020 is a key example, introducing clear rules for terminating undivided co-ownership and addressing intestate succession of agricultural land. In connection with the topic, *see also* Zsófia Hornyák, *A mezőgazdasági földek öröklése,* Bíbor, Miskolc, 2019; Zsófia Hornyák, 'Legal frame of agricultural land succession and acquisition by legal persons in Hungary', *Journal of Agricultural and Environmental Law,* Vol. 16, Issue 30, 2021, pp. 86–99.

6 Szilágyi 2017, p. 158.

7 János Ede Szilágyi, 'The Accession Treaties of the New Member States and the national legislations, particularly the Hungarian law, concerning the ownership of agricultural land', *Journal of Agricultural and Environmental Law,* Vol. 5, Issue 9, 2010, pp. 48–60.

most countries had a seven-year transition, some new Member States secured extensions – Hungary, for example, negotiated an additional three years,[8] extending the derogation to ten years to align its land laws with EU law.[9]

Following the end of the transitional period, the European Commission assessed the land laws of the new Member States[10] and found that specific provisions in their revised legislation restricted fundamental EU economic freedoms, notably the free movement of capital and the freedom of establishment. Consequently, in 2015, the Commission launched infringement proceedings against several new Member States.[11] It is worth noting that such proceedings related to land transfers were relatively rare in the past, with preliminary ruling procedures having been initiated instead.[12] Furthermore, the Commission's investigation and subsequent actions were focused exclusively on Member States that joined the EU in 2004 or later. This is significant because these countries had typically based their land laws on those of the 'older' Member States. This selective litigation approach of the Commission was criticized by a Hungarian expert, suggesting it could be discriminatory.[13] In light of this, it is worth conducting further investigations, and as some authors highlighted, it would be worth bringing the matter to the European Ombudsman for clarification.[14]

---

8 For instance, Poland had a longer transitional period, while most countries could extend theirs by three years with EU approval. Romania and Bulgaria, for example, were exceptions, with no extension allowed beyond the initial seven years. *See* Szilágyi 2017, p. 158.

9 Mihály Kurucz, 'Gondolatok a magyar földforgalmi törvény uniós jogi feszültségpontjainak kérdéseiről', *in* József Szalma (ed.), *A Magyar Tudomány Napja a Délvidéken 2014: Föld- és ingatlantulajdon, fenntartható mezőgazdasági fejlődés*, Vajdasági Magyar Tudományos Társaság, Újvidék, 2015, p. 151.

10 Except for Poland, given the longer transitional period.

11 *See* the press release of the European Commission: Financial services: Commission requests BULGARIA, HUNGARY, LATVIA, LITHUANIA and SLOVAKIA to comply with EU rules on the acquisition of agricultural land, at https://ec.europa.eu/commission/presscorner/detail/hu/IP_16_1827.

12 János Ede Szilágyi, 'Magyarország földjogi szabályozásának egyes aktuális kérdései', *in* József Szalma (ed.), *A Magyar Tudomány Napja a Délvidéken 2017: Migráció, környezetvédelem – társadalom és természet*', Vajdasági Magyar Tudományos Társaság, Újvidék, 2018, p. 185.

13 Ágoston Korom & Réka Bokor, 'Gondolatok az új tagállamok birtokpolitikájával kapcsolatban. Transzparencia és egyenlő bánásmód', *in* Klára Gellén (ed.), *Honori et virtuti*, Pólay Elemér Alapítvány, Szeged, 2013, pp. 266–267. *See also* Orsolya Papik, '"Trends and current issues regarding member state's room to maneuver of land trade" panel discussion,' *Journal of Agricultural and Environmental Law*, Vol. 12, Issue 22, 2017, p. 155.

14 *See* Szilágyi 2018, p. 186. Several Hungarian experts have proposed different solutions to address the issue of usufruct rights. For example, at the 2015 CEDR congress in Potsdam

As far as preliminary ruling procedures are concerned, the case of *Nemzeti Földügyi Központ*[15] represents the latest development in a series of legal challenges surrounding usufruct rights in Hungary[16] – and it forms the core of this study. The CJEU was asked to rule on the validity of restoring a previously annulled usufruct right, following Hungary's 2021 legislation adopted in response to a prior CJEU ruling. The dispute centered on whether a usufruct right originally granted to a German national had been lawfully registered.[17] This case is particularly interesting because, unlike previous cases where applicants sought reinstatement of their usufruct rights, the German-resident applicant in *Nemzeti Földügyi Központ* challenged the restoration of the previously deleted right.

To provide a better understanding of the issue, this study first briefly outlines the CJEU's jurisprudence on Hungarian land law, presents the infringement proceedings concerning land law legislation of the 'newly joined' Member States following the expiration of the transitional period, and provides a brief overview of the preliminary rulings before the CJEU in connection with the topic. As the primary focus of this study is the recent judgment of the CJEU regarding the rights of usufruct in Hungary, this case will be discussed in more detail. It should be noted that this study does not aim to provide a detailed description of the preliminary rulings or infringement procedures and related case law, as these topics have already been thoroughly covered in a previous issue of the Hungarian Yearbook of International Law and European Law.[18]

2. *The CJEU's Jurisprudence on Hungarian Land Law*

The jurisprudence of the CJEU concerning Hungarian land law legislation has become a significant body of EU case law on land issues. This develop-

---

and a 2017 Budapest conference, the topic was actively discussed. For additional insights on this subject *see also* Anikó Raisz, 'A magyar földforgalom szabályozásának aktuális kérdéseiről', *Publicationes Universitatis Miskolcinensis, Sectio Juridica et Politica,* Vol. 35, Issue 1, 2017, p. 441.

15 Judgment of 12 December 2024, *Case C-419/23, Nemzeti Földügyi Központ,* ECLI:EU:C:2024:1016.

16 Concerning this, *see e.g.* Miklós Zoltán Fehér & Réka Somssich, 'The Gradual Shaping of Hungarian Law by Consecutive Preliminary References', *Hungarian Yearbook of International Law and European Law,* Vol. 12, Issue 1, 2024, pp. 37–66.

17 *See* the press release of the CJEU, No 198/24.

18 *See* Szilágyi & Szinek Csütörtöki 2023, pp. 318–334.

ment is mainly attributable to the stringent regulatory framework enacted by Hungary, which is among the most restrictive in the region.[19] However, it remains open whether comparable legal constraints exist in the 'older' EU Member States – either justifying infringement proceedings against them or, conversely, supporting the argument that Hungary should not be singled out to face such proceedings alone.[20]

The Hungarian cases before the CJEU originated from the European Commission's assessment of national land laws across the 'new' Member States. It should be recalled that this review occurred following the expiration of the transitional period granted to these states upon their accession to the EU. The Commission identified numerous restrictive measures in the land law regulations of these 'new' Member States, which were deemed incompatible with fundamental EU freedoms – particularly the free movement of capital and the freedom of establishment. Consequently, the Commission initiated infringement proceedings against several Member States. According to its assessment, the national rules complained of imposed excessive restrictions on cross-border investment, discouraging the free movement of capital within the internal market.[21]

2.1. Infringement Proceedings and Preliminary Ruling Procedures

For the purposes of this paper, we must briefly examine the infringement proceedings initiated against Hungary concerning its land law legislation. In addition, a brief overview of the preliminary ruling proceedings before the CJEU will be given. Owing to scope of this paper, this analysis will only offer a concise summary of the cases rather than a comprehensive review, as this topic was already discussed in an earlier issue of the Hungarian Yearbook.[22] Nevertheless, it is essential to outline their substance to better understand the recent CJEU judgment.

---

19 János Ede Szilágyi & Hajnalka Szinek Csütörtöki, 'Conclusions on Cross-border Acquisition of Agricultural Lands in Certain Central European Countries', *in* János Ede Szilágyi (ed.), *Acquisition of Agricultural Lands: Cross-border Issues from a Central European Perspective,* Central European Academic Publishing, Miskolc-Budapest, 2022, p. 370.

20 János Ede Szilágyi, 'The International and EU Legal Dimensions of Agricultural Land Acquisition and the Room for Non-State Action', *in* János Ede Szilágyi (ed.), *Legal Protection of Farmers,* Wydawnictwo Instytutu Wymiaru Sprawiedliwości, Warszawa, 2024, pp. 52–70.

21 *See* Szilágyi & Szinek Csütörtöki 2023, pp. 318–334.

22 Id.

Regarding the infringement proceedings, it is worth mentioning that the European Commission initiated two infringement proceedings due to Hungary's land law regime: one concerns the *ex lege* termination of usufruct rights between non-close relatives[23] (*the usufructuary case*),[24] while the other addressed broader aspects of Hungary's land law *(the global case)*.[25]

In the global case, Hungary successfully defended several provisions,[26] leading to the removal of issues such as local land commission procedures, land acquisition limits, pre-emption rights, and lease durations from the scope of the infringement. However, ongoing challenges remain regarding the prohibition of legal persons to acquire agricultural land, the ban on transformation, professional competence requirements for farmers, non-recognition of foreign experience, self-farming obligations, and the approval condition for sales contracts.[27] Among these, the prohibition on legal persons to acquire land – an essential element of Hungarian land law since 1994[28] – remains particularly significant.[29] This rule applies to both domestic and foreign persons,[30] restricting ownership but not land use.[31] Experts argue that lifting this ban could undermine Hungary's rural land structure and require a fundamental legal overhaul.[32] A po-

23 Infringement number: INFR(2014)2246, decision date 18 June 2015.

24 For more one the usufructuary case, *see* Tamás Andréka & István Olajos, 'A földforgalmi jogalkotás és jogalkalmazás végrehajtása kapcsán felmerült jogi problémák elemzése', *Magyar Jog*, Vol. 64, Issue 7–8, 2017, pp. 410–424.

25 Infringement number: INFR(2015)2023, decision date 26 March 2015.

26 Andréka & Olajos 2017, pp. 410–424.

27 János Ede Szilágyi, 'Agricultural Land Law: Soft Law in Soft Law', *Hungarian Yearbook of International Law and European Law*, Vol. 6, Issue 1, 2018, pp. 193–194.

28 *Cf.* Péter Hegyes, 'A földforgalmi törvény a gyakorlatban', *in* Klára Gellén (ed.), *Honori et virtuti*, Iurisperitus, Szeged, 2017, pp. 116–121; Pál Bobvos *et al.*, 'A mező- és erdőgazdasági földek alapjogi védelme', *in* Elemér Balogh (ed.), *Számadás az Alaptörvényről*, Magyar Közlöny Lap- és Könyvkiadó, Budapest, 2016, pp. 31–41; Csilla Csák, 'Constitutional issues of land transactions regulation', *Journal of Agricultural and Environmental Law*, Vol. 13, Issue 24, 2018, pp. 5–32; Csilla Csák, 'Integrated agricultural organization of production system and the organizations carrying that', *Journal of Agricultural and Environmental Law*, Vol. 13, Issue 25, 2018, pp. 6–21.

29 Szilágyi & Szinek Csütörtöki 2022, pp. 362–363.

30 With some exceptions.

31 Martin Milán Csirszki *et al.*, 'Food Sovereignty: Is There an Emerging Paradigm in V4 Countries for the Regulation of the Acquisition of Ownership of Agricultural Lands by Legal Persons?', *Central European Journal of Comparative Law*, Vol. 2, Issue 1, 2021, pp. 29–52. Szilágyi 2022, p. 189.

32 Andréka & Olajos 2017, p. 410–424.

tential CJEU ruling on this matter could set an important precedent[33] at the EU level.[34]

The decision in the usufructuary case was preceded by a related preliminary ruling. The next sections will present key cases, including *Case C-235/17, Commission v Hungary.*

Turning to the preliminary ruling procedures, the first case to mention is *SEGRO and Horváth,*[35] which revolves around the *ex lege* termination of usufructuary rights over Hungarian agricultural land without compensation, a measure introduced by Hungarian authorities with new legislation. SEGRO, a Hungarian-registered company with foreign shareholders,[36] and Günther Horváth, an Austrian citizen residing in Austria, both held usufructuary rights over land in Hungary. However, due to changes in legislative, their rights were terminated, as the new provisions stipulated that such rights could only be granted to close relatives of the landowner. Believing this measure to be contrary to the principle of free movement of capital under Article 63 TFEU, they initiated legal proceedings before the Administrative and Labor Court of Szombathely, which referred the case to the CJEU for a preliminary ruling.[37] Advocate General Øe examined[38] the Hungarian legislation from the perspective of negative integration,[39] treating agricultural land primarily as a commercial good. However, a significant flaw in his reasoning emerged as he appeared to conflate usufructuary rights with the instrument of lease, even though Hungarian law distinguishes clearly between the two.[40] This confusion led him to conclude that Hungary's restrictions constituted indirect discrimination. This position does not fully

33 In its judgment of 23 September 2003 in *Case C-452/01, Ospelt and Schlössle Weissenberg,* ECLI:EU:C:2003:493, the CJEU held that an Austrian law restricting property acquisition by a Liechtenstein foundation was incompatible with EU law. However, the decision is not directly applicable to Hungary's land regime, as the underlying legal and factual circumstances differ fundamentally.

34 Szilágyi 2022, p. 190.

35 Judgment of 6 March 2018, *Joined Cases C-52/16 and C-113/16, SEGRO and Horváth,* ECLI:EU:C:2018:157.

36 *I.e.,* in Germany. *Joined Cases C-52/16 and C-113/16, SEGRO and Horváth,* para. 15.

37 Szilágyi & Szinek Csütörtöki 2023, pp. 318–334.

38 *Joined Cases C-52/16 and C-113/16, SEGRO and Horváth,* Opinion of Advocate General Saugmandsgaard Øe, ECLI:EU:C:2017:410, paras. 71–81.

39 Ágoston Korom, 'The European Union's Legal Framework on the Member State's Margin of Appreciation in Land Policy – The CJEU's Case Law After the "KOB" SIA Case', *in* János Ede Szilágyi (ed.), *Acquisition of Agricultural Lands: Cross-border Issues from a Central European Perspective,* Central European Academic Publishing, Miskolc-Budapest, 2022, p. 78. and 81.

40 The usufructuary rights *(haszonélvezet)* and the instrument of lease *(haszonbérlet).*

align with the structure of usufructuary rights under Hungarian jurisprudence, where such rights are typically granted to family members. Despite this information in the AG's opinion, the CJEU ruled that the Hungarian legislation in question constituted an unjustified restriction on the free movement of capital and failed to satisfy the principle of proportionality.[41] The judgment reinforced the primacy of EU law in governing cross-border investment and property rights while highlighting the limits of national regulatory autonomy in land law issues.[42] The case also raised expectations regarding the CJEU's potential assessment of the Hungarian legislation under Article 17 of the Charter of Fundamental Rights, which protects the right to property, and Article 47, which guarantees the right to an effective remedy and fair trial. However, the Court declined to examine these provisions, arguing that since the measure had already been found to infringe on the free movement of capital, an additional assessment under the Charter was not necessary to resolve the dispute. This outcome reaffirmed the Court's longstanding approach, whereby it tends to focus on fundamental freedoms under the TFEU before engaging with fundamental rights provisions.[43]

A related case, *Case C-24/18*,[44] further illustrated the strict procedural requirements for preliminary rulings before the CJEU. The Hungarian court had referred a question concerning the compatibility of national land law with Articles 49 and 63 TFEU, asking whether the *ex lege* termination of usufructuary rights, in cases where property had changed ownership through execution, constituted an infringement of EU law. However, the CJEU declared the reference inadmissible because the dispute was purely domestic in nature and lacked a sufficient cross-border element to justify an interpretation of TFEU provisions.[45] This decision underscored national courts' need to demonstrate a clear link between national legal disputes and EU law when seeking a preliminary ruling.[46]

While *SEGRO and Horváth* did not lead to a substantive assessment of Article 17 of the Charter, the case *Commission v Hungary*,[47] which also concerned usufructuary rights, provided the CJEU with an opportunity to address the right to property directly. The Court ruled against Hungary, hold-

41 *See* Szilágyi & Szinek Csütörtöki 2023, pp. 318–334.

42 It was also pointed out in a previous study. *See* Szilágyi 2017, p. 161.

43 Szilágyi 2022, p. 190.

44 Order of 31 May 2018, *Case C-24/18, Bán,* ECLI:EU:C:2018:376.

45 Szilágyi 2022, p. 191.

46 *Case C-24/18, Bán,* paras. 16 and 19.

47 Judgment of 21 May 2019, *Case C-235/17, Commission v Hungary,* ECLI:EU:C:2019:432.

ing that the national legislation amounted to unjustified deprivation of property under Article 17(1) of the Charter. The judgment emphasized that usufructuary rights, recognized under Hungarian law, constituted a legally acquired right subject to protection under EU law. By referencing case law from the ECtHR, the CJEU reaffirmed the principle that property deprivations must be accompanied by fair and timely compensation, which Hungary's legislative measures had failed to provide.[48] Consequently, the Court determined that the measure was incompatible not only with Article 63 TFEU but also with the fundamental right to property enshrined in the Charter.[49]

Similarly, *Grossmania*[50] arose from the legislation introduced in 2013 that imposed a blanket termination of usufructuary rights established by contract between non-close relatives. Grossmania, a Hungarian-registered commercial company owned by EU nationals, had acquired usufruct rights over agricultural land in Jánosháza and Duka,[51] but the legislative amendments *ipso iure* terminated these rights.[52] Grossmania's attempt to reinstate these rights through Hungarian administrative proceedings was unsuccessful.[53] The Hungarian Administrative and Labor Court in Győr[54] raised a key legal question: could a provision previously declared incompatible with EU law still be applied in a different factual context?[55] This issue challenged the primacy of EU law and whether national courts could uphold national provisions despite prior CJEU rulings. Experts, like Ana Bobić, argued that the CJEU had the chance to clarify whether national courts must disapprove of conflicting laws and render them inoperative for future cases. A decision extending this obligation would significantly shift the balance of power between national and EU legal systems.[56] *Grossmania* examined the conse-

48 Ágoston Korom, 'Requirements for the cross border inheritance of agricultural property. Which acts of the primary or secondary EU law can be applied in the case of agricultural properties' inheritance?', *Journal of Agricultural and Environmental Law,* Vol. 17, Issue 33, 2022, p. 67.

49 Concerning the topic, *see* Zoltán Varga, 'A termőföldre vonatkozó tagállami szabályozások az Európai Unió Bírósága előtt', *Európai Jog,* Vol. 20, Issue 1, 2020, pp. 6–7.

50 Judgment of 10 March 2022, *C-177/20, Grossmania,* ECLI:EU:C:2022:175.

51 Id. para. 16.

52 Press release no. 44/22, CJEU, Luxembourg, 10 March 2022, at https://curia.europa.eu/jcms/upload/docs/application/pdf/2022-03/cp220044hu.pdf.

53 Following the *SEGRO and Horváth* judgment.

54 Decision of Administrative and Labor Court of Győr, 10.K.27.809/2019/7.

55 Id. p. 7.

56 Ana Bobić, 'Constructive Versus Destructive Conflict: Taking Stock of the Recent Constitutional Jurisprudence in the EU', *Cambridge Yearbook of European Legal Studies,* 2020/22, p. 76.

quences of national authorities violating EU law, balancing legality and legal certainty. The CJEU ruled that the infringement was severe and manifest, recognizing restitution as the primary remedy. Compensation was deemed necessary if restitution wasn't possible, which was in line with national law. The Court also reaffirmed that Member States are liable for damages caused by serious breaches of EU law.[57]

These cases reflect the CJEU's evolving approach to land law in Hungary, highlighting the importance of the free movement of capital and the protection of fundamental rights. They limit national control over land ownership and underscore national courts' duty to uphold EU law. The tension between property rights, EU freedoms, and national sovereignty remains a live debate, with the CJEU guiding its direction. Notably, while earlier cases involved Hungarian citizens, the latest judgment concerns two foreign investors.

3. The Recent Fight over the Right of Usufruct in Hungary

As mentioned earlier, the *Nemzeti Földügyi Központ* marks the latest development in a series of legal challenges regarding usufruct rights in Hungary. This case reflects broader tensions between domestic land regulations aimed at protecting national (agricultural) interests and the EU's foundational principles – particularly the free movement of capital and the protection of property rights under the Charter.

3.1. Background of the Case

The events leading up to the dispute began on 30 December 2001, when the company Readiness Kft. and GW entered into a contract establishing a usufruct right over a plot of agricultural land in Kőszeg, Hungary. This usufruct right was duly entered into the Hungarian land registry on 29 January 2002 without any immediate objections, nor was it contested.[58]

Years later, in 2012, CN registered her ownership of the same agricultural land, and her ownership was officially recorded in the land registry.[59] In 2015, the Hungarian authority – the Szombathelyi District Registry, Vas Re-

57 Szilágyi & Szinek Csütörtöki 2023, pp. 318–334.
58 *Case C-419/23, Nemzeti Földügyi Központ,* para. 20.
59 Id. para. 21.

gion Administrative Department *(Vas Megyei Kormányhivatal Szombathelyi Járási Hivatal)* – deleted GW's usufruct right from the land register. This decision was based on the Hungarian legal provision that required the usufruct holder to be a close relative of the landowner for the usufruct right to be upheld.[60] Since GW was not a close relative of the landowner, the usufruct right was deleted from the land register, in line with the provisions of Section 108(1) of the 2013 Act on Transitional Measures, as well as Section 94 of the Act on the Land Register.[61]

However, the case took a significant turn in 2018 when the CJEU ruled on *SEGRO and Horváth,* clarifying that Article 63 TFEU (the free movement of capital) precludes national legislation that automatically extinguishes usufruct rights over agricultural land held by non-nationals of the Member State. This ruling emphasized that national laws that cancel usufruct rights solely because the holder is not a close relative of the landowner are incompatible with EU law.[62] In 2019, the CJEU issued a further judgment in *Commission v Hungary,* where it found that Hungary had violated EU law by adopting legislation that canceled usufruct rights held by non-Hungarian nationals, affirming yet again that such measures were contrary to the principles of the European Union, particularly the free movement of capital and the protection of property rights.[63]

In response to these rulings, Hungarian law was amended, and on 30 November 2022, the National Land Centre issued an order to reinstate GW's usufruct right in the land registry. This decision was based on the provisions of Sections 108/B and 108/F of the 2013 Act on Transitional Measures, as amended by a 2021 act[64] aimed at aligning Hungarian law with EU legal requirements. This reinstatement was crucial because, according to Hungarian law, the deletion of the usufruct right could only be undone if the usufruct holder was not considered to have proceeded in bad faith. CN, the current owner, was deemed to have proceeded in bad faith because she was the owner of the land when GW's usufruct right had been deleted and, therefore, could not claim good faith in the context of the reinstatement process.[65]

60 Id. para. 22.

61 Until 31 January 2023 Act CXLI of 1997. From 1 February 2023 Act C of 2021. *Case C-419/23, Nemzeti Földügyi Központ,* para. 22.

62 Id. para. 23.

63 Id. para. 24.

64 Act CL of 2021.

65 *Case C-419/23, Nemzeti Földügyi Központ,* para. 25.

Nevertheless, CN contested the decision of the National Land Centre, arguing that the original registration of the usufruct right in 2002 had been unlawful. The argument was based on Section 11(1) of the 1994 Act on Arable Land, which prohibited the registration of usufruct rights over agricultural land in favor of non-Hungarian nationals after 1 January 2002. Although the usufruct right was granted in 2001, it was not entered into the land register until 29 January 2002, when the law was already in force, rendering the registration unlawful in her view. Despite this, the registration decision had become final as it was not contested at the time, which complicated the legal situation.[66]

The National Land Centre and GW argued that the reinstatement of the usufruct right was valid and that there was no need to examine the lawfulness of the original registration. They pointed to the fact that the 2013 Act on Transitional Measures, as amended by the 2021 act, did not require an examination of whether the original registration of the usufruct right was lawful, and that the relevant legislation allowed for the reinstatement of rights that had been unlawfully deleted, provided certain conditions were met.[67]

The national court, Győr High Court *(Győri Törvényszék),* found itself grappling with the conflict between Hungarian national law and EU law, particularly the provisions of Article 63 TFEU and Article 17 of the Charter, which guarantee the right to property. The court noted that CN, a resident of Germany, was involved in an investment in agricultural land located in Hungary, which was subject to EU rules governing the free movement of capital. Additionally, it highlighted that GW's usufruct right, created by a contract signed in 2001 but registered only in 2002, occurred after Hungarian national law prohibited such registrations for non-Hungarian nationals. Although the court acknowledged the potential unlawfulness of the registration under Hungarian law, the decision became final due to the fact that it had not been contested at the time.[68]

The key issue raised at the Győr High Court was whether Hungarian legislation, which mandates the reinstatement of usufruct rights without examining the lawfulness of their original registration, is in compliance with EU law. The court sought clarity from the CJEU on whether Articles 63 TFEU and 17 of the Charter preclude national laws allowing the reinstatement of usufruct rights in the land registry without a mandatory consideration of

66 Id. para. 26.
67 Id. para. 27.
68 Id. paras. 28–37.

their (original) lawfulness. It also raised concerns about the principle of legal certainty and the compatibility of the reinstatement process with the EU's principles of effectiveness and sincere cooperation.[69]

3.2. Opinion of Advocate General Juliane Kokott

The Opinion of AG Juliane Kokott in the present case was delivered on 11 July 2024. Her opinion emphasizes that previous case law has established that national laws that violate EU principles – particularly those that annul usufruct rights to the detriment of EU nationals – are incompatible with EU law. In this case, the National Land Centre of Hungary reinstated the usufruct right following legislative changes adopted after a ruling declared the original law incompatible with EU law. However, the landowner, a German resident, challenges the reinstatement, arguing that the original usufruct registration was unlawful under Hungarian law at the time. The landowner asserts that the National Land Centre should have assessed the legality of the original registration before reinstating the usufruct to protect her property rights and the free movement of capital. This causes a conflict between the landowner's fundamental freedoms and the usufruct holder's rights. The key issue is whether the landowner can invoke EU law principles to demand the deletion of the usufruct despite the Court's prior ruling that protects the usufruct holder.[70]

The AG's Opinion delves deeply into the admissibility and substance of the preliminary ruling request, particularly the interpretation of Article 63 TFEU and Article 17 of the Charter. The case involves the reinstatement of a usufruct right after Hungary was found to have breached EU law. The Hungarian Government argued that the preliminary ruling request was inadmissible, contending that the reinstatement of the usufruct promoted the free movement of capital and did not warrant a review of the original registration.[71]

However, the Advocate General disagreed with the Hungarian Government, stating that there is a clear link between the case and EU law, justifying the referral.[72] The applicant, a legal person residing in Germany, is protected

69 Id. para. 37.
70 Opinion of Advocate General Kokott, *Case C-419/23, Nemzeti Földügyi Központ,* paras. 1–4.
71 Id. para. 35.
72 Id. para. 38.

under EU law, particularly Articles 63 TFEU and 17 of the Charter, guaranteeing the free movement of capital and the right to property. The reinstatement of the usufruct is directly tied to rectifying Hungary's previous violation of EU law, necessitating the referral to the CJEU.

On the substantive point, the AG assesses whether national authorities are required to examine the lawfulness of the original registration of the usufruct before its reinstatement. The main question is whether such an examination is mandated by EU law, even if the original registration was initially considered valid under national legislation. The Advocate General emphasized that, in this case, the rights of the usufruct holder may prevail over those of the landowner, as long as this aligns with EU law and internal market principles.[73]

The Advocate General further discussed whether the landowner, a non-resident of Hungary, can rely on EU law protections. The landowner benefits from the free movement of capital under Article 63 TFEU and the right to property under Article 17 of the Charter. However, these rights are not absolute and can be restricted if they conflict with the rights of others, such as the usufruct holder. In this case, the reinstatement of the usufruct is necessary to comply with EU law and rectify a previous infringement. The rights of the usufruct holder are equally protected under EU law, limiting the landowner's ability to exercise their right to property fully.[74]

The AG concluded that, in this context, the reinstatement of the usufruct is justified and proportionate under EU law. While the landowner's rights are safeguarded, the overriding objective is to ensure compliance with EU law and protect the usufruct holder's rights. The Court has consistently held that EU law must take precedence in situations like this, where national laws conflict with EU obligations.[75]

In conclusion, the Advocate General affirmed that the request for a preliminary ruling is admissible and that the reinstatement of the usufruct, in compliance with the judgment establishing Hungary's failure to fulfill its EU obligations, is consistent with EU law. The rights of the usufruct holder take precedence, given the need to uphold EU law and protect the free movement of capital and property rights. Additionally, the AG underscored that a landowner whose property is encumbered by a usufruct right that was originally lawfully registered but later deleted in violation of EU law cannot success-

73 Id. paras. 35, 40, 61, and 67.
74 Id. paras. 63 and 70.
75 Id. para. 76.

fully invoke their rights under Article 63 TFEU and Article 17 of the Charter to compel the competent authority to delete the usufruct once again. This is particularly the case if the original registration of the usufruct infringed Hungarian national rules that were in effect at the time.[76]

3.3. The Judgment and its Reasoning

The CJEU issued its judgment on 12 December 2024. It should be recalled that in this case, the CJEU was asked to assess whether EU law, specifically Article 63 TFEU and Article 17 of the Charter, prevented Hungarian national legislation from requiring the reinstatement of a usufruct right in a land register after it had been unlawfully deleted.[77]

As mentioned earlier, the case concerned a plot of agricultural land in Hungary, which had been subject to a usufruct right created by a contract between a foreign national and a Hungarian company. The usufruct was initially registered in the land register in 2002. Still, it was later deleted in 2015 following Hungarian national legislation introduced in 2013 that prohibited non-Hungarian nationals from holding usufruct rights over agricultural land.[78]

The referring court sought guidance from the CJEU on whether the reinstatement of GW's usufruct right, which had been unlawfully deleted, was compatible with EU law. The Hungarian government disputed the admissibility of the question, arguing that the EU law provisions cited by the referring court were unrelated to the facts of the case and that the applicant's conduct was in bad faith.[79] However, the Court found that the question referred was admissible, emphasizing that it was not for the Court to assess the merits of the instant case or the applicant's conduct, but to interpret EU law concerning the substantive issues raised.

The Court first considered whether the national legislation involved a restriction on the *free movement of capital* under Article 63 TFEU. It reaf-

76 Id. paras. 77 and 78.

77 The exact formulation of the question is: "Must Article 63 TFEU and Article 17 of the Charter of Fundamental Rights of the EU be interpreted as meaning that they do not preclude legislation of a Member State that, on reinstatement of a usufruct right, ordered following proceedings for failure to fulfil obligations – subsequent to the deletion of a usufruct right whose registration was unlawful but final –, does not provide for a mandatory examination of whether the usufruct right was registered lawfully?" *See Case C-419/23, Nemzeti Földügyi Központ,* para. 37.

78 Id. paras. 20–22.

79 Id. para. 38.

firmed that transactions involving non-residents investing in real estate, including agricultural land, fall within the scope of Article 63 TFEU. A national provision that imposes limitations on such investments could restrict the free movement of capital if it affects the position of investors from other Member States, particularly if it discourages investment. The Court found that the legislation requiring the reinstatement of the usufruct rights, which was detrimental to the land's value and reduced the owner's ability to enjoy their property, constituted a restriction on the free movement of capital.[80]

However, such a restriction may still be justified under EU law if it is based on overriding reasons of public interest and complies with the principle of proportionality.[81] The Court noted that the Hungarian legislation in question aimed to implement a previous judgment[82] in which Hungary had been found to violate EU law regarding the unlawful deletion of usufruct rights.[83] The Hungarian legislator's objective was to rectify this infringement and ensure that rights previously unlawfully were reinstated in the land register. The Court found that this objective constituted an overriding reason in the public interest.[84]

The Court then examined whether the national legislation complied with the principle of proportionality, which requires that measures do not exceed what is necessary to achieve the legitimate objective. It determined that the Hungarian legislation was proportionate, as it sought to ensure compliance with EU law by reinstating usufruct rights, even if the original registration had been considered unlawful under national law. The Court also noted that Hungary had amended its legislation in 2021 to allow for such reinstatement, reinforcing compliance with EU law. Additionally, the CJEU acknowledged that when reinstatement is impossible due to objective obstacles, compensation could serve as an alternative remedy. However, in this case, reinstatement was deemed feasible and did not disproportionately affect the property rights of the landowner, CN, who had acquired full ownership of the land after the usufruct was canceled. Moreover, the Court found that the technical illegality of the initial usufruct registration, based on an interpre-

80 Id. paras. 54–58.

81 Id. para. 59.

82 *See Case C-235/17, Commission v Hungary.*

83 The case at hand concerns a recent amendment to Hungarian law, which implements the judgment in *Commission v Hungary,* while previous case law focused on the 2013 Act on Transitional Measures.

84 *Case C-419/23, Nemzeti Földügyi Központ,* paras. 59–62.

tation of Hungarian case law, did not constitute an insurmountable obstacle to reinstatement.[85] It emphasized that the principle of legal certainty and the protection of legitimate expectations played a crucial role in the assessment.[86] The usufruct contract had been concluded in compliance with the law just before the 'restrictive' Hungarian legislation took effect. While the registration was technically unlawful, it remained uncontested for over 13 years, further supporting GW's position under the principle of legal certainty. The Court stressed that technical illegality should not result in disproportionate consequences, particularly when the usufruct had been exercised without objection for an extended period.[87]

Regarding the right to property under Article 17 of the Charter, the Court observed that reinstating the usufruct right did not undermine CN's ownership rights.[88] Although the original registration of the usufruct may have been contrary to national law, CN's full ownership of the land could not be considered 'lawfully acquired,' as it resulted from the unlawful cancellation of the usufruct.[89] The Court emphasized that reinstatement merely restored the legal situation that existed before the infringement and did not impose an excessive burden on CN. Therefore, reinstating the usufruct did not infringe upon CN's property rights under Article 17 of the Charter.[90]

In conclusion, the CJEU ruled that EU law does not prevent national legislation requiring the reinstatement of a usufruct right in the land register, even if the original registration was contrary to national law. Such a measure must comply with EU law and the principle of proportionality, aiming to remedy past violations and uphold EU principles.[91] The Court found Hungary's legislation justified,[92] as it sought to restore the legal situation after the unlawful cancellation of the usufruct right. Notably, the judgment emphasized that restitution should take precedence over financial compensation where feasible, reinforcing the obligation of Member States to fully rectify breaches of EU law. Furthermore, the Court acknowledged that longstanding and uncontested usufruct rights, even if technically unlawful under national law, may still be protected under the principles of legal cer-

85 Id. para. 69.
86 Id. para. 68.
87 Id. para. 70.
88 *Cf.* id. para. 35.
89 Id. para. 76.
90 Id. para. 68.
91 Id. para. 78.
92 *See also* paras. 59–77.

tainty and legitimate expectations. In my view, this case underscores the primacy of EU law and the binding nature of CJEU judgments, affirming that national authorities must ensure full and effective compliance. It also sets an important precedent for future cases concerning the enforcement of EU law in the field of property rights.

4. Comments and Proposals

Human rights are inherently linked to land tenure, with property rights being the most relevant. A significant development in this area is the growing influence of the European Union's human rights framework, which now exists alongside the long-established Strasbourg system under the ECHR.[93] This shift is evident in recent rulings by the CJEU, where the Charter of Fundamental Rights has been applied in Hungarian land acquisition cases. This highlights that Member States must also align their land policies with the Charter's requirements beyond the legal frameworks shaped by negative and positive integration. This underscores a key issue concerning the relationship between the EU's human rights framework and the ECHR in matters of land ownership. As the legal landscape evolves, Member States must stay vigilant and monitor these developments closely.[94] Regarding the specific case analyzed in this study, the judgment represents a significant development in the jurisprudence of the CJEU, as it offers an autonomous interpretation of the phrase 'lawfully acquired' within the meaning of Article 17 of the Charter. Notably, this phrase does not appear in the ECHR,[95] which is interpreted and applied by the ECtHR. As such, the CJEU is engaging with a legal concept that lies outside the established case law, thereby contributing to the evolution of European human rights law by clarifying the scope of property protection under EU law independently of the ECHR framework.[96]

Furthermore, the central issue in the present case was whether, from the perspective of the free movement of capital and the right to property, it is

---

93 Szilágyi 2024, p. 71.

94 Id.

95 *Cf.* Article 1 of Protocol 1 to the ECHR.

96 Patrick Leisure & Attila Vincze, 'Undoing undone Injustice: Nemzeti Földügyi Központ and the continuing Saga over Usufruct Rights in Hungary (Case C-419/23)', *EU Law Live,* at https://eulawlive.com/op-ed-undoing-undone-injustice-nemzeti-foldugyi-kozpont-and-the-continuing-saga-over-usufruct-rights-in-hungary-case-c-419-23/.

permissible to consider the unlawful nature of the original registration when deciding on the reinstatement of a usufruct right. The Court answered this question in the negative, which aligns well with the established practice of the CJEU. At the same time, this decision did not resolve the remaining concerns regarding Sections 108/F(6) and (7) of the 2013 Act on Transitional Measures. This is evidenced by the fact that a constitutional complaint procedure is currently pending before the Constitutional Court of Hungary,[97] which – among other things – seeks to establish the unconstitutionality of these provisions.[98]

It is also important to note that Hungarian law lacks provisions on liability for damages caused by legislative actions, raising the question of whether legislators can be held responsible for damages resulting from laws and the implementation of laws.[99] This also invites consideration of whether lawmaking itself can be unlawful.[100] It should be added that legislative actions are protected by state immunity and considered part of the state's legitimate authority. Moreover, no legal framework establishes a private legal relationship between the state and individuals harmed by legislative acts or omissions.[101] Judicial practice[102] has long hesitated to recognize liability for damages caused by legislation. However, two exceptions are widely accepted: when a law is deemed unconstitutional or conflicts with EU law as determined by the CJEU.[103]

Bodzási pointed out that case law recognizes two scenarios in which liability for damages may arise from legislative acts. In a case related to damages caused by Section 108 of the 2013 CCXII Act, which led to the removal of usufruct rights, the Budapest Court of Appeal *(Fővárosi Ítélőtábla)* ruled that the state is not exempt from liability for harm resulting from legislation,

97 No. IV/02518/2024.

98 Károly László Simon, 'A törölt haszonélvezeti jogok nyomában – A visszajegyezhetőség uniós jogi és alapjogi összefüggései az Európai Unió Bírósága Nemzeti Földügyi Központ ítélete (C-419/23) nyomán', *EU jog,* No. 1, 2025.

99 Balázs Bodzási 'Az Európai Bíróság a korábban törölt haszonélvezeti jogok ingatlan-nyilvántartásba történő visszajegyzéséhez kapcsolódó kérdéseket vizsgálta', *Magyar Jogász Egylet,* at https://jogaszegylet.hu/jogelet/az-europai-birosag-a-korabban-torolt-haszonelvezeti-jogok-ingatlan-nyilvantartasba-torteno-visszajegyzesehez-kapcsolodo-kerdeseket-vizsgalta/#_ftn6.

100 Ádám Fuglinszky, *Kártérítési jog,* HVG ORAC, Budapest, 2015, p. 579.

101 Attila Menyhárd, 'Az állam kártérítési felelőssége és állami immunitás', *in* Tibor Nochta *et al.* (eds.), *Ünnepi tanulmányok Kecskés László professzor 60. születésnapja tiszteletére,* Pécsi Tudományegyetem Állam- és Jogtudományi Kar, Pécs, pp. 400–401.

102 Particularly that of the Supreme Court *(Legfelsőbb Bíróság).*

103 Fuglinszky 2015, p. 582.

as no legal provision grants such immunity. However, additional factors, such as a ruling from the Constitutional Court of Hungary or the CJEU declaring the law unconstitutional or in breach of EU law, are required for the legislation to be deemed unlawful. Bodzási also highlights that even if the Constitutional Court does not annul a law but finds it unconstitutional due to omissions, this deficiency can still render the legislation unlawful. In this instance, the state failed to correct the identified shortcoming retroactively. While the Constitutional Court and CJEU decisions confirmed the unlawfulness of Section 108, the necessary conditions for establishing liability for damages were not entirely fulfilled.[104]

Moreover, Bodzási also pointed out that on the occasion of the reform of the Civil Code the proposal put forward by the Civil Code Committee aimed to establish rules on liability for damages caused by legislative acts. Under this proposal, the legislator would have been held responsible if the Constitutional Court of Hungary annulled an unconstitutional law *ex tunc.* If the annulment took effect later, liability would have applied only to damages occurring after that point. Furthermore, the proposal stipulated liability for damages arising from unconstitutional legislative inaction, precisely when the legislator failed to meet a deadline set by the Constitutional Court of Hungary. However, these provisions were ultimately not included in the Civil Code.[105]

Under EU law, compensation may be sought from a Member State if a directive is incorrectly transposed, leading to damages.[106] The ECtHR has also found Hungary liable in cases involving deficiencies in its legislative framework. Based on this, experts believe compensation for damages caused by legislation is possible, with Section 6:519 of the Civil Code as a potential basis.[107] However, applying this provision is challenging, as the *Kúria's* (the Hungarian Supreme Court) decision shows.[108] In this case, although the violation and breach of EU law were established, state liability for damages was not established. The court had to verify the causal connection between the unlawful conduct and the damage, which could not be established, leading to the rejection of the claim.[109]

---

104 Bodzási 2025. *See also* Court of Appeal No. 5.Pf.20.405/2019/8/II.

105 Bodzási 2025.

106 *See* the CJEU judgments of 5 March 1996 in *Joined Cases C-46/93 and C-48/93, Brasserie du Pécheur and Factortame,* ECLI:EU:C:1996:79.

107 Bodzási 2025.

108 *See* Case no. Pfv.VI.20.837/2022/9.

109 Fuglinszky 2015, p. 585.

Bodzási noted that Menyhárd proposes an objective liability framework, rather than a fault-based one, to solve damages caused by legislation. This framework should be outlined in a separate legal provision.[110]

In practice, the legislator has taken steps toward objective liability, notably by introducing provisions to compensate beneficiaries of cancelled usufruct rights.[111] As a general rule, the provision states that compensation is based on the annual value of the cancelled usufruct right. This annual value is defined as one-twentieth of the market value of the property encumbered by the usufruct right at the time of its deletion from the land registry. Importantly, in connection with this compensation, additional elements typically required under the Civil Code do not have to be evidenced – such as actual damage or a causal link between the legislative act and the harm suffered.[112]

5. Conclusions

Hungary's land law regulation has undergone significant reforms, particularly following its accession to the EU. These reforms included the revision of Act LV of 1994 on Arable Land, land restitution to address historical ownership issues, and the adoption of the 2013 Land Transfer Act to harmonize national law with EU regulations while protecting agricultural land as a national resource. As part of its accession negotiations, Hungary secured a transitional period during which it could uphold restrictions on the acquisition of agricultural and forestry land.

Following the expiration of this period, the European Commission launched infringement proceedings against several new Member States, including Hungary, for violating EU principles such as the free movement of capital. In parallel, preliminary ruling procedures were initiated to assess the compatibility of relevant national legislation with EU law.

This study set out to examine the evolution of Hungary's land law in light of EU legal requirements, focusing particularly on the challenges surrounding usufruct rights. Central to this analysis was the most recent case, *Nemzeti Földügyi Központ,* which builds upon earlier CJEU decisions such as *SEGRO* and *Horváth, Commission v Hungary* and *Grossmania.* These cases established that Hungary's termination of usufruct rights – particu-

110 Bodzási 2025.

111 *See* Section 108/K(1) of the 2013 Act on Transitional Measures.

112 Bodzási 2025.

larly those held by non-Hungarian nationals – constituted unjustified restrictions on fundamental freedoms, including property rights and the free movement of capital.

In its 2024 judgment, the CJEU ruled on the reinstatement of a previously cancelled usufruct right over agricultural land in Hungary. Hungary's 2013 law, which extinguished the usufruct rights of non-family members, was found to violate EU law. Hungary later enacted provisions to restore such rights. The CJEU confirmed that EU law allows for reinstating these rights, even if the original registration was unlawful, as the national law aimed to comply with an EU ruling. The Court emphasized that the reinstatement didn't limit the landowner's property rights, as the usufruct was registered before their ownership. It also introduced an autonomous interpretation of the term 'lawfully acquired' under Article 17 of the Charter of Fundamental Rights – offering a distinct EU perspective not found in the ECHR.

This study also highlights the unresolved issue of state liability in Hungary. While Hungarian law currently lacks a comprehensive regime for compensating damages caused by legislation, emerging proposals – particularly those advocating for objective liability – reflect a growing recognition of the need to modernize national law and align it with broader EU principles. Initiatives such as the 2013 Act on Transitional Measures offer partial remedies in this regard and suggest a direction for future legal development.

Protection of Journalists' Sources in the Recent Case Law of the ECtHR

Analysis of the ECtHR's Judgment in Csikós v Hungary

*Sándor Szemesi**

Abstract

Protecting journalists' sources is important in its own right as part of the institutional guarantee of press freedom. In order for the press to fulfil its public watchdog function, it is crucial that its staff can access information from a wide range of sources. This paper examines the extent to which this protection is upheld in Hungarian law, both generally and in the specific context of the Csikós v Hungary case, which was decided by the ECtHR in 2024.

Keywords: Csikós, ECtHR, freedom of expression, journalists' sources, Hungary

1. Introduction

The protection of journalists' sources is important in its own right as part of the institutional guarantee of press freedom. For the press to fulfil its *public watchdog* function, it is essential that its staff can obtain information from the widest possible range of sources. Particular attention should be given to information that is not (yet) available to the public. Conversely, for sources to provide journalists with credible information, it is also essential that they must be confident that their names will not be published or brought to the attention of the authorities against their will. Without this institutional trust, it would be difficult to expect whistleblowers to regularly provide substantive information to assist the press in performing their duties. However, source protection is not absolute. For exceptional reasons relating to *e.g.* national security, public order, criminal law considerations, or secrecy reasons, authorities may access journalists' sources, but only through a procedure secured by several safeguards.

* Sándor Szemesi: chief counselor, Constitutional Court of Hungary, szemesi@mkab.hu.

2. The Regulation of Protection of Journalists' Sources in Hungary – An Overview

In Hungary, source protection is regulated by Article 6 of Act CIV of 2010 on freedom of the press and fundamental rules on media content. At the time of its adoption in 2010, the wording of this Act obliged press staff (journalists) to protect sources of information, with the exception that "the right to confidentiality does not extend to the protection of the source of information which has disclosed classified information without authorization" and that "a court or authority may, in exceptional and justified cases, in order to protect national security and public order or to detect or prevent the commission of criminal offences, order the media or its staff to disclose the source of information".[1]

In practice, the provision was applied first (and perhaps only) time to Tamás Bodoky, editor-in-chief of the *Átlátszó* online journal. He was questioned by the police as a witness and ordered to reveal the source of information for a newspaper article. This case, known as the *Brokernet case* (which became famous because of this very procedure), in which unknown perpetrators approached Brokernet Zrt. to access its computer databases and obtained the details of several individuals connected to the company. An article about the crime was published by *Átlátszó*,[2] which also showed some of the files obtained. Following the publication of the article, Mr Bodoky was summoned as a witness by the police and ordered to reveal the source of the information. Bodoky refused and submitted a complaint, which was dismissed by the prosecution on the grounds that there was no public interest in the present case that could justify the protection of the journalist's source.[3] Moreover, according to the prosecutor's standpoint, there is no legal basis in the Hungarian legal system for refusing to testify in the specific case.[4] Bodoky lodged a constitutional complaint against the de-

1 Act CIV of 2010 on the freedom of the press and the fundamental rules of media content, Section 6(3) (no longer in force).

2 'Magyarleaks: meghackelték a brokernetet', *Átlátszó*, 6 July 2011, at https://atlatszo.hu/kozpenz/2011/07/06/magyarleaks-meghackeltek-a-brokernetet/.

3 The prosecutor justified their position by stating that the information in question constituted a trade secret of the company. *Átlátszó*, however, considered it to be in the public interest for the company's customers to be aware that their data could have been obtained by unauthorized persons.

4 *See* (in Hungarian) at https://atlatszo.hu/wp-content/uploads/2011/11/ugyesz1111071.pdf.

cision of the prosecutor's office,[5] which was examined by the Constitutional Court (together with other motions) in *Decision No. 165/2011 (XII. 20.) AB*.

In its decision, the Constitutional Court referred to *Goodwin*,[6] the leading case of the ECtHR. According to the ECtHR,

> "Protection of journalistic sources is one of the basic conditions for press freedom [...] Without such protection, sources may be deterred from assisting the press in informing the public on matters of public interest. As a result the vital public-watchdog role of the press may be undermined and the ability of the press to provide accurate and reliable information may be adversely affected. Having regard to the importance of the protection of journalistic sources for press freedom in a democratic society and the potentially chilling effect an order of source disclosure has on the exercise of that freedom, such a measure cannot be compatible with Article 10 (art. 10) of the Convention unless it is justified by an overriding requirement in the public interest."[7]

The Constitutional Court concluded that legislation which generally prioritizes the protection of classified documents over the disclosure of potentially related offences (*e.g.*, corruption) is a disproportionate restriction on freedom of expression. It is also a disproportionate restriction on freedom of expression if the burden is on the press to prove the public interest invoked to deny disclosure of the source rather than on the authority (or prosecutor) to prove the need to know the journalist's source. This is of particular concern where the reason for investigating a crime may itself justify an authority's access to the journalist's sources, as implied by Section 6(3) of the Act.[8] The Constitutional Court found that there had been a legislative omission, since, in its view,

> "the institution of source protection becomes a genuine defence when a journalist may refuse to make a statement or provide information, at least with a view to protecting his sources, in proceedings conducted by the investigating authority or by any other authority, and the procedural laws

5 *See* (in Hungarian) at https://atlatszo.hu/wp-content/uploads/2011/12/11–12-alapjogipanasz1.pdf.

6 *Goodwin v the United Kingdom (GC)*, No. 17888/90, 27 March 1996.

7 Id. para. 39.

8 Decision No. 165/2011. (XII. 20.) AB, ABH 2011, 478.

clearly regulate the exceptional cases in which they are nevertheless obliged to cooperate with the authorities, subject to judicial review."[9]

Following the decision, the Parliament has revised the Hungarian rules on the protection of journalists' sources. According to Act XC of 2017 on criminal procedure, in force at the time of writing this paper, a journalist may refuse to testify if it would reveal the identity of the source to whom (*i.e.*, to reveal the source) can only be ordered by a court if *(i)* the information is essential for the investigation of a sufficiently serious intentional crime, *(ii)* no other evidence can replace it, and *(iii)* the public interest in the investigation of the crime (in particular with regard to its gravity) is so overriding that it clearly outweighs the interest in keeping the source of the information confidential.[10]

3. The Factual Background of Csikós v Hungary

In November 2015, *Blikk*, one of Hungary's leading tabloid newspapers, reported the murder of an elderly couple in their home in Érd, a municipality in Hungary. The police only issued a press release about the crime after *Blikk* had reported it.[11] The *Blikk* article did not contain any further information other than the fact that a serious crime had occurred. Later, the National Defence Service *(Nemzeti Védelmi Szolgálat)* suspected a police officer of having informed the *Blikk* journalist Klaudia Csikós about the crime.[12] Documents from the criminal proceedings against the policeman revealed that, before the *Budai Központi Kerületi Bíróság* (Central District Court of Buda) authorized secret surveillance (wiretapping) of the policeman, the journalist, Klaudia Csikós, had also been wiretapped to identify the source of the information (*i.e.*, the policeman's name). This could be inferred from the fact that the interception documents included a note that the conversation

9 Id. 521, 527. For more on the decision of the Constitutional Court, *see* András Koltay & Gábor Polyák, 'Az Alkotmánybíróság határozata a médiaszabályozás egyes kérdéseiről', *Jogesetek Magyarázata,* Vol. 3, Issue 1, 2012, pp. 38 and 41–42.

10 Regarding the practical application of this rule, *see* Tamás Matusik & Kristóf Csépány, 'Az újságírói forrásvédelem határa a büntetőeljárásban – jogalkalmazói szempontok az európai alapjogi elvárások tükrében', *Eljárásjogi Szemle,* 2017/1, pp. 19–23.

11 *See* (in Hungarian) at https://www.blikk.hu/aktualis/tragedia-agyonvertek-az-idos-erdi-hazaspart-kutyajukkal-egyutt/tzjf3ht.

12 Criminal proceedings were ultimately initiated against the police officer (the source of the journalist) on suspicion of abuse of office and bribery, but he was eventually acquitted.

with Csikós was "identified by voice",[13] which would only have been possible if the interceptors had already been familiar with Csikós' voice (especially since the phone was not registered in her name). Under the relevant Hungarian law[14] the secret surveillance (wiretapping) of Csikós was not subsequently approved by a judge. The journalist was not questioned either as a suspect or as a witness. The alleged wiretapping was carried out by the National Security Service *(Nemzetbiztonsági Szakszolgálat)* on the instructions of the National Defence Service. In light of the circumstances of the case, the authorities were likely to have considered that the journalist could only have obtained information about the crime from a police officer. They also believed that the officer's identity could only be revealed through the journalist, which is why Csikós was subjected to preliminary wiretapping.

Csikós lodged a complaint against the interception under the Police Act,[15] which was rejected by the National Defence Service on the grounds that there was no room for a complaint against the use of the wiretapping. However, the National Defence Service also noted that the use of the special tool had otherwise been carried out in accordance with the law, but that no further information had been given to Csikós in view of the ongoing criminal proceedings.[16] Csikós also lodged a complaint with the Minister of Interior under the National Security Act,[17] but the Minister of Interior in his reply only made a general statement on the legality of the operation of the national security services and stated that the actions of the National Defence Service could not be challenged under the National Security Act.[18] Csikós also submitted a petition to the National Security Committee of the Parliament, which concluded that no violation had occurred in the specific case.[19] Csikós also brought an action against the National Defence Service under the law on the protection of classified information, but the court came to the

13 *See* (in Hungarian) at https://www.blikk.hu/aktualis/krimi/titkosszolgalati-modszerrel-figyeltek-meg-kollegankat/nf1cze8.

14 Act XXXIV of 1994 on the police, Section 72(1) as in force in 2015. The head of the investigating authority could order the use of a special instrument (in this case, wiretapping) for up to 72 hours in order to ensure the effectiveness of the investigation. According to the case file, the secret surveillance presumably took place between 3 and 6 November 2015.

15 Id. Section 92(1).

16 The National Defence Service thus *de facto* confirmed the fact of the wiretapping.

17 Act CXXV of 1995 on national security services, Section 11(5).

18 *Csikós v Hungary*, No. 31091/16, 28 November 2024, para. 15.

19 Id. para. 16.

final conclusion that Csikós was not entitled to know the identity of the person on whom the secret information was ordered to be collected, and that, failing this, he could not rely on the protection of privacy or the protection of journalistic sources.[20]

4. Procedural Considerations

Even in the context of well-developed case law, cases involving secret services present many procedural difficulties, since proving *victim* status is difficult. In the case of a properly conducted secret service operation, it is almost impossible for the victim to prove that they were involved (because of the absence of credible information). In the present case, however, the circumstances (in particular the criminal proceedings initiated and the available documents) enabled Csikós to prove that his phone had indeed been tapped.[21] In accordance with the ECtHR's established case law, the *'reasonable probability'* test is satisfied in similar cases.[22]

Another interesting question for the assessment of victim status is who qualifies as a 'victim' in the case of a secret service action: the person against whom the action is ordered or potentially everyone affected by the action. The question is relevant to the right to privacy and family life, and in particular to telephone interceptions, since each telephone conversation necessarily requires the simultaneous presence of at least two people (the caller and the recipient of the call). In the present case, this was not relevant because, on the basis of the case file, Csikós was able to establish that the investigative authority had specifically authorized the interception of her telephone for 72 hours. Generally, however, a regular telephone interception is likely to satisfy the requirements of necessity and proportionality from the point of view of those around the person concerned. From the point of view of ECtHR case law, those around the person intercepted are also unlikely to have suffered serious harm (disadvantage),[23] which is one of the conditions for complaints to be admissible.

In the present case, the question arose as to whether Csikós should have resorted to other forums in addition to the remedies mentioned above, such

---

20 Id. para. 18.

21 Id. para. 31.

22 *See* in detail *Practical guide on admissibility criteria,* Council of Europe, Strasbourg, 2025, para. 48 and the case law cited therein.

23 Article 35(3)(b) ECHR.

as initiating a damages action or proceedings with the National Authority for Data Protection and Freedom of Information (hereinafter: NAIH). Regarding the NAIH's procedure, the ECtHR has previously ruled in *Hüttl v Hungary* that NAIH's procedure is necessarily limited in similar cases as it can only access certain information through the Minister.[24] This calls into question whether the procedure is "sufficiently precise, effective and comprehensive as to the ordering, executing and potential redressing of surveillance measures."[25] As for the other (damages action) procedures raised by the Government in the present case, the ECtHR has stressed that the Government has not in any way suggested that these forums would constitute an effective remedy, *i.e.,* that Csikós would have had a realistic chance of winning the case on the basis of the relevant legislative context and case law.[26] This is all the more true because, if we accept that the 72-hour wiretap order against Csikós was lawful (as established by all authorities in Hungary), one of the fundamental legal grounds for awarding damages, namely the unlawfulness of the conduct, is clearly absent.

It is interesting to note that there is no indication in the case file that Csikós initiated proceedings before the Constitutional Court. According to the ECtHR's well-established case law, however, constitutional complaint procedure constitutes an effective remedy that must be exhausted before an application can be submitted to the ECtHR.[27] This is true even though the ECtHR only ruled it only in 2019, in *Szalontai,*[28] that the Constitutional Court's procedure (constitutional complaints) can be considered an effective remedy, and exhausting this remedy is a prerequisite for the ECtHR to proceed. Although Csikós submitted her application on 17 May 2016 (years before the *Szalontai* decision), the ECtHR has applied this requirement retroactively to complaints lodged prior the *Szalontai* decision.[29] Therefore, it

24 This is the so-called *'Section 23 exemption',* which refers to Section 23 of the Act CXI of 2011 on the commissioner for fundamental rights. The application of this act is provided for by Act CXII of 2011 on the right of informational self-determination and on freedom of information.

25 *Hüttl v Hungary,* 58032/16, 29 September 2022, para. 18; *Szabó and Vissy v Hungary,* 37138/14, 12 January 2016, para. 89. *Csikós v Hungary,* para. 35.

26 Id. para. 36.

27 Péter Paczolay, 'The ECtHR on constitutional complaint as effective remedy in the Hungarian legal order', *Hungarian Yearbook of International Law and European Law,* Vol. 8, Issue 1, 2020, pp. 157–168.

28 *Szalontai v Hungary (dec),* 71327/12, 12 March 2019.

29 *See e.g. Kiss v Hungary (dec),* 39448/14, 4 June 2019. In that case, the application was lodged on 20 May 2014 (almost five years before the *Szalontai* case was decided) and the case was declared inadmissible solely because the constitutional complaint was an effec-

is reasonable to question why the ECtHR failed to consider that Csikós did not initiate proceedings before the Constitutional Court. While there may have been procedural circumstances in this specific case that would have rendered proceedings before the Constitutional Court ineffective (similar to the excessive length of national proceedings cases), the ECtHR should still have explained its legal standpoint.

5. *Merits of the Case*

In its judgment, the ECtHR ruled that the wiretapping of journalists in relation to their work, including access to their sources by the authorities, falls within the scope of both Article 8 (right to private and family life) and Article 10 (freedom of expression).[30] *(i)* From the perspective of privacy and family life, wiretapping may be considered lawful if accompanied by a rigorous system of procedural safeguards, including regulations on the grounds and procedures for authorization, the duration of interception, and the handling of data obtained.[31] *(ii)* Given that Article 10 (freedom of expression, in this case the protection of journalists' sources) is involved, an even stricter system of guarantees is required:

> "the protection of journalistic sources is one of the cornerstones of freedom of the press. Without such protection, sources may be deterred from assisting the press in informing the public about matters of public interest. As a result, the vital public-watchdog role of the press may be undermined, and the ability of the press to provide accurate and reliable information may be adversely effected."[32]

In this case, the ECtHR could not establish that Csikós had indeed been wiretapped. One reason for this was that Hungarian law does not stipulate that the person intercepted must be informed afterwards.[33] Without such notification, however, the legal remedies available to the wiretapped person are necessarily limited. This is because the applicant (the person who was

tive remedy under the *Szalontai* case which the applicant should have exhausted. *See* paras. 11–12.

30 *Csikós v Hungary,* paras. 49 and 52.

31 *Roman Zakharov v Russia (GC),* 47143/06, 4 December 2015, para. 231.

32 *Csikós v Hungary,* para. 52; *Goodwin v the United Kingdom,* para. 39; *Sanoma Uitgevers B.V. v the Netherlands (GC),* No. 38224/03, 14 September 2010, para. 50.

33 *Csikós v Hungary,* para. 60. *See also Szabó and Vissy v Hungary,* paras. 83, 86, and 88.

allegedly wiretapped) must prove before the court that they were wiretapped. However, the essence of a properly conducted interception is that the person being intercepted is unaware of the proceedings against them.

While it is understandable that a third party should not be able to inspect the records of criminal proceedings against another person (even if their telephone was intercepted during those proceedings), it is hardly acceptable for a person to have no legal remedy against a wiretap specifically targeting them. In the present case, it is probable that the head of the investigating authority ordered a 72-hour wiretap between 3 and 6 November 2015 specifically to obtain Csikós' sources. This procedure did not provide any guarantees to protect the journalist's sources, such as judicial control, balancing of interests or an obligation to state reasons.[34] The ECtHR therefore found a violation of both Articles 8 and 10, ordering Hungary to pay compensation.

6. *Epilogue*

The case of *Csikós v Hungary* is especially interesting from the point of view of protecting journalists' sources. *(i)* On the one hand, the Constitutional Court clearly stated the constitutional importance of protecting journalists' sources in *Decision No. 165/2011. (XII. 20.) AB*. However, in this case, the authorities tapped Csikós' phone to obtain journalists' sources, clearly circumventing the spirit of the Constitutional Court's decision. In light of the Constitutional Court's findings, this procedure could not be justified as constitutional under Hungarian law, even though the interception formally complied with the relevant legislation. *(ii)* Conversely, under the current Police Act rules, similar interceptions may only be carried out with judicial authorization.[35] In other words, Hungarian law now provides procedural guarantees that allow for the reconciliation of journalistic source protection and the public interest of law enforcement. However, the legislator still does not provide for the person subject to secret information gathering to be informed of the surveillance afterwards, which is an obvious prerequisite for the exercise of truly effective legal remedies.

Finally, the case's specific procedural details cannot be ignored, namely the fact that Csikós did not initiate proceedings before the Constitutional

34 *Csikós v Hungary*, para. 70.
35 Act XXXIV of 1994 on the police, currently in force, Section 72(1).

Court. This was undoubtedly a precondition for initiating proceedings before the ECtHR at the time the application was examined by the ECtHR, as it follows from *Szalontai.* Csikós brought legal proceedings in Hungary, in which she was the plaintiff. She could have claimed before the Constitutional Court that the judgment and legislation applied in the case (Section 72 of the Police Act in force at the time) were contrary to the Fundamental Law. Therefore, it may be assumed that the Hungarian Constitutional Court, rather than the ECtHR, should have ruled on the case. While, from a journalistic perspective, it is commendable that the ECtHR found a violation of the ECHR,[36] it is nevertheless legitimate to question whether, in this case, the ECtHR,[37] which is usually so strict in enforcing procedural aspects, turned a blind eye.

36 This is confirmed by the commentary in the case. *Csikós v Hungary (case analysis),* Global Freedom of Expression, Columbia University, at https://globalfreedomofexpression.columbia.edu/cases/csikos-v-hungary/.

37 The ECtHR has recently ruled on several cases of exceptional importance. Notably, the KlimaSeniorinnen case and Ukraine and the Netherlands v. Russia stand out as being of outstanding historical significance. For more on this case, see Marcel Szabó: *The War Between Ukraine and Russia: From the Perspective of the ECtHR* (forthcoming, 2025).

Part V
– Hungarian state practice

The Solidarity Contribution in the Light of Municipal Autonomy in the Jurisprudence of the Hungarian Constitutional Court

*Olivér Ráth – Ádám Varga**

Abstract

In Hungary, the so-called solidarity contribution has been part of the annual central budget act since 2017, representing a payment obligation for local self-governments to the central state budget. Some argue that the solidarity contribution, which is based on local business tax capacity per inhabitant, is nothing more than a central tax on municipalities with high tax capacity. In its original form, the solidarity contribution affected only a small percentage of municipalities in 2017. However, as a result of annual changes to the rules, the number of municipalities paying solidarity contributions has increased almost fivefold (from 166 in 2017 to 855 in 2025), meaning that approximately one in four municipalities will pay solidarity contributions in 2025. Similarly, over the past nine years, the planned revenue from the solidarity contribution has increased almost eighteenfold (from 21 billion HUF to 360 billion HUF). This study examines the evolution of the solidarity contribution in relation to the financial autonomy of local self-governments, considering the decisions of the Constitutional Court regarding infringements of the European Charter of Local Self-Government.

Keywords: solidarity contribution, economic and financial autonomy, local self-government, financial distribution mechanism, Constitutional Court of Hungary

1. Introduction

According to the European Charter of Local Self-Government (hereinafter: Charter) "Local self-government denotes the right and the ability of local

* Olivér Ráth: visiting lecturer, Pázmány Péter Catholic University, Budapest, rath.oliver@jak.ppke.hu.
Ádám Varga: associate professor of law, Pázmány Péter Catholic University, Budapest, varga.adam@jak.ppke.hu.

authorities, within the limits of the law, to regulate and manage a substantial share of public affairs under their own responsibility and in the interests of the local population."[1] This is a powerful statement, but it also poses a serious challenge to local self-governments. It is also challenging for the state because transferring this competence is difficult. In other words, it is easier to declare that they have the 'right and ability' than to implement it. On the one hand, it requires a certain restraint on the part of the central government (*i.e.*, not to dominate local politics), and on the other hand, it is not easy to make a body capable of implementing autonomy. It requires not only knowledge and will, but also the provision of economic and financial resources. This is perhaps even more difficult to guarantee than political will, since resources are finite everywhere. For this reason, it is essential to guarantee financial and economic autonomy, otherwise self-government is only an illusion.

This is no different in Hungary, where the local self-government system has faced many challenges over the last three decades, many of these specifically related to economic and financial autonomy. The present paper does not discuss these impacts in general terms, but after exploring the general framework, focuses on one issue in particular, namely the so-called solidarity contribution.

The solidarity contribution was introduced in Hungarian public law in 2017. In our study, we follow the evolution of the solidarity contribution rule from year to year. Since its introduction it is essentially a payment obligation to the central state budget, primarily through the vehicle of withholding central grants. It is a unique feature and has not been properly evaluated in the past decade, that in some cases the deducted grants do not cover the required solidarity contribution and the municipality has to pay the difference to the central subsystem from its own funds.

In our study, focusing on the importance of economic and financial autonomy, and at the same time exploring the Charter's regulations (which serve as the framework for the analysis), we will examine the regulation of the subject and the interpretation given by the Constitutional Court. On this basis, an attempt will be made to gain a deeper understanding of the legislation and to formulate critical comments.

---

1 Article 3(1) of the Charter.

2. The Legal Context of the Solidarity Contribution

2.1. Autonomy in General

Without autonomy there is no self-government. While this principle is essential for self-government, it is not only linked to local self-governments. Freedom within the state, within certain limits, is made up of many components. In a narrow sense, autonomy is the right of a community within the state to create law for itself.[2] In a broader sense, it covers different aspects of independence, the right to decide on its own affairs and to implement decisions independently. This requires having competencies through which such autonomy can be exercised. It must also be stressed that autonomy never implies sovereign power, it must respect the limits set by the sovereign, it must not conflict with the acts enacted by the sovereign.[3] It can be created only because it is guaranteed by national or regional legislation. It is therefore necessarily limited: autonomy does not protect action that does not comply with the legal framework.[4]

Although the Hungarian Fundamental Law sets out just a list of groups of competences, in a practical sense these are the most important components of autonomy, ranging from regulatory autonomy to organizational and administrative freedom and economic-financial autonomy.[5]

2.2. Dilemmas Relating to Economic and Financial Autonomy

Following the change of political regime, in the local self-government-related cases examined by the Hungarian Constitutional Court the key concept was undoubtedly the principle of autonomy.[6] From among its components, financial autonomy is particularly important, since without this, the autonomy of local self-government is illusory.[7] Territorial self-government

2 Hans Peters, *Grenzen der kommunalen Selbstverwaltung in Preussen,* Springer, Berlin, 1926, pp. 37–38.

3 Paul Laband, *Das Staatsrecht des Deutschen Reiches,* Laupp, Tübingen, 1876, pp. 107–108.

4 Andreas Ladner *et al., Patterns of Local Autonomy in Europe,* Palgrave Macmillan, 2019, pp. 175–176.

5 Article 32(1) of the Fundamental Law.

6 László Sólyom, *Az alkotmánybíráskodás kezdetei Magyarországon,* Osiris, Budapest, 2001, p. 774.

7 Gábor Kecső, A helyi önkormányzatok pénzügyi jogi jogállása – A jogállást meghatározó jogintézmények modelljei a bevételi oldalon. Anglia – USA – Magyarország, ELTE Eötvös, Budapest, 2016, p. 97.

means more than just the decentralization of public administration, precisely because it has, among other things, ownership and financial autonomy.[8] In an ideal situation, the decentralization of public functions must necessarily go hand in hand with the transfer of the financial resources needed to carry out these functions.[9]

Regarding the economic basis for the functioning of local self-governments, it should be noted that Act CLXXXIX of 2011 on Local Governments in Hungary (hereinafter: LG Act) introduced a new system of task-based financing replacing normative financing, which brought about a new era in the local self-government sector.[10] In the early 2010s, the state took over municipal debts, but in return it introduced a centralized, task-based financing of public funds, opening the way for earmarked funds, the spending of which is subject to strict rules.[11] With the introduction of task-based financing and the centralization of some municipal functions (*e.g.*, education), a new basis for fiscal management was created for local self-governments. The decrease in local financial autonomy increased the significance of own revenue sources, in particular local taxes.[12]

The issue of financial autonomy is constantly on the agenda, as it is in constant flux in the context of changing economic influences. Following the 2008 economic crisis, a decrease in financial autonomy could be observed.[13]

The solidarity contribution is not the only interference in financial and economic autonomy that has affected municipalities in recent years. The restructuring of the education and health systems, the creation of special economic zones (whereby property was removed from settlements and transferred to the county self-governments) and the fact that borrowing is subject to government approval under certain conditions have also raised serious questions.[14] From a municipal point of view, the fundamental problem of

8 József Berényi, *Az európai közigazgatási rendszerek intézményei,* Rejtjel, Budapest, 2003, p. 308.

9 András Bencsik & Zsombor Ercsey, 'A helyi önkormányzatok pénzügyi autonómiájának átalakulása', *Glossa Iuridica,* Vol. 7, Issue 1–2, 2020, p. 226.

10 Id. p. 231.

11 Sándor Nagy, 'Hová lettél, hová levél, gazdálkodási autonómia?', *Új Magyar Közigazgatás,* Vol. 16, Issue 1, 2023, p. 12.

12 Péter Bordás, 'Kincs, ami nincs?', *Jogtudományi Közlöny,* Vol. 76, Issue 10, 2021, p. 471.

13 István Hoffman, Gondolatok a 21. századi önkormányzati jog fontosabb intézményeiről és modelljeiről – A nyugati demokráciák és Magyarország szabályozásainak, valamint azok változásainak tükrében, ELTE Eötvös, Budapest, 2015, pp. 25–26.

14 Sándor Nagy, 'Önkormányzati autonómia – Alkotmányos alapjog vagy személyiségi jog?', *Közigazgatástudomány,* Vol. 3, Issue 1, 2023, pp. 166–167; Katalin Adél Rámhápné

financial autonomy is therefore not caused by the contribution under examination in this study, but by the fact that municipalities are lacking financial resources. One reason for this is that the burden of financing mandatory functions (some of which are central administrative functions) reduces the scope for taking up voluntary functions.[15] Another cause of indebtedness is institutionalized 'collective irresponsibility'. Following the change of political regime the Hungarian State created acts for municipalities which it either did not take seriously (*e.g.*, requiring a quantity and quality of services that was far removed from the realities of the country) or did not create the conditions for their enforcement (*e.g.*, there was a municipal bankruptcy Act, but the institutional conditions for its application was lacking).[16]

To achieve economic and financial autonomy, it is important that the local self-governments have autonomous disposal over their property and the financial resources.[17] Autonomous management is guaranteed by the Fundamental Law, which states, among other things, that local self-governments exercise the rights of the owner over municipal property. In other words, although this property is part of the public property, the exercise of ownership rights is not dependent on any other body (not the government or its agency) but is decided by the elected local representative body.[18]

From the point of view of the central state power, the preservation of a balanced budget is also a significant task, and it is also obvious that the Fundamental Law places this above legal aspects[19] (*e.g.*, limiting the powers of the Constitutional Court; prior consent of the Fiscal Council for the adoption of the Act on the central budget). There is no doubt that an economic

Radics, 'Helyi önkormányzati autonómia: Mi változik, mi marad?', *Közigazgatástudomány*, Vol. 3, Issue 1, 2023, pp. 85–98.

15 Thomas Mann, 'Kommunale Selbstverwaltung durch wirtschaftliche Betätigung? Möglichkeiten und Grenzen in Ungarn und Deutschland', *Annales Universitatis Scientiarum Budapestinensis de Rolando Eotvos Nominatae: Sectio Iuridica*, Vol. 52, 2011, p. 47.

16 András Vigvári, 'A magyar önkormányzati rendszer (adósság)csapdában', *Fundamentum*, Vol. 16, Issue 2, 2012, p. 21.

17 In our view, the protection of property is more important in the context that autonomy is only illusory in the absence of ownership or by the partial deprivation of property. The management of property is therefore the other pillar of the system: property and its objects are just the basic conditions of management, (*i.e.* the static conditions), whereas management is the dynamic condition. András Patyi, 'Gondolatok a magyar helyi önkormányzati rendszer általános szabályairól', *in* Katalin Szoboszlai-Kiss & Gergely Deli (eds.), *Tanulmányok a 70 éves Bihari Mihály tiszteletére*, Universitas-Győr, Győr, 2013. p. 390.

18 Id. p. 390.

19 Article N(3) of Fundamental Law regarding local self-governments.

and a legal approach to the same issue can lead to different results, and it is also difficult to resolve the contradiction that, although local self-governments are autonomous, their debt (since they are part of the state) is also a debt of the state. And national assets must be managed in a way that is transparent to the whole nation.[20] Although national assets are far from being the same as assets under the control of the Government, the responsibility for the management of the State is undoubtedly primarily that of the Government.

2.3. The Importance of the European Charter of Local Self-Government

With the exception of the United Kingdom, Ireland, Norway and Latvia, all European countries have constitutional provisions that define the status of local self-government.[21]The Charter established within the Council of Europe, set out to define common minimum standards that all Member States would consider applicable to themselves. Hungary accepted the Charter, promulgated its entire text and considers itself bound by all paragraphs of Part I of the Charter.[22]

Any attempt to develop such a basic set of rules would have to face the challenge of the diversity and remoteness of the institutional systems already in place in Europe.[23] It is no coincidence that the Charter is more of a guideline, a summary of standards for local self-government, but in principle not directly enforceable.[24] Therefore, it did not attempt to standardize the legal framework for local self-government (which would have been impossible), but sought to establish a minimum set of criteria to be accepted by as many states as possible, despite the different state-specific factors.[25] This is also illustrated by the fact that the contracting states must undertake to recognize

---

20 János Zlinszky, *Az Alkotmány értéktartalma és a mai politika,* Szent István Társulat, Budapest, 2005, p. 36.

21 José Martínez Soria, 'Kommunale Selbstverwaltung im europäischen Vergleich', in Thomas Mann & Günter Püttner (eds.), Handbuch der kommunalen Wissenschaft und Praxis. Band 1 Grundlagen und Kommunalverfassung. Dritte, völlig neu bearbeitete Auflage, Springer, Berlin–Heidelberg–New York, 2007, p. 1017.

22 *See* Act XV of 1997.

23 Colin Crawford, 'European influence on local self-government?', *Local Government Studies,* Vol. 18, Issue 1, 1992, p. 70.

24 Hoffman 2015, pp. 55–56.

25 Anita Szabó, 'A Helyi Önkormányzatok Európai Chartája és Svájc', *Themis,* Vol. 3, Issue 2, 2005, p. 116.

at least twenty sections as binding, of which at least ten fall within a specific narrower core.[26] The provisions of the Charter are deliberately general enough, but its interpretation is nowadays so rich and detailed that a strict grammatical interpretation shows incompetence.[27]

Local self-government is clearly seen as a right (and also an ability) that should be granted to local authorities.[28] The Charter also stresses the importance of free and direct election of councils[29] and the protection of the boundaries of local authorities.[30] It makes provision for the principle of subsidiarity[31] – the first to do so from among all the international treaties.[32] The limits of state supervision are defined (monitoring of expediency over and above the supervision of compliance with the law is possible only in the case of delegated competences)[33] and the importance of judicial remedies is also enshrined.[34]

The Charter contains a detailed set of requirements to ensure the financial and economic autonomy of local authorities.[35] Article 9 of the Charter guarantees the right of local authorities to their financial resources and protects the principles of local self-government management. In light of the Constitutional Court decisions examined in this study, it is necessary to review Article 9 of the Charter, which lays down the basic principles of local financial resources in the following eight points:

	Content	**Restriction**
(1)	entitlement to and free disposal of own adequate financial resources	*"within national economic policy"*
(2)	commensurate financial resources with the responsibilities (provided for by the constitution and the law)	-

26 Article 12(1) of the Charter.

27 Zoltán Szente, 'Az Európai Önkormányzati Charta végrehajtásának monitoringja az Európa Tanács gyakorlatában', *Új Magyar Közigazgatás,* Vol. 7, Issue 1, 2014, p. 28.

28 Article 3(1) of the Charter.

29 Article 3(2) of the Charter.

30 Article 5 of the Charter.

31 Article 4(3) of the Charter.

32 Szabó 2005, p. 117.

33 Article 8 of the Charter.

34 Article 11 of the Charter.

35 Judit Siket, *A helyi önkormányzatok közigazgatási autonómiája Magyarországon,* Iurisperitus, Szeged, 2020, p. 198.

	Content	Restriction
(3)	the financial resources of local authorities shall derive from local taxes (and charges) of which they have the power to determine the rate	*"within the limits of statute"*
(4)	financial systems of a sufficiently diversified and buoyant nature (to keep pace with the real evolution of the cost of carrying out their tasks)	*"as far as practically possible"*
(5)	protection of financially weaker local authorities through financial equalization procedures or equivalent measures (designed to correct the effects of the unequal distribution of potential sources of finance)	*"Such procedures or measures shall not diminish the discretion local authorities may exercise within their own sphere of responsibility."*
(6)	consultation regarding redistributed resources	-
(7)	grants to local authorities shall not be earmarked for the financing of specific projects; the provision of grants shall not remove the basic freedom of local authorities to exercise policy discretion within their own jurisdiction	*"within the limits of the law"*
(8)	access to the national capital market	*"within the limits of the law"*

In light of the above, Article 9 of the Charter covers the main issues affecting the financial resources of local authorities, but it is also clear that it leaves a general and wide margin of maneuver for legislation and the central management of economic policy.

For the interpretation of the Charter, the Constitutional Court referred in two cases[36] to the non-authentic Explanatory Report to the European Charter of Local Self-Government (hereinafter: explanatory report).[37] The rele-

36 Decision No. 3383/2018. (XII. 14.) AB, Reasoning [22].
37 Explanatory Report to the European Charter of Local Self-Government, at https://rm.coe.int/16800ca437.

vant decisions of the Constitutional Court in relation to Article 9 of the Charter are discussed in Section 4.

3. Solidarity Contribution

The solidarity contribution was introduced in Hungary by Act XC of 2016 on the 2017 Central Budget of Hungary (hereinafter: 2017 Budget Act). Since then, the solidarity contribution has been part of the yearly acts on central budget. According to the explanatory memorandum of the 2017 Budget Law and the *amicus curiae* letter[38] of the Minister of National Economy sent to the Constitutional Court, two objectives can be identified in connection with the introduction of the solidarity contribution. The primary aim of the solidarity contribution was to provide the resources needed at the central level of public finances to cover the public education management tasks taken away from the local self-governments. Furthermore, according to the *amicus curiae*[39] of the Minister, the introduction of the solidarity contribution also serves to even out income differences between local self-governments.

According to the Constitutional Court's decision, the 2017 solidarity contribution was introduced as part of a horizontal equalization procedure in the financing system of local self-governments.[40] However, the Constitutional Court subsequently ruled in its decisions regarding the regulations assessed for the years 2017 and 2023 that there is a relevant difference in this respect. Unlike the legislation in force in 2017, the 2023 solidarity contribution does not contain an element providing additional financial grants to local self-government with a low tax capacity (coincidentally with the withdrawal of grants from local self-government demonstrating a high tax capacity).[41]

In connection with the decision of the Constitutional Court, it is worth referring to the policy report "Hungarian Local Government Finances: The

38 The Act CLI of 2011 on the Constitutional Court (hereinafter: CC Act) allows the initiator of an Act to inform the Constitutional Court (in the form of an *amicus curiae*) of its position on the matter.

39 *Amicus curiae* of the Minister of National Economy, p. 1, at https://public.mkab.hu/dev/dontesek.nsf/0/0562a7dfe9f34c4cc125814d0058eeb4/$FILE/V_1231_2_2017_NGM_amicis_curiae_anonim.pdf.

40 Decision No. 3383/2018. (XII. 14.) AB, Reasoning [36]; Decision No. 18/2024. (XI. 11.) AB, Reasoning [48].

41 Decision No. 18/2024. (XI. 11.) AB, Reasoning [58].

impact of the Local Business Tax and the Solidarity Contribution" [CEMGPAD(2024)4; hereinafter: policy report].[42] The findings of the policy report echo the findings set forth in the decision of the Constitutional Court, namely that

> "[c]urrently, there are no easily accessible data available on the amount of grants allocated for each specific task at national level making it difficult to assess how much of the solidarity contributions paid by municipalities are redistributed to which types of municipalities for cost or revenue equalization purposes. In the government's view,[43] the solidarity contribution is a crucial funding source for local government responsibilities and equalization purposes. At the same time, municipalities that make substantial solidarity contributions request greater transparency concerning the equalization measures and effects."[44]

3.1. Elements of the Solidarity Contribution as a Payment Obligation

The solidarity contribution can be considered a specific payment obligation [*see* in Section 3.2]. In view of this, our study summarizes the main points of the solidarity contribution regulation in a general way[45] along the following lines: subject/object/basis/rate/relief and exemption.

The *subjects* of the solidarity contribution are the local self-governments with a specified amount of local business tax capacity per inhabitant. It is worth noting that out of more than 3,100 local self-governments in Hungary, only 166 paid solidarity contributions in 2017, as highlighted by the cited *amicus curiae* of the Minister of National Economy.[46] However 855 local self-governments will be subject to this payment obligation in 2025 (according to the decree of the Minister of National Economy).[47] It should

42 The policy report formed part of the project "Local Government Public Finance Development and Municipal Capacity Building in Hungary", co-funded by the European Commission (DG REFORM) and the Council of Europe, at https://rm.coe.int/cemgpad-2024-4-hungary-pad-solidarity-contribution-and-local-business-/1680b213ad.

43 The report was agreed in April 2024 with both the ministries concerned and the mayors of some of the local self-governments concerned.

44 Id. p. 17.

45 We focus on the common points of the regulations appearing in the central budget acts of the given year (2017–2025), highlighting the consequences of the relevant differences.

46 In 2023, 724 local self-governments paid solidarity contributions.

47 *See* Annex 1 to Decree No. 1/2025. (II. 11.) of the Minister of National Economy on the amount of the local self-government solidarity contribution in 2025.

be noted that, on the basis of this ministerial decree, more than 65% of the total revenue foreseen for 2025 will be met by Budapest and its districts and the 25 cities with county status.

The *object* of the solidarity contribution – *i.e.* what the contribution is aimed at – is essentially the local self-government function (option) to introduce a local business tax.[48]

The solidarity contribution in force is *based* on the local business tax capacity per inhabitant of the local self-government. This is determined on the basis of historical and not current year data. The solidarity contribution is calculated using a formula based on a separate parameter table, which divides local self-governments into different categories according to their local business tax capacity per inhabitant and adjusts the contribution rate to these categories. For 2025 these calculations resulted in six categories of local self-governments, except for the first category each required to make a solidarity contribution up to 0.75% of the estimated local business tax capacity per capita.[49] A special rule applies to those local self-governments which have not introduced a local business tax, which regards the amount taken into account for calculating the tax capacity per inhabitant: this value is multiplied by the number of inhabitants to determine the tax base reflecting the local business tax capacity of the local self-government concerned.[50] Related to the basis of solidarity contribution the policy report points to the possible impact of demographic change. Accordingly, demographic changes, such as a declining population, can also disadvantage cities in per capita based calculations.[51] It should also be noted that one of the recommendations of the policy report is that in order

> "[t]o better reflect the fiscal capacity of municipalities, it is recommended to broaden the basis for calculating the solidarity contribution. Currently, the assessment of fiscal capacity relies solely on the Local Business Tax (LBT). Including other local taxes, especially where LBT revenue is not significant, would improve fairness and capture fiscal disparities more accurately. [...] For example, in Bulgaria, the equalisation system takes into

48 Decision No. 18/2024. (XI. 11.) AB, Reasoning [61].

49 It should be noted that the budget acts have changed almost every year with respect to the categories and also regarding the base (from 2017 to 2020 the regulation consisted of two interdependent elements, *see* Section 4.2.).

50 *See* Annex 2. II.1.3. of Act XC of 2024 on the 2025 Central Budget of Hungary (hereinafter: 2025 Budget Act).

51 Policy report, p. 5.

account a broad pool of 'fixed tax revenues' basically including all local tax revenues."

At the same time, according to the report, local business tax accounts for approximately 80% of local tax revenues.[52]

The solidarity contribution *rate* increased in a graduated scale (depending on the basis), with significant changes from fiscal year to fiscal year. Rather than tracking the change in individual percentages, the significant increase is best illustrated by the appropriations included in the budget acts. The table below shows that within the span of nine years, the amount of planned revenue from the solidarity contribution has increased almost eighteenfold.

Fiscal year	**Appropriations according to the central budget acts *(in million HUF)***	**Realized income according to the acts on the implementation of the central budget *(in million HUF)***
2017	21,321.2	26,566.1
2018	39,021.2	33,300.1
2019	43,021.2	44,623.5
2020	43,021.2	58,114.6
2021	165,452.5	155,044.8
2022	129,800.0	157,012.8
2023	217,000.0	237,240.2
2024	307,640.6	- *(Act not yet adopted)*
2025	360,160.9	- *(Act not yet adopted)*

The solidarity contribution was only explicitly *exempted* in 2017, with the 2017 Budget Act exempting the Municipality of Budapest from the payment of the solidarity contribution. As regards the Municipality of Budapest there have been special regulations for over three years, meaning their contribution rate for 2018 and 2019 was fixed individually in their respect (2018: 5 billion HUF, 2019: 10 billion HUF). Then, for the year 2020, a *discount* was introduced for the capital, with the solidarity contribution dipping 15% lower than the calculated amount. In this context, it is also worth mention-

52 Id. pp. 4, and 6.

ing that from 2019 onwards, a so-called correction factor is introduced for municipalities with a population below 500 inhabitants (from 2021 onwards, below 600 inhabitants). This reduced the amount of the solidarity contribution payable by a fixed 15 million HUF in 2019 and 2020, and by 12 million HUF from 2021 onwards.

The *main rules for the payment of* the solidarity contribution are contained in the subchapter titled "Additional rules for the provision of funds to local self-governments" of the yearly central budget acts. These provisions refer to net financing, which is regulated by Article 83 of the Act CXCV of 2011 on Public Finance (hereinafter: Public Finance Act). The key element of this is that the following are deducted from the grants received by the local self-governments: *(i)* public charges on staff benefits, and *(ii)* other statutory obligations. The remaining amount is then paid by the Hungarian State Treasury (hereinafter: Treasury) to the local self-governments concerned. In case the deducted grants do not cover the required amount of the solidarity contribution, then in addition to the deduction the municipality must pay the difference to the central subsystem. The Treasury first advances the amount and then issues a monthly direct debit order against the local self-government. If this does not produce a result within ninety days, the debt and the interest accrued are considered public debt and are collected by the State Tax Authority as taxes.[53]

3.2. The Tax Nature of the Solidarity Contribution and its Constitutional Status

The Government considers the solidarity contribution to be a central tax (based on the ministerial *amicus curiae* briefs on the solidarity contribution for 2017 and 2023). According to the *amici curiae* of Mihály Varga as Minister of National Economy [in the case underlying *Decision No. 3383/2018. (XII. 14.) AB*] and later as Minister of Finance [in the case underlying *Decision No. 18/2024. (XI. 11.) AB*] the solidarity contributions for 2017 and 2023 meet the definition of payment obligation under Article 28 of the Act CXCIV of 2011 on the Economic Stability of Hungary: the solidarity contribution is a public charge (tax) in substance, regardless of its designation. This is owed to the fact that it is a compulsory financial obligation on the part of the local self-governments to provide public expenditure. It is regul-

53 Section 83(4) of the Public Finance Act.

ated by an Act and there is no direct service provided to local self-governments in return. In the event of default, it is considered a public debt and is collected by the state tax authority in the same way as taxes.[54]

However, the Constitutional Court arrived at a different conclusion in its *Decision No. 18/2024. (XI. 11.) AB,* finding that the solidarity contribution contained in the contested provisions of the 2023 Budget Act is not a tax in the constitutional sense. This finding was based primarily on the fact that the obligation of local self-governments to pay solidarity contribution does not derive from the obligation of sharing public burdens.[55] Local self-governments are the beneficiaries, not the recipients, of this obligation contained in Article XXX(1) of the Fundamental Law. They are organizations that hold public power and shall decide on the types and rates of local taxes under the Fundamental Law.[56] And they can only be subject to sharing public burdens (in the constitutional sense) when they act as private parties.

Consequently, the Constitutional Court considers the solidarity contribution to be a public payment obligation (instead of a tax) from the local sub-system to the central sub-system of the public budget, which was embedded in the system of financing local self-governments.[57]

4. Related Decisions of the Constitutional Court

The Constitutional Court has so far examined the following four motions concerning the solidarity contribution, which obligation has been included in the central budget acts every year since 2017:

---

54 *See* the *amicus curiae* of the Minister of National Economy, p. 6, and the *amicus curiae* of the Minister of Finance, p. 2, at https://public.mkab.hu/dev/dontesek.nsf/0/56ce851847832753c1258af3005b236e/$FILE/III_1693_3_2024_amicus_PM_anonim.pdf.

55 It is also worth referring to a study that, due to the limitation of the powers of the Constitutional Court, the Court has not yet had the opportunity to express its position in detail on the new definition of the content of the principle of sharing public burdens, although it has done so in detail in relation to the previous legislation. Zsolt Halász, 'Néhány gondolat a teljesítőképesség alapú adózásról és az irányító adókról', *Iustum Aequum Salutare,* Vol. 15, Issue 3, 2019, p. 50.

56 *See* Article 32(1)(h) of the Fundamental Law.

57 Decision No. 18/2024. (XI. 11.) AB, Reasoning [62]-[63].

Decision/ order number	Initiator of the procedure	Procedure	Legislation challenged	Content of decision
Decision No. 3383/ 2018. (XII. 14.) AB	One quarter of the Members of the National Assembly	Examination of a conflict with an international treaty	Article 39(4) and further provisions of the Budget Act 2017	Rejection
Decision No. 3311/ 2019. (XI. 21.) AB	Municipality of the City of Budaörs	Constitutional complaint	Article 74(4) of Act CXC of 2011 on National Public Education	Rejection
			Article 39(4)-(6) of the Budget Act 2017	Declared inadmissible
Order No. 3028/2020. (II. 10.) AB	Municipality of the City of Tiszaújváros	Constitutional complaint	Article 39(4) and further provisions of the Budget Act 2017	Declared inadmissible
Decision No. 18/ 2024. (XI. 11.) AB	Budapest-Capital Regional Court	Initiative of a judge: examination of a conflict with an international treaty	Annex 2. point 57. of Act XXV of 2022 on the 2023 Central Budget	Rejection
		Initiative of a judge: revision of the conformity with the Fundamental Law	Article 83(3) of the Public Finance Act	Rejection
			Article 143(1) of Government Decree No. 368/2011 (XII. 31.) on the implementation of the Public Finance Act	Declared inadmissible

4.1. Limitation of the Powers of the Constitutional Court

The Fundamental Law currently limits the Constitutional Court's powers to review specific Acts regarding fiscal policy. The limitation of powers applies to specific constitutional court proceedings, for example the examination of constitutional complaints and is linked to the level of public debt as a percentage of GDP, with a target level under 50% (currently 72.6% – planned by the Act on central budget for the end of 2025). With regard to the current level of this indicator, the limitation of powers still applies in relation to certain fiscal acts, such as the act on central budget and acts on central taxes. Although this provision guarantees a constitutional review of these acts, the review is limited to certain fundamental rights reviewable in the above-mentioned procedures. From this point of view, it is decisive that the solidarity contribution is not regulated by a separate act, but by the act on the central budget, as well as the fact that the afore-mentioned *amici curiae* considered it as a central tax regardless of its designation.[58]

Consequently, these public finance acts are – as a general rule – exempt from the control of the Constitutional Court.[59] The limitation of powers does not apply to the examination of their conflict with international treaties. However, only one quarter of the members of the National Assembly, the Government, the President of the Curia, the Prosecutor General and the Commissioner for Fundamental Rights may submit a motion to this effect. In addition, a judge may initiate proceedings before the Constitutional Court if it considers that the law applicable in the individual case is in breach of an international treaty.[60]

It should be noted, however, that following the amendment of the CC Act[61] (in force as of 1 June 2023), local self-governments may no longer lodge a constitutional complaint against a judicial decision with the Constitutional Court (although this does not affect their rights to lodge a constitutional complaint against the law applied in a court proceeding).[62] Consequently, the right to challenge the possible unconstitutionality of judicial

58 Article 37(4) of the Fundamental Law.

59 László Klicsu, 'A gazdasági alkotmányosság alapjai', *in* Lóránt Csink *et al.* (eds.), *A magyar közjog alapintézményei,* Pázmány Press, Budapest, 2020, p. 976.

60 Section 32(2) of the CC Act.

61 Act X of 2023 on amending certain laws on judicial matters in connection with the Hungarian Recovery and Resilience Plan.

62 For more on this issue, *see* Ádám Varga, 'The Protection of the Right to Local Self-Government in the Practice of the Hungarian Constitutional Court', *Hungarian Yearbook of International Law and European Law,* Vol. 8, 2020, pp. 349–370.

decisions – even in the context of the solidarity contribution[63] – is no longer available to local self-governments.[64]

4.2. Motions Challenging the 2017 Budget Act

The Constitutional Court received three petitions concerning the 2017 Budget Act. Two of these were filed by local self-governments, but the Constitutional Court refused to admit these motions regarding the solidarity contribution. In both cases, the reason for the dismissal was that the arguments contained in the motions fell partly within the limitation of the Constitutional Court's powers (*cf.* Articles XIII and XV of the Fundamental Law) and partly because they failed to refer to provisions of the Fundamental Law that may be invoked in a constitutional complaint.[65]

Meanwhile, the Constitutional Court examined the merits of the motion submitted by Members of the National Assembly alleging a violation of an international treaty (the Charter). However, the Constitutional Court rejected the motion alleging a violation of the Charter on the following grounds. The Constitutional Court held that the contested legislation is not contrary to Article 9(1) to (2) and (5) of the Charter, as it applies only to local self-governments with a significant per capita tax capacity. Furthermore, the 2017 Budget Act simultaneously created the possibility of additional grants for municipalities with a low per capita tax capacity. According to the Constitutional Court, Article 9(1) of the Charter shall be interpreted within the framework of national economic policy, since only within this framework are local self-governments entitled to adequate financial resources of their own. The decision also refers to the Explanatory Report to the Charter, which states that this provision seeks to ensure that local self-governments shall not be deprived of their freedom to determine expenditure priorities.

In the Constitutional Court's interpretation, the solidarity contribution can be considered a horizontal public financial equalization procedure and is in line with Article 9(5) of the Charter. The 2017 regulation consisted of two interdependent elements. *(i)* First, it divided local self-governments into

63 *See* the case on which the judicial initiative is based in Section 4.3.

64 Order No. 3296/2024. (VII. 24.) AB, Reasoning [20]–[21]; Order No. 3400/2024. (XI. 8.) AB, Reasoning [19]–[20]; Order No. 3401/2024. (XI. 8.) AB, Reasoning [18]–[19]; Order No. 3425/2024. (XI. 28.) AB, Reasoning [12]–[14].

65 Decision No. 3311/2019. (XI. 21.) AB, and Order No. 3028/2020. (II. 10.) AB.

twelve categories according to their tax capacity per capita. It provided for additional support for the two lowest categories, while the other categories were subject to support reductions. *(ii)* Then, from local self-governments with a tax capacity per capita exceeding HUF 32,000, the portion exceeding the basis for calculating the reduction in support was withdrawn as a solidarity contribution (within the framework of net financing).

The Court considered that the equalization of the income inequality in the Hungarian local self-government sub-system is explicitly in line with the objectives of the Charter. According to the Constitutional Court, the mere fact that the legislation may generate revenue for the central budget does not in itself amount to a breach of Article 9(5) of the Charter.[66]

4.3. Decision of the Constitutional Court No. 18/2024. (XI. 11.) AB

The Constitutional Court rejected the motion of the Budapest-Capital Regional Court regarding the provisions on the 2023 solidarity contribution and the collection order issued by the Treasury.[67] In the proceedings underlying the judicial initiative, the plaintiff (the Municipality of Budapest), challenged the Treasury's procedure in relation to the 2023 solidarity contribution. The substance of the case is that the subsidies granted to the Municipality of Budapest under the 2023 Budget Act did not cover the amount of the solidarity contribution. Therefore, the Treasury advanced the difference and then submitted recovery orders to reimburse these amounts.

According to the judicial initiative, the rules on the 2023 solidarity contribution are contrary to Article 9(1), (2) and (4) of the Charter. The motion asserts that the solidarity contribution imposes a disproportionate burden on the Municipality of Budapest. It argues that its financial resources are not commensurate with the performance of its statutory tasks and that the financial system available is not sufficiently diversified and flexible. In addition, the motion alleges that the right to a fair administrative procedure [Article XXIV(1) of the Fundamental Law] is infringed by Section 83(3) of the Public Finance Act, since the Treasury's procedure is not based on a formal decision and the Municipality of Budapest was not involved in the procedure.

---

66 Decision No. 3383/2018. (XII. 14.) AB, Reasoning [35]–[37].

67 The Constitutional Court also rejected (for lack of necessary reasoning) the petition against the challenged provision of the Government Decree No. 368/2011. (XII. 31.).

The Constitutional Court found that the solidarity contribution cannot be linked in a constitutionally assessable manner to the relative freedom of disposal over own financial resources [Article 9(1) of the Charter]. This is because the contested provisions of the 2023 Budget Act do not restrict the possibility of using a municipal resource but impose a payment obligation instead. According to the Constitutional Court, the purpose of Article 9(1) of the Charter is to ensure that municipal revenue is not directly linked, within the limits permitted by national economic policy, to a specific legislative provision which specifies precisely what it may be used for.[68]

The Constitutional Court has pointed out that the 2023 solidarity contribution may conflict with the financial autonomy of the local self-governments [guaranteed by Article 9(2) of the Charter and the Fundamental Law], when the serious disproportionality of the financing system can be expressed in a constitutional argument and measured by the Constitutional Court's instruments for review. This supposes that a reasonable link be established between the extent of the net contributor position and the inability of the local self-government to legitimately pursue a balanced and sustainable budget management based on the resources of its financing system as a whole.[69] However, the Constitutional Court – also taking into account the report of the State Audit Office of Hungary – took the view that no such reasonable link could be established for 2023.[70] The Constitutional Court explained that Article 9(4) of the Charter imposes a requirement on revenue (flexibility and diversity), while the examined provision of the 2023 Budget Act is a municipal expenditure and in view of this, no direct link can be established.

With regard to the contested provision of the Public Finance Act, the Constitutional Court held that it does not in itself infringe the right to a fair administrative procedure. However, it identified as a constitutional problem the fact that the Treasury imposes the solidarity contribution without a formalized legal procedure (based on Act CL of 2016 on the General Adminis-

---

68 This may raise questions in the future in relation to Section 122(1a) of the LG Act (and Section 3 of the Act CXXXIII of 2006). Under that legislation, municipalities may use the revenue from local business tax primarily for the provision of their public transport services.

69 Reasoning [73]; The constitutional foundation on budget management principles is laid down in Article N of the Fundamental Law. For more on this issue, *see* Olivér Ráth, 'Az Alaptörvény N) cikke, jogirodalmi megközelítések', *in* Gyula Bándi & Anett Pogácsás (eds.), *Stability and adaptability – Állandóság és alkalmazkodás: Selected doctoral studies – Válogatott doktorandusz tanulmányok,* Pázmány Press, Budapest, 2023, pp. 449–473.

70 Reasoning [78].

trative Procedure), while at the same time imposing a quantified obligation on the local self-government.[71] Consequently, the Constitutional Court, while rejecting the judge's initiative for against the Public Finance Act, indirectly ruled against the Treasury's action on the points raised in the plaintiff's application.

5. Conclusions

In our study, we have demonstrated, through examples from the scholarly literature, that autonomy encompasses various aspects of independence. We have identified economic-financial autonomy as one of the defining aspects of autonomy, the essence of which is the acquisition and autonomous (independent) management of funds for own affairs. In this context, we have also pointed out that territorial self-government encompasses more than the decentralization of public administration, among other reasons, because it has own property and financial autonomy. In the ideal case, the decentralization of public functions should be followed by the transfer of the financial resources needed to carry out these functions, as set out in both the Fundamental Law and the Charter.

However, the topic of financial autonomy remains relevant in the context of changing economic influences. Through the studies and measures cited, we have shown that, following the centralized, multi-stage debt consolidation of local self-governments, the solidarity contribution is not the only intervention in financial-economic autonomy that has affected Hungarian local self-governments in recent years.

The solidarity contribution was introduced by the 2017 Budget Act with a dual purpose: *(i)* to provide the necessary resources to cover the public education management tasks taken away from the municipalities, and *(ii)* to even out the income differences between municipalities. Since then, the solidarity contribution has been included in the central budget acts each year, while the methodology of the regulation remained broadly similar. The changes highlight the following trends. A review of the regulations shows that the number of municipalities paying solidarity contributions is almost five times higher than when it was introduced (only 166 in 2017 and 855 in 2025). Similarly, the amount of the solidarity contribution set out in the 2017 Budget Act was around HUF 21 billion, whereas the 2025 Budget Act sets out a contribution of HUF 360 billion. This suggests that the extension

71 Reasoning [114].

of the solidarity contribution could further weaken the financial and economic capacity of local self-governments.[72]

In our study, we have reviewed the practice of the Hungarian Constitutional Court in relation to the solidarity contribution. However, the motions challenging the different regulations were ultimately rejected/dismissed on the grounds of the limited powers of the Constitutional Court and the deliberately general provisions of the Charter, in particular with regard to Article 9 in the context of national economic policy. Meanwhile, in the context of the aforementioned trend, the decisions of the Constitutional Court make it clear that the solidarity contribution can no longer correspond directly to the equalization procedure under Article 9(5) of the Charter, as reflected in the findings of the policy report. This is important because the aim of such equalization procedures, according to the Charter, is to protect the financially weaker local self-governments.

At the same time, the Constitutional Court has given guidance for the future in connection with Article 9(2) of the Charter, according to which the solidarity contribution may conflict with the financial autonomy of local self-governments guaranteed by the Charter and the Fundamental Law only if the serious disproportionality of the financing system becomes clear from a constitutional argument and can be measured by the Constitutional Court's instruments for review. Thus, in effect, it has designated the exceptional cases in which it may review the relevant legislation.

It should also be noted that the Constitutional Court has set out the constitutional guidelines for the Treasury's fair trial (the requirement to be included as a client and to establish the amount in a formal decision). Nevertheless the 2025 Budget Act expressly provides that the rules on the administrative proceedings do not apply to the determination and deduction of the municipal solidarity contribution in the context of net financing.[73] Instead, the Minister responsible for public finances has been empowered to publish by decree the amount of the municipal solidarity contribution for each municipality.[74]

Hence, the quantification of the solidarity contribution is now the responsibility of legislation rather than an administrative procedure. As a re-

72 Judit Siket, 'Veszélyben a helyi önkormányzatok funkcionalitása? – A pandémia hatása a helyi demokráciára', *in* Ádám Rixer (ed.), *A járvány hosszútávú hatása a magyar közigazgatásra*, KRE ÁJK, Budapest, 2021, p. 213.

73 *See* Annex 2. II.1.5. of the 2025 Budget Act.

74 *See* Article 78(4) of the 2025 Budget Act and Government Decree No. 368/2011. (XII. 31.).

sult, it is not possible to challenge the amount of the solidarity contribution before the courts in this way, but only to lodge a constitutional complaint directly against the Minister's decree under Section 26(2) of the Constitutional Court Act. However, the Constitutional Court has stated that it will not carry out a review of the quantification of the municipal financing system. In other words, the municipalities are not expected to be able to challenge the amount of the solidarity contribution applied to them on the merits.

Why Digital Transformation Is Needed in Minority Language Education

The Case of Hungary from the Perspective of Language Charter

*Balázs Szabolcs Gerencsér**

Abstract

This paper examines why digital transformation is essential for the future of minority language education, with a particular focus on Hungary and the European Charter for Regional or Minority Languages. As digital technologies become increasingly embedded in everyday life, they offer both a necessary and strategic opportunity to support linguistic diversity – especially in contexts where minority languages face institutional neglect, teacher shortages, and assimilation. The paper argues that digitalization can help bridge educational gaps by providing flexible, inclusive, and modern pedagogical tools, including digital content and online platforms tailored to minority needs. However, the Charter's monitoring largely overlooks the digital sphere in education, focusing instead on media. In Hungary, although legal frameworks support minority language education, implementation remains uneven, and digital technologies are underutilized. The COVID-19 pandemic accelerated digital education, revealing infrastructural and pedagogical shortcomings, particularly affecting disadvantaged groups. Despite improvements, such as broadband expansion and e-learning platforms, minority language content and teachers' digital skills remain insufficient. The paper concludes that while digital tools can greatly enhance language transmission and access, they must be integrated within long-term strategies, complemented with financial and methodological support, and sensitivity to community needs. Crucially, education must maintain its human core – digital solutions should complement, not replace, personal interaction, which remains vital in both learning and identity formation. Thus, digital transformation is not just a technical upgrade but a culturally and socially grounded imperative in sustaining Hungary's minority languages.

Keywords: minority language education, digital transformation, Language Charter (ECRML), education policy, linguistic diversity

* Balázs Szabolcs Gerencsér: associate professor of law, director of Ereky Public Law Research Center, Pázmány Péter Catholic University, Budapest, gerencser.balazs@jak.ppke.hu

1. Digitalization Is No Longer a Desire, but a Necessity

In an era of rapid technological development, digital transformation has become a key driver of innovation in many sectors, including education. Digital tools, platforms and pedagogies have a direct impact on minority language education, which in most countries faces challenges such as teacher shortages, declining speaker populations and institutional marginalization.[1] In Hungary, where linguistic diversity is shaped by historical, political and social dynamics, digital transformation offers both an opportunity and a necessity for the revitalization and sustainability of minority languages.

The European Charter for Regional or Minority Languages (hereinafter: Language Charter or Charter), adopted by the Council of Europe in 1992, provides a legal and political framework for the protection and promotion of linguistic diversity in the signatory states. Hungary, as one of the first parties to the Charter, has also committed itself to ensuring the rights of minority language speakers, *inter alia* in the field of education under Article 8 of the Language Charter. It is a constant question whether the digital environment offers a real alternative to overcome structural barriers through digital content development, interactive educational experiences tailored to minority language needs or even support for educational administration.

This paper examines whether the monitoring mechanism of the Language Charter, which is considered the most comprehensive European instrument for minority language education,[2] applies to the digital transformation of education in Hungary, and what phenomena and tools exist that could be further exploited to promote the preservation of minority languages and the development of education. In addition to pedagogical methods of education, digital tools can also serve the preservation of minority languages, either through institutional support for the education system, or through support for legislation or policy-making. It argues that digital transformation can bridge educational gaps, improve language accessibility and strengthen the transmission of minority languages to future generations, but it is important to leave room for human relations, as education is fundamentally based on the personal relationship between teacher and student. Through a critical examination of the efforts and challenges in Hungary, this

1 Mark Warschauer, *Technology and Social Inclusion: Rethinking the Digital Divide,* The MIT Press, Cambridge-London, 2003, p. 12.

2 Alexey Kozhemyakov, 'The European Charter for Regional or Minority Languages: Ten Years of Protecting and Promoting Linguistic and Cultural Diversity', *Museum International,* Vol. 60, Issue 3, 2008, pp. 26–36.

research contributes to the wider discourse on digital inclusion, language rights and sustainable education policies for multilingual societies.

2. *What Does the Language Charter's Monitoring System Say about the Digital Environment for Education?*

In 2012, Sarah McMonagle, looking back at 11 years of monitoring reports of the Language Charter, noted that the 'internet' is gaining an increasingly important place in the Charter's monitoring process.[3] In her quantitative study, she shows that in the 65 evaluation reports she has processed over the first twelve to thirteen years of the Charter, the internet is emerging as the most directly accessible form of the digital environment for an increasing number of countries as well as articles of the Charter each year.

It is also worth noting that according to the Telecommunication Development Sector (ITU-D) survey cited by McMonagle, the number of internet users in the world is growing steeply year on year.[4] While in 2008, the 10th anniversary of the entry into force of the Language Charter, 25% of the world's population used the internet, in 2018 it became 48% and in 2024 68%, that is 5.5 billion people. The growth in internet access and use is also accompanied by an explosion in technology, which nowadays, in addition to information and communication technologies (hereinafter: ICT), is also seeing the emergence of disruptive technologies such as big data, blockchain, 3D printing and artificial intelligence.[5]

When reviewing the documents related to the implementation of the Language Charter in Hungary, *i.e.*, mainly the country reports and the evaluation reports, there are few direct references to digital technology, internet use, ICT or digitalization in the context of the promotion of minority languages.

The above findings, *i.e.*, the general increase in references to the internet and the negligible reference to digitalization in the Hungarian reports, seem to contradict each other, but it is clear from the monitoring documents and other analyses of the Council of Europe that digital technologies are usually

3 Sarah McMonagle, 'The European Charter for Regional or Minority Languages: Still Relevant in the Information Age?', *Journal on Ethnopolitics and Minority Issues in Europe*, Vol 11, Issue 2, 2012, p. 8.

4 *See* at https://www.itu.int/en/ITU-D/Statistics/Pages/stat/default.aspx.

5 Adam Greenfield, *Radical Technologies: The Design of Everyday Life*, Verso, 2017, p. 300.

not associated with education (Article 8), but primarily with the media (Article 11).[6]

Thus, there seem to be valuable perspectives in the relationship between the Language Charter and new media. The Council of Europe report underlines that the Charter was created in an era dominated by traditional media forms. The emergence of new technologies, including the internet and social media, has significantly changed the media landscape, with implications for the use and promotion of regional or minority languages. The report stresses the need to adapt the implementation of the Charter to these technological developments so that minority languages can be effectively promoted in the digital age.[7] Indeed, these tools, used among others by children are also involved in education as we will see in the fourth chapter.

The EU has also carried out studies on the link between linguistic diversity and the internet. The study evaluating linguistic diversity online concludes that the internet presents challenges but also opportunities for minority and lesser-used languages. The development of language technology for all European languages is essential to prevent social exclusion and to exploit the potential of digital platforms to preserve and promote languages.[8]

The EU also published its Digital Decade 2024 country report for Hungary, which paints a digital landscape for Hungary, according to which 58.9% of the Hungarian population has at least basic digital skills, slightly above the EU average.[9] However, the share of ICT professionals in employment is below the EU average, suggesting that more efforts are needed to develop digital skills. Although the report does not specifically address nationalities (*i.e.,* recognized minorities in Hungary) or minority languages, developing digital skills can facilitate the creation and distribution of digital content in these languages.

---

6 Elin Haf Gruffydd Jones & Jarmo Lainio (eds.), *New technologies, new social media and the European Charter for Regional or Minority Languages,* Council of Europe, 2019, pp. 38–43.

7 Id. p. 19.

8 Dick Holdsworth (ed.), *Linguistic Diversity on the Internet: Assessment of the Contribution of Machine Translation,* European Bureau for Lesser Used Languages, European Parliament, Brussels, 2000. PE 289.662 /Fin.St p. 24.

9 European Commission's Hungary 2024 Digital Decade Country Report, at https://digital-strategy.ec.europa.eu/en/factpages/hungary-2024-digital-decade-country-report.

3. *The Legal Framework of Minority Language Education*

Today's Hungarian minority education system is based on three main legal sources: constitutional rules (the Fundamental Law of Hungary), the rules of the National Minorities Act,[10] and the rules of the National Public Education Act.[11] Its international framework is defined first and foremost by the Language Charter, to which Hungary has been a state party from the very beginning.

3.1. The Constitutional Rules

Constitutional rules, especially during the turbulent period of the 20th century in the Central European region, which was marked by world wars and successive dictatorships, became important as a guarantee and framework.[12] In Hungary, as in other Central European states, the constitution (Fundamental Law) lays down the framework for minority rights.[13]

The Hungarian Fundamental Law, which entered into force in 2012, essentially maintains the previous regulation, but makes necessary clarifications. The National Avowal (preamble) states that "the national minorities living with us form part of the Hungarian political community and are constituent parts of the State.", *i.e.*, minorities are equal members of the political nation. In addition to this political declaration, it also states that "we commit ourselves to promoting and safeguarding our heritage, our unique language, Hungarian culture and the languages and cultures of national minorities living in Hungary, along with all man-made and natural assets of the Carpathian Basin."

Article XXIX of the Fundamental Law contains the normative rules on national minority rights. It now states with legal force that nationalities are "constituent parts of the State" and have the right to use their mother tongue

10 Act CLXXIX of 2011 on the Rights of Nationalities.

11 Act CXC of 2011 on National Public Education (hereinafter: NPE).

12 Constitutional rules can be as decisive as the constitutions of the provinces. For example, Fedinec cites the constitution of the Province of Vojvodina as the framework for minority education. Csilla Fedinec, 'A kisebbségi magyar oktatásügy helyzete Közép-Európában, *in* Nándor Bárdi *et al.* (eds.), *Kisebbségi magyar közösségek a 20. században,* Gondolat–MTA Kisebbségkutató Intézet, Budapest, 2008. pp. 284–289.

13 Norbert Tóth & Balázs Vizi, 'The Legal Framework for the Protection of Minorities and Experiences in Law Application in States Neighboring Hungary: A Guide on Minority Rights to the Carpathian Basin', *Minority Review,* Vol. 9, Issue 1, 2024, pp. 10–12.

and to preserve and cultivate their culture. In this way, it adds the recognition and protection of nationalities to the scope of fundamental values, while preserving constitutional traditions.[14] The Fundamental Law continues to uphold a specific nationality (minority) status that goes beyond general human and civil rights.

The new constitutional arrangements retain the ombudsman's control over the implementation of nationalities' rights, as well as institutional protection. The only change in this respect is the restructuring of the ombudsman system: under Article 30(3), the deputies of the Commissioner for Fundamental Rights "shall protect the interests of future generations and the rights of national minorities living in Hungary." This way, the erstwhile Commissioner responsible for national minorities has been downgraded in their position to deputy, without the opportunity to act alone in submitting petitions to the Constitutional Court or producing reports.

Since the main field of study of this paper is education, it should be mentioned here that in addition to the above-mentioned Deputy Commissioner for Nationalities, as an institution of parliamentary control, the office of Commissioner for Educational Rights was created in 2000, which is a governmental ombudsman institution specialized in educational law issues.[15]

3.2. The Law on the Rights of Nationalities

Act CLXXIX of 2011 on the Rights of National Minorities is the fourth minority law in Hungary. The National Minorities Act defines the concept of "minority" in the first section, which uses conceptual elements that are identical to those of the previous Act: *(i)* centuries-old nationality, *(ii)* ethnic group, *(iii)* numerical minority, *(iv)* distinguished from the majority population by their language, culture and traditions, *(v)* they demonstrate a collective sense of identity, *(vi)* their purpose is to express and protect the interests of their historically established communities. The definition is close to the one used by the UN rapporteur, Francesco Capotorti, which takes into account both measurable, objective and subjective factors when defining minorities.[16] This may have been a conscious choice of the Hungarian

14 Ferenc Horkay Hörcher, 'The National Avowal', *in* Lóránt Csink *et al.* (eds.), *The Basic law of Hungary – a First Commentary*, Clarus, Dublin, 2012, p. 39.

15 The Education Ombudsman was created by the Public Education Act in 1999. Its operation is still based on the current NPE, Section 77(7) and (8).

16 Francesco Capotorti, *Study on The Rights of Persons Belonging to Ethnic, Religious and Linguistic Minorities,* Special Rapporteur of the Sub-Commission on Prevention of Dis-

legislator of the time, when faced with the fact that a consensual definition of the concept of minority would be difficult and challenging to establish, both in the 1990s and in the 2000s, or in fact, the present decades.[17]

The National Minorities Act maintains the system of individual and collective rights and gives special emphasis to language rights. This strong emphasis is not accidental: in Hungary minorities have a primarily linguistic character.[18] The Act divides the areas of language use into several areas: *(i)* language used in the functioning of national minority self-government, *(ii)* language used in official administration, and *(iii)* language used in the community.

The media (both national and public) and education are arenas of community language use. These powers are particularly evident in the autonomies, which are given a high priority in the law. As Hungarian law is one of the few that recognize and support collective rights, it defines autonomy as a collective right. A further element of autonomy in the law is self-determination in the administration of *education,* culture and media. The notion of autonomy in the law has mixed elements of territorial and personal autonomy, as it is closely related to national self-government. However, taking into account the characteristic features of the nationalities located in diaspora, the personal element is more characteristic.

Personal autonomy was widely discussed in the literature in the 1990s. According to Heintze, the concept of personal autonomy applies to members of a particular group within a given state, regardless of their place of residence, and includes the right to preserve and develop the religious, linguistic and cultural character of the minority through institutions constituted by the minority without interference from central power.[19] Personal autonomy is granted primarily to ethnic, cultural, religious or linguistic mi-

---

crimination and Protection of Minorities, United Nations, 1997, E/CN.4/Sub.2/384/Rev.1, para. 568.

17 Jelena Pejic, 'Minority Rights in International Law.' *Human Rights Quarterly* Vol. 19, Issue 3, 1997, p. 668.

18 The law recognizes 13 minorities, from which only the roma/gipsy population considered to be "ethnic", all other is considered to be "linguistic" communities. According to the Annex to the Act national minorities in Hungary are: Armenian, Bulgarian, Croatian, German, Greek, Polish, Roma, Romanian, Ruthenian, Serbian, Slovakian, Slovenian, Ukrainian.

19 Hans-Joachim Heintze, 'Autonomy and Protection of Minorities under International Law', *in* Günther Bachter (ed.), *Federalism against Ehtnicity?,* Verlag Rüegger, Zurich, 1997, p. 88.

norities.[20] Kovács presents three main arguments in favor of personal autonomy:[21] *(i)* it simplifies the drafting of the relevant legislative regulation, yet are easier to describe geographically; *(ii)* it provides a competent and legitimate partner *vis-à-vis* the central power; *(iii)* it simplifies the position of the elected national body *vis-à-vis* the central power, as both are "national in scope".

Minority autonomy is not the same as, but is linked to, the national system of minority self-government. These self-governments exercise powers that are primarily related to the cultural sphere. Chapter V of the law deals with the educational, cultural and media rights of national minorities. If we look at educational rights, the key to the regulation is Section 22(2), which states that the mother tongue of the national minorities in Hungary is a factor that binds the community together. This implies a regulatory attitude that if minorities are to be preserved, because they are an enrichment to the political nation, their identity must be supported, which in Hungary will primarily mean the support for preserving the minority vernacular.

Education, as the most important framework for the transmission of identity, is therefore given a prominent place in the law and the state therefore supports the use of the minority language in education, whether the school is state, minority or otherwise maintained, the costs of which are borne by the state.[22] In accordance with Article 8 of the Language Charter, Hungarian legislation also distinguishes between three types of national minority education: mother tongue education, in which education is provided entirely in the minority language and Hungarian is merely taught as a separate subject; bilingual education, in which a substantial part of education is provided in the minority language and Hungarian in parallel; and language teaching education, in which education is provided in Hungarian but the minority language and culture are taught as separate subjects. These educational models (with minor changes) have existed in Hungarian legislation since the beginning of the 20th century.[23]

The law gives priority to the fulfillment of public duties, *i.e.*, it does not tie minority education to a specific type of institution. It allows for this in

20 Ruth Lapidoth, *Autonomy – Flexible solutions to ethnic conflicts,* Institute of Peace Press, Washington DC., 1997, p. 37.

21 Péter Kovács, *Nemzetközi jog és kisebbségvédelem,* Osiris, Budapest, 1996, p. 184.

22 National Minorities Act, Section 22(2).

23 Sándor Balogh (editor-in-chief), *A magyar állam és a nemzetiségek. A magyarországi nemzetiségi kérdés történetének jogforrásai 1848–1993,* Napvilág, Budapest, 2002, p. 9. These minority education models were first regulated by the Ministerial Decree on Religion and Public Education No. 110478-VIII.a. in 1923.

the case of all forms of institutions and, in accordance with local possibilities and needs, education in the national minority language may be provided in national minority kindergartens, schools, classes or groups.[24]

And the provision of training and further training for teachers of the mother tongue of national minorities is a state responsibility by law. Within the framework of this task, the state also supports the employment of trained minority teachers as well as native language teachers as visiting teachers in Hungary.[25]

3.3. The National Public Education Act

Act CXC of 2011 on National Public Education (hereinafter: NPE) provides the complete set of rules for the Hungarian public education system, which also contains provisions on national minority education. The preamble of the Act already states that national minority education is closely linked to the realization of the human right to education. By establishing types of institutions and articulating rights and obligations, the Public Education Act creates the legal and institutional framework for the transmission of the national language and culture and thus for the strengthening of national identity.

According to Section 2 of the NPE, public education institutions are primarily maintained by the state. In exceptional cases, the national minority self-government, a religious legal person, a religious association[26] or any other person or organization may establish and maintain an educational institution within the framework of the Act, if it has acquired the right to do so.[27] Local governments may establish and maintain only kindergartens.

Non-state operators, *i.e.*, minority self-governments, churches, religious associations and other foundations and businesses, may establish and oper-

24 National Minorities Act, Section 22(4).

25 Id. Section 23(4).

26 In Hungary, the parliament recognizes churches by law. All other religious associations and are registered by the courts in a similar way as associations.

27 Before 2012, local authorities were the main providers of education and health services. By then, however, significant funding difficulties had arisen, and the financial capacity of local authorities had been overstretched. In addition, there was tension between the government's responsibility for education and the municipalities' ability to use their independence to implement the law to make decisions that went against the government's wishes. The 2012 reform therefore opted for centralization and gave municipalities powers in development policy decisions instead of education and health.

ate schools if they meet quality assurance requirements. Minority education is provided by law in the form of kindergartens, primary schools, colleges, gymnasiums, vocational gymnasiums, and from 2020 the category of "additional national minority language schools" has been created specifically for the purpose of teaching minority language and ethnic studies as extracurricular subject.[28] However, the establishment (and reorganization) of all of these is always subject to consultation with the national minority self-government (minorities) concerned.[29]

In March 2025, according to the Education Office's information database,[30] of the 5,686 educational institutions operating in Hungary, 108 are run by minority self-governments, of which 30 are run by national minority self-governments and 78 by municipal minority self-governments.

3.4. The Mother Tongue as a Community-bonding Factor; Assimilation and Loss of Minority Languages

However stable the institutional framework for minority language education may be, the country reports submitted under the Language Charter show that minority education faces significant problems.[31] The continuing assimilation of national minorities results in less use of their minority language and, consequently, less choice of minority-language educational institutions. Teacher training is similarly problematic, with few people applying to teach a language considered to be of lower prestige.[32]

The question is whether the resolute action constantly encouraged by the Language Charter's Committee of Experts is enough to preserve minority languages and identities. What else can the state do when identity is always the result of an individual and personal choice? Digitalization is considered to be an important tool for improving education, helping to foster innovation and create a supportive learning environment.[33] In the following, I will

28 NPE, Section 16/A.

29 NPE, Sections 50(10) and 83(4).

30 *See* at https://dari.oktatas.hu/.

31 Hungary has so far submitted 8 country reports which are available on the website of the Language Charter Secretariat, at https://www.coe.int/en/web/european-charter-regional-or-minority-languages/reports-and-recommendations.

32 *See* the Eighth Periodic Report presented in 2024. MIN-LANG(2024)PR3.

33 Olatunbosun, Bartholomew Joseph *et al.*, 'Digital transformation in education: Strategies for effective implementation', *World Journal of Advanced Research and Reviews*, Vol. 23, Issue 2, 2024, pp. 2785–2799.

explore the possibility of digital support as a substitute for traditional economic, methodological and institutional support tools.

4. Hungarian Digital Education During and After COVID

The rise of digital technology in education around the world has led to significant changes over the recent decade. Hungary has also taken several strategic steps in the field of digital education in the past years. The Digital Education Strategy (hereinafter: DOS) adopted in 2016 aims to promote the digitalization of education. One of the main goals of the DOS is to develop digital competences among both students and teachers, and to improve the digital infrastructure in educational institutions.

As a result of the 2020 COVID-19 pandemic, the Hungarian education system was also forced to make a rapid transition to digital education. This shift highlighted both the strengths and weaknesses of the education system. According to a survey by the State Audit Office of Hungary in 2021, the internet coverage of schools has improved in recent years, but not all families have the right technical background for digital education. This has been a particular problem for disadvantaged pupils, including Roma pupils, and the lack of technical equipment at home has widened educational inequalities. The government is seeking to bridge this gap by providing broadband internet access in education and free laptops for pupils who need them from 2022 onwards.[34]

The State Audit Office's investigation highlights that the Hungarian public education system has shown a quick ability to adapt to the exceptional situation. One advantage is the universal availability of broadband internet access, which has enabled the basic infrastructure for digital education to operate nationwide. This has also put lagging regions on the path to development. During the COVID epidemic, the majority of schools were able to provide some form of digital education, with around 95% of pupils participating in distance learning. A significant effort was made by both teachers and students to learn this new form of education, which helped to ensure a rapid transition.[35]

---

34 According to government figures, between 2022 and 2024, the Government provided a total of 450,000 IT devices.

35 Béla Czifra (ed.), *A digitális oktatás tapasztalatainak értékelése.* Állami Számvevőszék, Budapest, 2021, p. 36.

In addition, there was a challenge in that there were significant differences in teachers' digital competences and methodological skills, which affected the effectiveness of teaching. In addition, the availability, quality and structuring of digital learning materials were not uniform; the use of the National Public Education Portal[36] was not widespread. The fragmentation of online educational platforms, *i.e.,* the mixed use of platforms provided by the state or available on the market, and the lack of a unified educational administration imposed additional burdens on teachers and students alike. The report also found that during COVID, around 5% of pupils were completely excluded from digital education, which put them at risk.[37] The study showed that, although digital education has been rapidly implemented in technical terms, the quality, inclusiveness and sustainability of education are strongly dependent on the development of the pedagogical and organizational context. Experience shows that a complex, long-term digital strategy for public education is needed, integrating the areas of equipment, teacher training, curriculum development and administration.

In the years since the outbreak of the coronavirus, there has been a steady stream of digital developments, both in terms of the availability of digital learning materials and the modular development of the administrative framework (KRÉTA).[38] The framework now provides administrative support, a framework for communication between teachers, students and parents, and a framework for accessing online learning materials.

One of these is the Foreign Language Preparation Module, which also allows the use of artificial intelligence in language learning.[39] However, the service is currently only available in English and German, so it can only be used for national education by the German community, who are the largest linguistic minority in Hungary.

Digital hardware and software tools have been present in Hungarian mother tongue education for years. Sejtes notes that digital tools are used in education, but their real pedagogical integration – especially in humanities subjects such as Hungarian language and literature – still poses many chal-

36 *See* at https://www.nkp.hu/.

37 Czifra 2021, p. 5.

38 Core System for Public Education Registration and Studies (Köznevelési Regisztrációs és Tanulmányi Alaprendszer) abbreviated as KRÉTA, which means "chalk" in English. In March 2025, the KRÉTA system includes 38 modules supporting administration, curricula and teaching methods.

39 Foreign Language Preparation Module (IFM), at https://tudasbazis.ekreta.hu/pages/viewpage.action?pageId=71697082.

lenges.[40] Tools such as interactive whiteboards, student tablets, apps or social media can support the development of language competencies, deepening reading and comprehension skills, and expanding vocabulary through conscious pedagogical planning and integration into the curriculum.[41] However, this requires a change in teacher and learner attitudes, as the teacher is not only a knowledge broker, but also a mentor, a facilitator who guides and supports the learning process and makes learners active and collaborative participants in learning.[42]

If we accept that digital technology can be demonstrably used in the teaching of the majority language of the country,[43] then it is just a step further to properly apply it to minority languages. The use of technology in minority language education, just as in the case of the majority language, is needed both in administration and in preparing teaching materials, which also require the development of teachers' and students' competencies.

5. Conclusions

The use of digital tools in minority education poses additional specific challenges. The creation of digital teaching materials in the mother tongue, the development of digital competencies of teachers and the provision of appropriate infrastructure are all areas that require further continuous development. In order to address these challenges, targeted methodological and financial support for national minority educational institutions is necessary, just like the continuous training of teachers and the development of digital teaching materials in the respective minority language.

The Language Charter's Expert Committee continuously encourages the proactive involvement of the state in national language education. This proactivity, however, not only varies from state to state, but also requires different approaches and tools for each minority group. The precise content must always be adapted to the society, which presupposes a high degree of sensitivity and information on the part of policy-making. We have seen above

40 Györgyi Zs. Sejtes, 'Anyanyelvi nevelés digitális eszközökkel', *Anyanyelv-pedagógia,* Vol. 16, Issue 1, 2023, p. 62.

41 Id. pp. 67–71.

42 Gergő Fegyverneki, 'Új szerepben a magyartanár: digitáliskultúra-azonos pedagógia elméletben és gyakorlatban', *in* János Ollé (ed.), *Oktatás-Informatikai Konferencia Tanulmánykötet,* Budapest, 2014, pp. 274–288.

43 Gyöngyvér Molnár, 'Learning and Instruction: How to Use Technology to Enhance Students' Learning Efficacy', *Journal of Intelligence,* Vol. 12, Issue 7, 2024, p. 64.

that digital technology can now support both the administration of education and pedagogical methods. The real question remains: will minority language speaking children take up minority education, will they enroll in such schools? Does their language have 'value', 'prestige', *i.e.,* are they able to use their mother tongue in the labor market, in their own environment, in their official relations?

Overall, the digital landscape of minority education in Hungary is mixed. While significant progress has been made in the development of infrastructure and digital competences, we have not yet reached the end of the road, and there are still challenges to be faced in a number of areas. In the future, particular attention should be paid to improving access to digital education for disadvantaged and minority pupils, developing teachers' digital competences and ensuring opportunities for mother tongue training.

However, alongside the widespread use of digital tools, it is also necessary to develop *personal relationships* and skills. Schools are not only about knowledge transfer, but also about socialization and inclusion. In terms of minority education, education therefore serves two purposes: the preservation and transmission of minority identity, and the social integration and peaceful coexistence between ethnic groups.

Some Issues in the Regulation of Victim Protection in the Hungarian Legal System, with Special Regard to the Crime of Harassment

*Ágnes Czine**

Abstract

In today's legal system, victim protection is becoming increasingly important at international, EU and national levels. This paper focuses on one aspect of this: the protection of victims of harassment from a criminal law perspective. The paper covers Hungarian legislation on victim protection, based on relevant international and EU regulations. It examines the latest criminal law instruments and case law of the Hungarian Constitutional Court. The paper also examines whether current legislation on harassment can effectively protect victims.

Keywords: victim protection, victimology, EU victim protection directive, privacy, harassment

1. Introduction

Protecting victims is an important issue of our time and has been the subject of extensive literature and academic research. This has resulted in concrete measures to support victims around the world, including in Europe. Fortunately, Hungarian national legislation is largely aligned with the EU's directives on this subject, with only a few gaps in the legislation. The relevant harmonization is the result of a long development process, the most important elements of which I will outline briefly below.

* Ágnes Czine: professor of law, Károli Gáspár University of the Reformed Church, Budapest; justice, Constitutional Court of Hungary, czine.agnes@kre.hu.

2. On the Concept of Victim

The key problem with the concept of victim is that it can be defined from many different aspects, depending on the point of view of the analysis. We may approach victimized persons from different points of reference, for example, by what caused their harm – war, disaster, crime, *etc.* –, or by whether the harm caused was direct or indirect, or by categorizing at victim groups in terms of their characteristics. Defining the general notion of victim requires careful consideration. The impact of a single trauma can be wide-ranging, therefore, identifying those in need is a key issue when allocating resources and capacities.

The notion of victim has developed gradually, similar to other legal concepts. In the early centuries of known history, scarce resources did not allow for the possibility to help people who became victims and consequently had poorer life prospects. Not only did they lack the material resources, but also the expertise, the cohesion and the institutional system to assist victims. At the same time, there were always people who helped those in need, because they loved their fellow human beings. As with most social issues that affected many, the protection of the victims was addressed by the Church in the context of religion.

There were only a few people who took up the cause of helping the victims. A fine example of this is the life and deeds of Saint Elizabeth of the Royal House of Árpád – daughter of King Andrew II of Hungary. The wife, mother and then widow of the Margrave of Thuringia, she gave all her support to those in need. Although she was a royal heiress, she was admired as a saint for her humble life and her devotion to the poor and the sick. She was canonized by the Church a few years after her death in 1235.[1] Her life is just another example of how in Europe it was primarily the church, priests, nuns and monks who took it upon themselves to provide care and assistance to victims.

Suffice to think of *asylum,* which was essentially a refuge. It was an early approach to human rights, ensured for those who fled from aggressors and combat. In many cases, it was the walls of the temples and cathedrals that provided the protection that was necessary for physical survival. No wonder, therefore, that victim protection was closely linked to religion and church-related organizations in the early periods of history.[2]

1 Saint Elizabeth of the Royal House of Árpád (1207–1231) was a younger contemporary of Saint Francis.

2 Ágnes Czine, 'Néhány gondolat az áldozatvédelem kialakulásáról', *in* Andrea Domokos *et al.* (eds.), *Áldozati szerepek,* L'Harmattan, Budapest, 2025, pp. 189–206.

The secular approach to victim protection appeared relatively late. It is said that the word *'victim'* was first used in the 1660s to refer to a person who had been injured, tortured or killed by another person. However, the concept of a victim of a crime was essentially non-existent until the 17th century.[3] It was at this time that the victim was slowly recognized as a part of the justice system, and some argued that without a victim there would be no need for courts. As a result of these developments, research focusing on victims gradually emerged.

3. The Development and Main Elements of Victim Protection Legislation

It was mainly the second half of the 20th century that brought revolutionary changes in the scientific approach to, and institutional framework for the protection of victims, which emerged first at international, and then at national level. The horrors of World War II had an impact on the emergence of victimology and the shift of attention towards victims. This resulted in the replacement, or at least supplementation of church victim support by a range of secular solutions and institutions. For the purposes of this paper's topic, I would like to highlight two trends: *(i)* the scientific, theoretical development, *(ii)* and the development of international legal regulation related to victim protection.

3.1. Scientific Progress

Two fundamental approaches to the concept of victimhood have been identified: these are the active and passive approaches. *(i)* In the context of *active* approach, the term 'sacrifice' denotes the act of relinquishing something and bestowing it upon another, such as a deity or a superior. In English, the original form of the term is denoted by the word *'sacrificium',* which also conveys its religious character derived from the Latin version of the word. *(ii)* The *passive* approach emphasizes suffering, which implies helplessness and innocence. The notion of 'victim' in this sense comes from the Latin root *'vic-*

3 Jo-Anne Wemmers, 'A short history of victimology', *in* Otmar Hagemann *et al.* (eds.), *Victimology, Victim Assistance, and Criminal Justice, Perspectives Shared by International Experts at Inter-University Centre of Dubrovnik,* Niederrhein University of Applied Sciences, Mönchengladbach, 2010, at https://ssrn.com/*Abstract*=2482627.

tima.'[4] The latter concept is the basis for the discipline of victimology, which will be outlined below.

The development of victimology was given a boost by World War II as a sub-discipline of criminology: the scientific study of the victims of crime. Its aim is to study the relationship between victims and offenders; to identify those particularly vulnerable to crime and the victim within the criminal justice system.

The scientific study of victimology dates back to the 1940s and 1950s. Two criminologists, *Mendelsohn* and *Von Hentig,* began exploring the field of victimology by creating 'typologies' – as such, they are considered the 'fathers of victimology'. These scientists, the new 'victimologists', started studying the behavior and vulnerability of victims. *Mendelsohn* created a typology of six types of victims, in which only the first type was innocent, the other five types having contributed in some way to their own injury, having been involved in their victimization. *Von Hentig* (1948) studied homicide victims and said that the most likely type of victim was the 'depressed type', who is an easy target, careless and unsuspecting. This was followed by *Wolfgang*'s (1958) research, whose theory was that homicide victimization was in fact caused by the victim's unconscious suicidal urge.[5]

All these statements and typologies emphasize that victims are not entirely 'innocent', because they have certain characteristics that contribute to their becoming victims of crime. Victimologists have attributed this to a variety of factors, such as the external characteristics of the victims, their behavior, their social status and other causes. It should be added that the assessment of victimization is mainly a probabilistic approach, but there is no doubt that anyone, even the person with the best chances, can become a victim of crime. There are, however, factors that provoke criminals, offering perpetrators the opportunity to commit crimes based on certain personal characteristics, behaviors, situations, locations or motives.

3.2. The Main Elements of International Law on Victims

The emergence and further development of the scientific basis of the discipline of victim protection provided the theoretical foundations for the de-

4 László Levente Balogh, 'A magyar nemzeti áldozatnarratíva változásai', *Korall,* Vol. 59, 2015, p. 37.

5 Tiwari, Pramod, 'Victimology: a Sub-Discipline of Criminology', *Dehradun Law Review,* Vol. 4, Issue 1, 2012, pp. 88–89.

velopment of international legal instruments and then national legislation. First, I will look at the general rules on the protection of victims, and then at a specific category of victim, namely the victims of harassment.

From among the relevant international documents, I would like to highlight the declaration known as the Magna Charta of Victims, which has had a major impact on academic research. In 1985, the United Nations issued a declaration on the Basic Principles of Justice for Victims of Crime and Abuse of Power (hereafter: the 1985 UN Declaration), which for the first time defined at international level and in a general way *(i)* the concept of victim and *(ii)* the rights of victims.

Ad (i) Definition of victims. The definition of 'victims' is defined as persons who have suffered harm, individually or collectively, including physical or mental injury, emotional distress, economic loss, and whose fundamental rights have been substantially impaired by acts or omissions in violation of the criminal law of the Member States in force, including those prohibiting abuse of power. The term 'victim' includes close family members or dependents of the direct victim, as well as persons who have been injured in the course of intervening to assist victims in distress or to prevent victimization.[6] The new features of the general concept of victimhood: it *(i)* include not only the victims of crime, but also the victims of abuse of power and human rights violations, regardless of whether the state in question criminalizes the act in question; and it encompasses *(ii)* not only the person against whom the act is directly directed, but also those who suffer collateral damage, such as immediate family members or witnesses to the specific act, or persons who may have intervened or assisted in the crime; and *(iii)* the definition of harm has been extended, which may include physical, mental or emotional injury, as well as economic loss.[7]

Ad (ii) Rights of victims. The rights of victims are included in the document. These are the rights to be treated with dignity and compassion (point 4); access to justice, legal redress (points 4–5); immediate compensation (point 4); information (point 6/a); legal assistance (point 6/c); defence, witness protection (point 6/d); compensation and reparation (points 8–13); right to necessary financial, medical, psychological and social assistance (points 14–17).

---

6 1985 UN Declaration, approved by A/RES/34, 29 November 1985, points 1–3.

7 Ilona Görgényi, 'Az áldozat fogalmának és jogainak újraszabályozása az Európai Unióban',. *in* Andrea Borbíró *et al.* (eds.), *A büntető hatalom korlátainak megtartása: a büntetés mint végső eszköz. Tanulmányok Gönczöl Katalin tiszteletére,* ELTE Eötvös, Budapest, 2014, p. 175.

European regional international organizations have been at the forefront in the development of the relevant regional regulation. EU legislation on victim protection was created with the aim of strengthening cooperation between Member States and developing common values. The protection, safeguarding and promotion of victims' rights is an integral part of the EU's general objectives, in particular in the field of the rule of law and the protection of human rights. An important step in the development of the legal framework for the protection of victims is the Council's *Framework Decision 2001/220/JHA on victims' rights,* adopted in 2001, which requires Member States to guarantee respect and protection to victims.[8] The aim of the Decision is to improve the legal situation of victims and to provide them with adequate information and support regarding the consequences of crime. *Directive 2012/29/EU,*[9] which entered into force in 2012, further developed victims' rights and emphasized that all victims have the right to personal and psychological support. The Directive requires Member States to ensure that victims have access to the necessary information and the right to participate in criminal proceedings. Another important aspect of Directive 2012/29/EU is that it extends victims' rights not only to the judicial proceedings of criminal offences, but also to the pre- and post-criminal phases. This means that Member States must ensure that victims have access to appropriate psychological and financial support and legal assistance. Within the legal framework, EU law requires that victims are informed of their rights and of how to access these forms of support.

The EU has also launched a number of programmes to reinforce victim protection and support. These include national centers that provide comprehensive information to victims and help them receive the support they need. The programmes aim to ensure that the rehabilitation and reintegration of victims is smooth, despite cultural and legal differences. The EU system for victim protection is therefore evolving, with a steady increase in obligations and mechanisms to protect rights across the Member States. However, it is important that victims are aware of their rights and the resources available, as the support they can access can effectively contribute to their recovery and reintegration into society.

---

8 Framework decision 2001/220/JHA: Council Framework Decision of 15 March 2001 on the standing of victims in criminal proceedings.

9 Directive 2012/29/EU of the European Parliament and of the Council of 25 October 2012 establishing minimum standards on the rights, support and protection of victims of crime, and replacing Council Framework Decision 2001/220/JHA.

The Directive clarified the definition of 'victim' [Article 2(1)(a)] and did not link victimhood to the fact that it can only be the consequence of an offence under national law.[10] The importance of clarifying the concept lies in the fact that it is only on the basis of the determination of victimhood that it is possible to determine the means and benefits that may be provided to a particular category of victim. The Directive sets minimum standards for the rights, support and protection of victims of crime and ensures that victims of a crime are recognized and treated with respect. However, the European Commission's 2020 evaluation recognizes that there are shortcomings in the practical implementation of the Directive by Member States. This is due to, among others, the fact that some of its provisions are not specific enough. The review of the Directive is part of the EU's strategy on victims' rights 2020–2025, which aims to strengthen the rights of victims of crime across the EU.[11]

However, the EU has not stopped at this Directive in its quest for developing victim protection but continues to monitor the activities and implementation of the Directive in the Member States and develops the necessary programmes. As a result of this work, on 24 June 2020 the European Commission adopted the first *EU Strategy on Victims' Rights (2020–2025).* Its main objective is to ensure that all victims of crime, regardless of where in the EU and under what circumstances the crime occurred, can fully invoke and enjoy their rights. To this end, it outlines actions to be implemented by the European Commission, Member States and civil society.[12]

In July 2023, the European Commission adopted a *proposal to revise* Directive 2012/29/EU on victims' rights. The review was accompanied by an extensive consultation process and an impact assessment following the evaluation of the Directive.[13] The evaluation shows that, while the Directive has broadly delivered the expected benefits and positively affected victims' rights, specific problems remain regarding victims' rights under the Directive. The Commission's proposal to amend the Directive therefore foresees targeted measures to enable victims to better assert their rights under

10 Ágnes Czine, 'Néhány gondolat az áldozat, a sértett és a passzív alany fogalmi összefüggéseiről", *Magyar Jog*, Vol. 70, Issue 3, 2023, p. 145.

11 *See* at https://www.europarl.europa.eu/RegData/etudes/BRIE/2023/747432/EPRS_BRI(2023)747432_EN.pdf.

12 *See* at https://commission.europa.eu/strategy-and-policy/policies/justice-and-fundamental-rights/criminal-justice/protecting-victims-rights/eu-strategy-victims-rights-2020-2025_en.

13 *See* at https://www.brusselstimes.com/sponsored/840815/what-is-next-for-the-eu-rules-on-victims-rights.

the Directive. The proposal covers five areas: better information for victims, improving the assessment of the protection needs of vulnerable victims (*e.g.* children), increasing the involvement of specialized services, making legal advice more widely available, improving access to compensation.[14] The amendment is currently under negotiation before the European Parliament and the Council.[15] This is expected to have an impact on national legislation.

4. The Development of Legislation Tailored to Specific Victim Groups

First the UN and then regional international organizations have adopted conventions for specific categories of victims. The identification and separate treatment of the characteristics of specific categories of victims allows them to be treated individually, and the specific needs of victims to be identified as fully as possible, and their grievances to be addressed for further harm to be prevented. One specific group of victims is the category of victims of harassment.

4.1. Victims of Harassment

One in two women in the European Union has been sexually harassed at least once since the age of 15 and 32% of victims say the perpetrator was their superior, colleague or client. 75% of women in skilled or senior management positions; 61% of women in the service sector have been sexually harassed.[16] According to UNICEF's online survey conducted in Hungary, the majority of child respondents, 60%, clicked on the answer that they had been bullied online. When asked where the most cyberbullying occurs from among the platforms, 53% answered Facebook and 43% said Instagram. Online bullying is more prevalent among girls (55%) than boys (27%), but for both genders, the number of respondents who have experienced such

14 Directive of the European Parliament and of the Council amending Directive 2012/29/EU establishing minimum standards on the rights, support and protection of victims of crime and replacing Council Framework Decision 2001/220/JHA.

15 *See* at https://eur-lex.europa.eu/legal-content/HU/ALL/?uri=CELEX%3A52023PC0424.

16 European Parliament resolution of 1 June 2023 on sexual harassment in the EU and the evaluation of the MeToo movement (2022/2138(INI)), point E.

unwanted contact is high.[17] According to statistics from the Public Prosecutor's Office, the number of registered harassment offences in our country ranged between 4600 and 5300 annually between 2018 and 2022.[18] A large number of harassment offences remain undetected, as many do not know where to turn, or in which cases harassment is legally sanctioned.

The US led the way in criminalizing harassment. In 1990, the State of California became the first to enact a law making it a crime to stalk someone. Stalking is when one intentionally and repeatedly stalks or harasses another person, on at least two occasions, and makes serious threats with the intent to cause a reasonable fear for the victim's safety or that of their family.

Legal definitions became more varied and sophisticated over time, and around the turn of the millennium the crime of harassment appeared in the criminal codes of several European countries. For example, in Belgium *(Nötigung)* in 1998, in the Netherlands *(belaging)* in 2000, in Germany *(Gewaltschutzgesetz)* in 2001.[19]

The spreading of the concept of harassment and its criminalization in Europe dates back to the 1990s and the millennium. The instruments of European law and international law, in particular the recommendations, directives and resolutions drawn up by the EC, later the EU, and the Council of Europe, played a significant role. Suffice to mention the most important of these: the Commission's *Recommendation 92/131/EEC* of 27 November 1991 on the protection of the privacy of women and men at work[20] focused on so-called sexual harassment (at the workplace) and measures to combat it. The most recent provisions on discrimination and (sexual) harassment are set out in *Directive 2002/73/EC* of the European Parliament and of the Council of 23 September 2002 amending Directive 76/207/EEC on the application of the principle of equal treatment for men and women as regards employment, vocational training and promotion.[21] A third document is also worth mentioning, namely *Directive 2000/43/EC* of 29 June 2000 imple-

17 *See* at https://unicef.hu/igy-segitunk/hireink/keves-gyerek-fordul-felnotthoz-ha-a-neten-zaklatjak.

18 Information on crime data 2022, at https://ugyeszseg.hu/wp-content/uploads/2023/11/tajekoztato-a-bunozes-2022.-evi-adatairol.pdf.

19 Edit Fogarassy, 'Zaklatás: egy ismeretlen fogalom a magyar jogban', *Jogtudományi Közlöny,* Vol. 57, Issue 2, 2002, pp. 73–78.

20 92/131/EEC: Commission Recommendation of 27 November 1991 on the protection of the dignity of women and men at work.

21 Council Directive 76/207/EEC of 9 February 1976 on the implementation of the principle of equal treatment for men and women as regards access to employment, vocational training and promotion, and working conditions.

menting the principle of equal treatment between persons irrespective of racial or ethnic origin, which covers ethnic and racial harassment.[22]

As far as the more recent international instruments are concerned, the Council of Europe Convention on preventing and combating violence against women and domestic violence,[23] popularly known as the *Istanbul Convention* is most prominent, which Hungary signed on 14 March 2014 but has not ratified since. Article 34 of the Convention contains the threat of harassment, which refers to the general concept of harassment, while Article 40 sets out the internationally recognized concept of sexual harassment.

Traditionally, legal scholarship has distinguished three main categories of harassment. *(i)* Protection against ethnic and racial harassment is covered by Directive 2000/43/EC. *(ii)* Protection against harassment in the workplace, often identified as sexual harassment, is provided for in Recommendation 92/131/EEC of the Commission of 27 November 1991 on the protection of the privacy of women and men at work. *(iii)* Personally motivated harassment is when the perpetrator typically harasses the victim for a long period of time, persistently, continuously or repeatedly. This may be considered a third category, since there is a wide range of possible motives for such harassment.[24]

4.2. Regulation of Harassment in Hungary

The legal regulation of harassment is contained in several pieces of legislation in the Hungarian legal system. Victims' rights and protections – established through the implementation of the aforementioned EU Directives[25] – are enshrined in Act CXXXV of 2005 on assistance to victims of crime and

---

22 Fogarassy 2002, p. 73. Council Directive 2000/43/EC of 29 June 2000 implementing the principle of equal treatment between persons irrespective of racial or ethnic origin.

23 *See e.g.* Council Decision on the signing, on behalf of the European Union, of the Council of Europe Convention on preventing and combating violence against women and domestic violence. COM(2016) 111 final.

24 Ágnes Czine, 'Szerelmi téboly ellen nincs büntetőjogi védelem', *Acta Universitatis Szegediensis: Acta Juridica et Politica,* Vol. 81, 2018, p. 201. *See also* https://birosag.hu/hirek/kategoria/magazin/ne-valaszolj-ne-vagj-vissza-es-mentsd-bizonyitekot-zaklatas-elleni.

25 *See* Council Directive 2000/43/EC of 29 June 2000 implementing the principle of equal treatment between persons irrespective of racial or ethnic origin; Council Directive 2000/43/EC of 29 June 2000 implementing the principle of equal treatment between persons irrespective of racial or ethnic origin; Act CXXV of 2003, Section 65, points a, and f.

on state compensation. Owing to of the approximation of national law to EU law, the concept of harassment was defined for the first time in Hungarian law by Act CXXV of 2003 on equal treatment and the promotion of equal opportunities (hereinafter: the Equal Treatment Act). In essence, the concept contains the conceptual elements of the EU Directive cited above.[26] The Equal Treatment Act established the Equal Treatment Authority,[27] which may order the termination of the unlawful situation, may publish its decision and impose a fine on the offender.[28] A typical place of this type of harassment is the workplace.

4.2.1. Constitutional Protection of Privacy

It is also worth mentioning the constitutional basis of criminal law protection, or the protected legal subject matter: privacy. Since the formulation of the statutory definition of harassment, the Hungarian Constitutional Court has elaborated in detail the aspects of privacy protection, which contained a fundamental rights argument based on the pervious Constitution. In its *Decision No. 17/2014. (V. 30.) AB*, the Constitutional Court examined Articles II and VI of the Fundamental Law, recalling its interpretation of the right to privacy and its relationship to the right to human dignity laid down in *Decision No. 32/2013. (XI. 22.) AB*. It held that Article VI(1) of the Fundamental Law comprehensively protects the private sphere: the private and family life, home, relations and reputation of the individual. With regard to the core essence of privacy, the Constitutional Court upheld the Constitutional Court's previous practice that the essence of privacy is that it is not possible for others to enter, or be seen by others against the will of the person

26 Harassment is a conduct of sexual or other nature which is offensive to human dignity, which is related to a characteristic of the person concerned as defined in Section 8 of Equal Treatment Act and which has the purpose or effect of creating an intimidating, hostile, humiliating, degrading or offensive environment towards a person. Equal Treatment Act, Section 10.

27 The state initially performed these tasks within the framework of an independent administrative body. Later, legislation transferred this power to the ombudsman. According to Act CXXVII of 2020, the powers of the Equal Treatment Authority was transferred to the Commissioner for Fundamental Rights from 1 January 2021. Within the framework of administrative authority proceedings, the commissioner shall act in matters concerning equal treatment and the promotion of equal opportunities, in accordance with the relevant procedural rules.

28 Equal Treatment Act, Section 17/A.

concerned.[29] It pointed out that there is a particularly close link between the right to privacy guaranteed by Article VI(1) of the Fundamental Law and the right to human dignity guaranteed by Article II. Article II establishes the protection of the inviolable area of privacy, which is completely excluded from any state interference, as it is the basis of human dignity. However, the protection of privacy under the Fundamental Law is not limited to the internal or intimate sphere, which is also protected by Article II, but also extends to the private sphere in the broad sense (relationships) and to the spatial sphere in which private and family life unfolds (the home). In addition, personal image (the right to reputation) is also protected in its own right.[30] This private and intimate sphere is protected by criminal law through the criminalization of offence of harassment.

4.2.2. The Nature and Characteristics of the Criminal Law Offence

Harassment according to the Hungarian Criminal Code, is punishable if it is committed as a deliberate act with direct intent *(dolus directus)*. Since the act is aimed at achieving a specific goal as defined by law, e.g., instilling fear, it can only be committed with direct intent.[31]

The conduct of committing the offence is the systematic and persistent harassment of others,[32] making threats,[33] and creating the appearance of an offensive or threatening act.[34] Today's criminal law definition of harassment has been developed gradually in several stages and will certainly continue to evolve. In Hungary, Section 4 of Act CLXII of 2007 introduced the statutory definition of harassment into Hungarian criminal law, partly by adopting the wording of dangerous threat in Section 151(1)(a) of Act LXIX of 1999 on Administrative Offences, in force until 1 January 2008, and partly by criminalizing harassing, intrusive and annoying behavior.[35]

The new Criminal Code (Act C of 2012), in its Section 222(2)(b) included the new offence of harassment. Accordingly, a person commits har-

29 Decision No. 36/2005. (X. 5.) AB, ABH 2005, 390, 400.

30 Decision No. 3018/2016. (II. 2.) AB, Reasoning [27]–[29].

31 István Kónya (ed.), *Magyar büntetőjog. Kommentár a gyakorlat számára,* HVG-ORAC, Budapest, 2015, p. 856.

32 Section 222(1) of the Hungarian Criminal Code.

33 Section 222(2)(a) of the Hungarian Criminal Code.

34 Section 222(2)(b) of the Hungarian Criminal Code.

35 Anikó Gelányi, 'A zaklatás bűncselekményének jellemzése, különös tekintettel annak telekommunikációs eszköz útján történő megvalósítására', *JURA,* Vol. 16, Issue 2, 2010, p. 194.

assment who gives the impression that an event is occurring that is harmful to or directly endangers the life, physical integrity or health of another person. Section 2 of Act XLIII of 2012 amending Act C of 2012 on the Criminal Code amended the definition of offences and added to the list of aggravated cases the abuse of influence and the offence of harming a public official at a place or time that is incompatible with the official's official activities.[36]

The seventh amendment to Hungary's Fundamental Law reinforced the protection of privacy. Consequently, public officials also have the right to rest without any disturbances following their official duties, for example at home, during their holidays, and not to be harassed. In view of this, the legislator has provided in Section 222(3) of the Criminal Code adequate protection against conduct that constitutes harassment under criminal law, when it is carried out against a public official in a place or at a time that is incompatible with their official activities.[37]

Subsequently, a further amendment was made for the protection of the interests of the child. An aggravated case of harassment was introduced, applicable to cases where harassment is committed against a minor under the age of eighteen. The purpose of this was to deter perpetrators from harassing children by threatening them with a more severe punishment.[38]

The legal tools used to deal with harassment cases, while gradually evolving, face many obstacles in practice. The complexity of the evidentiary procedures and the difficulties in enforcing injunctions pose serious challenges to legislators and authorities.[39]

The amendment made to Section 222(1a) of the Criminal Code, which entered into force on 1 March 2025, sought to resolve the possible jurisprudential disputes as to whether an unlawful and purposeful contact with the victim following a clear official order (*e.g.*, a restraining order) based on an earlier criminal act constitutes harassment. The amendment clarifies that such conduct also constitutes harassment.[40]

---

36 Viktor Bérces, 'A zaklatás törvényi tényállásába ütköző cselekmények minősítése és bizonyítási kérdései', *Magyar Jog*, Vol. 64, Issue 7–8, 2017, p. 457.

37 Ministerial explanatory memorandum to Section 12 of Act XLIII of 2018 amending Act C of 2012 on the Criminal Code.

38 Section 21 of Act LXXIX of 2021 on stricter action against pedophile offenders and amending certain Acts in order to protect children.

39 Tamás Hornung, 'A zaklatás büntetőjogi szabályozása és gyakorlati kihívásai Magyarországon', *Magyar Rendészet*, Vol. 24, Issue 4, 2024, pp. 45–63.

40 Explanatory memorandum to Section 22 of Act LXIV of 2024a on the need to further effectively combat online fraud and other acts.

5. Some Remarks on the Regulation of Harassment

The concept and criminal law protection of harassment currently suffices to regulate this area of law, however, as with all rules, it is far from being fully satisfactory. Below, I list a few elements I believe are worth reflecting on to find new regulatory solutions.

(i) Evidence. Harassment is not always easy to prove, and the detection rate is not high. Not only because it is a matter of appreciation how regular or persistent the repeated harassing behavior is. The main problem is the difficulty of proof. The difficulties of proof stem from a number of factors. For example, harassment often takes the form of clandestine, ongoing behavior and is therefore difficult to document. Victims often do not have sufficient evidence, as most of the harassment does not take place in public. In many cases, the description of the harassment event is based on subjective experiences and may not reach the threshold to alarm an outside observer. It is often difficult for victims to accurately delineate what behavior of the harasser, rather than other circumstances, has caused them fear and distress, rendering legal action difficult. The involvement of witnesses is also problematic, as harassment does not always take place in the presence of others, so there is no witness testimony or witnesses are unwilling to take the risk of testifying. The applicable legal framework and the assessment of evidence may also pose problems, as harassment is not always obvious and the credibility of the victim can easily be questioned by the defence. These factors make it particularly difficult to prove harassment, and many victims are more likely to withdraw rather than to take legal action.

(ii) Harassment. Very often the perpetrator of harassment and the victim interact owing to their pre-existing relationship (*e.g.* sharing earlier emotional or family bonds, or them being neighborhood or workplace acquaintances). It has been suggested that the victim should not react to the harasser or take counter measures, as this will only fuel the fire, but also because it may confuse the facts and thus jeopardize criminal conviction. Why is this wrong? Harassment is essentially a unilateral activity, harassing, making threats, etc. If the victim does not tolerate this and immediately returns the harassment, a reciprocity is established, but it is the perpetrator and not the victim who will be held accountable. The *Kúria* of Hungary has already given a legal interpretation to this situation in a relatively early decision. Accordingly,

> "[t]he unlawfulness of the conduct in question is not in itself altered by the fact that the perpetrator is also the victim of the same conduct. In the

case of conduct which is distinct in time, this does not require any particular explanation. In the case of conduct which reacts directly to another at the same time, the succession of attack and defence may, as succession, confer on the defendant immunity from liability for his acts on the grounds of legitimate defence [...] The possible reciprocity of the conduct of the two parties is irrelevant, because the reciprocity of the conduct at the same time, which is an element of the legal situation, necessarily eliminates the arbitrariness of both parties, since it cannot be considered unilateral. Reciprocity with a give/take substance does not in fact lead (as does the acceptance of a challenge in the context of a legitimate defence) to the exclusion of criminal liability."[41]

(iii) Abnormal state of mind. In the case chosen as an example, the facts of the case show that the female defendant and the male victim worked at the same workplace. The female defendant was a colleague of the victim, had graduated from university, was married, and after her employment ended, she called the victim daily from two phone numbers. She not only phoned the victim, but also sent approximately 40 multimedia messages about herself and more than 15,500 text messages to the victim's phone over the course of a year. The calls, the multimedia messages and the thousands of text messages were intended to prove her love for the victim and she visited the victim in person on several occasions at his workplace and at his home. The victim did not answer the defendant's telephone calls and did not respond to her multimedia messages or her telephone messages. A year later, the victim filed a complaint against the accused for the offence of harassment in violation of Section 222(1) of the Criminal Code and filed a private complaint with legal effect, and requested the punishment of the accused. On the basis of the evidentiary proceedings conducted, the court accepted the opinion of the forensic experts and found that the accused had been suffering from a pathological mental condition known as love madness for several years, which clearly excluded her criminal liability in the case in question. The court found that the accused had committed the offence of harassment in violation of Section 222(1) of the Criminal Code, but her offence of harassment was not punishable, because her pathological state of mind precluded her criminal liability. Therefore, the court acquitted her of the charges brought against her.

The example is quite unique, as the presence of unaccountable perpetrators is rare in harassment cases, but the current criminal sanctions system

41 Judgment of the *Kúria,* BH2014.169.

cannot provide an adequate solution to protect victims in such cases. Compulsory medical treatment could be an option, but the legal conditions for this are not met in the absence of a violent crime against the person.[42] In such cases, instruments beyond criminal law could be considered. The victim can initiate the placement of the accused under guardianship with the prosecutor or the guardianship authority.[43] However, the defendant under guardianship can also text and phone the victim. Thus, she could make the victim's life difficult by sending thousands of harassing text messages over the next years. For the time being, however, there is no doubt: there is no criminal law protection against love madness.[44]

(iv) Private motion and date of commission. Harassment can be committed in a systematic and sustained series of acts, so in practice it can be problematic to determine the date when the crime was committed. This, however, is particularly important because under Section 231(2) of the Criminal Code harassment is prosecuted upon private motion and there are 30 days to file such a motion. In practice, in criminal proceedings for harassment, it is understandably difficult to determine the date of the threat to commit any criminal offence of violence or public nuisance against an individual. The victim, particularly in the case of offences against relatives, is often the victim of a long process of harassment and cannot, afterwards, tell the exact date on which the threats were made.

According to the relevant judicial practice the person submitting a private motion cannot, at the time of doing so, seek to hold someone liable for future, as yet unrealized acts. When a private motion is filed, the criminal claim is only valid for the act alleged therein; the criminal claim must be refiled for any subsequent acts of the same nature.[45] Thus, a new private motion is required for further acts committed after the private motion has been filed.[46] The aforementioned prosecutorial investigation found that this was rarely enforced in the practice of the public prosecutor's office or the courts.

The Prosecutor General's Office suggests that a new practice should be applied by the investigating authority to solve the problems raised by the validity of private motions. The victim must be informed by the investigating authority that it is not sufficient to make a statement about the private

42 Ágnes Vadász, 'Hogyan tudnék élni nélküled? Avagy a párkapcsolatok megszűnése utáni zaklatás szankcionálásának aggályai', *Ügyészek Lapja,* Vol. 28, Issue 5, 2021, pp. 17–30.
43 According to Act V of 2013 on the Civil Code, Section 2:28(1).
44 Czine 2018, p. 200.
45 *See* BH.2014.169.
46 *See* ÍH.2014.86.

motion when filing the report or during the witness interview. If the perpetrator continues his activities, the victim must also make a statement about maintaining the private motion within 30 days with regard to subsequent acts.[47]

6. Outlook

The protection of victims of harassment can only be ensured through adequate legislation. In particular, for the purposes of the case mentioned above, the legal system should provide for a regulatory mechanism which offers proper protection against a harasser suffering from a pathological state of mind when committing the crime, for which they cannot be punished. It is clear, that the solution to such situations for the protection of victims is to resort to instruments within the realm of the health care system and to develop a procedure to avert attacks from abusers suffering from love madness.

47 *See* (in Hungarian): *Összefoglaló jelentés a zaklatással kapcsolatos ügyészségi gyakorlat vizsgálatáról.* Legfőbb Ügyészség, Budapest, 2015, at https://ugyeszseg.hu/repository/mkudok7747.pdf., p. 7.

Part VI
– Review of Hungarian scholarly literature

Part VI
Review of Hungarian scholarly literature

Tamás Molnár and Ramses A. Wessel, Interactions Between EU Law and International Law: Juxtaposed Perspectives (Book Review)

Edward Elgar, Cheltenham, 2024, 328p, ISBN 978 1 80088 875 3, eISBN 978 1 80088 876 0

*Birgit Hollaus**

1. Introduction

Interactions Between EU Law and International Law is co-authored by Tamás Molnár and Ramses A. Wessel. Tamás Molnár is Legal Research Officer at the EU Agency for Fundamental Rights and Lecturer at Corvinus University of Budapest, Hungary.[1] Ramses A. Wessel is Professor of European Law and Head of the Department of European and Economic Law at the University of Groningen, the Netherlands.

Both authors are recognized experts in the law and practice of the ever-expanding field of EU external relations law, where international law and EU law are set to meet and interact. For this reason alone, the co-authors are a perfect fit for the present exploration of the multi-layered interrelationship between international law and EU law. Yet, there is something even more intriguing about this author pairing. Each of the co-authors has strong roots in both the international law and the EU law communities,[2] and this is re-

* Birgit Hollaus: postdoctoral teaching and research associate, WU Vienna University of Economics and Business, Institute for Law and Governance, Vienna, birgit.hollaus@wu.ac.at.

1 At the time of this book review, Tamás Molnár is also affiliated with the Institute for Law and Governance, WU Vienna University of Economics and Business.

2 *See e.g.* their engagement with the European Society of International Law (ESIL), and, in particular, its interest group 'The EU as a Global Actor'.

flected in their approaches to their topic of common interest, as they move between international law and EU law perspectives, never losing sight of the other. By teaming up and putting on both sets of 'lenses', Molnár and Wessel are a living example of what they hope to achieve with this book: to initiate a constructive dialogue across – artificial – disciplinary divides for the advancement of the study of the interactions between international law and EU law.

In their book, Molnár and Wessel have skillfully crafted 10 harmonious chapters to cover the broad topic of interactions between international law and EU law. Each chapter could be read in isolation and still enrich the reader. However, the reader should be encouraged to follow the thoughtful sequence of chapters for an enlightening tour d'horizon of the two-way process of interactions between two legal orders. Whether one belongs to the international law or EU law camp, this enjoyable read will invigorate everyone with its wealth of insights.

2. Juxtaposing Perspectives: Need, Value and USP

It may not come as a surprise that a book which focuses on the interactions between international law and EU law takes as its starting point the claim for 'EU autonomy'. After all, the (now) CJEU's famous assertion that the founding Treaties have created a new legal order[3] – as Molnár and Wessel go on to show – laid the 'necessary' foundation for its conceptual separation from the international legal order.[4] What began with *van Gend en Loos* is thus the very reason for the need to investigate how the separate legal orders interact.[5] However, Molnár and Wessel direct our attention to the (even) broader consequences that follow from an autonomous EU legal order.

Molnár and Wessel highlight how the separation of EU law from international law, as established by the Court, explains why international law and EU law have become separate fields of study.[6] This is a fact that we may simply accept. Yet, its repercussions are particularly visible in the study of the EU's engagement with the international plane, where each field applies

3 Judgment of 5 February 1963, *Case C-26/62, Van Gend en Loos*, ECLI:EU:C:1963:1.
4 Tamás Molnár & Ramses A Wessel, *Interactions Between EU Law and International Law: Juxtaposed Perspectives*, Edward Elgar, Cheltenham, 2024, p. 57.
5 Id. p. 260.
6 Id. p. 11.

its own perspective and narrative to what are essentially questions of shared interest, be it the participation of the EU in international law-making efforts or the EU's international responsibility for internationally wrongful acts. However, the "picture is so complex that a single narrative can hardly capture it",[7] so that the picture remains blurred.[8]

In their book, Molnár and Wessel seek to provide a compelling counterexample to the usual practice by taking both an international law and an EU law perspective on the complex interplay between the two separate legal orders. Molnár and Wessel do not present these perspectives in isolation, but juxtapose them. By juxtaposing perspectives, the co-authors are able to direct our focus to real – as opposed to perceived – differences between the two legal orders, and also draw our attention to parallels and commonalities as a basis for mutual learning. Thus, as also Jan Klabbers highlights in his foreword,[9] the book's presentation of a juxtaposed perspective sets it apart from competing titles and thus provides a unique selling proposition (USP). In this way, the co-authors offer not just another book on the EU's external relations, but a stimulating, fresh approach to the legal theoretical conundrums that, in the words of one of the co-authors, "keep many scholars off the streets" these days.[10]

3. *The Power of a Shift of Perspective(s)*

While Molnár and Wessel use both an international law and an EU law perspective throughout the book, they make a conscious choice to use general international law as the starting point for each analysis.[11] This choice has its doctrinal justification in the fact that the EU is still an international law experiment[12] – a fact often forgotten in the 'EU bubble'. Readers, such as the present reviewer, who have been 'raised' primarily in an EU law mindset are thus challenged to leave their default position and take a different perspective on familiar issues. However, it is clear that accepting this challenge and

7 Id. p. 266.
8 Id.
9 Id. p. viii.
10 Id. p. 1.
11 Id. p. 2. This is done by conceiving consecutive chapters, *e.g.* Chapters 2 and 3, or by switching perspectives within an individual chapter, *e.g.* Chapter 4.
12 Bruno de Witte, 'The European Union as an International Legal Experiment', *in* Grainne de Búrca & Joseph H.H. Weiler (eds.), *The Worlds of European Constitutionalism*, Cambridge University Press, Cambridge, 2011, pp. 19–56.

making this shift in perspective is a powerful way of identifying blind spots. A particularly illustrative example of this is the co-authors' examination of the intra-EU responsibility of EU Member States in Chapter 8. Taking international law as their point of departure, Molnár and Wessel show that Article 55 on the Responsibility of States for Internationally Wrongful Acts (hereinafter: ARSIWA) does not apply when dealing with the consequences of internationally wrongful acts of Member States in their intra-EU relations.[13] Although its logic differs from international law,[14] the EU infringement procedure in particular would provide a specialized rule of state responsibility to compel Member States to comply with EU law.[15] However, Molnár and Wessel entertain the idea whether, should this 'EU machinery' fail, recourse to general rules of state responsibility would be allowed.[16] The co-authors point to two "theoretical scenarios" in which the general rules of state responsibility as codified in the ARSIWA could play a residual role.[17] One of them, however, namely the continuous violation of EU law by a Member State, does not seem too theoretical anymore in today's rule of law crisis. The residual use of the general law of state responsibility could thus assist with ensuring the effectiveness of EU law where it cannot ensure it itself – to the benefit of EU law.

Naturally, readers identifying primarily as international lawyers will feel at home with Molnár and Wessel's approach of starting from the vantagepoint of general international law. However, as each topic is eventually addressed from the perspective of EU law, these readers will still face the same challenge to their default perspective – and will ideally find it equally useful. Chapter 7, in which Molnár and Wessel examine the international responsibility of the EU, serves as a vivid example of this assessment. Here, the co-authors acknowledge that from the vantagepoint of international law the EU is just another international organization, and therefore responsible for its internationally wrongful acts.[18] However, the composite structure of the EU and its unique division of competences would make it difficult to attribute a specific act to the EU based on the traditional effective control test.[19] Turning smoothly to the perspective of EU law, Molnár and Wessel specifically

13 Molnár & Wessel 2024, p. 200ff.
14 Id. p. 205.
15 Id. p. 205ff.
16 Id. p. 214ff.
17 Id. p. 218.
18 Id. p. 176f.
19 Id. p. 179.

point to military and civilian missions in the framework of the Common Security and Defense Policy (CSDP) and EU-coordinated cross-border missions as a specificity of the EU legal system that is not taken into account by international law,[20] thus risking a responsibility gap with respect to violations of international human rights and humanitarian law. The co-authors therefore propose a solution in which the EU would act as a 'portal' for all questions concerning accountability and responsibility.[21] Such a solution may be one of the rare cases where it is the international legal order that – rightly – demands EU exceptionalism.

4. Past and Future Flexibility – on both Sides

From the outset, Molnár and Wessel make it clear that they understand interactions as a two-way process, not a one-way street. While this understanding underpins their entire analysis, its significance becomes particularly apparent when the co-authors explore the influence of the EU and EU law on international law. While such influence depends on the EU's possibilities to participate in international efforts, these possibilities are not determined solely by EU law. The EU Treaties may provide the EU with objectives, procedures and institutions to this effect.[22] Ultimately, however, it depends on the willingness of international partners to accommodate the EU as a non-state actor and, in particular, its needs and wishes, which it derives from its special features, whether claimed or real. And there is change on the horizon.

The co-authors note that, in the past, the EU has succeeded in "forcing the international legal order to accept it as a new and relevant legal entity and to adapt its rules accordingly".[23] The composite nature of the EU is an illustrative example of this. This special feature of the EU, resulting from the division of competences between the EU and its Member States,[24] has led to special international rules, including the so-called REIO clauses, which relate exclusively to Regional Economic Integration Organizations, effectively, the EU.[25] However, such EU-friendly treatment no longer seems to be the

20 Id. p. 188.
21 Id. p. 197f.
22 Id. p. 134ff.
23 Id. p. 173.
24 *See* Chapter 4.
25 Id. p. 151.

default position at the international level.[26] Instead, the claim for the autonomy of the EU legal order and the judge-made requirements for its protection seem to have an increasingly constraining effect on the EU in its international relations.[27] In this respect, Molnár and Wessel aptly observe that "the global system is not made for composite entities that continue to claim legal autonomy and exceptionalism".[28] To do so was "certainly not helpful to convince international partners of its valuable contribution to world society".[29]

As in any good relationship, Molnár and Wessel see a need for more flexibility on both sides.[30] However, they stress that such flexibility is a real necessity for the EU, which otherwise risks seeing its own objectives remain an illusion. Accordingly, the co-authors see particular potential in "a less dogmatic approach by the CJEU" with regard to the EU's autonomy, which would "allow the EU to fulfill its brief to participate in the international legal order".[31] Undoubtedly, such a less dogmatic approach should still be based on strong doctrinal structures.

5. Keep Putting Theories to the Test

Not satisfied with examining the rules, theories and concepts governing the interactions between international law and EU law in the Abstract, Molnár and Wessel put them to the test. To do so, the co-authors use two deliberately different fields of law. On the one hand, the field of international dispute settlement mechanisms (IDS) offers insights into procedural and perhaps even institutional interactions.[32] The topical field of migration and refugee law, on the other hand, allows for a sector-specific examination of interactions, especially substantive interactions, which are indeed manifold.[33] In addition to providing a valuable illustration of the earlier, more conceptual analysis, it is this second case study that leads the co-authors to an equally important and perhaps humbling discovery: the reality in this policy field

---

26 *See* to this effect, in particular, the case study of the EU's participation in international dispute settlement systems: Id. p. 242ff.
27 Id. p. 139.
28 Id. p. 103.
29 Id. p. 263.
30 Id. p. 262.
31 Id. p. 257.
32 Id. p. 242ff.
33 Id. p. 233ff.

"does not fully reflect the grand theories that describe the relationship between international law and EU law".[34] Molnár and Wessel see this as clear evidence that more sector-specific research is needed, as well as a feedback loop between such thematic research and the more conceptual research, in order to further develop the general and Abstract design of the relationship between international law and EU law.[35] Such a feedback loop seems indeed to be missing at the moment. Their call should therefore be taken as an open invitation to join forces: Studying interactions between international law and EU law is not the sole task of a selected few, but feeds on the insights of many. It is ultimately, as the authors show with their case studies and their book, a collaborative project. However, the need for collaboration does not stop there.

Commendably, the co-authors also use their case studies to highlight the value of interdisciplinary research, which is, unfortunately, still rare in the legal sector. Having identified contradictory patterns in the CJEU's migration case law in terms of its openness towards international hard and soft law instruments,[36] they point to the possibility that these instruments may still have influenced the judges' decision-making and decision.[37] However, such insights are not accessible through the legal methodological toolbox alone. Thus, the co-authors recognize a particular need for further legal sociological research to help us understand attitudes and approaches that pervade legal acts and *(quasi)* judicial decisions,[38] whether at the EU or the international level. This goes to show just how diverse the study of the interactions between international law is, or should be.

6. Conclusion: Continued Interactions between Law – and Lawyers

Molnár and Wessel did not set themselves an easy task. Yet, as they indicate in their book, what is easy is not always interesting.[39] By not shying away from a difficult task, they have given us the gift of a truly remarkable book that will have a lasting impact on the study of the fascinating phenomenon of interactions between international law and EU law – a phenomenon, which is here to stay.

34 Id. p. 242.
35 Id.
36 Id. p. 236f.
37 Id. p. 237.
38 Id. p. 237.
39 Id. p. 1.

The co-authors show true skill in tackling with ease their vast and complex topic. With an elegant sequence of chapters, assisted by careful transitions between perspectives, the co-authors take the reader on a journey through these complexities – without denying these difficulties. With an impressive command of the every-growing body of (case) law and honest appreciation for the work of their colleagues Molnár and Wessel manage to make incisive observations that offer meaningful insights for seasoned experts while remaining accessible to new members of the club, whatever their home discipline. The result is a truly unique appraisal of the multifaceted topic of interactions between international law and EU law.

With their timely book, Molnár and Wessel have unraveled the potential of bridging the disciplinary divide in the study of an exciting phenomenon and its future development. They provide us with concrete ideas as well as fresh inspiration for tapping into this potential, and for continuing the conversation in order to establish – ideally – a lasting dialogue as we meet on and off the streets. In this and many other ways, Molnár and Wessel have done the community a great service.

Péter Mezei – Hannibal Travis – Anett Pogácsás (eds.), Harmonizing Intellectual Property Law for a Trans-Atlantic Knowledge Economy

Brill–Nijhoff, Leiden–Boston, 2024, 436p, ISBN: 978-90-04-68620-5

*Dávid Ujhelyi**

1. Introduction

It is beyond doubt that the Fifth Annual Workshop on Intellectual Property Rights in the city of Szeged, Hungary of 2021 (or WIPS for short)[1] was a successful international conference. Among the fruitful conversations and exchange of ideas that took place, the fifth WIPS also provided a successful starting point for scholars, guided by Péter Mezei, Hannibal Travis, and Anett Pogácsás, to develop the volume "*Harmonizing Intellectual Property Law for a Trans-Atlantic Knowledge Economy*", the focus of this book review (hereinafter: Volume).[2]

In the Introduction (authored by the editors),[3] the editors articulate a compelling rationale for the Volume: the convergence of IP regimes is not only about doctrinal alignment, but also about balancing the interests of the many stakeholders and purposes, goals and objectives of IP law – incentivizing authors and other rightsholders, fostering innovation, strengthening market integration, while preserving cultural and unique, national constitu-

* Dávid Ujhelyi: head of department, Department of Competition Law and Intellectual Property, Ministry of Justice of Hungary, Budapest; senior lecturer, Pázmány Péter Catholic University, Budapest, dr.ujhelyi.david@gmail.com. The views expressed in this paper do not necessarily reflect the views of the above institutions.

1 The programme of the conference can be accessed at https://wips.copy21.com/schedule/.

2 Péter Mezei *et al.* (eds.), *Harmonizing Intellectual Property Law for a Trans-Atlantic Knowledge Economy,* Brill–Nijhoff, Leiden–Boston, 2024, 436 p.

3 Péter Mezei *et al.*, 'Harmonizing Intellectual Property Law for a Trans-Atlantic Knowledge Economy – an Introduction', *in* Mezei *et al.* (eds.) 2024, pp. 1–37.

tional identities. This balancing act becomes more precarious in light of dynamic technological advancements, such as artificial intelligence (AI), 3D printing, and streaming economies. In my view, the Volume's main strength lies in addressing these tensions in both depth and breadth, traversing traditional boundaries between copyright, trademark, and patent law, while also incorporating critical, interdisciplinary, and comparative methodologies.

As a short overview, the Volume is structured into four thematic parts. Part 1, titled "*Pursuit of Harmonization*" focuses on the successful aspects of harmonization, while providing a historical and theoretical foundation for understanding IP law harmonization. Part 2, "*Divergences in Harmonization*", delves into areas where harmonization efforts have faced significant obstacles, or could be deemed outright unsuccessful. Part 3, titled "*Innovation for or against Harmonization?*" is concerned with emerging new technologies and their effect on IP law harmonization. The fourth and final Part of the Volume, "*The Challenges of Technological Advancements to IP Doctrine – Any Space for Harmonization Yet?*" focuses on specific technological disruptions to IP doctrine. Each Part contains chapters that interlace legal scholarship with practical policy insights, while the Volume itself is generally based on comparative and analytical methods, dividing its focus between legal, technological, business, and policy perspectives. Together, the 16 chapters illuminate how trans-Atlantic IP harmonization is as much a regulatory necessity as it is a deeply contested and evolving ambition.

2. An Overview of the Selected Papers (Chapters)

On the positive side of harmonization effort, Laura R. Ford's chapter, "*From Plato to WIPO: Old and New in Legal Harmonization*" aptly navigates through the historical philosophical underpinnings of IP law, highlighting how ancient principles still resonate in modern legal frameworks. Ford's exploration offers a rich narrative that combines philosophical discourse with legal evolution, calling attention to the perennial tension between the protection of creators and the public interest.[4]

Hannibal Travis's contribution, "*Augmented Creativity in a Harmonized Trans-Atlantic Knowledge Economy*" further delves into the implications of emerging technologies for creativity and IP law. Travis argues convincingly

4 Laura R. Ford, 'From Plato to WIPO: Old and New in Legal Harmonization', *in* Mezei *et al.* (eds.) 2024, pp. 45–66.

that while technological advancements can facilitate creativity, they also challenge existing legal paradigms. The chapter points to the need for dynamic legal frameworks that can adapt to technological innovations, thus ensuring equitable protection of rights while promoting progress.[5]

On the more challenging side of harmonization, Péter Mezei and Caterina Sganga's chapter, "*The Need for a More Balanced Policy Approach for Digital Exhaustion,*" underscores the complexities of digital exhaustion and its legal ramifications. Their analysis reveals the stark differences between EU and US approaches to digital content and the need for a balanced policy that considers the rights of consumers and creators alike.[6]

Anett Pogácsás, in her chapter "*To Waive or Not to Waive? – Some Thoughts on the Role of Copyright Waiver*" examines the rarely analyzed concept of copyright waivers, highlighting the fundamentally divergent approaches of the different legal systems and their potential to be mitigated and to provide flexibility within IP frameworks.[7]

Giulia Dore in her chapter "*Experimenting with EU Moral Rights Harmonization and Works of Visual Arts: Dream or Nightmare?*" critically assesses moral rights[8] harmonization in visual arts within the EU, raising questions about whether uniformity is feasible or desirable in culturally sensitive areas, while exposing the persistent gap between the civil and common law approach.[9]

In the opening Chapter of Part 3, Hannibal Travis contributes with a second paper titled "*Spooky Innovation and Human Rights*". This chapter critiques how emerging technologies, such as quantum computing and neural networks pose normative risks to legal coherence and individual autonomy. This chapters reveals how technological advancements necessitate adaptive legal frameworks while posing risks to traditional IP regimes.[10]

---

5 Hannibal Travis, 'Augmented Creativity in a Harmonized Trans-Atlantic Knowledge Economy', *in* Mezei *et al.* (eds.) 2024, pp. 67–84.

6 Péter Mezei & Caterina Sganga, '*The Need for a More Balanced Policy Approach for Digital Exhaustion*', *in* Mezei *et al.* (eds.) 2024, pp. 133–153. *See more* Péter Mezei, '*Copyright Exhaustion: Law and Policy in the United States and the European Union*', Cambridge University Press, Cambridge, 2022.

7 Anett Pogácsás, 'To Waive of Not to Waive? – Some Thoughts on the Role of Copyright Waiver', *in* Mezei *et al.* (eds.) 2024, pp. 175–194.

8 *See on* moral rights and parody: David Ujhelyi, 'The Long Road to Parody Exception', *Iparjogvédelmi és Szerzői Jogi Szemle*, Vol. 17, Issue 2, 2022, pp. 65–81, 94–95.

9 Giulia Dore, 'Experimenting with EU Moral Rights Harmonization and Works of Visual Arts: Dream or Nightmare?', *in* Mezei *et al.* (eds.) 2024, pp. 195–219.

10 Hannibal Travis, 'Spooky Innovation and Human Rights', *in* Mezei *et al.* (eds.) 2024, pp. 237–263.

Mauritz Kop offers a provocative theory of public property from the machine, in which AI-generated works could fall into a new category of commons-based output. His argument, while still nascent, opens up important debates about the future of authorship and ownership in algorithmically driven systems, also offering a new, alternative solution faced by copyright law regarding generative AI services.[11]

David Linke's analysis of AI training data, wittily titled "*AI Training Data: Between Holy Grail and Forbidden Fruit*", represents one of the Volume's most timely and technically detailed contributions. He describes the fine line between lawful training practices and unauthorized exploitation of protected works. Linke offers a nuanced comparative analysis of evolving case law in the EU and the US, highlighting how legal uncertainty could inhibit both innovation and harmonization.[12]

The final Part of the Volume further expands on the question whether doctrinal IP law can keep pace with rapid technological shifts. Peter Menell's chapter on design protection is a standout contribution. He dissects the historical divergence between US and EU design regimes and explores how differing policy rationales and institutional frameworks obstruct harmonization.[13]

Bohdan Widła addresses the thorny issue of copyright protection for application programming interfaces (APIs), comparing the landmark *Google v Oracle* decision in the US_with evolving European jurisprudence. He shows that while both systems recognize the centrality of interoperability, their doctrinal foundations differ significantly.[14]

3. *(Un)successful Harmonization?*

In an era characterized by rapid technological advancements and globalization, the quest for harmonizing intellectual property law across jurisdictions has become paramount. The Volume is unquestionably an ambitious schol-

---

11 Mauritz Kop, 'Public Property from the Machine', *in* Mezei *et al.* (eds.) 2024, pp. 264–288.

12 David Linke, 'AI Training Data: Between Holy Grail and Forbidden Fruit', *in* Mezei *et al.* (eds.) 2024, pp. 289–310.

13 Peter Menell, 'Navigating the Trans-Atlantic Design Protection Quandry', *in* Mezei *et al.* (eds.) 2024, pp. 311–352.

14 Bohdan Widła, 'No More Convergence? Copyright Protection of Application Programming Interfaces in the USA and the EU', *in* Mezei *et al.* (eds.) 2024, pp. 375–394.

arly endeavor that addresses the complexities of intellectual property law harmonization between the EU and the US. It explores how globalization, technological advancements, and differing legal traditions shape IP regimes in these two major jurisdictions.

The editors deserve credit for curating a volume that strikes a balance between doctrinal depth, comparative rigor, and policy relevance. Their introduction not only synthesizes the key themes but contextualizes the Volume within the wider evolution of international and EU IP law.[15] They identify several crucial trends – the rise of digital platforms, the challenges of AI, the influence of multilateral and regional treaties, and the evolving role of fundamental rights – that structure the Volume and give it analytical coherence. Importantly, the Volume does not assume that harmonization is necessarily desirable or always achievable. Rather, it invites the reader to consider harmonization as a spectrum of legal, institutional, and normative processes. In this respect, the Volume is in line with contemporary scholarship that treats harmonization as a contested and pluralistic phenomenon, rather than a unidirectional goal. This Volume enriches the literature on comparative IP law and offers valuable insights to policymakers, academics, and practitioners alike. Its strengths lie in its interdisciplinarity, its responsiveness to current debates, and its careful balance of theoretical and empirical perspectives.

That said, some areas could have benefitted from deeper exploration. While the Volume includes detailed discussions of copyright and, to a lesser extent, trademarks and design rights, it pays comparatively less attention to patents, trade secrets, and the role of international enforcement mechanisms. Similarly, while – as the title of the Volume suggests – the trans-Atlantic axis is thoroughly analyzed there is limited engagement with emerging economies that are increasingly shaping the global IP landscape.

Applying a holistic approach to technology and platform regulation, including the impact of regulations like the DSA[16] or the DMA[17] would have

---

15 *See* Anett Pogácsás, 'One Hundred Years of International Copyright', *Hungarian Yearbook on International Law and European Law*, Vol. 10, Issue 1, 2022, pp. 246–259.

16 Regulation (EU) 2022/2065 of the European Parliament and of the Council of 19 October 2022 on a single market for digital services and amending Directive 2000/31/EC (Digital Services Act).

17 Regulation (EU) 2022/1925 of the European Parliament and of the Council of 14 September 2022 on contestable and fair markets in the digital sector and amending Directives (EU) 2019/1937 and (EU) 2020/1828 (Digital Markets Act).

further strengthened the discussion, especially given the EU's global regulatory influence (the so-called "Brussels Effect").[18]

4. Conclusion

The Volume captures the complexity and urgency of aligning IP regimes in a digitized, globalized world. It resists simplistic calls for convergence and instead offers a thoughtful, multifaceted, and critical approach to harmonization. The Volume's blend of doctrinal analysis, technological literacy, and normative reflection makes it essential reading for anyone engaged in the study or practice of intellectual property law today.

The editors have successfully curated a diverse array of perspectives that encompass historical, theoretical, and practical dimensions of IP law harmonization. Each chapter, rich in content and insights, addresses critical questions and controversies that underpin the current landscape of intellectual property in the digital age.

In sum, the Volume is not only a scholarly achievement but also a practical toolkit for navigating the challenges and possibilities of IP law in the 21st century. It marks an important step toward a more coherent, equitable, and innovation-friendly regulatory landscape.

18 Miriam Vogel *et al.*, 'Is Your Use of AI Violating the Law? An Overview of the Current Legal Landscape', *New York University Journal of Legislation and Public Policy*, Vol. 26, Issue 4, 2024, p. 1113.